THE FUNERAL

Chimo died this morning.
Chimo was not a friend of mine. But he died.
He used to talk nonstop as if he was paying
   back an old debt to words that were about to
   abandon him.
Tomorrow I will wear my black coat and go to
   his funeral
and when I'm back home I'll smile to myself.
Today Chimo died,
an acquaintance of mine.
And here I am now, no longer a stranger in
   this country.

Ahmad Yamani
Egyptian poet

Translated from his collection *Amakin Khatia'a*
(Wrong Places), Cairo 2008

DIGITAL BANIPAL
– complete archive now available to subscribers

Banipal's digital edition offers readers all over the world the chance to flip open the magazine on their computers, iPads, iPhones or android smartphones, wherever they are, check out the current issue, search through the back issues and sync as desired.

A digital subscription now gives full access to the complete digital archive, back to Banipal No 1, February 1998 – for individuals (£24.99) and for institutions (rate based on FTE). Print and digital subscriptions are still separate for the moment.

Download the free iTunes App. Preview the digital archive, preview the current issue or check out the Free Trial issue:
Banipal 53 – The Short Stories of Zakaria Tamer

For more information, go to: **www.banipal.co.uk/subscribe/**

Trial issue

A MARSHLANDER HAS LEFT US
TRIBUTE TO HUSSAIN AL-MOZANY
BY STEFAN WEIDNER – PAGE 202

Photo by Samuel Shimon

The Banipal Visiting Writer Fellowship

St Aidan's College of the University of Durham and Banipal magazine of modern Arab literature, with the support of the British Council, announced in October 2016 the establishment of an annual writing fellowship of three months for a published author writing in Arabic, based each year at St Aidan's College.

The first Banipal Visiting Writer Fellow (2017), selected from 92 applications, is Ali Bader, a well-known Iraqi novelist and essayist, whose work is making an important contribution to contemporary Arabic literature. He is the author of thirteen works of fiction, two of which were long-listed for the International Prize for Arabic Fiction, and several works of non-fiction. His best-known novels include *Papa Sartre* and *The Tobacco Keeper* (both published also in English translation), (*Running after the Wolves*), (*Kings of Sand*) and (*The Sinful Woman*), and a number have won awards. Ali Bader was born in Baghdad, where he studied western philosophy and French literature, and now lives in Brussels.

The Fellowship is based on the three cornerstones that have formed the core of Banipal magazine: that Arab literature is an essential part of world culture and human civilisation; that dialogue between different cultures needs to be continually deepened; and that the joy and enlightenment to be gained from reading beautiful poetry and imaginative writing is an integral part of human existence.

The Fellowship will encourage dialogue with the Arab world through literature. The cultural exchange and dialogue that it will enable, and create, will open windows for non-Arab audiences in the UK onto the realities of Arab cultures in all their diversity and vibrancy, enabling fruitful discourse to develop. It is hoped that this will lead to further exchange, to mutual respect, to new writings, to deeper understanding, and to contributing to Arab literature taking its rightful place in the canon of world literature.

Each year the Fellowship will provide a unique space for a published author writing in Arabic to reflect and to write, and to also have the opportunity to share their work with British audiences.

The application process for the 2018 Fellowship will open on 1st June, with the deadline for receiving applications being 1 September 2017. Applications will be assessed during September.

For enquiries, please email: Banipalfellowship@gmail.com

Postal address:
The Principal, St Aidan's College, University of Durham, Windmill Hill, Durham DH1 3LJ, UK

BANIPAL
Magazine of Modern Arab Literature

Banipal, founded in 1998, takes its name from Ashurbanipal, last great king of Assyria and patron of the arts, whose outstanding achievement was to assemble in Nineveh, from all over his empire, the first systematically organised library in the ancient Middle East. The thousands of clay tablets of Sumerian, Babylonian and Assyrian writings included the famous Mesopotamian epics of the Creation, the Flood, and Gilgamesh, many folk tales, fables, proverbs, prayers and omen texts.

Source: *Encyclopaedia Britannica*

PUBLISHER: Margaret Obank

EDITOR: Samuel Shimon

CONTRIBUTING EDITORS
Fadhil al-Azzawi, Issa J Boullata, Peter Clark, Raphael Cohen, Bassam Frangieh, Camilo Gómez-Rivas, Marilyn Hacker, William M Hutchins, Adil Babikir, Imad Khachan, Khaled Mattawa, Anton Shammas, Paul Starkey, Mona Zaki

CONSULTING EDITORS
Etel Adnan, Roger Allen, Mohammed Bennis, Isabella Camera d'Afflitto, Humphrey Davies, Hartmut Fähndrich, Saif al-Rahbi, Naomi Shihab Nye, Yasir Suleiman, Susannah Tarbush, Stephen Watts

EDITORIAL ASSISTANTS: Annamaria Basile, Yen-Yen Lu, Maureen O'Rourke, Valentina Viene

ADDITIONAL TRANSLATIONS: Adil Babikir, Jonathan Wright

COVER ARTIST: Yahya al-Sheikh

LAYOUT: Banipal Publishing

WEBSITE: www.banipal.co.uk

EDITOR: editor@banipal.co.uk

PUBLISHER: margaret@banipal.co.uk

INQUIRIES: info@banipal.co.uk

SUBSCRIPTIONS: subscribe@banipal.co.uk

ADDRESS: 1 Gough Square, London EC4A 3DE

PRINTED BY Short Run Press Ltd
Bittern Road, Sowton Ind. Est. EXETER EX2 7LW

Photographs not accredited have been donated, photographers unknown.

BANIPAL, ISSN 1461-5363, is published three times a year by Banipal Publishing, 1 Gough Square, London EC4A 3DE

Supported using public funding by
ARTS COUNCIL ENGLAND
LOTTERY FUNDED

www.banipal.co.uk

Yahya al-Sheikh

Naguib Mahfouz

Muhammad Khudayyir

Shahla Ujayli

Elias Farkouh

Excerpts from IPAF shortlist 2017

BANIPAL 58
Magazine of Modern Arab Literature

Arab Literary Awards

PLUS Naguib Mahfouz, Muhammad Khudayyir, Alaa Khaled, Elias Farkouh, Shahla Ujayli, Mahmoud Saeed, Ashur Etwebi and Yahya al-Sheikh

Cover painting by Yahya al-Sheikh

Mahmoud Saeed

Abdo Wazen

Fatma Alboudy

Stefan Weidner

Fadia Faqir

For information on all contributors in *Banipal 58*,
go to pages 222-224 or
www.banipal.co.uk/contributors/

EDITORIAL

The first issue of 2017, our 20th year of continuous publication, includes features, Literary Influences essay and works by a range of authors as well as its title feature. It opens with Sally Gomaa in conversation with Egyptian author and essayist from Alexandra Alaa Khaled, founder of Amkenah magazine, whose works always defy boundaries, and includes an intriguing chapter from his autographical novel.

The short story from veteran Iraqi author Muhammad Khudayyir, entitled "The Three Wise Men", retells in his own way the ancient Akkadian epic of Atraharsis, invoking the ancient Mesopotamian gods of Ea, Shamash and Sin, al-Jahiz and Basra's poet hero Badr Shakir al-Sayyab. Shahla Ujayli's very short story is packed with ideas, images, situations and concepts while reliving a nightmare.

There is a splendid story by Naguib Mahfouz, published four years before he became a Nobel laureate, the title story of the collection *The Secret Organisation*, in which secret "family" cells require complete obedience in carrying out their demands, working as they say for "Perfection, Love, Obedience", striving to come nearer and nearer the Supreme Leader, but never managing it.

The chapter from Jordanian author Elias Farkouh's novel *Drowned in Mirrors* has the protagonist, retired builder Shakib Effendi, wondering if changing his walking route on the very day the Prime Minister was assassinated was a sign. He had risen early, as usual, and was waiting to meet his old friend Hafeedh from his days in Haifa, where Shakib had first heard "Star of the East" Umm Kulthum sing, but instead there were enormous explosions . . .

Iraqi author Mahmoud Saeed, who has five of his 20 novels in English translation, writes in his Literary Influences essay how Mosul Public Library, recently found ransacked and destroyed by ISIS, was where he discovered and read great literature. Libyan poet Ashur Etwebi writes a lyrical essay describing how Iraqi-Norwegian artist Yahya al-Sheikh (our cover artist) captures the essential spirits of day and night in his unusual drawings, many of which are reproduced in the essay.

We include a tribute by Stefan Weidner to our dear friend Hussain al-Mozany, who died suddenly last December. Till now we can hear his voice in our heads, his laughter, we can picture his serious mien, his humour, his quiet endurance and his enthusiasm for learning English. Banipal also pays tribute to Herbert Mason, a consulting editor for many years, and finds a space here to remember with sadness our colleague Ben Hollander and his untimely passing in November 2016.

As usual in the Spring issue of Banipal, we present excerpts from the six shortlisted novels of the 2017 International Prize for Arabic Fiction – the winner will be revealed at the award ceremony on 25 April in Abu Dhabi. This year, the prize, described as the "most prestigious and important literary prize in the Arab world", reaches its 10th year of rewarding "excellence in contemporary Arabic creative writing" and encouraging the reading of "high quality Arabic literature internationally through translation".

Complementing the forthcoming award ceremonies of two of the biggest Arab literary awards, and not forgetting also the Saif Ghobash Banipal Prize for Arabic Literary Translation, which is starting its 12th year of awards, Banipal's title feature presents views and opinions from around the Arab world on the impact of the growing number of Arab literary awards on encouraging reading, on creative writing and on the literary scene. Banipal magazine, from the beginning, has not taken any position itself, but its pages have been opened up for publishers, critics, authors, and literary journalists to express their thoughts freely on this hot topic. All of the articles, bar one, were written especially for this feature. Khalil Suweileh's article that he published in the Lebanese *Al-Akhbar*, is reproduced here in translation with his permission.

Cultural editor Abdo Wazen, in Beirut, writes that there has been "an unprecedented upsurge in literary awards" in the Arab world, heavily funded ones, and when you look at who the winners are they are turning out to be "democratic and inclusive awards". The most effective prize for him is the IPAF which has "lent vigour, enthusiasm and passion to the literary scene in the Arab world", and he concludes that that is only because of the prize's association with the UK Booker Prize.

Fatma Alboudy, publisher of Dar Al-Ain in Cairo, takes a long view of the IPAF prize in terms of how it has affected Arab publishing both positively and negatively. Ibrahim Farghali looks at the revival of the novel genre as a result of these relatively new literary awards and the general impetus they have given to increasing readers. But he warns that awards need "to regularly revise their procedures to protect authors' rights and to maintain their credibility".

Publisher Hassan Yaghi is an adroit observer of the Arab literary scene and the impact of prizes on readers. He assesses how the IPAF prize has enabled winning works "to appeal to the readers", with relatively unknown authors becoming widely known after winning. However, he writes that he is "duty bound" to put forward suggestions to boost the status of IPAF, the main one being the addition of missing readers to the judging panels.

Apart from the biennial Al Owais prize, which was set up in 1988 by the Sultan Bin Ali Al Owais Cultural Foundation, with five categories of awards for achievements rather than specific works, most of the major Arab literary prizes have been established in the last decade or so, indicating an important shift. In 1996, the Naguib Mahfouz Medal for Arab Literature was launched by the AUC Press, and is awarded every 11 December, the Nobel laureate's birthday.

In 2006, the hugely funded (US $1.9m) Emirati Sheikh Zayed Book Award was launched with nine categories, not all awarded each year. In the last couple of years the Award has introduced long lists and short lists before the announcement of the winners. This strategy makes prizes more attractive and grips people's attention. Increasing the appeal of a literary prize to the reading public should perhaps be the top priority for prize administrators. However, after the shortlists have come suggestions to make awards to those shortlisted, with the huge prize pot for the winner being redistributed to enable such additional awards. The SZBA, about to make its 11th edition of awards, is a very important prize in the Arab world. It keeps on developing and improving its public image and reputation, and hopefully this can continue with more openness regarding its judging systems and the widening of awards offered.

A point made by a number of the contributors above is that increasing readers is one of the important purposes of prizes, and that is what the International Prize for Arabic Fiction, above all others, has succeeded in doing. Launched in 2007 in Abu Dhabi, for the first time an Arab literary award explained all its procedures from the start, and reached out to the public with a long list, a short list and then winner, with the panel of judges named for all to know. These open procedures were new in the Arab world, as many contributors bear out.

Since 2014 two prizes, also hugely funded, have emerged from Doha, Qatar, one for the novel – Katara Prize for the Arabic Novel, and the other for translation into and out of Arabic and for organisations working in and promoting translation from Arabic – Sheikh Hamad Award for Translation and International Understanding.

A final word from Fadia Faqir, who writes her novels in English, and in this issue reflects on being a judge for the inaugural Al-Multaqa Prize for the Arab Short Story. She writes that she "thoroughly enjoyed the experience of reading 184 collections of short stories and further exploring the literary map of the Arab world" and concludes with a comment that Banipal can wholeheartedly agree with, that "in an Arab world riddled with wars, civil and uncivil, and conflicts, to pick up a pen and write is a triumph in itself".

Comments on the Literary Awards feature by readers, prize administrators, judges and nominees are very welcome. Just email them to editor@banipal.co.uk.

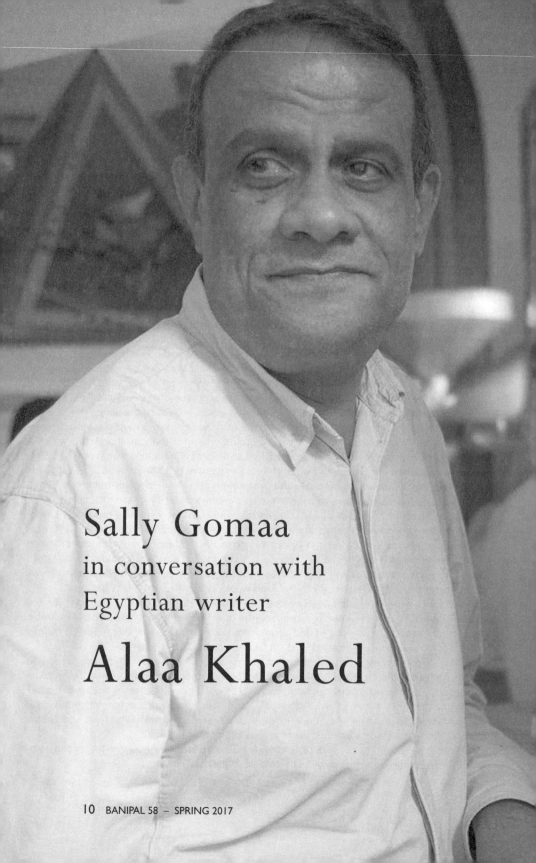

Sally Gomaa
in conversation with
Egyptian writer

Alaa Khaled

In Search of a Map

Poet, novelist, essayist and editor **Alaa Khaled** *was born in 1960 in Alexandria, Egypt. He has published six collections of poetry, three books of essays and reportage, and two novels. In 1999 he founded* Amkenah *(Places) literary and cultural magazine. He is well known for relentlessly ignoring the formal boundaries that are supposed to separate literary genres, creating his own style and narrative.* **Sally Gomaa** *went to interview him about his work and ideas, and also translated a chapter from his autobiographical novel* A Pain as Light as a Bird's Feather Floating Quietly from One Place to Another.

We met at the Delices Café in Alexandria. If we were in a novel, Delices would have been the perfect setting. In addition to its European flair, which dates from the 1920s when it first opened its doors, Delices has two entrances. One faces a busy commercial street and the other a central square with the Mediterranean Sea gleaming in the distance. According to Alaa Khaled's poetic vision, Delices's architecture symbolizes the building's ability to occupy two worlds at the same time. Alaa always writes about restoring this "other" world that lies between the visible and the invisible, the real and the unreal. Whether used in his fiction or poetry, the concept of the other implies freedom and contains the potential for transcendence.

Alaa Khaled is always looking for holes in the fabric of everyday life through which the sublime is manifested. Even in the most difficult circumstances, he is able to find a portal to a richer, more complex, more fulfilling life. Sometimes the portal is as simple as an orange. In *The Trail of the Sad Blue*, a book that details his stay at an intensive care unit after a simple surgery went wrong, he describes the hospital ward as "a long season of orange". The orange skin "glows" and "glitters" until its freshness drowns out the odors of Detoll, Clorox, and rancid urine. Although the orange is a symbol of life, it still remains an orange. Alaa Khaled writes, here and elsewhere, to restore to the orange its orangeness.

Mixing playfulness with purpose and lyrical style with sparse prose characterizes Alaa Khaled's writing. His autobiographical novel *A Pain as Light as a Bird's Feather Floating Quietly from One Place to Another* depicts both the ordinary and the divine in everyday life with equal eloquence and grace. See below pages 19-24 for a chapter. Like its title, the novel seems to flutter from one memory or reality to another. But in actuality, it is a tightly woven work of fiction. Alaa Khaled writes to mythologize his own family with all its quirks and dysfunctions and to historicize an era he witnessed growing up in Alexandria in the 1960s and 70s. He is able to bridge the distance between the individual and the collective in this novel by depicting "Alexandria" as somewhere between the public and the private, the hidden and the revealed, the self and its other. In everything he writes, he is a gifted poet, a great storyteller, and one of the leading intellectuals in Egypt.

I have to start this interview with a confession. When I initially told you that I liked your novel A Pain as Light as a Bird's Feather, *I lied to you. I didn't like it at all. [Alaa Khaled appears neither defensive nor angry, just intrigued]. What I mean is when I started reading your "novel", I expected a story with different elements of fiction, like character, plot, setting, etc. It took me a while to understand that you were writing bits and pieces, snapshots of a life without any central or focal point. So, what is your definition of the novel as a genre?*

The novel is a network or an intersection between different worlds. Different threads are interwoven throughout the novel. It does not have to have a neat beginning, or even an end, as long as the lines converge and diverge. Reading my novel should be almost like watching a movie: different scenes and different characters with multiple trajectories. My first book *Points of Weakness* was a confession of sorts and an attempt to confront the other. But in *A Pain as Light as a Bird's Feather*, I use the language of stories. This time I have found the true other, the one I can share stories and chat with as opposed to the one I want to fight or grapple with. In *A Pain as Light as a Bird's Feather*, the narrator is just a voice among many other voices. His perspective is only part of the texture of the narrative without trying to dominate it. I hope that others find bits and pieces of their own histories in mine.

One key concept throughout your writing is the concept of the other. What does otherness mean to you?

We are all suspended somewhere between two worlds. One is available to us, the one we live in on a daily basis. The other world is unseen. It may be hidden in our memories or buried in our unconscious minds. The fact of its being hidden or unseen makes it more significant or revealing than the world we readily have because we have to constantly work to unveil it. We should not privilege one world over the other. But if we let go of this other world, if we don't work hard to trace it, we could lose the core of our being.

There is no stable definition of this "other" world because every person has his or her own private world. Instead of trying to define it, which is a dogmatic way of thinking anyway, we should live in relationship to our awareness of it. In other words, the two worlds exist in a dialectical relationship. It is in the tension between them that a new truth emerges. You can see this tension at work, for example, in the way space is transformed by memory so that it becomes two spaces at the same time: the one we can see and the one we have stored in our minds.

Otherness also implies freedom and dialogue. The other could be another version of oneself. This version inhabits a world hidden yet accessible. To access this world, one has to have a flexible sense of self. The constant dialogue between the self and its other allows one to re-examine one's beliefs and values. Even writing has an other. Writing is a way to reinvent the narrative that one has internalized until it becomes, mistakenly, one's identity. Writing, almost like psychotherapy, is a way to reconstruct the past. But in the new narrative we're no longer victims or passive receivers. We get to map out a new trajectory out of the twists and turns of our lives.

The Trail of the Sad Blue *is a personal account of your own fight with death and your miraculous recovery. You had gone into the hospital for a simple operation, but your physician made a terrible mistake and you almost lost your life. To be blunt, why should this personal crisis matter to your readers?*

It matters because this is our story: the story of the death we all confront and the other we all pursue. There are points in each person's life which may appear random, but if a line were drawn across those points, they would reveal a hidden trail. For example, the cannulas that were inserted into my body at the hospital outlined a map I was able to trace. Each person has his or her own map. Therefore, I'm writing about a collective experience or at least an experience that lies somewhere between the personal and the collective.

In *The Trail of the Sad Blue* I was looking for a methodology or a taxonomy to classify my experience and its objects. The suspended place from which I wrote this book was not religious but it was not completely void of spirituality either (as in, say, the discourse of Enlightenment's rejection of all irrational or subliminal knowledge). It was a place that allowed me to encounter the divine on an equal basis. By "equal", all I mean is having a conversation with the divine. This type of conversation is one of the mechanisms or tools through which we can authenticate existence.

Could you explain what you mean by "authenticate existence"? This ex-

pression appears frequently in your writing. For example, in The Trail of the Sad Blue *you talk about death as a way to illuminate the relationship between the individual and the whole. Death, you write, "helps us authenticate our existence and renew our connection to life in its broader sense beyond the subjective and the finite".*

The term "authentic" is currently contested. When I use it, I mean returning to the core of our being when all our defences are down. That could only happen when one undergoes a traumatic experience, such as being in prison or in hospital. When one confronts death, either symbolically or literally, one is stripped of all the accoutrements or layers that isolate one from the larger world, whether represented by society or nature or the universe. What remains in this case is a hybrid of the conscious and the unconscious. When we get to this point, we can encounter being in its purest form. Part of this form is physical but another part is metaphysical. Somewhere precariously positioned between the material world and our perception of it, we can glimpse our true selves. This is the vantage point from which we can authenticate our sense of being.

As an accomplished poet, how different do you find writing fiction from writing poetry?

Unlike the novel, which is preoccupied with the other, poetry reveals the essence of being where there is no otherness. Poetry exists in a purely existentialist state. Every existence has a rhythm and poetry captures this rhythm. Yes, we are all poets because we are all suspended between two worlds. Childhood is a bridge into the Poetic Idea. But there are other bridges such as obsessive compulsiveness, guilt, and sacrifice. Like poetry, they all require imagination. Guilt is an expression of our responsibility towards the universe. The poet is like an obsessive compulsive person, but rather than fearing the object of his/her obsessiveness, the poet wants to confront it. Therefore, poetry is like obsessive compulsiveness in that it is a way to imagine a complete other world but without fear.

You write prose poetry, a misunderstood or vague term in contemporary Arabic literature. How do you define it?

The prose poem enables the poet to write about everyday life and about ordinary objects while revealing truths about being. Moreover, the prose poem can be an act of violence because it forces the poet to reconstruct the personal scene. It is like turning a sock inside out. It can be an unveiling and a state of actualization.

The traditional Arabic poem (which has specific rhymes and meters) has become an empty ritual because it depends for its existence on the exterior. It turns its gaze to the outside rather than the inside. The more it depends on form, the less vital and the less dynamic it becomes. This is why it has reached a standstill. The prose poem, on the other hand, opens up an existentialist space. I write from this space because I'm against all static, stagnant, and stifling ways of thinking.

Alexandria occupies a prominent place in your writing. It is the main subject of your book Alexandrian Faces. *But to a certain degree, it is the subject of every book you have written so far. How does Alexandria fit your idea of otherness?*

To begin with, there is no "single" or "real" Alexandria. Currently, most of the questions that have to do with the Alexandria express a desire to restore an ancient version of it, like a paradise that was lost. Therefore, the myth of return is the strongest myth in the history of the Alexandria. As if what we have now is the shadow of another city. Perhaps this is because Alexandria is a concept rather than a city. Perhaps the complexity of its history has caused it to become invisible in its actuality and visible only within a system of symbols and ideas.

Throughout its history, Alexandria exemplified tolerance and coexistence. This role reached its peak towards the end of the nineteenth century and the beginning of the twentieth when Alexandria was home to different nationalities. This period has since become rooted in the city's subconscious mind and the source of its nostalgia. Even those who have not witnessed this period, still feel the same nostalgia as if it were part of our collective memory. Although this period was not perfect, our nostalgia is a complicated one. It expresses our current desire to play another role on the global scene.

Cover of Amkenah No 9, August 2008

We should still treasure this part of our history the way we treasure old wives' tales. We love those tales because they provide a way to engage the past and the present. Today, what could link the past and the present more dynamically than the idea of the City – or the memory of the City? Alexandria, in this sense, is not just a coastal port. Alexandria is a question that opens the door to the Self and its Other.

What is the idea behind your superb literary magazine Amkenah *(Places)?*

The idea for *Amkenah* was born in 1997. Back then, literary magazines did not pay attention to social trends or movements. We wanted to create a magazine that would highlight the social dimension of literature. We decided to locate this dimension in the culture of space.

Since its inception, each issue of the magazine has focused on a place where multiple cultures coexist, such as the mall or the university. Through the ordinary, everyday experience, the magazine examines how those different cultures interact. In case one culture ends up dominating all others, we try to chronicle this transformation as indicative of larger social patterns.

For example, the first issue of *Amkenah* published in 1999 took

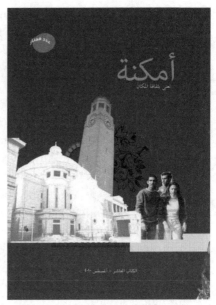

Covers of Amkenah *magazine: No 3, October 2003, and No 10, August 2010*

place in what was called the French Market in Alexandria. This Market was first opened in the 1920s. It was like a farmer's market with shops and cafés where people from different nationalities gathered. Over time, the place started to change to reflect the new dynamics of the people who lived in it. You can see this change in the types of shops and small businesses that survived. The second issue of the magazine took place in Mar Girgis. This is the area in Old Cairo where you have a Coptic church (the Hanging Church), a synagogue (Ben Ezra), and a mosque ('Amr Ibn al-'As). We found there that the idea of death was the hidden thread that tied those different cultures together. And so on. This magazine studies culture as it interacts with space.

Although your questions to me will not be part of this interview, I want readers to know that you have interviewed me as much as I have interviewed you. I'm grateful for the way you viewed my life as if it contained the same Poetic Idea that inspired yours. I know that you treat everyone with the same respect and kindness. Thank you for being so humble, gracious, and gifted.

Thank you.

ALAA KHALED

The Hidden Treasure

A CHAPTER FROM THE NOVEL
A PAIN AS LIGHT AS A BIRD'S FEATHER FLOATING QUIETLY FROM ONE PLACE TO ANOTHER
TRANSLATED BY SALLY GOMAA

When my grandmother Ra'eefah passed away, my brother Salah was nowhere to be found. As if he had vanished. He took off to the streets and did not come home until the body was carried away. Around that time, he was almost thirty and had yet to learn how to shield himself from the waves of terror that swept over him in the Angel of Death's presence. Four years earlier, he was at home when my other grandmother Rateebah died. It was around 9:00 pm and the smell of bread burning in the toaster was coming from the kitchen. As part of our night-time rituals, my mother was making dinner. My brother could not leave the house that time partly because he dreaded my father's reaction. The Angel of Death had taken him by surprise and left him with no escape route. While my grandmother's body was wrapped in white sheets, we were busy working under the supervision of my aunt Zeinab to empty the room out and prepare for the washing to take place the following morning. When I happened to absent-mindedly hand Salah the slippers my grandmother used to wear, he gave me a hard slap on my face. Until this day, I have no idea why he did that. Perhaps he was scared to touch something that belonged to the deceased. At any rate, the waves of terror that attacked him that night found nothing to hit except my face.

Salah used to take out all his frustrations and disappointments on my helpless mother. She sensed that deep down he held a grudge against her, but he did not have the courage to openly or secretly acknowledge his feelings. So he was always ill-tempered whenever he had to interact with her. Perhaps, deep down, he blamed her for his chronic illness. Sometimes when pain is beyond our comprehension, we try to share it with someone. Usually, this is the person we love the most because the channels through which we express love are the same ones we have at our disposal to express all other emotions, including those that have nothing to do with love.

Salah's life consisted of one crisis after another. He suffered from insomnia, anxiety, and excessive fear of the future. For every year he spent in college, he turned the entire household into a study camp. He would be upset if we talked loudly. The least noise, even my mother yawning, would throw him into a tizzy. He would tap the glass door with his pen like a conductor to signal that we had crossed the line. The whole house resembled a temple where nothing was to be heard except prayers. Not only that, but before final grades were posted, he would always expect the worst and wallow in misery over what would happen if he failed or even if he did not earn enough grades.

Those critical junctures, when he felt his fate was suspended between heaven and earth, were the best times to ask him for favors. "What gift would you give me if you passed your exams," I would ask. Having a book to study, an exam to take, or a hurdle to pass must have been his tools for self-actualization. Fear, more than joy, gave him a sense of accomplishment. In my father's absence, his ability to serve as head of the family was impeccable. If he knew that my mother, my brother Adel, or I did something that would upset my father, he would be sure to tell him without missing even the tiniest detail. This was not driven by revenge; it was driven by his blind faith in complete honesty. For this reason, we excluded him from our circle. We did not share our secrets with him or discuss intimate details of our lives. Even in small things, he never stopped acting like a father. If I happened to be on the phone for too long or if I kept the fridge door open while I was taking a sip of water, he would impatiently say, "Shut the door to the fridge." If I misplaced a book on the desk, he would not fail to notice and would be upset. Due to his illness and his temperament, life at our house had a nervous quality like a cord ready to snap.

Despite the small gap between Salah and Adel in age, they were very different. Unlike Adel, Salah never followed fashion. He did not

Alaa Khaled

have a favorite singer, other than Farid al-Atrash and the occasional song by Umm Kulthum. However, he owned every book written by Tawfiq al-Hakim. He heard in the cynicism that rang through all of Hakim's writings an echo of his own. He shared with Hakim the same cynicism combined with an irrational pessimism that seemed to suck the joy out of life. But perhaps his indifference towards life gave him a way to harness the energy that enabled him to pursue the highest academic degrees. Perhaps it afforded him a little shade from his burning desire to succeed academically. But, unlike his genera-tion, he did not care much for his appearance. Every now and then, he was driven into depression and despair by an unshakeable ni-hilism. But his love for knowledge and his superb academic perform-ance were the only bonds that tied him to this life and gave him both pain and pleasure, anxiety and ease.

Despite the fact that both Salah and Adel went to college during the highly political times of the late sixties and early seventies, they had no political interests. Adel's leftist classmates used to call him "Hafez" because he resembled the romantic idol Abdel Halim Hafez in the way he did his hair and in the way he was sweet and adorable. (Years later, when I ran into one of those classmates at a public event, he told me more about Adel in those days and had a hard time be-lieving I was his brother). Yet, Adel's adorability did not serve any purpose. He took risks and had great adventures, but he made no sacrifices. He wanted to be "popular" in the full sense of this word because its superficiality allowed him to hide his real self. But the minute he walked in, all traces of this "romantic" version of himself disappeared to be replaced by his hardcore stubbornness. Abdel

Halim Hafez was a legend that had such a hold over the women of that age, which was precisely what Adel wanted. He literally watched one of Hafez's movies thirteen times to memorize all his lines. Salah was the opposite. He did not know how to act romantic and had no myth to cultivate of himself. The only icon he admired was the writer Tawfiq el-Hakim who had already belonged to an earlier generation.

While he lived in the Gulf after he completed his PhD and before his marriage to an Egyptian teacher in his early forties, he did something out of character. Perhaps it was the first and the last risk he ever took. He knew an Indian janitor at the university where he taught who needed to pay for a complicated heart surgery. Salah gave him the money for the down payment and agreed to pay the rest in the form of a loan he took out on his salary. The janitor died only a few days after the surgery, but Salah continued to pay the hospital for years after. That was an unexpected turn, but he took it to see another side of himself or to make sure that side existed if it was ever called upon. When I got married, he deposited a large sum of money he had saved for that day into my bank account. Perhaps I was wrong to be surprised by this generosity but I never expect love from others and it always comes to me as a surprise.

Salah hid this treasure within himself and allowed only rare glimpses of it for reasons no one else could comprehend. Perhaps knowing that he had access to this hidden treasure, which he did not hesitate to share with a complete stranger, was one of the reasons behind his success in life.

His marriage to Fatma was mere coincidence. He had happened to be at the scene when her father was killed in an accident. Fatma's father was one of the members of the Muslim Brotherhood who were forced into exile during Nasser's era. He went to the Gulf with his wife and children. They settled there and had nothing left of their life in Egypt except fear and distrust. Fatma's adolescence in the Gulf was dreary and unexciting. After the accident and brave testimony Salah delivered, their relationship developed. So when he proposed to her, she agreed. I believe it was fortunate for Salah to have fate play this major part in his personal life. Left to his own devices, he would not have had the courage to make a marriage proposal or even pursue a long-term relationship. Unlike Adel, he did not know how to play the role of the romantic lover. Fatma had a great impact on his life. She put up with his temperament and his natural inclination to be asocial especially during the first few years of their marriage when they had their two children, Yaseen and Aisha, though she rarely accompanied Salah on his trips to Egypt, preferring to stay with her mother and sisters.

We were shocked to find out that Salah had been married without telling us. The wedding was a simple ceremony, especially given that the bride's father had died only a few months earlier. But shocking people was Salah's trademark. It was his way of spicing up his otherwise dull, uneventful life. Naturally, my father was very angry when he found out, but Salah needed to make this decision on his own. However, by the time Salah and Fatma came over for a visit, my father was ready to forgive him. The other bit of information Salah did not share with us was the fact that Fatma was six years his senior.

It was Salah's early awareness of the hard facts of life prompted by his asthma that forced him into isolation—he needed a quiet space where he could patiently coax the air back into his lungs. But his loneliness had an aesthetic dimension. It was his portal into another world that existed within this one. His voracious reading and his accumulation of all sorts of books, for which he had to save from his meagre allowance, were signs of his search for answers to the questions that usually haunt the chronically ill or afflicted. "Why me?" "Why do we fall sick?" Some people respond to those existentialist problems by ignoring them as long as they do not interfere with their lives. Others ponder those questions through art and literature. Salah belonged to this second category. Even the pessimistic disposition, which shrouded his entire life and which he nourished by espousing certain philosophies and reading certain genres of fiction, acted like a vaccine to provide him with immunity from the fear of death. The times he elected to spend alone and the pessimism he cultivated on his own were his way to prepare for the solitary confinement of the grave which is part of the human destiny, where, regardless of the season, we would all have to wait for resurrection.

He was paranoid, but his paranoia was fueled by his desire to find the truth whether in the people he met or the books he studied. He picked the economies of developing nations to be his area of academic expertise because it was a field that used hard numbers and statistics as means to operationalize suffering. The sad eyes of the poor people whose conditions he analyzed must have haunted every page he wrote. He picked this field despite the fact that he had no political interests. But sometimes the search for facts inevitably collided with politics. We all attended his dissertation defence, my father, my mother and Madeleine (Adel's wife). How inspired I was to hear his poetic rendering of the theories of economic development. For whenever there is suffering, a poetic discourse should be made to describe it. This was the angle from which he viewed life.

He always had faith in something. Perhaps he found God during his stay in the Gulf and his decision to marry the daughter of one of the leaders of the Muslim Brotherhood. There was a luminous side to his isolation and his paranoia as if there was a lighthouse sending signals to a ship that must have been sailing somewhere in the depth of his darkness.

As much as reading and collecting books helped him cope with his loneliness, they helped me cope with my own. His books opened up a vast horizon of ideas for me to explore. I will never forget the day I had my first asthma attack. He bolted through the house as if he were stung and insisted that my father take me to the doctor immediately. He wanted to protect me from the disaster that ruined his life. Perhaps my father would have taken me to the doctor anyway, but Salah's decisiveness, "Right Now," was ruthless. That was the first time I received this tremendous love from him or from the "other" that lived within him.

The love others bestow upon us is like random dots on the course of our destiny. We, the ones who need this love, should find a way to connect those dots. Sometimes we don't have the means or the time to do so, especially given our short lifetimes. But we still have to spread those dots on our paths or at least look for them. Someone else might come along and be able to draw the line. At that point, a whole map would unfold, a map we have been unconsciously following all along because we all come from the same origin. I don't know what love is, but I know that the more we are humble in the way we perceive ourselves and others, the more we are likely to find it.

From the novel *Alam khafif ka-rishat ta'er tantakil min makan li-akhar* (A Pain as Light as a Bird's Feather Floating Quietly from One Place to Another), published by Dar El-Shorouk, Cairo 2009

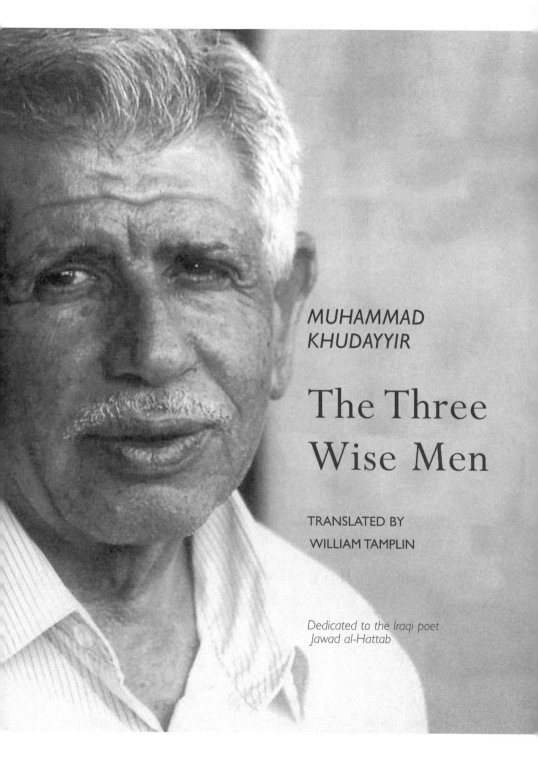

MUHAMMAD
KHUDAYYIR

The Three
Wise Men

TRANSLATED BY

WILLIAM TAMPLIN

*Dedicated to the Iraqi poet
Jawad al-Hattab*

The three wise men appeared in the city. They were emissaries, and they came at daybreak. They walked its streets and entered its markets without raising suspicion amid the tumult, the sirens of hurried ambulances, and the rousing songs.

The three wise men wandered in the city, they wandered all over the city, they walked here and there, and no one paid them any attention. The city itself was crowded with throngs of people who were pouring in from other cities: soldiers, journalists, correspondents, fathers following their sons on their way to the front. People filled streets, squares, hotels, and roadside tents.

The wise men descended upon the city—or ascended to it—on a rainy dawn in February. They disappeared in the daytime but reappeared the following evening covered in the mud of battles that had raged for fourteen days on a spit at the mouth of the Gulf, eighty kilometres to the south.

Then the rain stopped, the sky cleared, and the wise men mixed with the people of the city. The wise men mingled with the dense crowds, full of intent, searching faces and leisurely, distracted ones. They gazed into faces big and small but could glean nothing from them. They listened closely to the different dialects tripping off people's tongues, and walked with the new arrivals from the city's outskirts to the wide, clamorous main square that contained most of the city's coffee houses, hotels, restaurants and bars. The square would inhale deeply, drawing people to it, and then exhale, leaving the crowds to heave and scatter, reassured of the city's lively, throbbing heart.

With the exception of their flowing beards, straight gait, piercing glances, and the perfume they left in their wake, nothing about the three emissaries' appearance was cause for wonder. They wore Bedouin garb and instead of sceptres carried the slender staffs of shepherds. None of the city's people was in a position to recognize in the wise men's faces anything to distinguish them from the messengers who had come to the city in days past, sent from the Divine Council in Ashur to review the frontline.

The three wise men were the last of the messengers who had arisen from the land of stones and silence to the clamor of the city at the river's mouth, the city on the shores of the marshes. One could liken their long journey to climbing ten terrestrial storeys' worth of stairs. The first of them was called Atrahasis, in addition to three titles the gods had bestowed upon him in appreciation of his wisdom. The wise man of many names chose his two companions from among the recorders of epic and didactic literature, both of whom had only one name composed of two syllables.

Despite their differences in stature, the three were equally able to communicate internally, an ability which allowed their reflections and revelations to circulate between them in a telepathic way as if a thin cylinder was slowly revolving around itself, gathering its surroundings, then revealing in images, thoughts and words what was taking shape within. With the same ability to attract and combine, the cylinder drew to itself clouds of words and thoughts circling over the heads of the crowds and swept into its tranquil interior hundreds of movements and forms: sidewalks, food and tea stands, shoeshines' boxes, trucks, rifles, helmets, and crutches. The cylinder revolved, digesting its contents and storing them for the content of the report the three wise men would present to the Divine Council. And the report could take months or years to complete.

The sagacious Atrahasis was familiar with the city's streets, alleys and markets, for he had passed through them time and again. Because the city was renowned for its rivers, the wise men crossed many bridges. Atrahasis, who knew the city's markets better than his two companions, led them to an area far from the clamorous main square. He proceeded with them into the city's markets.

The commotion of people dwindled, the voices drifted away, and the lights of the city ebbed, but the full moon lit the buildings surrounding the junction of the inner markets, where the wise men stopped. From this junction the different markets branched off— the perfume, cotton and rope markets, as well as another complex of winding markets, whose doors had closed at sunset and where silence and darkness now reigned. The staff in the wise man's hand indicated a path that cut through the market on its way to the dockyard.

The river was close by, and the wise men caught a whiff of refreshing air laden with the fragrance of oiled wood from ships anchored in the port with their empty holds. Then they heard the twelve strokes of the old clock tower bell. It rang, always, from a stunning shrillness to a broad, hoarse echo that faded gradually as though it had so pervaded the city that it echoed through all its pipes. After the ringing died down, the wise men pricked up their ears to the whistle of a steamship, commandeered since the war's outbreak, that was moored on the river's wide, flat surface. Its whistle resounded at the same time every night.

Atrahasis paused, murmuring to himself, and told his companions they were nearing the inn where he stayed the first time that he came to the city, in the retinue of King Sennacherib twenty-seven centuries ago. He pointed with his staff toward a gentle light pouring from chinks in a wooden balcony overlooking a wide, open space inside the market.

At that time, the city, close to the mouth of the Euphrates, was called Bab Salimti, which means "Gate of Safety". It was there, in 696 BC, that Sennacherib's fleet met his army, which was accompanying his ships along the banks of the Euphrates. The king then took his fierce warriors to the eastern marshes to fight the Elamites. But Atrahasis, who was accompanying the Assyrian king, stayed behind in the city and spent days in a lodging that his friend called the Dwelling of the Wise. Throughout the succeeding centuries, the city was demolished several times and ceased to exist; then it would reappear in the same spot. After each disappearance or reappearance, the Dwelling of the Wise was never uprooted from its location near the docks, near the junction of the city's inner markets.

The oldest man in the city trusted the guidance of his staff. Following his tracks the other two wise men moved towards the thread of rays streaming from the balcony into the depths of the dark market as they tapped on the thresholds of the closed shops with their long staffs. The three wise men proceeded towards the Dwelling of the Wise.

Stares greeted their arrival. Men seated in the wide entrance hall observed the three Bedouins with flowing beards who stood in the arch of the gateway, opened onto the moonlit night. Atrahasis let his eyes wander about the familiar hall and was comforted by the warmth issuing from the dense group of bodies and their incongruous clothes before he was drawn to the rays emanating from vents in a large cylindrical heater. It lay in the corner nearest the staircase, which led to the upper floor of the inn. They were standing on the threshold, raised a few steps above the floor of the hall. The stares drew the two wise men to follow Atrahasis towards an empty table in the middle of the hall. It was next to another table at which sat three soldiers. The centre of the hall was well lit by a canvas-shaded lamp suspended from one of the high ceiling's wooden beams and hanging just above people's heads. Its grainy light illuminated the shiny chair backs and the soldiers' sallow hands that were devoid of watches or rings, and rested quietly on the polished, newly painted table. Though the faces of another group of men, sitting at one side of the hall, were draped in shadow, beads of light from the heater's vents and the lamp's halo revealed their coarse clothing, their head coverings, their beards, and their bags of personal effects.

Atrahasis estimated—and related to his companions—the number of stairs that each one of the withdrawn-looking men had climbed. There were twenty or thirty men. They were gathered around a long table and sunk into silence, and in partial shade; they exuded the scent of medicinal herbs, old wood, saddles, trousers and slippers worn out by long journeys, many washings, and many repairs.

A tiny man who looked like al-Jahiz was accompanied by his favourite storyteller, Khalid ibn Yazid, known as the beggar. Not far from them were three poets who could have been al-'Attabi, Ibn Lankak and Abu Dulaf. According to a wise man, who had climbed an even longer staircase, the unchanged hall in the Dwelling of the Wise included three or four scholars from Transoxiana and a similar number of teachers from state schools. Neither was the hall empty, on closer inspection, of dervishes, madmen, and storytellers, all gathered around their masters Badi' al-Zaman al-Hamadhani and al-Hariri. On the other side of the hall was another long table, at which there were a number of explorers, rulers of faraway provinces, and military leaders.

The crowded hall appeared to the two wise men as it had appeared to Atrahasis centuries earlier. It looked more like a caravanserai than the foyer of a hotel, tavern, coffee house, hospice, or mosque. The hall was located on that tranquil side of the port, nearest the sea, which was free from radios, televisions, clocks and mirrors. The hall contained a few lanterns on a small shelf, two decorative works of calligraphy in Thuluth script, three wooden columns that supported the ceiling, a door to the left of the stairs that led to the cellar, and a huge heater hidden behind a table in the corner. Its cylindrical, black-painted neck rose five feet high and had a circular covering with numerous glowing holes that transmitted heat throughout the room. The warm air of the hall mingled with rising clouds of smoke from the burning tobacco in the nargilah funnels, scattered about the men's legs.

The warmth was widespread, few people spoke, and movements were rare, when the main gate opened. A thin man leading a blind man appeared in its moonlit frame, and the hum of voices spread throughout the hall as suppressed cries of amazement erupted, signaling the new arrivals. The delicate communication cylinder detached itself from Atrahasis's memory, hovered about people's heads, and slowly revolved through the smoky air, displaying the pure, noble features of the two approaching faces.

The first was the city's ailing poet Badr Shakir al-Sayyab, accompanied by the old blind man from his village of Jekor. Entrusted with the secrets of al-Sayyab's poetic inspiration, the old man was the transmitter of his poetry in kingdoms of darkness and the isthmus of light. Hand in hand, the two men made their way between the tables, stopping by the table of the three wise men and sat down. The poet al-Sayyab raised his hand to shield his weary eyes from the lamplight while his other hand still clasped the blind man's under the table. Then he lowered his free hand to his inside jacket pocket and tossed a small notebook on the table. It had a green cover.

A light tension spread through the hall, and chair legs scraped on the tiled floor. Then a firm, rugged voice broke the silence: "Hey, poet! Sayyab! What took you so long? We thought you'd never reach the Dwelling!"

The resounding voice came from the edge of the hall and belonged to the inn's proprietor, who squatted at the bottom of the stairs. Everyone awaited the poet's response, but it was the blind man's figure that arose amid the tables.

The blind man said: "Forgive our poet, friends. Let him rest awhile in the warmth. His legs are weak and worn out, and his head is split to bursting from the wondrous things he's seen. Ever since that winter long ago he's been dragging his feet along the pathways in search of this inn. A long time has passed. The city's landmarks have changed; new roads have been laid. You all remember that rainy October evening twenty-one years ago when the poet's coffin was lowered to the pavement in Umm al-Brum Square in Basra centre. I was one of three in the cortège.

"The poet's wish after returning to his city was simple and modest: to go to the White Rose Tavern. That didn't take long—just a few steps and we were there. The square, Umm al-Brum, was built over a cemetery and brought together the places frequented by the poet, not just his tavern but his coffee house, the newspaper and used books kiosk, and his barber's shop.

"When we finally decided to make our way here, we said goodbye to our companions and roamed all over the city by night. Every night since that faraway winter, we've explored the depths of this city, returning to the same square—the old cemetery—and relaxing in the same tavern or in a nearby hotel. Then we'd repeat our excursion the next night in search of the lost inn. We were only led here once we'd been led to the simple truth: 'Go to the old part of the city, enter any dwelling, and you'll find yourself in the one you were looking for.' When we finally decided to apply that bit of wisdom, the missing inn suddenly appeared before our eyes."

The blind man paused for a moment and then said: "These long years of searching have worn out the poet's body and reopened the wounds on his legs. But his spirit, which followed him like a cool shade and wiped from him blood and pus, inspired in him new poems that he's written down in this notebook."

The old man pointed, without sight, to the notebook resting on the table between the poet's hands. Then he said: "More poems on the city, death, and women. Isn't the notebook there, Sayyab?"

The poet raised his weary hand and tugged on the abaya of the blind speaker, who sat down. The poet rose, wrapping his jacket tightly about his teetering body. His dry, wrinkled palm pressed the green notebook to his chest, and in no time his words materialized in the grainy lamplight and quivered like the strings of an out-of-tune violin.

"Friends, I have to clarify something. My blind friend didn't tell the whole truth. It's his wont to exaggerate, to concoct marvellous stories. I didn't in fact record my new poems in a notebook. This notebook belonged to another poet by the name of Yusuf al-Tahhan. I met him one night in a hotel. He was a soldier who had been wounded in battle. Indeed, his notebook still bears traces of dried blood.

"He was lying on the bed opposite mine when I entered the hotel room with my friend—the proprietor of the hotel had thought the other bed in the room was empty. So my friend lay down on the floor and sank into a deep sleep. Anyway, I couldn't tell where the sleeping man was wounded, but his bandages showed from under a wrap that covered half his body. When the young man awoke, he found me staring into his calm, broad, handsome face. That really startled him.

"According to him, he awoke from a dream that had just ended. In his dream he had seen me calling out to him from the bank of a fast-flowing river that was covered in mist and surrounded by mirrors and beautiful women. Its swift current was dragging at a boat where the poet lay with some wounded soldiers. I was trying to pull the boat out of the water before the river swept it away. He awoke to find me bent over him. Later, he was able to recall the details of his dream, and arranged them in a poem. He called it 'The Trap' and read it to me the next night. Like him, the poem was poignant and hurting like his wound.

"After a few nights I returned with my friend from my outing to the city and found the wounded poet's bed empty. He must have gathered his strength and left—to where, neither I nor the owner of the hotel knew. That gloomy night I slept in the bed of the wounded poet and let my elderly friend sleep in mine."

Exhausted from so much talking, the poet paused to wipe the blood from his long, bony face. Then the violin continued transmitting the poet's low cadences.

"I spent the night trying to recall the features of that shining face as I stared at the high ceiling. My hands went looking for a pack of cigarettes under the pillow but instead found something else. I brought it out, it was the poet's green notebook, its edges stained with dried blood."

Then al-Sayyab glanced at the soldiers around the nearby table and said: "I figured that in the end I'd meet him here. Unless he recovered from his wounds and is still alive, in which case he wouldn't be here."

Al-Sayyab opened the cover of the green notebook and flipped through the pages with his delicate fingers, saying:

"His poem, inspired by his dream vision, is recorded here. He also transcribed my poem about Umm al-Brum Square and another one about the return of the gravedigger, which I read to him one night in the hotel room. It's all here—poems, diary entries, stories. Friends, it's a marvellous little notebook. And it's also where the young poet wrote down his friends' addresses, the names of books he read, telephone numbers, unpaid bills, and his leave dates. A strange little notebook."

He filled the hall with his weary glances and continued, almost shouting: "Permit me now to read you his poem 'The Trap'. It's my duty to read it to you, out of loyalty to him. It's a poem crafted with a confident hand and a fresh, keen imagination.

> Waiting for the young man
> the old man plants his mirror in the road
> When the young man passes
> the old man will give him a large comb and a woman's picture
> When the young man begins to
> groom himself for the belles
> the old man will catch him unawares
> and open his chest
> and extract a veil embroidered with blood and jasmine
> The young man will sleep beside her
> He'll sleep deeply, deeply.
> Waiting for the young man
> death plants his mirror in the road.

The poem weighed on the chests in the room like an imaginary warm stone, and the men in the hall yielded to that comforting pressure until the weight of the stone receded and vanished and their spirits were freed. One of the three soldiers stood up, and the lamplight revealed a deep scar on his forehead and a stain in the middle of his shirt. He said: "I'm a soldier, as you can see. These two are soldiers from my unit. You're waiting for us to say something. Well, okay. I've picked out some words. I had a lot of words to say, but my short life wasn't long enough to say them. You're absolutely right, dear friend, great poet. You had the good fortune of knowing that poet-soldier. If we'd known him like you had, we too would've considered ourselves lucky. Friendship with someone like him allows you to gain an additional life in which you can travel to many different cities. They give you a feeling of existing everywhere, whenever you wish. It's true, we never met the poet. But that's strange, because that old man and his belle blocked our path on the way to this very inn."

The revolving, diaphanous cylinder recorded the soldier's wisdom just as it did other, unstated words of wisdom from the men in the hall, withdrawn into the shadows. It continued spinning amid the silence and calm where freed spirits floated, making blind, ghostly im-

Statue of Badr Shakir al-Sayyab in Basra

pressions of them. It returned to the three wise men to give them a summary of the invisible but reliable communications. They sent it back, and it transmitted signals informing the men in the hall of the wise men's thoughts at that moment.

Atrahasis was thinking about a meeting that had occurred in the Divine Council. The gods had summoned him to inform him of Sennacherib's terrible dream about torrents of blood flooding the ancient land of Bab Salimti. The gods ordered him to go there to draw up a report on the ongoing battles.

Ea, the water god, said to him: "Let the sweet water flow with ease in the large river."

Ishtar said: "Shoot the arrow with all your might to pierce the body of Pazuzu."

The stormy Adad supported her, saying: "Tremble, quake, snarl, and shake the earth beneath your feet!"

But the shining Shamash said: "My sun will rise on the land of the south, and my rainbow will stretch over the sea as a gate to the boats of the world."

The luminous Sin said: "The dust shall be scattered. The bloody rain shall cease. Gushing streams shall pour forth and wash the land of blood and bodies and carry off the remnants of destroyed weapons. The fertile plain shall appear, split by the River of Life, flowing towards the faraway sea."

Then came the calm, deep voice of Ashur: "After this, peace will reign, and people will love one another. You, peaceful land, shall become magnificent! Make our commandments known, wise old man—hurry off there!"

Atrahasis began to think of the opening words of the report that he would submit along with the wise men. An invisible translation machine translated his words and communicated them immediately and telepathically, allowing the men of the hall to understand his words in their own language.

For the men in the hall, the jet-black night strengthened their bones and enlivened their spirits. But the day's approach shook their serenity and erased their forms. No sooner had the first rays of the sun appeared than the men of the hall packed their bags and hastened soundlessly to the stairs and up to their rooms on the second floor. Others descended to the cellar through the door next to the stairs. At the end of the dispersing procession, the wise men stood up and vanished, just as they had appeared.

The three wise men departed from Bab Salimti.

No one told me this story. I was an integral part of it. Indeed, my name, address, and phone number appeared in the poet Yusuf al-Tahhan's notebook. I was lying on my bed in the small hotel at the junction of the inner markets, where I seek shelter many a gloomy winter night, when my hands happened upon something under the pillow. It was a green notebook, the corners of whose pages were stained with drops of dried blood. To my great astonishment I found my name in it, on a list of many names. Beside each name there was an address. On another page the names of thirty men from different eras were recorded under a single address: the Dwelling of the Wise. On the following pages I read the poem 'The Trap', as well as other poems, including two by Badr Shakir al-Sayyab. On the cold nights that followed, I confined myself to the hotel room and, without stopping, threw myself into combining the fragments of the notebook and arranging its events and names to compose this story.

March 1986

Translated from his collection *Ru'ia Kharif*, published by Dar Azminah, Amman 1995

SHAHLA UJAYLI

A Dead Hand

A SHORT STORY

TRANSLATED BY AYANE EZAKI

I was driving my grey Honda Civic on the main road that leads from Naour to the village of Um Bastin, on my way to the free clinic where I work. A white van was in front of me, resembling an ambulance, except that the light on its roof was green instead of red and it was surrounded by high glass windows. At times, I passed it, and at others, it passed me. I wanted to overtake it so I could get away from the smell of death on the road that calm morning, but the driver gave me no opportunity to do so. When we were side by side, I turned and noticed a coffin through the glass window. The mere metre that separated my living body from the dead one scared me, as did the face we were subject to the same traffic laws.

I recited the fatiha prayer in my head, avoiding looking at the van next to me. We both turned onto the side road leading to Um Bastin, a narrow and quiet road. The van was in front of me and I stared at the words written on the back door under the glass: To the righteous it will be said, "O re-assured soul, return to your Lord well-pleased and pleasing to Him". I looked above the letters, then suddenly a hand grabbed the back window from the inside, twisting towards the roof, tensing a little then loosening.

Behind the steering wheel I sat up. The dead man raised his hand in my face and waved it towards me persistently, as if he were calling to me. I tried to convince myself that it was the person accompanying him, but I was sure I hadn't seen anyone in the back of the car. The dead man continued to show me his hand, as if he were grabbing my neck or my collar, as if he were calling for help. I knew that tortured souls, the kidnapped and the killed, call for the help of the living to take their vengeance or to expose the circumstances of their deaths. Or maybe the dead man was still alive!

I followed the van and we turned towards the graveyard. I considered that the dead man might be a member of the political opposition and that a member of the police had killed him through torture, or that he might be a regime soldier assassinated by the opposition. But then I realised there was no war between the opposition and the regime in this country, there was no war at all!

When we arrived to the graveyard, the ambulance passed through the gates quickly, and the dead man's hand rose, banging on the glass, as if someone other than me did not see it. A woman, carrying an automatic gun and wearing a military uniform and a keffiyeh, stopped my car and asked me where I was going. I responded that I wanted

to accompany the coffin, and she refused. She said that women do not attend the burials of the dead and there were no exceptions. I noticed a woman inside, a gravedigger, carrying a shovel, clearing the soil for a grave. She wore a pair of plastic shoes and a dress with the ends tucked into her leather belt. I said to the guard: "But you're a woman, and the one digging the grave is also a woman, and I'm a doctor, maybe they need me for something." The guard responded with a resoluteness that stopped me from asking a second time, saying: "They forced us, me and that woman, to do this. Few others were qualified as all the men died in the war. Also, the dead do not need doctors."

The honking of the cars behind me roused me from this waking nightmare. I pressed down on the accelerator and took off. The ambulance was not next to me and not even in the area. When I listened to the radio broadcast at eight o'clock sharp, the news presenter announced that a prominent leader in the area had died in a neighbouring country, killed by two women who had lost their families in the war.

NAGUIB MAHFOUZ

The Secret Organization

A SHORT STORY, TRANSLATED BY

NATHANIEL GREENBERG AND HAGAR HESHAM AHMED

In the corner of the club where we gathered opinions flared like explosions. We grappled with our ideas until our voices were hoarse. There was no controversy, small or large, that would not get torn to shreds. Everyone participated in this ritual, with the exception of one old friend. He would ramble on about some passing matter, but when it came to something serious he would zip his mouth and slink away into himself, gazing absently ahead. In a way, he lived on the sidelines of our world. But still, it was his friendliness that kept him rooted in our hearts.

One day, I received a call from him at the office. "I would like to speak with you," he said. "Meet me at the Tutankhamun Shop tomorrow morning."

I agreed immediately. On the date of the appointment, there I sat, right on schedule, waiting for him. When he arrived we greeted each other and sat down to take our coffee. As we exchanged glances I noticed him staring at me rather gravely. As he did so, I began to imagine a person almost entirely different from the one I knew. Tilting his head closer to mine he said: "Think before you speak because your words here will commit you forever."

Naturally, this sparked my interest. I intensified my stare to solicit more.

"If this warning has not escaped you," he said, "we can address the topic directly."

"We have to begin with the warning and then we can talk." I repeated. "Go on."

Clenching his massive fist he looked at me with solemn eyes and said: "You're looking for work, right?"

I was astonished. A flutter of hope flashed across my heart. "How did you know that?"

"I've been following your discussions."

More surprised still, I said: "I never thought you were paying attention."

He smiled, not saying anything.

"Let's have it," I said.

He leaned forward with his elbows on the table and asked: "Do you really mean what you're saying?"

"Every word, every word!" I said in earnest.

"So, then you want to work?"

I realized the significance of his warning, but my cup was overflowing and I said with an exuberant sense of destiny: "Yes."

"Work, unlike talk, is expensive," he said.

"I understand that completely," I said with a slight tone of defiance.

"To feel regret after the fact is pointless," he said.

"That's what I believe too."

"There's no turning back."

"Of course, of course."

"My intuition was correct then," he said with satisfaction.

"You are very shrewd," I exclaimed, barely able to contain my excitement.

In a manner almost apologetic he replied: "Well, that's life."

"Or even death. Whatever God so pleases!" I said sharply.

"That's a good start."

"Give me what you have," I said eagerly.

"What I have is something small," he said quickly. "Smaller even than what you might think. This evening you will meet a family consisting of me and four others. Besides them I know only the person providing me with the orders."

"But the family is part of a greater whole, and at the head of everything is a leader," I stipulated cleverly, adding "What do you know about that?"

"Nothing . . ." he said simply.

"The family works in shadows, so we stay in the dark," I said.

"Maybe, and maybe you move to a family of higher rank."

"And when do you reach the Supreme Leader?"

"You know what I know," he said. "The work is what matters. That and the goals."

He examined me with a piercing look. "They know best how to achieve security and success."

It was a day unlike any other in my life. I was like a man whose flesh, blood, cells and soul had shifted. I seemed to have been in a new world with new laws. It was as though I had said farewell to a life of creature comforts and indifference and hello to adventure and death. There was nothing left of my past but my name, and even that would soon change.

That evening the first meeting of the family was held in a small house in Old Cairo. We were five. In charge was the old friend from the coffee shop. We referred to him as "A". Why not? We had become symbols to achieve the goals.

Sitting at the head of the table, A surveyed us, peering at us with a penetrating kind of gaze.

"Welcome to our family, gathered here for the best. It is with this family that we will free ourselves from slavery and purify ourselves of idolatry. Perfection, Love, Obedience, this is our motto and our bond. Let us work with what we know. Let us not ask about what we do not know. And beware of mistakes, because a mistake will not go unpunished."

Meetings followed one after another. We would discuss goals and means. Or learn answers to some pressing questions and consider suggestions. As time progressed, my admiration for our immediate leader A increased. He was bright, perceptive and upright. He possessed extraordinary strength, as though he were a champion of Greco-Roman wrestling. His seriousness, however, perturbed me at times. He was stingy with his smiles and jokes. But, still, I found solace in the knowledge that if it were not for these qualities, which are quite integral to his work, the Supreme Leader would not have chosen him. The Supreme Leader no doubt picks the appropriate man for the job. Shadowy agents with orders in hand would slink away from his unknown residence. Even A himself knew but one individual from amidst this complex apparatus.

At one of the meetings, after a weighty discussion, I found him sitting in silence. I approached him and said spontaneously: "Is it not better that the heads of the families meet with the Supreme Leader on a regular basis to see how things are going?"

He awoke from his silence and threw me a stern gaze. "All at once you have committed multiple mistakes," he said. He counted them on his fingers.

"You interrupted my thoughts, you interfered with something that does not concern you, and you disobeyed one of the commands."

I was terrified by the seriousness of the matter and said, emphatically: "Sir, I am sorry."

"There must be a punishment. I sentence you to stop smoking for one month, starting now."

His sentence shocked me. But despite its severity, I obeyed in good faith.

We felt at the same time that we lived under the surveillance of our mysterious apparatus and in constant pursuit by the police. This is what we volunteered for, out of a mad, sacred desire to change the world. Incidents and secret fliers proliferated. Security forces tried to root out the sources and often by any means necessary. But we persevered. It was enough for us to believe that we had been selected to join a chosen elite and that our role had been outlined by the Supreme Leader who, along with his apparatus, was now a legend on everyone's lips.

One day, as we were gathered around the table, A looked at me and asked: "Where is the pencil that was in front of you at the last session?"

I replied innocently. "Maybe I took it with me."

"What made you think that the pencils were for taking?" he replied coldly.

I said indignantly: "I will return it next time, or else I can buy you another one."

He said even more icily: "We consider that a kind of thievery."

I retorted angrily: "We have pawned our very lives and asked nothing in exchange. How can we be accused of stealing a pencil?"

He said: "Your sacrifice is no favour to us. You are not sacrificing for our sake. We are all sacrificing for the sake of the goal. I now sentence you to stop using your left hand for one month."

An immense feeling of regret bubbled up inside me. In a sullen mood I left the meeting and made my way to the Palestine Restaurant, out along the New Highway, to have my supper. I sat down at a table near a girl who was alone. Shrugging off my worries, I saw she had not ordered anything and that the waiter had not approached her. I also noticed she was staring at me with the kind of boldness and firmness that only a sex worker projects. She was beautiful, but her appearance also suggested that she was poor and hungry. With her eyes she was asking me "Please invite me for a meal". My heart was touched and I smiled at her. She instantly returned a trite grin. This one walks a rough road, I said to myself. I pointed to the empty seat in front of me and she moved over without hesitation. We ate a dinner of macaroni and bread, which she devoured ravenously and shamelessly. An air of satisfaction replaced her look of distress. Not having introduced ourselves, we smiled at one another.

Just to break the silence, I asked her: "Are you from here?"

"My apartment is just above the restaurant," she said in a meaningful sort of way.

With no real plan in mind, I glanced at my watch.

"Shall we go?" she asked.

I surrendered, neither with enthusiasm, nor lassitude. She took my arm and led me to her building by the back alley. I am not an addict of this sort of thing. But it's not my hobby either. What fate is she offering the single man!

She became soft and even talkative, and not very professional in my opinion, chatting about the noise of the city.

"What's wrong with your left hand?" she asked me.

"A mild case of rheumatism," I said with annoyance.

"But you're a young man," she said, as though it were a compliment.

"Ailments these days don't discriminate between the young and the old," I said impatiently.

As I was leaving, she turned to me: "Don't let this be your last visit!"

Problems at home and at the office persisted because I would not use my left hand, not to mention my bad mood caused by the moratorium on smoking. The following meeting with the family resulted in more unexpected annoyances.

A turned towards me and said: "You are still deviating from the right path."

I looked at him in astonishment.

"Adultery after thievery," he said.

I began to flush and looked away.

"Do you not recognize the gravity of your mistake?" he asked.

"One personal slip won't affect my public behaviour," I said desperately.

"Bullshit. Women are more dangerous than the cops."

I said, defending myself: "Marriage is very difficult these days."

"If the goal is clear," he said coldly, "everything else in life is dispensable."

After a short pause he continued: "You are proficient in argumentation but when will you learn obedience?" After thinking a little, he continued: "Due to your circumstances, you can pay your penalty of a hundred pounds in instalments."

I found myself in a predicament. I almost regretted volunteering, but the consequences of bowing out now did not escape me. I took solace in knowing that I could score points when we were asked to share our opinions or when tasks were assigned that I could easily execute. I imagined our Supreme Leader in the mould of A: a massive figure commanding both fear and respect. My longing to meet him was mixed with the hope that I might never find myself in his presence. As time progressed, my behaviour became flawless and my work was error free. I excelled in my studies and training, receiving great praise for my efforts. The punishments and embarrassments soon vanished from my life. Following one important meeting with the family, A asked me to stay behind. He placed a sealed envelope in front of me and said: "You will travel to (. . .) and meet (. . .) the courthouse clerk. Slip him the letter and then do as he tells you."

This mission was right up my street, as my particular skill set consisted of knowing the precise locations of places around town, the schedules of trains and buses, and how to communicate discreetly in public. I began the task, step by step, until I had successfully delivered the letter to the man in question, who then told me to book a room in a hotel and wait. In the morning, an old Ford car came to pick me up. The driver told me to sit beside him then drove away without introducing himself or speaking. Halfway there, he said to me: "In the back of the trunk you'll find a leather suitcase."

He pulled over, not too close to the house in Old Cairo where the family met.

It was heavy, but I carried the suitcase to the house. Despite the delicacy and seriousness of the situation, I overcame my nerves and placed the suitcase on the table right before A. A sense of pride filled my heart and I was overwhelmed with the sensation of having abandoned the mundane world once and for all. A opened the suitcase, turning it away from me so that I could not see what was inside. He examined the contents for a quarter of an hour, then closed it and said: "You spent some time at a café, forgetting that a stranger draws attention in small towns."

My heart pounded in anticipation of a new punishment. But then he said: "Still, everything went smoothly."

I was filled with a sense of satisfaction and confidence, feeling victorious in my quest. The task I had achieved had a long-term impact on the operations of the family, and through a series of consecutive leaps and turns, I finally achieved high status. One day, A summoned me. I found him waiting alone in the meeting room. He seated me in the chair closest to him and said: "It has been decided that you will be leaving us for a new family."

Trying to overcome my emotions I stared at him in silence for a time; then I asked cautiously: "Would you allow me to ask you a question or two?"

He nodded in the affirmative. So I asked: "What does it mean 'a new family'?"

"It is the family of the only colleague I know outside of our own family. His name is B and his unit is one notch further up the ladder than ours. I have no idea how many units there are, but at the top is the Supreme Committee."

Relieved, I asked: "What kind of work is there with this new family?"

"I don't know."

"Who nominated me to this new family?"

"Your work spoke for itself," he said simply.

He rose, took my hand and led me to a small interior room and said: "Let me introduce you to your new boss."

We found him seated, waiting for us. To my surprise, he looked nothing like I had imagined. I figured he would be stronger than A, bigger. But here stood a young man, just a few years older than me. He had a handsome face and was friendly. To look at him was to be captured by his charm and sweetness. How could this young man head a family that was close to that of the Supreme Leader, carrying out tasks that were doubtless ever more dangerous and more violent? How could our Leader trust two such disparate personalities? When would I ever be allowed to meet this strange Leader who keeps the police awake at night, who whips up public opinion into a state of frenzy? B and I exchanged a few friendly words. He captured my heart immediately. We rode in his four-door Fiat 128 to the White Rose Gardens along the highway to Sakkara.

Before entering the gardens, I asked him: "What do you know about this park?"

Smiling, he took my arm and lead me in. I soon found myself in a cabin overgrown with evergreens and flowers. The rays of a warm winter sun crept across the roof. I found all the new family present. Like my first family, this one consisted of five members. But I was surprised by his choice of meeting place. No one tended to visit these gardens, which had a bad reputation, except for students in pursuit of forbidden love. I said to myself: "Perhaps, in his shrewdness, he is like an onion that must be peeled." We drank tea happily and contentedly.

"Welcome to our new family," he said.

After reflecting briefly, he continued: "Each of you has a commendable record of taking risks and braving danger. We have before us now a new task that requires a new approach and hence a new family. We are not rejecting the past, but rather, pursuing our objective through novel means. Beware, however, of ridiculing your new work because of its deceptive appearance. You are to be like gardeners sowing a barely visible seed that will one day grow into a great tree in whose shade all the wretched of the earth will seek shelter."

After a brief silence he said: "Your previous mission was to confront the ugly face with truthful words. Your new task will be to sing about the beautiful new face that we desire. Today's dream and tomorrow's reality. But what lyrics and melodies? New lyrics and new melodies. Only new ones."

Our eyes gleamed brightly. He said: "I will be your lyricist and your composer, and you will be my choir. For every throat I will supply the appropriate melody."

Our faces clearly showed our astonishment. He continued: "On the surface, our task will appear trivial, but in actuality it is one of great import, with danger lurking around every turn. Each of you must be prepared to make sacrifices." Scanning our faces, he asked: "Are there any questions?"

"Should we understand your remarks metaphorically?" I immediately asked.

"No," he replied quite simply.

"Are you really going to teach us melodies to sing?"

"Absolutely. Yes."

"But we are not singers."

"Each one of you will sing in a public park and anyone who chooses to listen may do so."

"But I have no talent for singing," I said.

"That does not matter," he replied. "The important thing is the tune. The song is a new kind of love song."

"Don't you think the public might consider our singing annoying?"

"Perhaps."

"You don't think they'll make fun of us?"

"Perhaps."

"They might attack us."

"Perhaps. They might. And this is why you must be prepared to make sacrifices."

A colleague interrupted emotionally: "Our previous work was easier, even despite the violence!"

With a smile, he responded: "Very probably."

I hesitated a bit and then said: "I have a question but am afraid of being punished."

B quickly responded: "Punishment is not a word in our dictionary."

So I asked: "What's the use of the songs, melodies, and singing?"

"More than you can imagine," he replied calmly.

With yet greater courage I asked: "Has the Supreme Leader approved the work of our family?"

"We are nothing but tools," he said with a smile.

He added enthusiastically: "Allow me to invite you all to a dinner of grilled meat and wine so that we may pledge ourselves to love and work in the best circumstances."

We began training immediately, memorizing our new songs. Before we knew it, we had begun our assignments. I was exposed to endless ridicule and embarrassments. I believed my new work was harder than my former job. I felt that I worked in a choir conducted by a poet and composer. I marvelled at his character. I marvelled even more at our Supreme Leader who employed so many contradictory tricks and methods to reach his goals. Something B said stuck in my mind: "Punishment is not a word in our dictionary." This encouraged me to relieve my tension with another visit to my girl from the Palestine Restaurant, whom I had not seen for quite a while, despite my having been previously reprimanded and warned that women are more dangerous than the police, and despite knowing that my actions, like those of everyone in the team, would not be a secret from my boss. She was so happy to see me that I soon forgot all my anxiety and worries. I began to discover a sweeter side of her personality, one that was often wanting among those in her profession.

At the following meeting, after my little adventure, B said to me: "I have no objection to love."

I blushed.

"But love without a bond sullies the soul," he said.

I understood what he meant and responded critically: "But . . ."

He interrupted me to say: "Don't cite clichés that we've declared war against." That was his final word on the matter and he moved on to the topic of the meeting.

My marriage to the girl was as perilous an adventure as any of the tasks I had performed when I was a member of A's family. On the

evening of the wedding, B arrived, without an invitation, and pre-
sented us with the finest bottle of red wine. At the end of the
evening, he whispered in my ear: "Keep your secrets deep in your
heart."

My life continued as normal between the office and the public gar-
dens and my "nest" above the Palestine Restaurant. But then, sud-
denly, things changed. One of our colleagues was absent from a
scheduled meeting. Nothing like this had ever happened. B pointed
at the empty chair and said sorrowfully: "He's been arrested."

The news stunned us, bewilderment filling our faces.

"Perhaps he failed to keep his mouth shut."

"His torture may lead to a confession," one colleague said, "that
would threaten the security of the entire family."

"That is why we are postponing our meetings indefinitely," B said.
"At least until we choose a new location. But I am certain he would
die rather than confess."

I returned to my original solitude. Anxiety and fear crept into my
soul as I expected an iron grip to seize my neck at any moment. Yes,
it was true, the identity of every colleague was concealed from the
rest of us. But what was our guarantee of that? These were days of
fear and feeling lost. One day, a colleague ran into me by chance at
Ataba Square. In defiance of our code, he shook my hand.

"Pardon me," he said, "but I have urgent news."

Before he even spoke I was overcome with fear. With my eyes I
implored him for clarification.

"They have arrested our chief, B, himself."

"Where did you learn that?" I shrieked in terror.

"Rumours were flying around my workplace," he said. "And where
I work, rumours are considered news."

He frowned grimly. "It's said he died while he was being interro-
gated."

"How horrible!" I cried.

"The rumour is that our previously arrested colleague confessed.
He sold himself and turned the boss in."

"We should flee," I said nervously.

"He presents no further risk," came the furious response. "He was
found dead, poisoned in prison. With everyone else, the investiga-
tions are already underway."

I followed the papers but there was no mention, small or large, of our group. We were left in complete darkness and our connection with the apparatus was severed. Alone with my secret and with no one to confide in, any hope of solace became an impossibility. Alienation enveloped me in a hostile world where I did not know when desperation would extricate me from torture. My supervisor at work called me into his office and asked: "What's wrong with you? You're not yourself. Is it your marriage?"

I claimed I was ill.

"So, take some leave to avoid making any more mistakes."

I fled from the office, retreating into myself.

Sensing my level of stress, my wife tried to lighten my mood by saying: "Darling, you're going to be a father."

I tried to feign happiness, though it was a feeling I could hardly recall. My thoughts were with the Supreme Leader. I wondered how he would mend the fabric of our torn apparatus. How would he bridge what was broken? Did he know how we were suffering from this loss? Or was he thinking to get rid of us, as he did our traitor colleague, all for the security of the organization. My leave was over and I went back to work. With every day that passed without a new surprise my anxiety subsided slightly. I began to believe that I would return to a mundane state of life, full of daily bitterness, becoming again just one among the millions who suffer and complain and wait patiently in vain. I said to comfort myself: perhaps a mundane ending is more merciful than fear and lost hope. Months followed and my first child was born. I became absorbed in the daily routines of life. One morning, when I had been a father for a month, the doorbell rang. My wife opened it to see who it was.

"He says he's a representative of the Eastern Insurance Co.," she told me, appearing surprised.

I went to the door and asked what he wanted.

"Listen to me for five minutes," he said heartily. "I've come to talk to you about your son, may God be with him."

We sat in the living room, facing one another. He was of modest height, strong build, and elegantly dressed. He had a smile on his face, like all good salesmen. His eyes were piercing. In his hand was a briefcase. Out of curiosity, my wife came in. He waited for her to sit down, then said: "I came on a Friday to make sure I would find you. My task here is central to my work. Our job is to follow up newborns. We visit families to encourage them to purchase insurance for their children. Lucky is the one who plans today for tomorrow."

"Can we afford it?"

"After hardship comes relief," he said encouragingly. "The insurance is for those with nothing. There is a policy for every income level."

He opened his briefcase and handed me a booklet. "Inside you will find a list of the different plans. God willing you will find something suitable."

He stood up and I escorted him to the door. As he shook my hand, he slipped me a piece of paper and whispered: "I have no connection with the insurance company. Read what this says out of sight of your wife. You'll find the place and the time. Don't be late."

That was all he said before he departed.

I wanted him to stay a moment longer, to say something more. But this is how I was suddenly resurrected. My buried spirit was reawakened with holy fire. I returned to life and to feeling responsible.

On the appointed day, I was in an old house, deep in the district of al-Qal'ah. The building was located on the border between a crowded block and the City of the Dead. As usual, the new family was composed of five members. At its head was "C" (the salesman from the Eastern Insurance Co.). Of the other four, two, including myself, were from the family of the late B. Another was a colleague from the family of A, and the fourth was someone new I had never seen before.

"It's been one year without communication," C said.

"A year of hardship and torture," I said immediately.

My colleague from B's family asked: "Is our old family back together under new management?"

C said: "B's family has been reassembled with a new leader. But for all of you this is an entirely new family."

He cleared his throat before continuing. "The past year has not been in vain. No. It was a year spent investigating, tracking, and observing. Our Supreme Leader – and this is only my opinion – needed to be sure he could trust you. He had to test how much the police know and what they are capable of. It is my belief that I have received his orders precisely at the right time."

I told myself this man means what he says. He is capable of filling the void with confidence. I liked him right away.

He continued: "Welcome to your new family – the ultimate one.

The Supreme Apparatus is all that remains above it. In truth, I receive my orders directly from the general secretary of the Supreme Leader, may God preserve him."

He lit a cigarette and gestured that we could smoke as well. Then he said: "Perhaps you're wondering how we work here. The first thing I'll tell you is this: our family runs by the same rules as your two previous families. There's no need to fix what works. So, in addition to what you will learn, don't forget your previous training in your first and second family. And don't forget that all the families are part of a single family with one goal and one Leader."

After searching our faces he continued: "In each family you were asked to love your colleagues. And this is my first request for this family. But you are also requested to love everyone, without distinction. Even if they do not reciprocate your love because they are ignorant of your family's existence, you must still honour the source from which you all came."

He slowed down a bit and then said: "To the thoughtless, our work seems strange. It requires patience, as well as impulsiveness. One must be ready to sacrifice money and soul, but to guard them as well. To rely on oneself, but also to rely on God. To abstain from everything and to be thankful for every benefit. To love life and to love death."

He waited until his words had dug deep into our souls and then continued: "You are already familiar with the mandate of obedience. You are still requested to obey the orders transmitted to you. But in addition to that, you are charged with thinking creatively. Do not rest. Abstain from laziness. Don't have recourse to me unless I give you a clear order. From your training, you have all the skills you will need. But you are free to add to your toolkit whatever you deem appropriate. Your cleverness will determine your destiny."

I sensed for the first time that this assignment would be more difficult than anything I had ever imagined.

He said: "And so what's the outcome? You could be arrested, God forbid. Face a heroic death. Or be promoted to the executive office."

Unable to contain myself, I raised my hand. He granted me permission to speak.

"I thought that the closer I got to the executive office the more I would have to obey and the less I would have to depend on myself."

"That's a wrong assumption," he said confidently. "Because our

Leader is a free man and his revolution has always been on behalf of freedom."

Adding to my previous question, I said: "But why doesn't the Leader allow us to draw courage and strength from him?"

"There is no other way to do that but through your work," C responded. "Which he will follow closely."

Pushing my question yet further, I said: "But he allowed B to meet his death."

C cast a long gaze at me and I felt deep remorse.

"No one can say with certainty what the fate of our dear colleague was," he said in a whisper.

We exchanged agitated, concerned looks.

"This meeting was intended for introductions only," he said quickly. It's time to end it now. Goodbye."

Meetings followed each other, and orders arrived in succession. Our endeavours multiplied, and we accomplished major tasks until victory began to materialize on the horizon like a sunrise. Many fell in heroic fashion, which only made us more courageous and determined. Our chief C would say to us: "Truly, you are men." Or he would say: "As evil vacates the soul, so too will evil aspirations vanish from the earth."

His self-restraint encouraged discussion. So I asked him: "Isn't it time for me to meet the Leader?"

He furrowed his brow, though not in anger. Reproachfully, he asked me: "Do you doubt the fairness of my evaluation?"

I responded quickly and honestly: "God forbid, sir!"

"Is the work you're doing not enough for you?"

Almost begging, I replied: "Sir, I am but a love-starved madman."

He laughed lightly and said: "Who knows? Maybe you've seen him already, but didn't realize it."

I looked at him with astonished disbelief.

"To my knowledge, he does not live in an ivory tower. Rather, he lives his life among the people. He's possibly been to the very same places you visit for work or relaxation."

In denial, I said: "If I had seen him, the force of his character would have caught my attention."

"There's much of great note that would catch our attention," he said smiling, "were we not blinded by so many trivial matters."

I repeated this saying to myself over and over. If it was not for the deafening and ceaseless call of work, all the world would have faded away but for those words.

***

Success followed success and the new dawn was at hand until an opinion burst out. Unconvinced by the recent string of achievements, this opinion yearned for final victory. From which family did it emerge? Or did it emerge from all three families at once? It began with a call to hold a general conference, under the direct supervision of the Supreme Leader, to reconsider the entire plan from beginning to end. The call was met with immediate disapproval, sparking the first rebellion our organization had known. Representatives from the families met and vied in presenting their new concepts. In the heated discussion, each clamored to defend his position and mocked the others' methods. A general call was made for each to serve under their own flag. Anger erupted and insults were hurled. Soon blows were exchanged and in a moment our unity was torn apart. The good ones stood aside, shedding tears. It was the perfect moment, they knew, for the police to arrive and to dismantle our structure from its very foundation. I could not believe what I was seeing and hearing. Sorrow tore at my heart. I rushed to the head of my family and said to him: "What has happened is unbelievable."

"These things happen," he said.

In distress, I wondered: "How can we collapse in despair when we're so close to victory?"

"Keep your gloom at bay," he called out sharply. "Do you still have hope?"

In a powerful and clear tone he said: "Wait. No, don't wait. Hasten without hesitation to do what is truthful and kind. It is only a test and like every other test, the correct answers are known in advance."

I received his words like a thirsty man receiving a drop of pure water.

This is the title story of Naguib Mahfouz's short story collection
Al-Tandheem al-Serri (The Security Organisation),
first published in 1984.

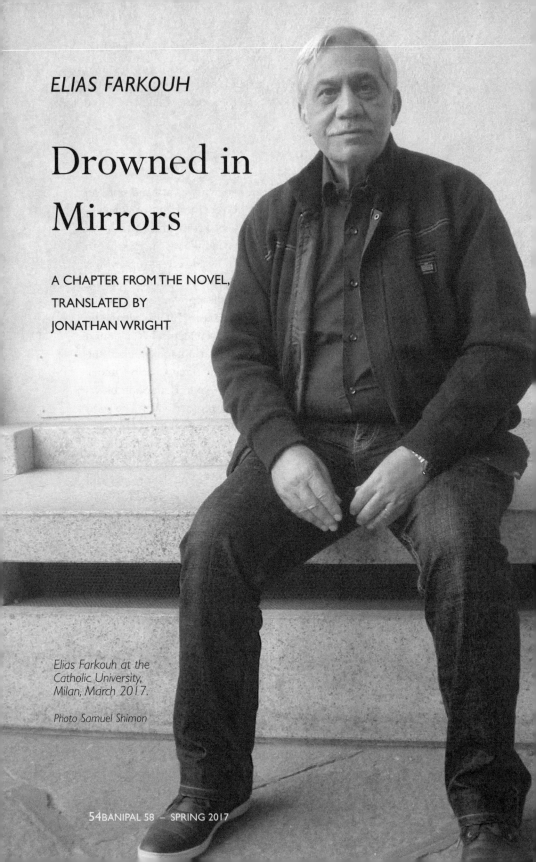

ELIAS FARKOUH

Drowned in Mirrors

A CHAPTER FROM THE NOVEL,
TRANSLATED BY
JONATHAN WRIGHT

Elias Farkouh at the
Catholic University,
Milan, March 2017.

Photo Samuel Shimon

Haifa, Star of the East and Amman

It wasn't until three o'clock in the afternoon that Shakib Effendi learned from Radio Amman what was really behind the events of that morning. He was looking out of the window at the roofs of the tall houses when the booming voice declared: "Weep for the martyr, Karak; weep for the martyr, Hebron; weep for the martyr, Salt; weep for the martyr, Nablus; weep for the martyr, Irbid; weep for the martyr, Galilee!"

"They've blown up the Prime Minister*. They've assassinated him. That's a bad omen."

He went back to wondering sceptically whether the fates left stubborn marks on people's minds.

Was the fact that on that day he, Shakib Effendi, had changed his usual itinerary a sign, and had he missed its meaning?

* * *

Not for any known reason. Even he didn't know why he might have done that – taken a different direction on his morning walk. Ever since retiring from the Ministry of Public Works he had been meticulous about taking a route that was the opposite of the one he had established by virtue of his job. Now it went from his house in al-Malfouf, down the steps that would take him to King Talal Street, past the small open space where there was the entrance to the cinema and the ticket office, and then there were the remaining thirty steps that his shiny dark brown shoes with their pointed toes and their sturdy English-style laces needed to take along the dusty pavement. He then faced, on the pavement opposite, the shops in the building owned by his friend George – single-storeyed, with corrugated metal shutters that were now raised. At that moment he could imagine the sound of them. His damned memory did so automatically, without him needing to hear them. The sound came from the rust that had accumulated in the roller axles because they were seldom oiled. His body shuddered involuntarily and he knitted his reddened, wrinkled

---

* Hazza' al-Majali (1919-1960), Prime Minister of Jordan, was assassinated at his office on 29 August 1960

brow. He would advise George to give his tenants a warning or else the mechanism was liable to break down. He would remember that when he visited George in the afternoon. For the moment the flood of pedestrians and vehicles had not yet started in either direction. The August sun, blazing afresh, was still bearable. The morning was serene, like every morning, and his spirit took comfort in the docility and meekness of life. There was nothing to detract from his love for life today. At the first corner of the Husseini mosque there was cold fresh water that he could scoop out of the earthernware jar covered in damp sacking, using the aluminium mug held by a cord tied to its handle. Then he had to climb up to the coffee shop opposite.

"If life was a little girl," he thought, "I would give her a piece of candy and kiss her cheek." One idea led to another. "And I'd call her Haifa!"

He often had visions of an imaginary girl he thought of as his daughter – the outcome of the wild oats he had wasted in the frivolity and aimlessness of his youth. Then in his mid-thirties he had obstinately adopted the maxim that "Women put a piece of sugar on everything they say to men" – a proverb he was used to reading in newspapers and magazines that happened to fall into his hands. His conviction that his bachelorhood was the right choice was corroborated when he chanced to read a sentence that became a guiding principle in his life and appeased the doubts that remained after he passed the threshold of middle age. He found it on the back of a page on one of those wall calendars: "Marriage in the East is a deal that can be struck only with the consent of fathers."

A deal! He would never make that deal. And so among his acquaintences he came to be known as "the eternal bachelor".

Now he was living the first elation of the morning, and an old song buried deep inside him had free rein to rise up and cheer his soul. He sang the words to himself: *I would give my life for him, whether he remembers our love or lets it go*. The song was not only engraved deep in his memory; it had also spent long evenings with him when he was alone and found it hard to sleep, as on the previous night. Then he would pour a glass from the bottle of Zahle arak that one of the drivers on the Amman-Damascus-Beirut route had recommended to him. He diluted it with a little water and dropped in three lumps of the ice that he got from the waiter at the coffee shop in exchange for five piastres. He savoured each sip. He would chop a slice of cu-

cumber and play the ancient record of the song, which was kept carefully inside its sleeve on top of the expensive gramopohone turntable he had bought from Butaji's shop in Haifa. It was a His Master's Voice, with the picture of the dog seated next to the trumpet speaker. And Butaji himself was now in Amman.

Today was Monday, August 29, 1960, or 6 Rabie al-Awwal ,1380, in the Hijra calendar. That was what it said on the Istiqlal calendar. He pulled off yesterday's day, looked at the back of the new piece of paper and read: "Happiness in life is a phantasm that is sought, but if it becomes a reality, people soon tire of it." He nodded in agreement and looked at his precious watch, a Jovial with a strap that had faded to yellow: it was ten past seven.

There was no one like Shakib Effendi in the neighbourhood for making an early start, except for Khalil, the widower who owned the coffee stand. The one-room shops on either side of the steps were usually locked up and there was mop water, cloudy with soapy suds, spilling out from under the wooden doors – doors painted green and starting to flake, rather like the door of his house. Whenever he closed his own door, to go out or when coming home, even if he did it with great care, he found it swaying and making a groan that suggested it was coming off the hinges, and his old heart would sink. He promised himself every time that he would fix the hinges on Friday but, as they say, there's a Friday in every week.

On one occasion – he forgot when it was, since his memory had started letting him down – he had wondered why people insisted on this green colour. Maybe he was the only one who broke this convention and stubbornly insisted on painting his own door navy blue. Yes, specifically "navy" blue, and he used the English term to describe it, but in a Cockney accent, having picked up some of the Cockney words used by the soldiers in the British army. He had learnt such words in his years working in Palestine and mixing with the soldiers, and he was proud that his complexion, particularly his face with its aquiline nose, was just as red as those of the Englishmen. Perhaps he had acquired his obstinacy and persistence from the English engineers and assistant technicians, from the time in his early youth when he worked in the workshops of the project to expand and develop Haifa port. It was there that Shakib Effendi learned the art of doing things properly, and how to tackle and overcome any difficulties or complications that arose.

"It's a new day," he told himself, repeating the refrain as if it were an incantation he must not forget. "It may be a blessed day, by the glory of our Prophet Muhammad," he added, though that did not imply there was any deep religious faith in his heart. Unlike Hajj Kheireddine al-Warraq al-Bukhari, who read books, thought about them and traded in them near the church, and spoke about things he sometimes did not understand and that did not necessarily concern him, Shakib Effendi saw religion as only a sound moral tradition to civilise people and straighten out the kinks in their moral character. He knew he had not chosen his religion over others as an act of free will. It was a tradition with which he was content without deep introspection, exactly like the ruddy complexion he had inherited unwittingly from ancient forefathers living in the villages of Jabal al-Arab, the area around al-Suweida in Syria. In Amman people with this skin colour were known as "gingey" – a pinkish skin, mostly white with freckles, and reddish hair and eyebrows with that fiery hue produced by some varieties of henna.

"And what took you from Jabal al-Arab to Palestine, Shakib Effendi?" asked George, wearing his usual fez that was always firmly upright on his head. That was on the day when they were preparing the foundations for his building, digging them deep because the ground was liable to flash floods in winter. Shakib Effendi advised him to be generous with the quantities of cement. He even supervised the operation himself and worked hard on the project. Above and below the frame of bent steel bars he laid sacks of pure cement next to each other, just as they were, layer upon layer. Shakib Effendi said he had learnt this technique from the English engineers when he was working with them on building breakwaters as part of the project to expand Haifa port and extend the shore towards the sea. It meant George had to borrow more money from the Ottoman Bank and the debt weighed on him for years. This was after World War Two and the price of imported cement was sky-high, but it had proved its worth since the building was still standing. Their friendship and mutual affection was underpinned by the eternal bachelor's visits to George's family home in the back section of the building. The house had an extended balcony with a view over the gully, which was tranquil in summer but sometimes full of torrential floodwater in winter. You could look out over a group of sheds where potters sold their wares and that looked as if they had appeared overnight but planned to stay forever, and over Abu Mazhar the Circassian's stable, which had piles of straw around it, along with his cows and his two horses and the pungent smell of dung that brought swarms of blue flies in summer. The Italian hospital was also visible, on the hill opposite with its red tile roof. The Muhajireen bridge was to the right with its police station, where the police chief was so strict, and the Hammam bridge was to the left with its public baths and the shops that sold leftovers from slaughtered animals. You could also see the corner where Hajj Bukhari set up his mobile bookshop on the pavement, at the wall of the lower entrance to the church.

"My father took me, George. He took me as a child of eleven or twelve down from Jabal al-Arab to the Houran. We travelled on the Hejaz railway from Deraa station to Haifa. We rode on a goods wagon for free, and if you want to know the truth, we did in fact hide in the wagon. We had hardly any money. We went through Samakh, Beisan and Afula before we arrived."

"In Haifa?"

"Yes, at Haifa station. It was the first time I'd seen the sea. The train station is by the sea."

"And then?"

"He had me working with him in everything, laying concrete, as a porter in the docks, filling bags and loading them at the cement factory, as a navvy in the grain silos, as a seasonal worker in the olive and grape presses, assistant night watchman at the refinery for the Kirkuk oil pipeline. Then he abandoned me and died."

"And then?"

With the indifference of someone who does not want to remember, Shakib Effendi continued: "Kind people buried him in the city cemetery. At the time I was seventeen years old, I think. I packed up his clothes in a bundle, adding the two gold sovereigns that were our savings from a year's labour, and sent them to my mother with someone I trusted. I told him to tell her I'd be away a long time. I wanted never to go back. I'd fallen in love with the place."

"And the English?"

"I worked with them to learn a trade that would be useful. Construction, George. Proper construction. I started like my father, laying concrete, and a day wouldn't go by without me getting a splinter of wood in my arm or a steel nail stuck in the bottom of my shoe and then in the sole of my foot, or a rusty piece of baling wire sticking out and scratching my face. I became a master builder, and if you like you can say that the English made me into an assistant engineer."

He let out a brief laugh but the tone of his voice suggested great pride and confidence.

George changed the subject and offered his guest a bowl filled to the rim with *barbara*, a hot dish made of spiced wheat, raisins and nuts. "And how did you come to be called *effendi*? Did you have a government job there?"

Shakib played him along: "Not at all. You can consider it an afterthought. Maybe it was a matter of wearing clean clothes and looking smart, the way I liked in the gentlemen I met."

Shakib Effendi started picking up the raisins and blanched almonds with a spoon, then with trembling fingers coarsened by working with cement and with soil. His ring finger was adorned with a golden ring crowned by a red stone. He dived spoon-deep into the richness of the wheat and between one mouthful and another, each well-chewed by his strong set of teeth, he spat out fragments of his aphorisms and precepts.

"Everything, George, has a price we have to pay for it. I haven't accumulated wealth. All my life. It's not important. I've lived all over the place. All the treasures of Qaroun are lies. Ours and not ours. I don't belong to anyone. She disappears like a whore. Just as she appears, and God's the one who's running this world. Isn't He its creator? I'll tell you something that life has taught me, something you should teach your son so that he doesn't go astray: with every piastre I earned and that went into my pocket, I was losing a piece of my freedom, so I would hurry up and spend it."

When he had finished off the bowl of wheat, he licked his lips and drank from the cup of water. The sound of church bells announcing a funeral turned his thoughts to death and money.

"Did you see the funeral procession for Hamdi Manko?" he asked, referring to the biggest merchant in Amman.

"I heard about it like everyone else. Many people took part and the streets were packed. Did you see it? Tell me."

"I saw it and, as you may have heard, the final truth stuck its head out of the coffin when they carried it on their shoulders."

"The final truth?"

"He said in his will that they had to leave his hand hanging out of the coffin at the funeral."

"That's really strange, Shakib Effendi."

"Not at all. So that people could see that his hand was empty and not holding anything." Without thinking that what he said might be contrary to polite conversation and the etiquette of social gatherings, Shakib Effendi continued: "I spit on wealth, George. I piss on it. That's what the bastard deserves."

And then, as if remembering something, he finished up by laying out his argument: "Wasn't your Jesus Christ the innocent handed over to the Jews in exchange for thirty lousy pieces of silver? He, the salt of the earth and of mankind, in exchange for base metal covered with the dirt from people's hands."

* * *

"Good morning, Shakib Effendi."

Shakib turned to Khalil, who was busy sorting out the tools of his trade. He kept to himself his sympathy for Khalil on his loss of his wife and threw him a question: "You were a stonemason and your father before you, before you started this tea and coffee work of course. Do you know what the best kind of Palestinian stone is?"

"Of course, Qabatiya stone, Shakib Effendi."

"Incorrect. Atlit stone is better. Did you know they brought the stone for the seawall in Haifa port from Atlit?

"What I know from my father is that Atlit's a long way from Haifa, so how can that be?"

At that point, Shakib Effendi tapped Khalil on the shoulder as if admonishing him. "True," he said, "but they carried the stone to the port on wagons on the railway tracks. The English are devils."

While Khalil stopped to imagine what the route might have been, Shakib Effendi continued: "Is Akram still with his grandparents in Anata?"

Khalil sighed: "Still there," he said. "Until the good Lord steps in and provides him with a good woman to marry."

Shakib tried to console him. "Don't worry, my friend, it's not so serious. I'm sure it won't take long and you'll just have to wait. Well, I'll be off if you don't mind."

The widowed coffee man said goodbye: "Off you go then and God be with you." He added a prayer to the Lord.

Shakib walked off at a leisurely but sprightly pace. The pavement was dappled in soft sunshine as he made his way to his morning objective. On his right he left the end of George's building, where Shourbaji's laundry lay like a deep cave between the street above it and the street that went to the shops in the building below, then the entrance to the vegetable market that overlooked the flood drainage channel, and the fish shops and grocery shops on the other side of the street. He turned when he heard the clattering of one of the metal shuttters there. He saw a tall thin man rubbing his hands together and then slipping into the darkness of the Najma grocery shop, at the corner of the next building.

The sun came out, with such beautiful light, the sun of suns...

He accompanied Fairouz's voice in a whisper: *Come on let's go fetch water and milk the water-buffalo*, in time with the song that came from the coffee shop radio. He didn't have a nice voice. He knew that, but it didn't stop him giving free rein to his high spirits. He planted his copy of *al-Jihad* newspaper on the surface of the marble table, close to the pane of the large window that looked out on the mosque square. He gazed around at the space. Little puddles of mopping water still stood here and there, and he could see tiles coated in sawdust. Then he buried his eyes in the lines of the newspaper, and there was that distinctive smell as well – the coffee shop smell that the big ceiling fan spread around, heavy with a mixture of compacted Ajami tobacco, cigarettes, a trace of that putrid smell found in hidden corners, the aroma of brewed tea and the steam blowing out of the kettle in the distance.

It was now twenty minutes to eight according to the clock hanging on the wall behind the owner's desk alongside a picture of the king, still young and in his twenties, in air force uniform, with his recently grown moustache and a mole clearly visible on his left cheek.

Hafeedh hadn't come yet. It wasn't yet time. It was still early and, except for the two waiters moving around and three other customers, the coffee shop was deserted. Two of the customers were sitting opposite each other in a far corner, conversing inaudibly. The third, in white Arab dress under a brown cloak and with a white keffiyeh over his head, had his back to the left wall and his eyes on the entrance. He looked as if he was expecting someone to come, or was resting from travel until it was time for an appointment. Shakib had a chance to browse through the newspaper. He didn't have to call the waiter because the waiter would know his order: a cup of tea with milk to clear his throat of the strong Rothmans smoke, a large cup, and about half an hour later a cup of Turkish coffee with very little sugar. Then it would be close to nine o'clock and Hafeedh would turn up.

Hafeedh was Hafeedh Eissa al-Akkawi, the man who had turned Shakib Effendi into a man who read the daily papers. He had encouraged him to learn how to read at the time when he worked in Haifa port. He first met him on a Saturday evening, when Shakib was sitting alone at a table in the Shatt al-Sayqali coffee shop overlooking the sea. He pulled up the chair opposite and sat down without asking permission. He said he felt bored and that, like him, he was sitting alone and that he wanted to talk. This Hafeedh was strange. He was the same age as Shakib, in his early twenties or a little less. His immediate family was in Acre and he was living in Allenby Street with his married sister and working at the magazine *al-Zohour*. Shakib had never heard of it or, more precisely, would not have taken any interest in it or in any other magazines or newspapers. Shakib at that time could hardly tell one letter from another. They got along well and they chatted. They shared a bottle of Guinness, which was usually expensive but the coffee shop owner bought it from soldiers who smuggled it out of the camps, along with other goods available in their canteens. They smoked four local cigarettes produced by Karaman Dick & Salti – excellent Turkish tobacco before Virginia tobacco invaded the world. Hafeedh took the cigarettes out of a square box. It was a Saturday, and Saturday was his weekly day off, when he left the breakwater project behind him and, exhausted, walked out through the gate where the salty seawater had rusted the signboard of the English company contracted to carry out the project, the one hanging at the top of the high fence. He forgot, or pretended to forget, his labours at the port. He went back to the room he rented in Wadi Salib, Haifa. He washed, he changed out of his work clothes and headed for a cinema. The Ein Dour, or the Carmel, the Cinema Jaffa or the Cinema Armon. He would chose the cinema according to the film that was showing. It would usually be foreign, in black and white of course. Sometimes they would show an Egyptian film. He sauntered into the cinema, enjoying its cleanliness and the comfortable seats. He came out of the cinema into the street and its soft lighting to buy a cone of roasted peanuts from the cart parked at the cinema wall opposite the telephone kiosk. He would wander around aimlessly, enjoying the night air that was heavy with the smell of the sea and with the mixture of humans coming out of the auditorium, and the chatter that gave their origins away: middle-class Palestinians, Arabs from Syria, Lebanon and Egypt, Ashkenazi Jews from Europe in short trousers and shirts with the sleeves rolled up, civilian and military English people, Germans coming in from their own suburb on the sea. He visited the Germans once on a job there and saw with his own eyes the Nazi flag with the swastika flying high and in the corner of the flag the word Palästina. On another flag he saw the German eagle and the same swastika across the bird's breast, with the same word Palästina above the eagle's head on a curly scroll.

Because Shakib was still in his early youth and a simple labourer absorbed in life as it was, he gave little thought to the unusual political situation. He lived his life day by day, earning money and working till he was exhausted. He was happy-go-lucky and it never occurred to him that disaster might strike Haifa in the near future. Maybe not that near because his memories went back to the year 1928 and that wonderful night in the middle of October when Hafeedh invited him to an Umm Kulthum concert.

"Where did you get the ticket?"

"Never you worry. Jamil Hanna, the owner of the magazine, gave them out to us. He's the founder of the Rabita literary club." He took a printed piece of paper out of his shirt pocket and unfolded it. It was a picture of Umm Kulthum, the diva of the masses. He gave it to Shakib, saying, "Keep it as a souvenir."

As he pressed it into his trouser pocket, Shakib asked what the club had to do with Umm Kulthum. "I heard that she sang in the Aden theatre in Jerusalem a few days ago," he added.

"It's the club that's organising it and sending out invitations. Do you like Umm Kulthum's singing?"

"I don't know. I haven't been following her."

"Come along and you won't regret it. We sea people know how to enjoy ourselves."

It was her second concert in Haifa and she had come by train. She had given the first concert in Mulouk Street and now his friend Hafeedh al-Akkawi was taking him to hear her sing in the Pleasure Park Theatre.

It was a real evening of pleasure with a novel flavour that Shakib would long treasure. He wouldn't forget the Haifa woman who stepped out of the crowd and went up to where Umm Kulthum was standing and said, "You're not the Singer of the East; you're the Star of the East." Whenever he felt elated, for whatever reason, as on this morning in Amman, the words of her song welled up from somewhere deep inside him, in the voice of Umm Kulthum:

I would give my life for him, whether he remembers our love or lets it go,
he has possessed my heart and there's nothing I can do about it.
If anyone has tasted torment by their beloved as I have done, and does not
* find it sweet,*
then they know nothing of love and are only pretending.

* * *

Did Shakib Effendi, now a perpetual bachelor, ever fall in love at the time? Did he ever burn with the fires of passion?

No one can know for certain and no one ever heard him speak openly about this aspect of his life. Just as nothing presaged what would happen on that day – Monday, August 29, 1960.

Hafeedh didn't come to the coffee shop and Shakib Effendi didn't leave his seat. He continued to scan the lines of the newspaper in search of an adage other than the one he had read on the back of the calendar page at home. With his Parker pen in his hand, peering through his thick glasses, the hunter of words skimmed through the text to find an aphorism that might explain to him the meaning of what he was going to hear, now that the small hand of his Jovial watch was on ten and the big hand on six.

A massive explosion shook the whole city. An explosion nearby. The coffee shop windows shook and the customers raised their heads to look each other in the eye. Shakib Effendi looked around: there were the same faces as there had been when he lost himself in his newspaper, except that the man in the white Arab dress was no longer there. Maybe the time for his appointment had come and he had gone off. Outside, when he stood surveying what was happening, he saw people rushing around and shopkeepers coming out of their shops into the street. At a distance equal to the width of the road opposite, scattered groups had congregated in the open mosque square. He looked back inside and saw the coffee shop owner turning the dial on the radio is search of a response. No one was getting any response so far. The newspaper was open and on top of the paper his favourite Parker pen was rolling around. Many of the customers had left, driven by curiosity or by fear of what might yet come, but he still didn't know what to do. Then, as if he were slightly dizzy, he collapsed on his chair and put his head between his rough hands. He didn't know how much time passed but from where he was he heard a convoy of vehicles and a big commotion coming from the direction of the Raghdan bridge. It wasn't a long time but when he raised his head his blurry eyes fell upon a Japanese saying where the tip of his heavy pen lay on the newspaper, but the letters were indistinct and he couldn't make out the words.

At that point, at ten past eleven, a second explosion took place.

Everyone were stunned, and a panic spread through the city.

A secret evil was flying through the air and people hold their breath.

In order to reach home, Shakib Effendi had to inch his way down King Talal Street, where everyone was suddenly rushing in all directions. Some of the shops had closed their doors. One thing he remembered was the pieces of paper kicked up by people's feet in the Petra Cinema side street, to the left of the roadway. The old Haifa explosions, a few months before he left the city, came back to him, and the bodies thrown outside the Jaffa Cinema.

There was a curfew until eight in the evening and he couldn't visit George as he had arranged. All he could do was whisper to himself: "They've ruined my day, those people who are obsessed with politics! Never mind."

He turned around. He switched the radio off. He took the old record out of its sleeve, placed it on the turntable of the gramophone, and turned it on. He walked towards the window to look out at what he could see of a city sinking into a night that trembled. The voice of the "Star of the East" swept away his melancholy and soared, albeit accompanied by a familiar scratching that was now an inseparable part of her song.

Selected and translated from the novel *Ghareeq al-Maraya*
(Drowned in Mirrors), published by Dar Azminah, Amman, 2012

arab
literary
awards

Abdo Wazen
Fatma Alboudy
Ibrahim Farghali
Chip Rossetti
Khalil Suwaileh
Hassan Yaghi
Ismail Ghazali
Fadia Faqir

ABDO WAZEN
POET AND CULTURAL EDITOR

Arab awards: the novel in the lead

The Arab world has recently seen an unprecedented upsurge in literary awards, driven by a growing interest by governments and private entities in patronizing cultural activities. While those awards cater for different genres, the novel seems to have won the lion's share. The local, country-level awards are sponsored either by the government, such as Egypt's State Creativity Awards, or by private institutions, such as the Sawiris Cultural Club, also in Egypt. Other awards go beyond national boundaries and open up the competition for talent from across the Arab World. Examples of these are the International Prize for Arabic Fiction (IPAF, known in the region as the Arab "Booker"), Sultan Al Owais Cultural Awards, Sheikh Zayed Book Award for Literature, and the lucrative Katara Prize for the Arabic Novel (which every year honours five published novels with $60,000 each, and three unpublished ones with $30,000 each).

These heavily funded awards are turning into a magnet for Arab writers like never before. They are also giving rise to some kind of competition among those patron states to attract literary talents, but without imposing any custodianship upon writers or demanding anything in return. Whatever the driver behind such lavish generosity, those awards are surely lending substantial financial support desperately needed by the writers, most of whom are financially distressed, some even hanging on the poverty line. Indeed, those awards have enabled many novelists, poets, and thinkers to secure houses for their families, pay for the schooling of their children and meet their essential needs. A quick glance at the names of the winners would tell you how democratic and inclusive these awards have been, with the avant-garde and progressive represented on equal footing with the conservative and traditional, and with left-wing writers featuring prominently on the lists.

An interesting feature of these award programs is that the vast majority of prizes go to the novel, with very little dedicated to poetry, short stories, and theatre. Some awards are exclusive to the novel. These are more lucrative and have a higher profile than the others. Two prominent examples are the IPAF and the Katara Prize. The attractiveness of these awards has prompted many poets, critics, and short story writers to try their luck with the novel. In contrast, the poetry awards are significantly leaner, fewer, and of lower profile.

These awards give rise to many questions that need answers: to what extent can they impact the quality of writing? Can they inhibit the writer's freedom and audacity? Can they throw cold water on his/her enthusiasm to break taboos?

We might need to wait for some time before we can find answers to such thorny questions. But how about this one: has money corrupted the Arab literary awards? Most of the Arab writers would emphatically say no, although they are pretty sure that money has a negative bearing on literature, particularly when prizes become an obsession for writers. But prizes without money are surely deficient, no matter how high their so-called 'moral value' might be. Such prizes are little more than souvenirs, a certificate to hang on the wall for some time. Money lends appeal and glamour to the award, and turns it to a goal in its own right, a legitimate means of earning, particularly when its value is substantial. Most of the Arab writers feel they deserve compensation for the efforts to which they have de-

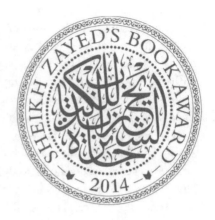

voted half of their lives or even more. Sales of their books earn them only peanuts, except for the "popular" writers, whose books receive wide circulation for reasons that sometimes have nothing to do with their creative value. Only a few Arab writers are making a living from writing, unlike many writers in the west. None of the literary awards in the west, except for a few, offers substantial financial value. However, winning such prestigious awards as the French Goncourt, the British Man Booker, the US Pulitzer, and the Spanish Cervantes, will guarantee high sales, and hence, decent income for both the writer and the publisher. Western critiques of these awards may be right in portraying them as a struggle, or even covert plotting, between publishers and judging panels. Arab awards, on the other hand, rarely help in promoting the winning works. One exception may be the IPAF.

The rise in the number of Arab literary awards is an interesting development. I mean here the transnational awards, rather than the local ones, and the ones with high cash value rather than the 'moral' ones. The latter type is declining, with the exception of Naguib Mahfouz Medal for Literature, a $1,000 (USD) prize sponsored by the American University in Cairo, which also sponsors translation of the winning novel into English.

The International Prize for Arabic Fiction was launched in Abu Dhabi under the patronage of the Emirates Foundation, as an Arabic version of the famous English Man Booker in Britain, Ireland, and the Commonwealth. The IPAF has on its Board of Trustees such figures as Jonathan Taylor, long-standing Chairman of the British Booker, along with other British and Arab figures. The IPAF is clearly modelled on the British Booker, which has given birth to two other offshoots: one in Russia, and another, based in the UK, under the name of the Caine Prize for African Writing (which includes the Arabic-speaking countries of Northern Africa). It can be claimed that the partnership with Britain lends IPAF a touch of "legitimacy" and "objectivity" and protects it from being associated with any particular

Katara Prize for Arabic Novel

political or regional background, although some names on the Board of Trustees may not help give strong credence to such a claim.

Another important question that needs to be answered is to what extent can IPAF help in promoting the winning works in the Arab world? Could it, like all international awards, serve as a catalyst for boosting sales and readership or would it remain as a prize without readership? It is a well-known fact that literary prizes in the Arab world rarely help boost the sales of winning works. Even the Nobel Prize did little to trigger the sales of Naguib Mahfouz's novels in the Arab world, but it opened up wider markets for him worldwide. Another example is the Algerian novelist Waciny Laredj. Although his novel, *Kitab el-Amir* (The Prince's Book), won the high profile Sheikh Zayed Book Award for Literature, that did little to endear it to a wider readership in the Arab region that would have encouraged its Beirut publisher Dar al-Adab to reprint it. Yet whatever the sales proceeds might be, they can never come close to the $200,000 (USD) Laredj received in prize money.

The real merit of IPAF lies in the fact that it gives its laureates an invaluable international exposure through translation into several languages, as stipulated in the contract terms. As such, it offers the new Arab novel the chance to reach out to international readership. This promotion is not based on any external, or commercial, considerations but rather purely on the merits of the work as a creative text, not as an "exotic" text that appeals to the Western reader or because it is light, entertaining and makes a good read on the train.

The upsurge in the number of literary awards is a promising development. Although most of the funding for these awards comes from the GCC states, the majority of the winners are non-GCC writers, which adds to the credibility of those awards. Most of the laureates of the Sultan Al Owais Cultural Award are prominent Arab writers, predominantly with progressive inclinations. The same applies to the IPAF, which has propelled many names to fame – and to the Katara prize, despite some negative points raised by some critics.

These are the most sought-after awards in the Arab world. Some other ones are open only to the nationals of the particular country. The State Creativity Award in Egypt, for instance, is exclusive to Egyptians. Sudan has two literary awards, both named after its world-renowned novelist, the late Tayeb Salih. The first was launched in 2002 by the Abdel Karim Mirghani Cultural Center to recognize homegrown talent in fiction. The second, launched in 2010 by a major telecommunications company, opened the door for writers from across the Arab world to compete over the $200,000 (USD) total prize, distributed between the novel, short story, and poetry.

Of all the novel-focused awards, the IPAF stands out as the most important, despite some flaws here and there. It is the only award that has attracted considerable readership to the novel. Winning the IPAF will guarantee the writer, no matter how obscure he is, high publicity, promotion, and wide review. This is apart from its cash value, although that is not as big as some other awards. It is a "promotional" award *par excellence*. Its true value lies in its ability to propel winners to a sometimes unwarranted stardom. A novel that would normally have occupied the shelves for a long time will be sold out in a few days, and will even go into multiple reprints. Yet that fame hardly goes beyond the confines of the Arab world. The Arab Booker has not yet managed to put any of its laureates on the world map. The translations into English, mostly by medium-size publishers, are still too far from giving the winning works access to the English reading world anywhere comparable to the stature of their counterparts in the English Booker.

The IPAF is an Arab award, first and foremost. One of a kind, with a significant publicity machine – and if I may say, it has acquired a "regional" status. If awarded to an Egyptian, the credit goes to his country. If the winner is a Saudi, the credit goes to Saudi Arabia, or perhaps to the wider GCC. Criticism circulated for some time about the Maghreb countries being left out; at other times, some voices complained about Iraq and Jordan being neglected. It is obvious that the award has come to allure Arab novelists across identities and generations. There is hardly any novelist who is disinterested in popularity, or more of it, in high sales and circulation, and who can resist the temptation of media cameras. Many novelists have been tempted to come out of their self-imposed solitude. When Gamal el-Ghitani won the Sheikh Zayed Award, which coincided with Youssef Ziedan winning IPAF, he said, almost in jest, that he would have preferred the Booker, although the latter offered much less prize money. Ziedan's win provoked a wave of angry sentiments from many Egyptian novelists who dismissed him as a researcher intruding into their world of the novel. A big controversy arose over the winning novel *Azazeel* (see my article about it in *Banipal 34 – The Word of Arab Fiction*). According to some Arab publishers, many novelists would submit manuscripts only on condition that their works be nominated for awards. Many short story writers and poets have recently forayed into the novel in order to enter the competition although they are aware that they have no chance of competing with long-established novelists.

Controversy aside, one thing is beyond doubt: this "Arab Booker" prize has created an environment of keen competition between veteran and new novelists, and has lent vigour, enthusiasm and passion to the literary scene in the Arab world. It has come in "the time of the novel", to quote critic Gaber Asfour, which has dwarfed all other genres. The IPAF has become a highly anticipated event. Each year, novelists and readers wait in suspense for the longlist, then for the shortlist, and finally for the winner. It is an occasion for celebration, but also for criticism and gossip. This time each year, much ink is shed, reflecting divergent views.

Could the International Prize for Arabic Fiction have had all this glamour and appeal among Arab novelists, critics, and readers without the "Booker" name attached to it? The answer is definitely no. For it is a name strong enough to lend the prize glamour and prestige experienced by none of the other Arab awards, some of which are more important and real than this "imported" one. The British Booker prize seems to have woven its spell on the Arab novelists, and particularly on the readers who have grown confident that any novel that wins this award is worth reading. The secret power of IPAF lies in its ability to promote the selected works and to invade the "bestseller" lists. It is an unprecedented phenomenon. Even Naguib Mahfouz had never experienced the luxury of reprints that "Booker" laureates today enjoy. Had it not been for that promotional effect and "imported" aura, the IPAF would have been undistinguishable from the other awards.

Flanked by Etihad stewards are the 2015 IPAF six shortlisted authors (l to r): Ahmed El-Madini (Morocco), Jana Elhassan (Lebanon), Shukri Mabkhout (Tunisia) who was announced the winner, Lina Hawyan Elhassan (Syria), Hamour Ziada (Sudan) and Atef Abu Saif (Palestine)

Authors Ibrahim Nasrallah (Jordan), Yahya Yakhlif (Palestine) and Elias Khoury (Lebanon), three of the five laureates of the 2016 Katara Prize for the Arabic Novel (for published novels)

The 13 winners of the 2016 Sheikh Hamad Award Award for Translation and International Understanding, presented in Doha, Qatar last December. The awards were for translation between Arabic and Spanish and Achievement awards for organisations including Banipal Publishing. See: http://www.hta.qa/en/winners-2016/

Amin Maalouf is presented with the 2016 Sheikh Zayed Book Award of Cultural Personality of the Year by UAE Deputy Prime Minister H.H. Sheikh Mansour bin Zayed Al Nahyan. See: http://www.zayedaward.ae/2016/04/

FATMA ALBOUDY
EGYPTIAN PUBLISHER

The role of the literary editor

There is no doubt that literary prizes are very important for creativity. They are a sort of literary recognition. Recently, they have become a material form of recognition, too. Unfortunately, the national prizes in Egypt have not paid due attention to the feelings of the competitors that there is favouritism, nepotism and cronyism because these prizes are awarded by the state, and most members of the judging panels are state employees in one way or an other.

When the International Prize for Arabic Fiction, known as the "Arab Booker", was launched precisely ten years ago, there were great reverberations in Arab intellectual life. The translation of a novel into different languages is the dream of every creative writer. Building on that, year after year, translating novels has become the main concern of most publishing houses, even the academic ones that previously only published academic works. It is not an exaggeration to add that new publishing houses have opened with the precise aim of publishing novels that could be nominated for the IPAF prize, even though most of them have not paid attention to the selection process or to the specifics of book production. My own publishing house, Dar El-Ain, on the other hand, has had five novels shortlisted. It is true to say that the prize has greatly increased demand for these novels and has made Dar El-Ain a reference point for their authors.

One of the merits of literary prizes is that they have compelled Arab publishing houses to pay attention to the role of the literary editor, a job that didn't exist in Arab publishing, and now has been taken into consideration.

The novels announced on the long or short lists obviously receive great recognition and that goes to show the readers' trust in the prize.

As for the Katara Prize, it bestows a large monetary award but doesn't achieve the hoped-for literary importance, nor the popularity. I would also say that one downside of prizes is that they make some writers produce novels that are not creative, in the sense that they base their concepts on those prickly topics that attract translation, ie, where the three taboos of sex, religion and politics are broken, and are hence devoid of literary value. This happens a lot and some judging panels have even hinted at it in their speeches.

In conclusion, if we disregard the huge number of religious books in print, I can say with certainty that the novel is the main format making headway in Arab publishing today.

Translated by Valentina Viene

IBRAHIM FARGHALI
AUTHOR AND JOURNALIST

Reviving the Arab literary scene

I still remember how most Arab publishers used to claim, especially during the 1980s and 90s, that there was no readership for fiction in the Arab world. But no one paid attention to the simple fact that most publishers had no venues for selling their books. In Cairo, a city of more than ten million people at the time, there were no more than ten bookstores.

Today, it would be ridiculous to make similar claims. This is not because reading has become a definitive quality of Arab societies where illiteracy rates are still a source of horror as well as disgrace, even though the internet is now a fierce competitor for reading, especially among young people. Still, compared to the previous two decades, the Arab world has taken a great interest in novels in particular and literature in general. A quick look at websites such as Goodreads, confirms this trend.

It is possible that the stardom some novels have achieved through untraditional means since the turn of the century has created a new market for "bestsellers". A great example is the Egyptian novelist Alaa al-Aswany's novel *The Yacoubian Building*, which was marketed aggressively before it was turned into a feature film.

But, more importantly, a number of literary awards have appeared in the Arab world. Not only have they increased readership but they have also created a cultural milieu and an excitement for novels even before they hit the market. The awards themselves are a popular topic on social media, especially Facebook. There are also several Facebook groups sponsored by literary associations dedicated to introducing readers to novels. Sophisticated readers have online venues to exchange critical perspectives, which may, in turn, shape public opinion.

These signs of the Arab novel's revival would not have been visible had it not been for the new literary awards, the most important of which is the International Prize for Arabic Fiction. Launched in the United Arab Emirates in 2007 and modelled after the prestigious Man Booker Prize, the IPAF maintains its regional character by reflecting the map of contemporary Arab literature from the Atlantic Ocean to the Gulf.

There is no doubt that the IPAF, often called the Arab "Booker" prize, has given the novel genre unprecedented attention. It has succeeded in introducing Arab readers to novels from countries other than their own. This is especially important for nations such as Egypt whose cultural hegemony has kept them isolated from the rest of the Arab world. The IPAF has given Egyptian readers the chance to read novels from the Gulf to the Levant, and vice versa.

The announcement of IPAF shortlist has become a literary event that boosts the sales of novels in a way that has never existed before. As for the winner, its sales double. For example, the number of reviews posted on Goodreads for *The Bamboo Stalk* by Kuwaiti novelist Saud Alsanousi, winner of the 2013 IPAF award, reached 40,000. This shows the extensive readership the winner enjoys. So far, this novel has had 30 editions in Arabic, in addition to multiple translations.

Within a short period of time, more awards for different categories have appeared on the scene. For example, the Sheikh Zayed Book Award was established in the Emirates in 2006, one year before the

IPAF. However, this award is open for literature, translation, literary studies, children's literature, publishing, in addition to having a special track for young writers. But despite its high value, it is not as popular as the IPAF, possibly because of its administration. There are no clear guidelines for nominations and the names of the judges are not shared. Still, it promotes Arab literature and encourages competition among writers.

There are also two important awards in Egypt. First, there is the Naguib Mahfouz Medal for Literature founded by the American University in Cairo in 1996. It was immediately highly regarded because there were very few others at the time and because it was named after the pioneer of the modern Arab novel, Naguib Mahfouz. It was also open for all Arab writers and not just Egyptians. The winner receives a small cash prize, $1000, in addition to a translation of his or her work into English. Initially, it was criticized for its lack of transparency. In addition, its board members remained the same for many years. However, in the recent years, improvements have been made regarding publicizing the rules of entry and excluding novels published prior to a certain date. Today, the award has great credibility in the Arab literary scene.

The second Egyptian award is the Sawiris Cultural Award. This may be the first prize offered by a private agency in the Arab world. It is run by the Sawiris Foundation for Social Development. Its board of trustees consists of Egypt's most prominent intellectuals. Each year a new board is selected according to specific rules. The Award is offered only to Egyptian writers in the fields of novels, short stories, drama, screenplays, literary criticism, and poetry. It also features a special category for emerging writers. As a result, it has helped many young writers at the beginning of their career, especially given its high value: 180,000 LE (EGP) for the first place winner; 80,000 LE for first place in the emerging writers category; and 40, 000 LE for second place. Due to its transparency, this award has been successful in prioritizing talent over any other consideration.

Recently, Qatar has entered the scene with the Katara Prize for the Arabic Novel, which, in addition to a large sum of money, gives the winner the opportunity to turn his/her work into a feature film. In my opinion, this does not necessarily serve literature since judging a novel's potential for film requires a cinematic vision different from the writer's literary achievement.

Saud Alsanousi, the author of The Bamboo Stalk, *the IPAF winner in 2013*

Kuwait has also started a new award known as the Cultural Circle Prize for the Arabic Short Story. The purpose of the award is to recognize the great art of the short story.

There is no doubt that all these awards have revived the literary scene after years of inertia and have energized the market for Arab novels. They have also introduced Arab readers to authors from different regions and made those authors familiar to international readers through translation. However, in my point of view, these awards are not yet in the service of great literature.

As evidenced in the criticisms many of the Arab awards face, the Arab literary scene is still partial. For example, some awards pay more attention to geography or favour political and social themes over literary merit. This may be due to the fact that the awards try not to promote novels that would be considered bestsellers. Finally, these awards may have encouraged some writers to enter the field of literary production regardless of their talent.

However, there are more positives than negatives. The awards need to heed these criticisms and to regularly revise their procedures to protect authors' rights and to maintain their credibility. In the end, I'm optimistic because the more awards are offered, the harder they will have to work to achieve transparency and fairness.

Translated by Sally Gomaa

CHIP ROSSETTI
EDITOR AND TRANSLATOR

On book prizes in the Arab world

B efore I began learning Arabic, I was just another acquiring
editor at a New York publishing house, and would occasion-
ally attempt to persuade my colleagues to publish a book in
translation. But at the time (the late 1990s), that was a futile effort:
for my various bosses, it was a truism that American readers didn't
read foreign books. As a result, my projects never got farther than
the conference table at the editorial meeting. The number of trans-
lations that make it into the US book market, and eventually into
the hands of American readers is still woefully small, but the situa-
tion is better than it was then, thanks in large part to an array of
smart new independent presses dedicated to translation; some of

the large trade houses have also come around to the idea that international fiction can find a readership in the US.

But there was another hurdle for the translation titles I proposed as a young editor: without being able to read the book in question before it was translated, and with little sense of the book's reputation in its original language, my publishing colleagues knew they were in uncharted waters about just how good or mediocre the book in question was. In those cases, it's difficult to underestimate how important awards and shortlists can be in steering foreign publishers to books they might not otherwise hear about.

In that sense, one great benefit from the growth of literary prizes for Arabic-language fiction in the last decade is that they focus the attention of publishers and readers from elsewhere in the world. I am sympathetic to the criticisms lodged against these prizes— whether the Naguib Mahfouz Medal for Literature, the IPAF, or a more recent prize such as the Sheikh Hamad Award: namely, that they encourage authors to anticipate what judges are looking for, and that they encourage a certain kind of novel or narrative, one that caters to the tastes, assumptions, and stereotypes of a European or American readership. And as much as awards can highlight and champion new writing, by their very nature they exclude other writers and texts.

But it's no bad thing that prizes lend a note of urgency and interest to books that are competing for attention in a media-saturated environment; nor is it a bad thing that prizes make publishers feel they need to be more alert to new voices coming out of the Arab world. Another reason why publishers from outside the Arab world often don't know which books they should pursue is that few Arabic-language publishers compile rights lists for the books they publish. A prize or the presence of a book on a shortlist can at least signal to a foreign publisher that a particular book is worth going after.

On the other hand, as a translator, I am particularly fond of prize

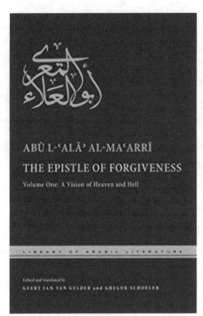

ABŪ L-'ALĀ' AL-MA'ARRĪ

THE EPISTLE OF FORGIVENESS

Volume One: A Vision of Heaven and Hell

LIBRARY OF ARABIC LITERATURE

Edited and translated by
GEERT JAN VAN GELDER and GREGOR SCHOELER

Abu l-'Ala' al-Ma'arri's The Epistle of Forgiveness (Risalat al-Ghufran)

shortlists as a way to keep myself up to date with new books I somehow missed when they came out. Inevitably, there will be books that are new to me, and that I will make a note to get hold of when I can. Even more than the IPAF prize itself, the annual longlists are a real boon for translators, or really, anyone trying to keep track of new fiction coming out of the Arab world. The creation of new awards depends on enthusiasm, institutional support, and funding, but I hope at some point even more awards will spring up, perhaps for specific book categories—such as an award dedicated solely to Arabic-language graphic novels, or awards for specific genres (Best Young Adult Novel? An award for best historical fiction in Arabic? An annual science fiction prize, like an Arabic-language Hugo Award?)

In terms of the book series I work for, the Library of Arabic Literature, I can say we were all enormously surprised that the Sheikh Hamad Award for Translation and International Understanding gave two of our books the top Arabic-English translation award two years in a row, first to Geert Jan van Gelder and Gregor Schoeler for their translation of Abu l-'Ala' al-Ma'arri's *The Epistle of Forgiveness* (Risalat al-Ghufran), and then more recently to Michael Cooperson for his translation of Ibn al-Jawzi's *Virtues of the Imam Ahmad ibn Hanbal* (Manaqib al-Imam Ahmad ibn Hanbal). It was particularly gratifying because book awards are almost always aimed at contemporary texts—newly published novels, poetry, and non-fiction—but rarely for new translations of ancient texts. Even if the authors that LAL publishes are long dead, we are committed to new Arabic editions and new translations into lucid, contemporary English, so it was good to see a new award that honors the hard work that goes into translating pre-modern texts.

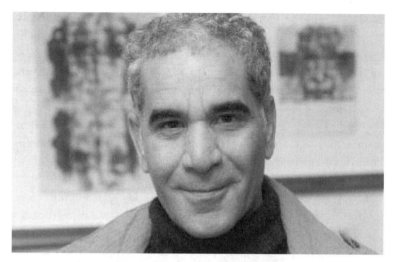

KHALIL SUWAILEH
NOVELIST AND JOURNALIST

Awards, what have you done to the Arabic novel!

W hat have the awards done to my fellow Arab novelists? There is an unprecedented fever to break into a race, as if we were in front of a deafening Ramadan TV drama season. The novelist who has never won a prize is made to look like a failure or, at best, as if he needs the acknowledgement of an award's stamp of approval, which would give him exposure, though he has no record of this sacred stamp. But has the way been paved already before an author can knock on the doors of these prizes?

With some awards, the battle begins with the nomination of this or that novel by the publisher. Some novelists pose the condition of candidacy of their work in advance before the publishing house has agreed to publish their work. Such an author is driven by the belief that one of the prizes will harvest his fruit and satisfy his secret conviction that his "product" is sought after, that the standard requirements for the prizes are met and will stimulate an appetite for translation.

On this basis, we are no longer surprised to find in a novel a character who is a terrorist, or a brutal dictator, or to have oppressed homosexual characters in an Eastern society that suppresses individual freedoms. They are made to measure!

Lately, an Arab writer has refused to make his opinion public, fearing the anger of judging panels, especially since he has just finished a new novel, which, he says, meets all the conditions for victory as required by the judging panel of a remarkable award. To add to that, there is the critical attitude of the "overseer" of the award and mouth-watering spicy seasoning added by the reader, the translator and the judges – all at the same time. This novelist has made sure to not let go of a single thread when weaving his magic carpet or preparing his sumptuous banquet. It would put any judge in an awkward position if they were to think of putting such a novel aside.

On the other hand, some awards for the Arab novel look as though they emulate those contests on satellite TV channels, where the best singer, actor, acrobat or dancer is selected, and is seen to reach the top one step after another. That is how the longlist appears. Then comes the shortlist, then the "Big Brother", the moral coronation and its material twin, while tens of other novels exit the sorting mill.

Finally, one of the trustees of the "Arab Booker" has admitted to having excluded in advance about 90 novels nominated for the prize, while helping members of the judging panel to read 200 novels. In view of the impossibility of reading and assessing so many novels in a limited time, to continue the process of evaluation seems like some sort of Theatre of the Absurd.

So, a large number of serious works are overlooked, and remarkable novelists put in the embarrassing position, when an unknown novelist or amateur wins, of being placed among novices whose works are full of mistakes, and barely eloquent. This is what happens again and again without the judging panels offering any convincing critical justification.

But do prizes undermine the production of novels or do they encourage it? Some believe that prizes contribute to multiplying the number of readers of fiction, which increases the circulation of the winning novel. As soon as a certain novel appears on a prize list, we find the stamp of the second edition, just days after the book is listed. Some novels might even reach a 20th edition, while this never happened to the novels of Naguib Mahfouz, the sole Arab Nobel Prize laureate.

Some have accused the awards of being an obsession, a booby trap, an attempt to subvert literature and dilute its essential core.

There is a third group that hints at the bias of judging panels, at their connections with notable publishing houses, or the writers themselves, and maintain that the "booty" is distributed on a geographical basis rather than according to the importance of this or that text.

With all the arguments for and against literary awards, no one can deny the seduction of the "gold fever" that comes with victory. If he were to win, the Arab author would think of settling financial debts he has accumulated and improving his living standards, that is, if he is still young. Finally, this is perhaps what made Bahaa Taher (Ed: winner of the first year's International Prize for Arabic Fiction for his novel *Sunset Oasis*) suggest, after winning the Prize for the Arabic Novel awarded by the sixth Cairo Forum for the Arabic Novel in 2015, that the award should be equally shared between an older writer and one from the young generation. As for Zakaria Tamer, he once answered the question of how important awards are in an author's life by saying: "The problem with Arab prizes is that they arrive at the very end of life."

Someone has suggested to the secretary of an honorary award to add to the works of an author selected for the prize a list of all the illnesses he has suffered from: diabetes, rheumatism, chronic inflammation of the lungs, ideally even open heart surgery. And in this manner his chances of winning may increase.

Translated by Valentina Viene

FOR PRINT BANIPAL go to: http://www.banipal.co.uk/print/
FOR DIGITAL BANIPAL go to: http://www.banipal.co.uk/digital/

HASSAN YAGHI
LEBANESE PUBLISHER

Reversing the course of regression

A ny observer of the cultural scene in the Arab world cannot help but wonder at the remarkable increase in the number of literary awards – and in the lavish prizes offered.

But the question remains: how successful are these awards in bringing good works to light? A glance at famous awards across the world will show that the prizes for creative works are more popular than the ones dedicated to studies and research. The latter category is confined to academic circles, its main domain. And given the current deterioration in the quality of research and university education in general in the Arab world, particularly in the field of humanities, awards of this category hardly make any impact on readers. Because research works worthy of recognition are in short supply, these awards are increasingly becoming consolation prizes whose laureates are selected on the basis of such extraneous factors as nationality and religion rather than merit. But we cannot blame the patrons for this situation because humanities colleges have become a dumping place for students who do not score well enough to join colleges that guarantee good jobs and prosperous careers for their graduates. In such circumstances, one can hardly expect good research worthy of recognition.

Given the weak impact of these awards on the quality of research, I will focus my discussion on literary prizes, though they are relatively less lucrative. There are numerous literary awards, but most have little impact on readers, even though some have big names on their judging panels. Examples include, from Egypt, the Sawiris awards, the State Literature Award (recently renamed the Nile Prize for Literature) and the Arab Novel Conference Award, which have big names among its laureates list. Yet, these awards did little to boost the sales for the works of such prominent authors as Abdulrahman Munif, Sonallah Ibrahim (who in 2003 rejected the State Literature Award), Tayeb Salih, Bahaa Taher, and others. Besides, there are many other novel and poetry awards, such as the Naguib Mahfouz Medal for Literature that has been awarded to famous names such as Mourid al-Barghouti, Hoda Barakat, Ahlam Mosteghanemi, Ibrahim Abdel Meguid, as well as many obscure ones.

At the regional level, there are plenty of literary awards, but most of them are not widely known. Examples of these are the Riyadh Book Fair Award, a grand prize but with a very limited impact, being exclusive to Saudi writers. Other examples are the Tunisian Comar d'Or Award and the two Tayeb Salih Awards in Sudan.

The awards that are in the spotlight today are the International Prize for Arabic Fiction (Arab "Booker"), the Katara Prize for the Arabic Novel, and the Sharjah Book Fair Award. Due to limitations of space, however, I will comment only on the IPAF, which has attracted me as a publisher although I care little about awards and do not nominate any of my titles except at the request of the author.

One year after its high profile launch, which took advantage of the big name of the British Booker, the Arab "Booker" began to elicit interest from readers in the novels that had made their way onto its long and short lists, and an interest like never before in the winning works. Its strong impact began to be felt with the selection of Youssef

IPAF winner 2012 The Druze of Belgrade
by Rabee Jaber

Ziedan's *Azazeel* as a winner, and continued to build up with subsequent winners, and to a lesser degree, with the short-listed ones.

A lot has been said about the Arab "Booker", both negative and positive. I, for one, look at it from a highly positive perspective. I believe the trustees are duty bound to preserve the unprecedented status this award is enjoying with readers. They need to make it an award that presents only the most attractive. I say "the most attractive" to assert the fact that the literary value of the titles, though important, is not the crucial point. It is rather how the winning work is likely to appeal to the readers. This has already been the case with many of the winning works, such as *Azazeel*, *The Druze of Belgrade*, *The Bamboo Stalk*, and *The Italian*. Three of the laureates were not widely known novelists, but once they won the award their works became widely circulated and produced a passion among readers that far exceeded the imagination even of someone like me, who has been in the publishing business for more than 30 years.

That winners are not well-established novelists is one of the advantages of the IPAF. It has hence introduced new names that would have had to wait long years before getting the recognition they deserve. One of these is Rabee Jaber. The Lebanese novelist had written around 16 novels before *America* put him on the IPAF short list, and then *The Druze of Belgrade* won him the title and moved him to the top rank of Arab novelists. Arab readers are now going back to his early works and are waiting enthusiastically for his new ones. Not only that, his novels are being translated into many languages and gaining wider interest.

Again, the IPAF is neither a "critics" award nor a "bestseller" one. Rather, it is one that has to present high quality literature. At the same time, however, its trustees must realize that it needs to target a wider base of readership, which has recently grown less confident and less enthusiastic towards the award.

It is the award's overall objectives that should guide selection of the judging panel. Those same principles should also guide the work of the judging panel, which needs to strike a balance between literary merit and an appeal to readers. As regards interference, I can testify as a publisher that in no time have I ever felt the judges were under any pressure to favour a particular work. Were there any interference from the trustees, at least four novels would have been disqualified for challenging taboos. The latest of these was *In the Spider's Room*, by Mohammed Abdel Nabi, which I did not have the guts to publish. Based on my close association with many of those who served as judges, including three chairpersons, I can say clearly that they are not the type of people who would condone outside influence from any source.

The IPAF has gained an unprecedented status in Arabic culture and I feel duty bound to testify to this, and also to put forward some suggestions I feel could help boost that status. I feel these suggestions are timely because the Award is at risk of losing some ground. The problem is not organizational, as the Board of Trustees seems to have thought, and which informed their latest amendments to the rules of nomination. It rather goes deeper into the criteria and method of selection of the judging panels themselves. The absence of readers from these panels is a point to consider. They have writers, critics, and journalists present on these panels, but no representatives of those who have elevated this Award to its present status – the readers.

The selected judges need to be independent-minded, impartial, and of proven integrity. This is crucial because the final decision rests with them alone. If their decision is influenced by any inclinations – political, national, literary, or personal, that would deal a fatal blow to the reputation of the prize. The Chairperson can play, or is supposed to play, a major role in restoring the award to its well-merited stature, and reversing its current course of regression.

Translated by Adil Babikir

ISMAIL GHAZALI
MOROCCAN WRITER

Pushing open frontiers

In my opinion, what unites the writer and the writing is purely an existential relationship. He writes in complete isolation, irrespective of whether his writing will or won't be welcomed, applauded and kept in high regard.

The question of the prize and of recognition comes next, and is not pre-determined nor is it a list of the mysterious reasons behind the strange and amusing act of writing.

For sure, some literary prizes have created a new dynamism in the Arab cultural scene, with the effect comparable to a stone being thrown in a stagnant pond. This means that it pushes open the frontiers, shedding light on a specific new Arabic narrative that would otherwise have been relegated to silence, oblivion and neglect.

Some of these prizes deserve credit for turning the attention to

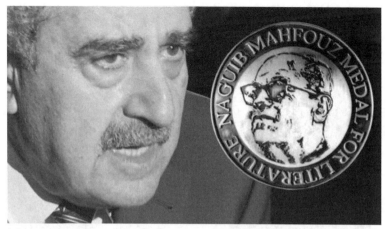

Lebanese writer Hassan Daoud was awarded the 2015 Naguib Mahfouz Medal for Literature for his novel La tareeq ila al-janna *(No Road to Paradise)*

emerging authors (young and not so young), to the artistic value and distinction of their texts, to the creativity achieved in narrative style, and to the unique aesthetic qualities of their work. Whereas before the list of the names nominated would have been decided by official cultural institutions, and would not have been based solely on the value of writing and the quality of the texts.

We can disagree on the criteria that the judging panels use to look at the texts, just as we can disagree on the cultural references, their knowledge of literature and their taste, but we cannot deny that the specific frontier opened up by the prizes has given the works a purpose and an impact within the cultural process.

One thing that has not been raised with regard to prizes is that they have become a centralizing power that appears entitled to dictate the tastes and methods of evaluating Arabic creative narrative. We should not forget that the scope of the prizes is limited; it is not an overall universal scene.

It is a trap into which many writers fall if they start writing for a prize, and rush their work haphazardly. It is a vulgar thing, in my view, and most of such works are born dead.

To conclude, a good piece of literary work does not need the help of a prize since it has a life of its own, with different readers in different places and times, independently from its author.

Translated by Valentina Viene

FADIA FAQIR
AUTHOR AND ACADEMIC

Reflections on my experience as a judge of a literary prize

I was delighted to accept the invitation to join the judging panel of Al-Multaqa Short Story Prize 2016, the new award for the Arab short story, sponsored by the American University in Kuwait (AUK) and Al-Multaqa al-Thaqafi (Cultural Circle), founded and managed by Kuwaiti author Taleb Alrefai.

Prominent Moroccan author Ahmed el-Madini was appointed as chair of the panel. My colleagues on the judging panel were Egyptian author Ezzat al-Kamhawi, Iraqi writer and critic Salima Salih, and Kuwaiti writer Ali al-Enazzi.

On 27 April, 2016, the panel met in Abu Dhabi in the presence of Taleb Alrefai, founder of the prize, to set the criteria for the selection. We agreed on the following yardsticks: content and creativity in presentation, language (accuracy, beauty etc.), use of imagination, impact (emotional and otherwise), and overall vision.

What made the process successful is that both the chairman and members of the judging paned observed total confidentiality, and never disclosed the procedure or discussed nominees and their works with any outside parties. This resulted in a first round free of xenophobia, cliquism, preferential treatment, and also immune to outside influences.

As an academic and writer of fiction, I thoroughly enjoyed the experience of reading 184 collections of Arabic short stories and further exploring the literary map of the Arab world.

However, the volume of simple and simplistic works that get published in the Arab world is staggering and perhaps one reason behind that is the way the publishing industry functions and publications are processed. In many cases, authors pay publishers to get published, not the other way round, which eschews standards and corrupts the measures that commissioning editors apply when selecting a work. Alas, most works that see the light should have been left in the dark. Another symptom of the lack of professionalism in Arab publishing is the number of language and typographical mistakes. So, the author pays to be published and the publishing house spends very little on copyediting and/or printing the text, and the result is poor indeed.

Most of the collections are either reportage, autobiography, memories, or confessional writing thinly disguised as fiction. They are hurried, shallow, crude and single-layered with little dramatisation, and in addition are riddled with clichés without any plot or structure. In a few cases pornography is superimposed on the text where sexual scenes are not justified within the text or the context.

The descriptions in most collections are stilted and the characters one-dimensional and static. And in many cases, you encounter sentimentality and emotions that are not justified within the text, and therefore could not be evoked in the reader on the receiving end, this being a lack of what T.S. Eliot called the "objective correlative". Most collections fail at both form and content levels, which are interconnected of course.

There is a confusion concerning literary genres, for prose is not poetry and no matter how beautifully written a paragraph is that does not turn it into a short story. Some writers use the twist or the surprising ending of poetry in a prose piece. But poetic prose does

Founder of Al-Multaqa prize Taleb Alrefai, inaugural winner Mazen Maarouf and Chair of the American University of Kuwait Board of Trustees Sheikha Dana Nasser Al-Sabah

not turn a text into a short story, which is a specific literary genre with its own prerequisites. There is also some over-writing and flexing of linguistic muscles without much success.

There is a marked difference in the levels of works considered for the prize and unevenness within the collections themselves. Many authors are full of good intentions, but they rarely realise them. Many authors suffer from shortness of breath and sloppiness where the movement of the hand is not completed. A disjointed literary work can be classified as "trauma literature", where there are absences, but the text would normally be complete and realise its full potential. However, that does not apply to some of the collections I have read. Writers, in some cases, are not distant enough from their material in order to turn them into resonant and meaningful literary texts, and many use writing as exorcism or a way to vent anger.

Luckily, a few authors have mastered the art of writing fiction and are in control of their tools. They use a multitude of techniques: the interior monologue, stream of consciousness, a variety of perspectives, unreliable narrators, mixing of registers and voices, operatic chorals, intertwining of fantasy and reality, intertextuality, and mythology. Some can be classified as modernist and others as postmodernists, and very few are feminist. Some texts are original, creative and the imagination of their writer soars high.

In his multi-media collection "Massahhat al-Duma (Doll's Infirmity), Moroccan author Anis Arafai challenges the boundaries between fiction, essay writing, reportage and photography and the result is a tour de force. The collection cannot be classified as a photo essay or as graphic literature, for that would be to reduce its character. Some of the prose rises to the level of poetry. Arafai uses the second person, which readers don't encounter very often, adding to the uniqueness of his narrative. Overall his work is original, tightly plotted, beautifully written with a surprising ending.

It is no mean feat for Arab authors to produce such works under the present circumstances. Some tackled political issues, such as how corruption permeates and destroys the social fabric of a country, with grace and lightness of touch. For example, in his collection *Nukat lil-Mussallaheen* (Jokes for Gunmen) Palestinian writer Mazen Maarouf, who unanimously won this inaugural al-Multaqa Short Story Prize (2016), writes most of the time from a child's point of view about oppression, lack of control over his surroundings, and other issues. This collection, in which each story is mature and complete, reminds us of the writings of the late Emile Habibi, but Maarouf takes Habibi's writing to another level, and a touch of surrealism is added to the combination of tragedy and comedy. The unusual and bizarre are mixed with the mundane to produce texts that are deceptively simple but raise existential questions. The brutality of the occupier is always present in the background and is portrayed indirectly or metaphorically without any mention of the political realities against which Maarouf's texts are set, or were produced.

Very few writers succeed in transposing us to their unique world, where reality is not only presented, but also reshaped. Some create rich multi-layered texts with a unique vision, which might help readers understand the complex realities of the region. In an Arab world riddled with wars, civil and uncivil, and conflicts, to pick up the pen and write is a triumph in itself. Furthermore, to produce unique and original texts that would stand any scrutiny whether local or international is a victory for Arabic literature and culture.

Durham, 25/2/2017

الجائزة العالمية للرواية العربية

INTERNATIONAL PRIZE FOR ARABIC FICTION

10TH ANNIVERSARY · في عيدها العاشر

THE SHORTLIST 2017

•

A Small Death
MOHAMMED HASAN ALWAN

•

The Slave Pens
NAJWA BINSHATWAN

•

Al-Sabiliat
ISMAIL FAHD ISMAIL

•

The Children of the Ghetto – My name is Adam
ELIAS KHOURY

•

In the Spider's Room
MOHAMMED ABDEL NABI

•

The Bookseller's Murder
SAAD MOHAMMED RAHEEM

The Award Ceremony and announcement of the winner is on 25 April in Abu Dhabi.

For latest updates, go to:

www.arabicfiction.org/

MOHAMMED HASAN ALWAN

A Small Death

EXCERPT FROM THE NOVEL,
TRANSLATED BY PAUL STARKEY

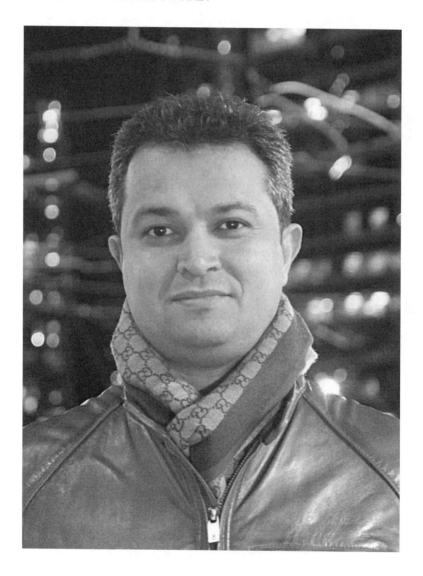

I left the house at midday choking with frustration. Wasn't it enough that the city had already been oppressing us, without the caliph harassing us further with his commands and prohibitions? What was there left for us to read in the books of the Zahiriyya[1], which stir neither heart nor mind? Seville had become really intolerable. The markets were dead. The people were scared. Emotions on edge. Repeated clashes between Christian and Muslim youths loafing around on the river bank. Strange rumours being circulated by the women hairdressers about Andalucia surrendering to the Franks. News of Crusader fleets anchoring in the harbours of Portugal. A massive rebellion in Africa threatening the Almohads. Even winter had arrived biting cold, with winds so strong that I couldn't walk on the river bank or wander through the bazaars.

My last refuge had been Frederick's house and farm. Even this refuge had not been free of annoyances. He'd grown cautious after the new laws and held his gatherings on only a few days every month. Even when we got there, we could hardly find anything to read, for he had put all his books into boxes, covered them with leather, and sent them with a caravan to his brother in Marseilles for fear that they would be discovered in his possession and burned. When he invited us to his farm one night, half of those we usually saw there had stayed away. One of the musicians hadn't come, and there was nothing to drink in the bottles except for a bitter fruit concoction, instead of the usual wine made from grapes. I sat there with al-Hariri, Frederick, Gala, Jidu, al-Samh, and Frederick's Slovak slave that he hired from his owner. They talked about things that didn't interest me, I don't remember what. I chose a bottle for myself and drank, then drank and drank more. Then I told them to stop talking, took Jidu's hand, and stood her up. The others exchanged looks of amazement, as well as disapproving smiles. The musician played what he could without a drummer. Al-Hariri tried to grab the bottle from my hand, and as I danced, the contents began to spill onto the floor. I pulled the bottle towards me, fastened it to my lips and drank until my mouth was full and the liquid went down inside me like a tongue of fire. I held the mouth of the bottle up to Jidu's mouth, but she drew back and gently pushed it away from her. Al-Samh and Gala stood up to dance, inserting themselves between Jidu and me to keep us apart. I emptied the rest of the bottle down my throat and went to get another. Frederick laughed and patted me on the shoulder.

"Take it easy!" he said, "The night is still young!"

I stumbled, and al-Samh held me up. I grabbed another bottle and started to gulp it down. Two threads of liquid dribbled from the sides of my mouth. I carried on dancing. I held Jidu tight and tried to lift Gala up but they both preferred to stop dancing and sit on the edge of the gathering. Al-Samh and al-Hariri stood on either side of me and started to dance with me, exchanging meaningful glances and uneasy smiles as they did so. Several times they tried to snatch the bottle from my hand, but I held onto it as if it were the elixir of life. I stood on the table, grabbed the drum (the drummer had still not come) and started to thump on it in a rhythmless way, shouting "Louder, louder!" to the musician as I did so.

I started to twirl around myself. Time and time again I twirled. I lifted my right arm, which was holding the bottle, and let my left arm hang downwards. I felt light as a feather, as if I were soaring like a dragonfly. I shut my eyes and found myself closing them over a bright white colour, which became even more intense as I turned more quickly. I felt I had plunged into a fog, and my turban had become a cloud. I felt immersed in a light bright as the sun. Stars and planets orbited around me. I seized a star, kissed it, then stopped a planet and embraced it. All were naked before me, and I threw myself on top of them all.

Suddenly, from behind the veil of the universe, there emerged a featureless man, who shouted at me, then pulled me so roughly that I fell to the ground. The table I had been dancing on was smashed, and the drink and everything else in my belly flowed over the floor. I opened my eyes to find myself confronting frightened, frowning faces. I was gripped by a fear like none I had ever experienced in my life. They sat me down, and sprinkled water over my face. They loosened my turban. They undid my shirt and poured water over my chest. Time and again, my name was on everyone's lips. They joined forces, lifted me, supported me, and sat me up. As soon as I could sit up straight and take in my surroundings, I felt that the place was choking me, almost killing me. The walls were oppressing me, almost encircling me, the people's faces were weird, almost tearing my own face. I stood up, slipped away from them, and made for the door. I ran from the gathering, not knowing where I was headed, leaving behind me a crowd of confused drunks who didn't know what had come over me.

I ran through the fields on a pitch-black night. Their voices could at first be heard behind me, then gradually they grew softer until I could no longer hear them. I ran over ground that was at first solid, then muddy. Over grass, then earth. Sometimes flat, sometimes sloping. I could not see where I was putting my feet. Several times I stumbled and fell, picked myself up and ran as though chased by all the devils on the earth. I cried as I ran, and the tears flowed over my temples and ears. Eventually, I found myself before the walls of Seville, where I slowed down and started to walk, panting and coughing. I heard sheep bleating and walked towards them, until I saw the shepherd, who was wearing tattered rags and dirty trousers. I walked towards him, put my hand on his shoulder, and said to him, in a panting voice: "Hey, you, give me your clothes, and take mine!"

I didn't wait for his answer, but proceeded to take off my clothes, as he stared at me apprehensively. I took off my soft cotton shirt, my cloak, and new trousers, and gave them to him. He felt them carefully with his hands. They were fine quality, and I don't think he had ever worn clothes like that in his life. He raised his head to look at me, and I was completely naked. He took off his own clothes immediately and gave them to me. I put on his dirty shirt and ripped trousers, and left him behind me. He didn't know whether I was man or jinn, or whether he was awake or dreaming. Then I carried on walking alongside the wall, the echo of a voice ringing inside me continuously. Finally, I found myself in the graveyard. I went in, paid my respects, and wandered among the graves, feeling at peace. Then I noticed a dilapidated grave, more like a small cave, where I sat down and began to recite the Qur'an.

On the morning of the fifth day, I was found by Salloum. He was at his wits' end with despair as he started to talk, and his eyes were flooded with tears in which hope mingled with weariness. If I hadn't left the graveyard having made up my mind to return to the city, the waiting might have been even longer. With permission from the governor, my father had enlisted ten soldiers to search for me in the area surrounding Seville. Al-Hariri told him that the last time he had seen me was on Frederick's farm, and he described to him the state I had been in when I left them, everything . . . everything, even the clinking of cups and what the singer had been playing.

I went into the house in the shepherd's clothes, which had by then become even dirtier. My face was covered in dirt. I had turned pale, and my eyes were sunken with hunger. My mother was appalled when she saw me. She sat on the ground as she always did when she had a fit of weeping, one leg stretched out, and the other underneath her, and wailed like a mother who had lost her child. My father continued to hover around me, not yet having worked out whether I was a prisoner to be treated gently, a wanderer to be pitied, or a drunkard to be rebuked. My two sisters stood clinging to each other beside the door, their faces a mixture of astonishment and fear, which hadn't left them for four days.

I sat beside my mother and answered as many of my father's questions as I was able to. Then I heard him call Durrah, my father's Castilian concubine, and tell her to clear his bath chamber for me to use. In the bathroom Durrah left me soap, a bottle of rose water, and a new loofah, and Salloum brought the bathing vessel filled with water to the top, which he didn't usually do. I washed as much as I could, got dressed, and left the bathroom, hair and feet still wet. Then I went into my room and slept until the noon prayer. When I woke, I found beside me a plate of fruit and some bread and cheese, which my mother had placed beside me while I slept. I ate a pear and some grapes, which stirred my guts into action, so I went to the bathroom and stayed there, squeezing my insides out and feeling dreadful pains in my stomach. I complained to my mother, and she sent Salloum to bring me some apple vinegar, cinnamon and sage. She mixed the cinnamon with the apple vinegar, olive oil, and saffron, and gave it to me to drink as soon as I came out of the bathroom. Then she boiled the sage leaves for me in hot water and left them beside me, while she massaged my shoulders and back with her hands and stroked my face. I put my head on her chest, and warm tears flowed from my eyes as I wept.

In the evening, my father returned from the palace, and immediately made for my room. He sat on my bed, checked that I had recovered, then asked me: "Where were you, my son? And what has done this to you?"

"I was in the graveyard, Father."

"Four days in the graveyard? We thought you must have been kidnapped!"

"I swear on God I didn't know it had been four days, until you told me just now . . ."

"How come? What happened?"

I avoided answering and turned my face away. My father repeated his question. When I didn't answer, he took my chin in his hand, turned my face toward him, and repeated his question, looking me directly in the eye.

"My son," he said, "tell me what happened to you!"

Then the gentleness disappeared from his voice, to be replaced by a decisive tone. "You dare hide anything from me!"

I took a deep breath, turned my face away again, and said: "It's *jadhba*, attraction, Father!"

"Attraction? What is this attraction?"

"Sufi attraction!"

At this point, my father lost patience with my answers, which he found impossible to comprehend, and raised his voice. "And what is this Sufi attraction?" he asked.

"It is the perception that the Divine Providence has of His servant, through his attraction to the state of proximity!"

"And how does this come about?"

"God perceived me in a state that was not the state for which He chose me, so He drew me to Himself through His Providence, and God's attraction puts reason to flight. Tell me, if a sheikh admonished you, and delivered the admonition well, would not your heart be confused and your soul disturbed?"

"Yes."

"So how would it be if God Himself, may He be honoured and exalted, were to admonish you?"

"But why should He admonish you in particular, rather than the rest of creation?"

"Because I am a *wali*[2]!"

My father was silent for a moment then turned his head left and right, looking in the empty room for something to help him steady his nerves. He gave a great sigh then said: "Wake up, my son, awake from your present state, and do not continue indifferent to your error! What sort of holy man is this, who is twenty-two years old and spends his nights with whores and singing girls?"

"God decreed that I should become drunk and seek pleasure so that I should experience the divine attraction and be truly restored to God's favour."

"Just like that? Is it that straightforward? We get drunk to become holy?"

I did not answer my father's question, which was a mixture of anger and sarcasm. I remained silent as I digested his rebukes, which were repeated several times. My father was at a loss what to say. "Why the graveyard?" he asked. "Why didn't you come back home?"

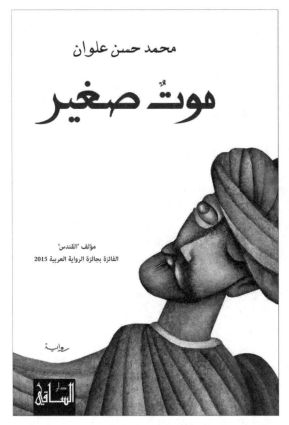

"In the graveyard I suspended my soul with God. A thousand thousand times I asked Him to employ me in whatever might please Him and not to employ me in what would take me away from Him."

"A thousand thousand times?"

"Yes, Father, a thousand thousand times! And when I had completed that number, I left and came to you, and now you say that it was four days according to your calculations. But in the

---

A Small Death *is the fictionalised account of the life of a Sufi saint, Muhyiddin Ibn 'Arabi, from his birth in Muslim Spain in the 12th century until his death in Damascus. It follows his mystic Sufi experience and heroic travels from Andalusia to Azerbaijan, via Morocco, Egypt, the Hijaz, Syria, Iraq and Turkey. Of a sensitive and anxious nature, Muhyiddin struggles with inner turmoil throughout the course of his travels. Witnessing fictitious events including savage military conflicts, he attempts to fulfil his mission against a backdrop of states and numerous cities where he meets countless people.*

Published by Dar Al-Saqi, Beirut, Lebanon, March 2016

estimation of my solitude, it was a thousand thousand prayers. Such is my time. And how great a difference between that and your time!"

My father stood up, as if his patience had been totally exhausted. He was about to go out but he stopped by the door of the room, turned toward me and said in a despairing voice: "God knows, my son, I have seen doers of good and doers of evil, saints and sinners, innocents and profligates, but I do not know which sort you are. I believe that your mind has simply been warped by delusion, so that you have started to think yourself a holy man when you are no such thing, and consider yourself pious when you are not, and to my mind this has come about through though an excess of leisure and a lack of occupation!"

"I am occupied with the remembrance of God and my leisure is filled with His light!"

"Oh, get lost! First you occupy yourself with whores and drink, then jostle the dead in their graves! Now, you have heard that the caliph Ya'qub has ordered drinkers of alcohol to be flogged, and be put to death if they re-offend, and I am afraid you may meet an end that is not that of a sheikh or a holy man. So put your affairs in order!"

My father's despairing tone encouraged me to say: "Then let me travel, Father!"

My father was angered by my request. He stood in the middle of the room and raised his arms in the air as he shouted: "Travel? I cannot trust your reason in Seville where I can keep my eye on you, so how could I trust you somewhere else, out of my sight? Stay here where you are, and stop wasting my time!"

This time, he really did leave the room. Suddenly, however, he came back in. "Be informed" he said, "that I am putting you under surveillance, and I swear by God, if I hear about you anything that I do not wish to hear, I will show you things that you will not wish to see!"

Notes:
1. A school of thought in Islamic jurisprudence founded by Dawud al-Zahiri in the ninth century CE, characterized by reliance on the manifest (*zahir*) meaning of the text of the Qur'an and the hadith, as well as rejection of analogical deduction (*qiyas*). The Zahiri school enjoyed only limited success in the Middle East, but briefly flourished under the Almohads in Spain in the twelfth century CE, particularly under the leadership of Ibn Hazm.
2. An Islamic saint, or 'friend of God', in the Sufi tradition.

NAJWA BINSHATWAN

The Cloak and
the Family Tree

A CHAPTER FROM THE NOVEL *THE SLAVE PENS*,
TRANSLATED BY RAPHAEL COHEN

My Aunt Sabriya was dealing with something in the city, then came back and was horror struck at the sight of the Pens ablaze and in flames. The authorities were stamping out the plague in one fell swoop. Death was running rampant and their colony might die too if they did not confront it decisively. That meant they had to burn the Pens to the ground. And, honestly, that's what they did!

My Aunt Sabriya dropped the fava beans and chickpeas she had brought for us. In the distance, she screamed in disbelief at the catastrophe that had befallen the Pens. The Pens were on fire while Benghazi, enclosed by a high wall, absentmindedly sucked up the smoke in front of the people. It was said that the plague had been carried by the tears of black Libyans and that day the same tears became an ocean to rival the sea before them.

That ill-fated day my aunt felt an affection for the Pens unlike the way she had left it. She started running, the fear making her heart fail. What was happening? The situation needed no interpretation. We had only to take in what we saw with our own eyes, which confused and shocked us. None of those crowding like ants at the entrances to the Pens noticed my aunt. In that apocalyptic scene, it was barely possible to be aware of yourself. Fire, not water or the wind this time, was destroying everything. My Aunt Sabriya took no notice of the rows of soldiers preventing access, simply shouting as she pushed past them: "Don't you dare stop me, I must get the cloak and the family tree!"

All that could be made out was her grey cloak flying around her, her voice that had turned into a strangled wailing, and her dusty bare feet. Giuseppe tried to catch up with her, but the head of the contingent grabbed hold of him and reminded him that the people in there had the plague. In tears, my Aunt Aida was shouting at the soldiers: "Don't pour petrol on the entrances. She's coming back. Give her a chance. Half the Pens haven't burnt down yet."

Aunt Aida addressed a senior officer and a medic with a Red Cross badge on his arm. The doctor shook his head that it was no use and with great sorrow lifted her hands off him. The soldier carrying the jerry can of petrol refused to stop, and executed his officers' orders. He emptied out the jerry can and sealed the last living part of the Pens with fire. I realised then that I would lose my Aunt Sabriya in the inferno. I scrabbled at the earth with my fingers to prevent the fire taking hold. Giuseppe hurried to help strew earth over the petrol on the ground. Aunt Aida and other blacks joined in, while yet others charged to the sea to scoop up water to help put out the fire. They were desperately trying to save their devastated homes. But they could only try.

From every direction, the inhabitants of the Pens battled to put out the fire. They grew tired, but the fire did not tire. Giuseppe started to pull me away. He gripped my arm and dragged me backwards as best he could. His hands were dry and my body a heavy corpse.

I had begged them to put the fire out, and later I remembered that Giuseppe, in his still clean clothes and dust-covered face, scraped up the dirt like me to put out the fire while Auntie Aida struggled with the soldiers and, together with a black translator who was part of the campaign to eradicate the plague, shouted at them. They just pushed her away as she asked the translator to tell them that Aunt Sabriya was healthy and had not caught the plague. "Tell them she's getting her savings and will come back. Tell them she won't take long. Give her a moment to survive, don't burn her alive when she's healthy."

We lost Sabriya. No one came back. Exhausted people started to gather together like an infected herd of cattle. The soldiers threatened to open fire if people refused to walk to the quarantine in Jalyana. We were filled with despair and grief, while their vehicles filled the air around us with dust. Aida's screams grew louder; what was happening was driving her mad. She slapped herself and tore her clothing. Her terror-stricken eyes sought me out. When she found me the look in her eyes was truly frightening. She pulled me hard by the shoulders, jolting me out of the vacuum in my head, until she had wrenched me out of Giuseppe's hands and was leading me back towards the Pens. All the people were going in the opposite direction. I was in a state of delirium, unable to believe that my Aunt Sabriya had been trapped inside by the fire. I wanted any kind of miracle to happen that would bring her back to us at any moment. I looked around through the vast clouds of smoke. I could see only a giant furnace consuming everything. I reckoned that she would suffocate, then burn: her lungs were weak and would succumb first.

My Aunt Aida was in shock like me. When it seemed as if everyone was actually burning alive, I became certain of something she had started to hint at. "Weep for the woman who isn't coming back. Weep for your mother. Weep for your mother."

She shook me hard in Giuseppe's hands, who had caught up with us in an effort to get me out of her clutches. "Taawidha is your mother. Your mother, not your aunt. Sabriya is your mother, not your aunt."

Some soldiers hit Aunt Aida with their rifle butts and warned her to move off as she was obstructing their mission against the plague. Giuseppe was in despair, he pulled me away and hid my face in his chest so I would not witness any more. I had become a real orphan. I had lost my root in life at the very moment I discovered it. I missed her as though she had been my mother my whole life, not my aunt. To escape harm and fearful for me from man's evil she had disguised herself to disguise me. She was my mother, who had stepped into many fires for my sake, not just that final one to rescue the family tree that acknowledged who my father was, and was supported by his cloak, the man's protection, covering, and honour. She was my mother, whom the burning ground did not allow to come out alive and back to me. I was crying and wailing and Giuseppe took me in his arms in sympathy with my plight, shocked like me by what Aida had said. He told the commander of the medical mission that he would take me in his cart with him.

I shouted the word "Mummy" for the first time in my life: "Mummy, don't leave me. Mummy, come back. Mummy, don't go."

Argh, the misery! I called out what I had lost at the moment I lost it. I was ignorant of what I knew at the moment I was aware of it.

Was it the work of man, or the work of fate?

Giuseppe did not leave me. As we were riding the cart he said: "They'll take us somewhere where we all have to shower and be disinfected, and they'll get rid of our clothes and things." He cried like me, and fought the tears, placing my head on his shoulder, while a crazed person left my body leaping towards the Pens. Giuseppe screamed at me: "Don't look back! Don't look back!"

But I was reviewing the heritage of my ancestors whom my ancestors enslaved, with my eyes shut, so that my death did not see my death.

The last thing I saw of the tragedy of the Pens was the thick black smoke obscuring heaven and earth. A foul stench of human and animal bodies roasted alive. My mother's spirit, untouched by the

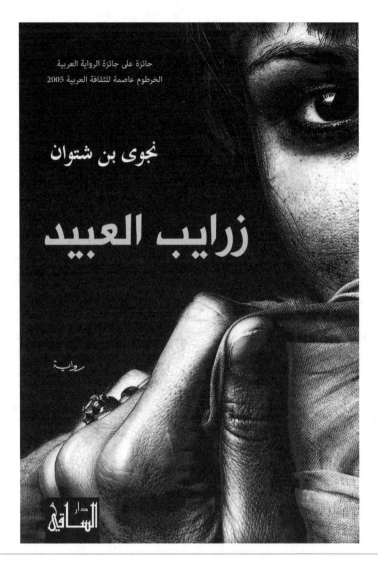

جائزة على جائزة الرواية العربية
الخرطوم عاصمة للثقافة العربية 2005

نجوى بن شتوان

زرايب العبيد

رواية

The Slaves' Pens *lifts the lid on the dark, untold history of slavery in Libya, of which the effects can still be felt today. Slave owner Mohammed and his slave Ta'awidha have fallen in love, but their relationship is considered taboo. Living in a community where masters take female slaves as lovers as they please, Mohammed's father sends him on a trading mission in an attempt to distance him from Ta'awidha. During his absence, his mother forces her to miscarry by serving her a spiked drink, and she is married off to another slave. On his return from his trip, Mohammed learns of his family's activities and he begins searching for his beloved.*

Published by Dar Al-Saqi, Beirut, Lebanon, May 2016

plague, had asphyxiated, dust to dust, ashes to ashes, she and those trapped there by the fire. They were still alive when the authorities splashed petrol over the huts and set them on fire with their inhabitants inside. I clung on to the fading vision, crying, until I imagined I could see my mother in the Pens moving away into the sky as if she were stepping between the shacks and huts heading for the sea to wash her clothes, to wash the mats, to vanish like little girls did with unworldly beings never to return. That was the first and last time, full of sorrow and grief, that I uttered the word "Mummy", yet my mother did not hear it, nor my Aunt Sabriya, as she had chosen for me to call her always to protect me.

At the Josephite Mission two nuns sedated me with an injection. I think I must have slept there for days from the shock of my loss. Whenever I raised my head I fell back into my coma. Perhaps that was for the best. For days it kept me away from the pain. I just knew I was still breathing when I opened my eyes and saw the white sisters in their clean outfits wandering around me, saying something to me, holding my hand and smiling. It was as if I only opened my eyes to get one of those smiles and then went back into my coma again.

I knew that Giuseppe was with me. He assiduously checked up on everyone he knew from the Pens. Most of them were no longer around. He searched for my Aunt Aida to find out the truth about all the things whose truth was hidden from me. He said that the people would go back to the Pens once the grief had subsided to pray over the remains of the dead and bury the remnants according to Islamic law. Then the Italian government would build them a new camp.

The Pens died, but lived on in us in another form.

Giuseppe said he would go with them and try to find our tin shack if he could and bring me what he could find. Hesitantly, in recognition of the inanity of the question, he asked me: "What would you like me to look for there?"

He hung his head when he saw me cry and wiped my face with his hand. I was laid up in a bed in a whitewashed room, empty except for a small table and a large crucifix on the wall opposite. Around me were the faces of three Italian nuns talking with Giuseppe. I imagined I was in a place whose like I had never seen. I heard them talking about me because I was only present as a poor body from the Pens. I had lost everything. My life would not be easy from now on. I was a young orphan. Where would she go after coming out of the coma?

That silent room and that phrase, which the sisters often repeated when talking next to me whether on their own or with Giuseppe, remained swaying in my mind, lay in wait in a distant corner of my soul, and raced like a hungry beast towards its prey whenever the pain of the loss touched me again.

"The poor child! No mother, no father, no family!"

It was not just the loss of my aunt, who was my mother, but of the Pens and everything about them: my childhood, my work, my life, my aunts, my friends, the sea, the large riddle for sifting sand, love, song, dance, tears, the slave Iltiqaz, Muftah who always came from afar, the heart of Buqa, about whom an Italian surgeon who sold dead bodies to the medical school in Rome said: "This heart, my friend, which looks like the heart of a sheep, is from a fabulous corpse."

The Pens could not possibly fade away for me, or burn down, so what could Giuseppe bring me from the ruins of me there?

I thought that Muftah had been spared witnessing that black day, but I saw that he was not spared the sorrow it caused him. He venerated the site of our shack in the Pens and visited it. He would sit there on the ground and cry alone, not wanting anyone to comfort him.

Once, on the morning of his wedding day, we couldn't find him. I figured where I might find him and rode the cart with Giuseppe to the sea. I spotted him there in the distance, in the Arab robes of a bridegroom. He was sitting with his head on his knees, telling my mother that he had got married, and that he missed her on his happiest day. He promised her he would do all he had promised her, give her name to the child, go on the Hajj for her, and never abandon me.

I heard his words as we drew nearer. He broke down in tears when I came up and hugged him. As the tears dripped down his cheeks he said: "I miss her, little sister, I miss her."

I am the legacy of those whose death was never seen. They closed their eyes to them so as not to see the cruelty, just leaving an opening for the tears.

I sprouted from what fell from those eyes.

ISMAIL FAHD ISMAIL

Al-Sabiliat

EXCERPT FROM THE NOVEL,

TRANSLATED BY WILLIAM M. HUTCHINS

As the pace of the Iraq-Iran War of September 1980 to August 1988 began to accelerate, the Iraqi government issued a binding decree, the gist of which was: "To protect the safety of our citizens who dwell in villages and towns located near battle fronts we have ordered that . . ."

Umm Qasim remembers that a military jeep with a loudspeaker came down the only road traversing the village of al-Sabiliat. That imperious voice would brook no dissent. All citizens had to vacate their dwellings in three days at the latest. Anyone who wondered where he could go received an immediate reply. The other Iraqi governorates are prepared to accommodate all persons displaced from the Basra Governorate. Reassuring words were attached to the response. The current mobilization will not last more than three months, perhaps less. Then you will return to your homes and orchards.

Umm Qasim struggles to remember more. She recalls the first day of the specified period in a confused way. How can we be forced to leave, turning our backs on all our ties to this place? Another important question tormented her mind as it did her husband's and those of her three sons and two daughters. What would become of their nine donkeys? They weren't able to sleep that night. The next morning they were surprised by the reactions of most of their village's residents who had begun bundling their possessions together. Each one of them had acquaintances or relatives who lived in other governorates. The members of Umm Qasim's family gathered and debated what to do. The father said: Our living relatives are in al-Ahsa in Saudi Arabia. Still incredulous, as if speculating, he added: Reality or possibility? Reaching al-Ahsa would require crossing international boundaries. And that would mean everyone would need to acquire travel documents, but circumstances have been impacted by the

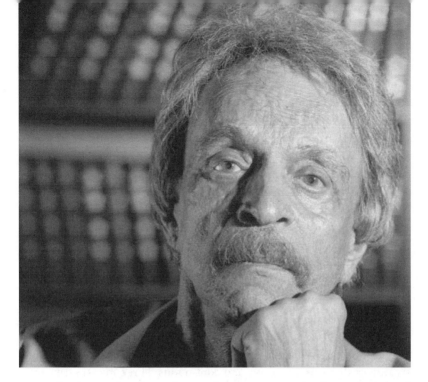

war's chaos. There's no hope of this. So our only choice is to head north till we find land that can accommodate us and our donkeys. Umm Qasim remembers her comment on her husband's statement: I doubt we'll find land that suits us. She received his acknowledgement, which was preceded by a sigh of pain: God's earth is vast.

Deciding to leave for parts unknown took up their second day. The attempt to choose items they would load on the backs of their donkeys and those they would leave behind unguarded till they returned occupied the third day. Before sunset that day they were surprised by another military vehicle that drove down their only street. Anyone who had not left by the time specified would be subject to imprisonment and a fine. We aren't people who would dare disobey orders. They reviewed their selections of possessions they needed to take: clothes, bedding, cooking utensils, and the documents that established their identities as Iraqis. Then they jostled each other as they set off, heading north at dawn with their heavily laden donkeys.

Umm Qasim remembers what her eldest son, Qasim, said as they crossed the bridge spanning the Hababa River during the first hour of their journey, when they were approaching the dirt road leading to the village of al-Sanqar: If we didn't have our donkeys with us, we could have hired a vehicle that would have transported us faster. Her mind begins recalling what her middle son, Hamid, commented:

We would never find a vehicle to transport us. Why not? Because we're a clan with more than twenty members. Her daughter Zahra's voice rang out: We ought to hire a large lorry. The voice of her other daughter, Hasna, protested from the depth of her memory: That's assuming we knew where we're heading. Umm Qasim cowered inside herself at the time, astonished by her children's conversation, which showed their nonchalance about a surprising event that could bring untold devastation. Did she envy them their nonchalance and indifference to eventualities? Just then, she was caught off guard by her husband's plaintive refrain: The only power and might are Almighty God's.

She cannot calm the pounding of her heart. Abu Qasim suffered from a mysterious ailment that the doctors referred to as a heart defect. Some years earlier a doctor had given him an ultimatum: You either quit smoking or face an imminent death. Finally he had chosen to quit smoking, but a hidden, life-threatening illness like this needed treatment that was expensive and continuous. Three months earlier he had stopped buying his medicine. It's no use. When he said that, he reminded her of a person washing his hands of his reasons for living. She had once asked him what type of pain he was experiencing. He had smiled sadly. I feel like a person being ground between two horrid millstones. Even though she had not grasped what he meant by this, she had nodded to show she understood, and listened as he continued: Pain becomes a face of death when it is alone with a person who prays to his Lord to honour his trust. He concluded that perhaps he would be relieved of his sufferings. She looked him straight in the eyes, reproachfully. How could you think of leaving me alone? He answered to mollify her: You have the children and grandchildren to compensate you for me. It hurt her spiritually that he died the third night of their trip north. This pained her as much as it angered her, because he had celebrated with her that night, laughing and embracing the world despite its defects. He had fallen asleep and when he was late waking up, she had chided him for being lazy, but he had not responded.

So they would know how to find his grave on their return, they buried him between two nearby male date palms beside the national highway on the northern outskirts of the city of Nasiriyah. Her oldest son, Qasim, told her: Necessity legitimizes forbidden deeds. He clarified: In view of the present circumstances, you are excused from observing the widow's months of *iddah*. She personally hadn't even considered that. Her sorrow was unbearably heavy. She criticized her husband for leaving her without asking her permission. She focused her eyes and senses on her sons and daughters, their spouses, and her grandsons and granddaughters as well. She observed nothing more than a transitory grief and a passing sense of loss. The living had a right to carry on with their lives so far as that was possible, committing their loved ones to God's mercy. But Umm Qasim's condition was completely different. The matter for her meant the loss of her companion. When you find yourself deprived of the irreplaceable person you live for, the hurt and pain within you intensify without your being conscious of that until they come to resemble a lump of lead that is concealed in your gullet and that digs into you each time you take a breath. Her husband was no longer beside her. She had left him back there concealed beneath the hard dirt, between two palm trees. Their trip had lasted for days when the men all agreed that there would be no harm in establishing a temporary residence on the fringe of the desert overlooking the southern edges of the great cemetery of Najaf – after they noticed that groups of refugees from Basra had settled there. They set about collecting palm fronds and purchasing the wood and ropes they would need from Najaf's markets.

Since you were talking about living temporarily in a place for no more than three months you could erect six huts to house as many people as would fit. They assigned a relatively spacious nest to her. She didn't tell them: Abu Qasim isn't beside me. There's no need for any luxury. This isn't the time for it. When he was alive, she would make sure he was comfortable. Now, though, he was beneath the dirt in a desert that was alien to him and to her. In one of his visits to her in her dreams he inquired plaintively: When will we be able to reunite? After they had stayed there three weeks, someone asked to lease their donkeys to carry brick from Dogha village, which was near where they were living, to a work site a few kilometres away. Thus they acquired a way of making a living, praise to God the Exalted. Her sons and the husbands of her daughters negotiated energetically and fixed a rate. Requests to hire their donkeys continued to come. The improvement of her children's financial situation coincided with their growing familiarity with the place. The three months specified by the decree for the evacuation of the villages and settlements south of the city of Basra passed without any word of the time to return. What happened was that the Iraqi military authorities ordered the evacuation of the areas around al-Tannouma, Ashar, and al-Khura to the west of the Shatt al-Arab.

The war intensified over the next six months. Her children and grandchildren were preoccupied with their lives, and Umm Qasim's time began to follow another course unrelated to the numerous children and grandchildren around her. The flow of time slowed to the point of stopping. This feeling constantly pressing on your ribs and making it hard to breathe causes you to sense a yearning for your original home, while you huff and wheeze. The mind is continually crowded with memories that all relate to the place there, to childhood, to youth, and to Abu Qasim's proposal to her. One afternoon, her son Hamid brought them an orange from the market in Najaf. Her heart pounded. She remembered a time long ago, before any of her children were born. Eighteen years old then, she had fallen ill, and her husband surprised her by bringing her four oranges. Where did you get them? From the Pasha's orchard. She looked at him anxiously. He reassured her: I didn't steal them. Her eyes focused on his lips. He continued: Once Makki, the farmer in charge of the Pasha's garden, learned you were sick, he picked these four oranges. That was the first time in her life she had tasted an orange. The taste was magical. She had never tasted anything like it in any other fruit. She remembered the Pasha's orchard, which was on the far side of the street – where some village women gathered to wash cooking utensils and clothes. The Chumma River, which branched off from the Shatt al-Arab, separated them from the orchard. Oh stupid heart, why are you so flustered? My imagination soars to settle there in that place with all its taste, fragrance, view, and smell. She could sense herself dozing off as if she were back where she had lived. Closing her eyelids, she saw her husband moving from their bedroom to the date palm located in Hajj Mahmud's orchard and then heading to the donkey paddock. She could hear him call out "Darling!". When they were alone, he insisted on calling her darling. She opened her eyelids. Here, now, everyone was preoccupied with his own life. In the past, back in her days in the village of al-Sabiliat, she used to wait impatiently for the arrival of Ashura when they would travel to Najaf to perform the ritual visit of the shrines. Dedicating days to visiting sacred sites was one thing; being forced to reside near them nonstop after leaving your first home was something else. This was not a type of suffering she had ever experienced before. You were alone with your longing to be back there where your heart focused.

When the new school year began, the adults were busy enrolling their children in Najaf's schools. Once the children had gone off to their schools, Umm Qasim's solitude became ever more intense. After it had been almost two years since they left home, she gathered her sons and daughters around her and told them frankly: I can't stay here any longer. What do you mean? I feel a queer type of asphyxiation. If you want, we'll take you to a doctor. He will diagnose the causes for your illness. She didn't tell them it wasn't an illness in the usual sense of the word. Her audience did not include people capable of understanding what was gnawing at her spirit. I'll wait patiently for a couple of days before I decide. Two days later they asked her: Shall we take you to a doctor? She told them they had no reason to be concerned. Her health had improved. She knew what they were like. None of them would have been able to take seriously the suffering that her dislocation was causing her. She herself decided to return to her distant house under her own steam. They have their life. I will take responsibility for mine.

Making her way to the village of al-Sabiliat from Najaf would not be easy. She would need to reflect carefully for some time about the logistics and then make her preparations. She would have to be careful to keep the matter a total secret. If she didn't, her grandchildren, almost more than her children, would cling to her. We won't let you embark on a crazy adventure like this. She agreed that it was an adventure or a fool's errand that they would attribute to elderly people who were senile. Call it what you want. She could not bear to linger where she was for an unspecified period without any set end date. The idea of spending the remaining years of her life in the house in al-Sabiliat took control of her. She weighed her options. She could make do without many of the personal possessions she had accumulated during her time here. She had a lot of stuff at her first home. All the same, the trip would be arduous. Riding there in some vehicle never crossed her mind. Civilian transport was banned in regions that had been cleared of civilians by the military. She had to reach her house the way she had left it. She would need one of the donkeys to guide her, one capable of retracing its steps. She brooded about this. She knew each of their nine donkeys as individuals. She knew their temperaments, how much they could bear, and which ones were ornery or rebellious. Her considerations led her to select the donkey her husband had named "Lucky Foot" the day it was born.

They had gone without any jobs for many weeks, and anxiety was starting to take its toll on her husband. If this lack of employment lasts another week, we'll need to borrow some money. The morning this donkey was born someone knocked on their door and asked to hire all their donkeys. Her husband's face had relaxed at that moment into a cheerful smile. This was a lucky colt. He explained: We'll call him 'Lucky Foot'. That had been five years ago. Now their auspicious colt was a full-grown donkey. Lucky Foot. Umm Qasim seized a moment when only the donkeys were in their paddock to begin a whispered conversation with him: I know you're ready to bear the hardships of the road patiently – and there will be a lot of them – but you're headstrong only occasionally. She gazed deep into his eyes and continued whispering just as quietly: Do you promise to care for me till we reach our house in al-Sabiliat? That last word penetrated deep into Lucky Foot's consciousness. He was not used to hearing any member of the large family call him by his given name – except for the patriarch, who had disappeared some time ago. Now here was Umm Qasim; by mentioning his birthplace she had awakened his senses. Whatever their matriarch had in mind, he was ready to do her bidding. He flicked his tail through the air and moved his head nearer to her. Delight spread through him when his visitor spread her palm and stroked his neck. She continued: If I take you with me, I have one condition. She moved her mouth a little closer to his ear: You must refrain from your usual braying. When he jerked his head away dismissively, he might as well have been asking frankly: Who's speaking now?

Her decision and initial preparations to execute her plan omitted references to what the army might do if they encountered her on the trip home or as she neared her goal. She knew she would struggle to convince them of her point of view. Every living person has an hour of death appointed for him whether he is on a battlefield or asleep in his own bed. She prepared to confront whatever might happen, and that resolve made her all the more energetic. She put aside some money to buy what she would need and chose suitable provisions for the trip. A supply of dry dates, ma'moul short bread pastries, and a container of drinking water. She did not forget a scythe to cut grass to feed Lucky Foot when that was necessary. It would take them a week or more to reach there. She began to visit the donkey paddock daily with the goal of affirming her intentions to Lucky Foot. The month of February ended, and three weeks remained before Nowruz*. She wanted to be home by then. She left at dawn one Friday, because all the members of her large family had the day off and slept till noon. This would allow her time to travel a good distance before they realized she had departed. Her

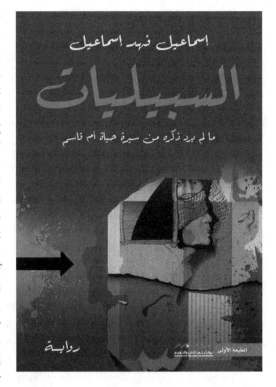

preparations were followed by her execution of the plan. She was pleased to find that all the donkeys supported her plan. At least that was what she surmised.

* Nowruz is a traditional Festival on the vernal equinox, 21st March, marking the beginning of Spring.

Al-Sabiliat *explores the reason behind the existence of a green artery in the midst of a vast wasteland in Iraq following the longest war of the 20th century, that between Iraq and Iran. Iraqi forces blocked the entry points of the tributary rivers and streams of the Shatt al-Arab river. This prevented water flowing to the forests of palm trees situated on the western side. Years passed and the palms dried up, no longer bearing fruit. Eventually, all the trees, vegetation and fruit died apart from one green strip of land stretching from the Shatt to the edge of the desert to the west, in an area called "Al-Sabiliat". One old woman is responsible for this green lifeline, which supplies the village and the soldiers living in it.*

Published by Nova, Kuwait City, Kuwait, April 2016

ELIAS KHOURY

Betrayal by the Fathers

EXCERPT FROM THE NOVEL

THE CHILDREN OF THE GHETTO – MY NAME IS ADAM,

TRANSLATED BY HUMPHREY DAVIES

The historian went off, leaving me bewildered. I wanted to run after him so we could discuss the meaning of truth, because I'm certain, given the fragmentary stories Manal had told me about her first husband, that my father must have been sympathetic towards Marxist thinking, even though he didn't belong to the Communist Party. That would explain why, in the ranks of the Holy Struggle Organization, they'd called him the Red Warrior.

If I'm to believe my mother, my father's supposed communism was the result of the effect on him of what he'd been told of his father's, the martyr's, relationship to Bolshevism.

Why had the even-tempered Dr. Hanna Jreis flown off the handle when I suggested adding a short paragraph to my father's letter, thus solving the problem of the text he was searching for? That way he could put forward his new thesis that the foundation of the Palestine Communist Party wasn't the doing of Jews alone: Palestinian prisoners of war in Russia who were members of the Turkish Red Brigades had played a role too.

I hadn't suggested forging history, just filling in the gaps. He said the imagination was all right for literature but not for writing history, though how in that case does the historian expect us to write it? Are we supposed to leave it to the Zionists? And who told him that the histories that have been written of Palestine are true and not an out-and-out carnival of forgery?

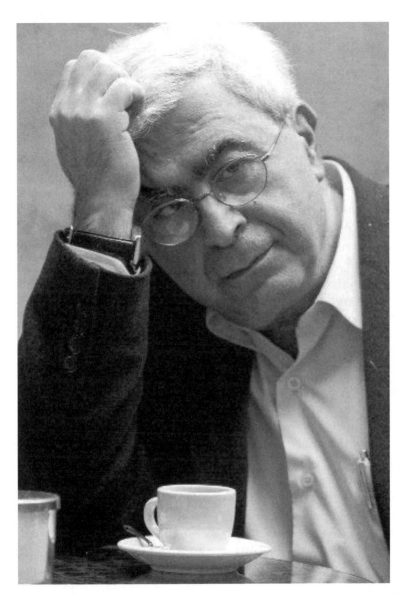

I should have discussed the matter with him when he came to the restaurant in New York to eat stewed beans, but I'd forgotten about the whole thing, and it only came unstitched from the folds of my memory today, as I sat alone trying to gather together the threads of my life.

What do I want, and who am I?

God protect me from the word "I", as the Arabs say! When I look for myself in these stories I tell, I find myself in others' mirrors. Each person is the mirror of another, each story the mirror of another –

that's what my solitary existence in New York has taught me. When I came to this city, in flight from a love that had died, I expected to experience solitude, live with myself, forget that world so crammed with people and events, and sit around in idle boredom.

"Nothing's better than boredom!" I told myself as I set down my bags in my small apartment in New York. Even writing the story of Waddah al-Yaman had been part of what backgammon and card players call "killing time". From the day I let myself into this hell, however, I discovered that I was surrounded by people who'd been hiding in the crevices of my memory, and instead of luxuriating in my boredom, I found myself under duress, forced to set aside time for all those ghosts who hemmed me in, and to organize their introduction into this text, so there could be some thread for me to follow.

This world is made up of mirrors that, when we break them, shatter into a thousand little pieces that are transformed in turn into new mirrors that need to be broken. The mirrors that hem me in today are those of my three fathers, who abandoned me.

I shall begin at the end, as I was never interested in the issue of the relationship to the father. I came to consciousness as the son of Hasan Dannoun the Martyr, and as a child of the Lydda ghetto, and that's enough. Even my mother's marriage to Abdallah al-Ashhal in no way altered that conviction. I am a descendent of the great Sufi, Dhul Nun the Egyptian, a son of the city of al-Khidr, and a citizen of the Arab world, or a Palestinian living in the State of Israel. And when I left my mother's house, I discovered that I was my own son, and that all those legends about my father's heroism that she'd planted in my head meant nothing to me. I know the man only as a name and a picture, and names and pictures mean nothing till transformed into a voice that takes you by surprise when recalled from you know not where.

My running into Blind Ma'moun here in New York, and the fragmented stories he told me about my other, real, father, stirred up lots of questions. When those questions encountered the film that presented a forgery of the truth about Dalia and her friends and made no reference to Yibna, my grandmother's village – as one would expect for a village whose inhabitants were viciously expelled in 1948 – my soul exploded and my memory flowed.

To keep it short, I'll just say that when I took classes in psychology at Haifa University, I read avidly about the Oedipus complex, as fashioned by Freud, not because I felt that the killing of the father was something necessary, but because, on the contrary, I felt I was devoid of the complex, someone having taken it upon himself to kill my father before I was born.

Even when my mother married (I was eight at the time, i.e., had passed the penile stage presided over by the Oedipus complex), I didn't feel jealous of the man. On the contrary, I felt disgust, and disgust has nothing in common with jealousy. I felt pity for my mother at the thought that she could sleep next to him.

They don't, however, teach the Oedipus complex's twin, the Abraham complex. I now, based on personal experience, believe that the Abraham complex is the more firmly rooted in the collective human unconscious. The only place I've come across it is in contemporary Jewish Israeli literature, which has a strong focus on the sacrificing of the son.

(Note: Oddly, the Jewish religion has no feast day dedicated to the sacrifice of Isaac – even though there are so many Jewish feast days and despite the foundational centrality of the story of the sacrifice of the son – while the Muslims have transformed the tale into their greatest feast, which they name the Feast of the Sacrifice, when they perform the duty of pilgrimage and slaughter sheep as a ransom for the son who was saved at the last moment: the oldest son, called Ismail, grandsire of the Arabs. The Christians, for their part, call it, in our country, the Great Feast, and celebrate the killing of the son and his resurrection from the dead.)

To return to the Abraham complex, I'd say the whole thing stems from the killing of the son, whereas the killing of the father in the story of Oedipus is no more than a reaction to the father's nailing of his little son's feet to a piece of wood and then casting him aside to die. Oedipus only killed his father because the father wanted to kill the son, from fear of the prophecy of the oracle and as a step toward its fulfilment.

Now, in my solitude, I discover that all three of my fathers wanted to kill me. Indeed, symbolically speaking, they did kill me, and I ought to have killed them, to defend my very existence. I am the murder victim who ought to turn into a murderer who feels pity for his wretched victims.

My first father, meaning my biological father (according to Ma'moun's account of how he found me lying on my dead mother's breast), I know nothing of. I don't even know his name. It seems that the wife, with her baby son, waited too long to join the march of death, so the man kept going, like all the others who'd lost members of their families but were sure they'd meet up with them once they got to the areas under Jordanian army control. And when he reached Naalein, he looked for his wife but couldn't find her, so he joined the ranks of the other searchers, who were stricken by everyone's indifference to their plight. On that terrible July day, people lost their souls and were transformed into living corpses. Heat and thirst devoured them, and they experienced the great fear that frees the survival instinct of all constraints. Sons abandoned fathers, fathers sons. Small children got lost under feet and people died of heat and thirst.

People talk of fear as though it were an individual experience. They speak of the knees giving way, of the emptying of the heart, of the annihilation. But it is the fear that turns into waves that is the greatest: fear that undulates through thousands of people who have been cast into the wilderness, beneath the lead of the bullets and amongst the faces of the soldiers gloating at their misfortune, soldiers scattered along the length of the rocky road, who take everything the stream of fugitives possesses by way of money and jewellery and gaze at the wandering throngs with indifference.

A wave of fear rises and my father walks alone, a youth of twenty-five who has lost his wife and only child. He walks next to his aged father and keeps turning around to look for his wife. Then the wave sweeps him up and he finds himself alone, wrestling with fear. His thirst becomes a choking feeling. He raises his head above the wave to breathe, before being swallowed up again.

I don't want to go looking for excuses for this man about whom I know nothing. The truth is, ever since I found out about what happened between us, I've felt nothing for him but pity and contempt. I mean tell me, tell me how he could have left his son, who wasn't more than four months old, to save his own skin?

I'm assuming here that my first father escaped death on the march of death, that he reached Naalein safely and from there kept going with the caravan of refugees to Ramallah, but it's not certain, and I'm not prepared to go searching for him. Most likely, he's dead now, or on the brink of the grave! Meeting him would do neither me nor him any good. Indeed, it wouldn't even have the savour of that melodramatic meeting at which tears flow. In fact, it would be a meeting of strangers.

Let's suppose the blind youth hadn't rescued me and given me to Manal. Probably, I would have died of hunger. I don't want to go now into Ma'moun's description of the rigidity of the child he picked up, it makes my skin crawl. However, ever since Ma'moun told me that story, I've had strange headaches and feel as though my "I" is drowning in fog, as though I weren't I.

My first father killed me. He left me to die on a dead woman's breast and fled towards his life. That's my first story with fathers. A cowardly and impotent father, a people herded like sheep towards the wilderness and death, and a child, its body rigid with thirst, lying on its mother's dry breasts.

All I needed was a drop of milk. One drop, which my mother's breasts were incapable of offering me, so I lay on them awaiting my death. My relationship with death began that torrid day in July, the day I died and Manal had to rub my body with oil and feed me boiled ground lentils with her finger until the people of the ghetto came across the milking cow that saved me and the rest of the ghetto's children from death.

Ma'moun said the moment when they found the cow was the most beautiful of his life. "Imagine, lad, how we were. To this day I'm convinced the cow was a gift from God, Great and Glorious."

I don't want to submerge myself in the days of the ghetto now: that's a story I need to write from beginning to end, at one go, and without digressions. I've told Ma'moun's version of my first father's story, which has no story, because of my feeling that I'm the murdered son, and that my father was my murderer.

Perhaps in saying this I'm being somewhat unjust towards the man, whom I didn't know. He was a victim and I'm the victim of a victim. I don't care for such justifications. Being a victim doesn't grant one the right to make victims of others – on the contrary, it makes one doubly responsible for them. This is what I tried to explain so many times to my Israeli Jewish friends, though with no great success. True, to be honest, my beloved Dalia once surprised me by adopting the same idea and, indeed, expressing it eloquently, when she said, "The Palestinians are the victim's victim and the Jewish victim has no right to behave as his own executioners did. That's why I'm not just Jewish, but Palestinian too."

We were walking that day on the shore at Jaffa, close to the Cemetery by the Sea, where the Palestinian academic and writer Ibrahim Abu-Lughod is buried. I told her about this man whose voice still rings in my ears and of how, after he died, his daughter Lila took him by car from Ramallah to Jerusalem so that his death could be announced in that city and he could claim, as a non-Jewish American, the right to be buried in Israel, which is to say, in the cemetery where his fathers and forefathers had been buried. An expression of grief passed over Dalia's brown, oval face and she announced that she had become a Palestinian.

As for how and why Dalia came to abandon me and her Palestinian identity, that's another story, one that is intertwined with sorrow and ambiguity.

My first father didn't look back, and so failed to see me being pulled from my mother's womb a second time so that I wouldn't die. I can imagine the man weeping, or pretending to weep, for his only child and proclaiming me a martyr, then marrying a relative, having a boy, and giving him my name.

Though I don't know what that name was and don't want to know.

My name is Adam and I don't care that my first father doesn't know that, because the man means nothing to me. He appeared on the screen of my life as a man made up of words spoken by the blind man. A man without features, like a black spot in my eye.

Maybe I'm doing the man an injustice! I'm basing everything on the assumption that he kept going and didn't make a serious search for me. But what if the man had already been killed? What if he was one of the victims of the massacre that took place at the Dahmash mosque? If that were so, my mother would have fled with me on her own.

It's a serious possibility but I'm not in a position to prove it, which is the case with all the other possibilities concerning my first father. I'd rather not, however, place him among the ranks of the martyrs, because having one father who's a martyr is enough.

The Children of the Ghetto — My Name is Adam, by Elias Khoury, will be published in 2018 by Maclehose Press, translated by Humphrey Davies

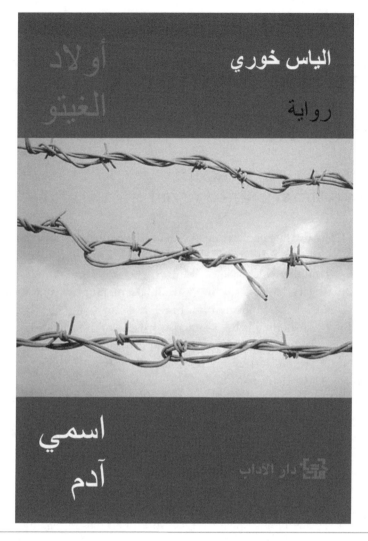

Children of the Ghetto – My Name is Adam *tells the story of Palestinian Adam Danun and his attempt to write a novel after emigrating to New York. A retelling of his own personal story, the novel recounts his childhood in Lud, Palestine, where in 1948 the city fell to occupying forces who drove out the majority of its inhabitants. Adam's mother remained in the city with her baby and his story is that of the barbed wire encircled Palestinian ghetto created by the occupying army. It is a tale of remaining and an attempt to interpret the victims' silence.*

Published by Dar al-Adab, Beirut, Lebanon, November 2015

MOHAMMED ABDEL NABI

In the Spider's Room

AN EXCERPT FROM THE NOVEL,

TRANSLATED BY JONATHAN WRIGHT

The further my writing advances, the bigger this small room grows and the more the walls recede until they disappear completely. The pages of the notebook in front of me is the only place left that exists. I'm evasive. I take memory as far as it can go, to put off the confrontation. I feel as if I'm saying goodbye to my life by shrouding it in lines and words. I haven't gone close to the open wounds yet. I'm still twisting and turning on paper, just as I walk around letting my body lose its way in the downtown crowds every night.

Two days ago, I went out for my evening roam and I realised I'd forgotten my dark glasses and had gone out with my face uncovered. I'd raised my right hand to adjust the position of the glasses on my nose and I was surprised to find they weren't there. I felt as if I'd gone out in the street naked with nothing to cover myself. I had gone only a few paces from the door of the building that has the hotel on its top three floors. I looked around quickly, just to be safe, and didn't see anything suspicious. Even so I found myself shaking – at least my fingers were clearly trembling. I pretended that everything was normal, on my guard for anyone monitoring me, as though a great big eye, open day and night, was watching my slightest move-ment and maybe my thoughts as well. I feel I'm not alone, and I haven't recovered yet. I looked through the pockets of my coat and trousers, though I was sure the glasses were still on the glass top of the dressing table in the room. I behaved as if I had forgotten some-thing, just to send the right message to that hidden eye. I turned and went back, almost tripping over. All this happened in less than three minutes, but it was enough for me to know I was still a long way off.

I still wake up in a panic in broad daylight. I don't know where I am. In one of these suffocating fits I went and looked at the packets and strips of pills in the drawer of the bedside table, tempted to take them all, to put an end to it all and feel relieved. Suppressing my tears, I reached out for them and started to tear the plastic bubbles over the Xanox tablets, which were a sad pale pink. My only friend turned up right then – the small black spider I had met in the same room weeks ago when I came out of prison. It started to climb up my fingers casually and affectionately and without fear, as though it were holding back my hand, trying to stop me taking the pills and whispering to me to calm down and think again. I backed down and kept watching it walk over my wrist and the palm of my hand, then

I went back to writing, imagining myself as a dumb spider spinning a frail web around himself in the hope that it won't be destroyed.

My psychoanalyst, Doctor Sameeh, said: "Write, Hani, please, send me emails regularly, or even text messages on your mobile. You may have lost your ability to speak but you can still write. Whenever you feel you're suffocating, write. Say what happened on paper, if only for yourself. Cleanse yourself of everything that made you feel dirty there." When he said "cleanse yourself" I felt he could see inside me. Maybe he knew that since coming out of prison I'd spent a long time under the shower trying to get myself clean. I started thinking seriously about his suggestion. I wrote the first sentence that night on a page in one of the little notebooks I use for communicating with other people. "My name is Hani Mahfouz," I wrote. But I tore it up and threw it away, then took a sleeping pill and was gone within minutes.

I sleep. I sleep all the time. I sink into long periods of stupor interrupted only by the need to stay alive. I'm woken up by thirst or when I want to urinate, or by nightmares of course. I hardly remember anything of them other than the shock of how they end. I might have ordinary dreams sometimes. Some of them take me back to prison, with the most intricate details of the cell and my fellow prisoners, and during those I feel a warm familiarity, like someone who's finally gone back to his home and family. I still haven't come out of the long nightmare, though physically I have distanced myself. The black bird is still perched on my head. I keep avoiding looking other people in the face, in streets and public places, and if any of them stare at me, even for seconds, I get flustered and I look away, then I move off quickly, with my fingers trembling and my throat dry.

I've confessed to Dr Sameeh in an email that sometimes I imagine the worst possibilities. It's like I enjoy being frightened and sinking into the dark, oozy mud of my fear. When I'm walking around aimlessly, I imagine a heavy hand landing suddenly on me, a living pincer on my neck. I expect it to come down on me at any moment and at every step. I feel it's a small victory when I manage to ignore this threat and steer my thoughts far away from it. But within five minutes it comes back to me again and I can sense that unknown person coming up to me, pinning me down and taking my glasses off my face in one violent gesture. The glasses fall to the ground and other people gather around us in the blink of an eye. Some of them recog-

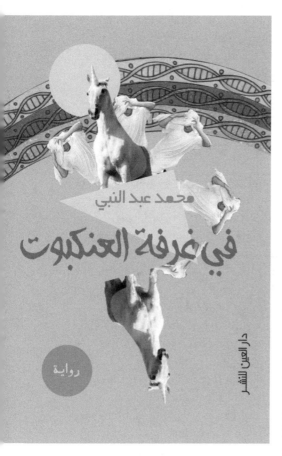

nise me or he introduces them to me, like a hunter who's happy to have finally found his prey. I see them taking his side, all of them without exception, some of them laughing, and others upset and disgusted when they find out the truth about me. One of them joins in the public performance with a well-aimed spit right in my face, and another with a firm slap on the back of my neck. Then the others pull at my clothes, which tear easily in their hands and fall off my body like paper handkerchiefs. I'm soon naked among them. I try to cover up my genitals but they prevent me. I curl up on the ground while they kick me. The exquisite horror keeps toying with my imagination. Cigarettes are stubbed out on my back and stomach, stiff fingers reach towards my arsehole, and I don't even have the energy to scream or cry. I run between their legs on all fours like an animal looking for a gap between them, but there's no way out.

In the Spider's Room *is a coming-of-age novel with a difference in which Hani Mahfouz recounts his life in Cairo, his marriage (in order to get a loan from his mother), his boyfriends, and a host of colourful characters, but above all his horrendous experience of getting caught up in the notorious "Queen Boat" arrests, in Cairo in 2001. During his trial he loses the power of speech, and when released from prison, finds that writing is the best way to allay his nightmares.*

Published by Dar al-Ain, Cairo, Egypt, May 2016

I don't describe these imaginary details to Sameeh in as much detail as I do here. There's also a clear distance between what I write to him by email and what I write for myself here in my notebooks. He wrote to me saying I was trying to overcome my fears by imagining them and magnifying them as much as possible, which is a good start but not a proper solution, and he again encouraged me to write.

When I'm writing, facing the dressing table mirror yet trying not to look at it, I succeed in forgetting, not just forgetting what has happened to me over the past few months but also forgetting what I have to do now, and tomorrow and the day after tomorrow. Every day I'll have to carry it on my shoulders until death relieves me. I avoid the pressing questions and escape to the happy past, to my grandfather and the workshop and the family house in Abdeen and my first relationship. But as soon as I go out roaming every evening questions hover around my head like birds of prey with horrible cries. What will I do with my life? Should I emigrate like some of the people released with me are trying to do? If I wanted to go, how could I go through with the procedures when I'm still completely unable to speak. I'll have to get my voice back first, and to get it back I'll have to have regular therapy, act on Dr Sameeh's orders, make an appointment to see the speech therapist he recommended and do endless other things. All this and I feel like a dead man walking, a corpse that fights the smell of its own decomposition every day and that has nothing but this rabid wandering every night.

When my feet flagged, I would head to that small local bar I recently discovered. It was not one of the places I was in the habit of frequenting in my former life, before the nightmare. There I drink one beer after another, and my hand might loosen up enough for me to write in the little notebook I keep with me all the time. The damned questions keep swarming me. As soon as a new question is born, within seconds it branches out into other questions, each one hurtling off in a different direction, until I envision a network that branches out to infinity. The new question becomes in turn a new hub from which new questions branch out, and so on. It's not like the web that the little spider would spin – my friend that I check up on every now and then in his place in the drawer. I once addressed him without speaking. "I would have liked to sing to you, but now I can't even speak," I said.

SAAD MOHAMMED RAHEEM

Sami al-Rifai's email

AN EXCERPT FROM THE NOVEL

THE BOOKSELLER'S MURDER,

TRANSLATED BY JONATHAN WRIGHT

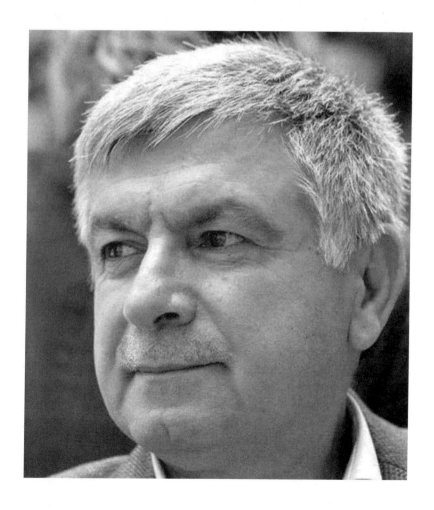

He didn't wait a month. Three days later I was surprised to receive an email from Sami al-Rifai. In his last year at the Academy of Fine Arts he began to ensnare her. That was at the time when the leftist wave was in ferment, at the beginning of the 1960s. He sat next to her on the bus from Baghdad back to Baquba. It didn't happen by chance. He had started monitoring her more than a month earlier. He would wait for her at the bus stop in Maydan Square every day. Her short jet-black hair, her almond eyes, the dimples in her cheeks, her elegance, or rather her intelligent choice of clothes, her polished legs that were uncovered till six inches above the knee – all this and other things enthralled him. She stole his heart. He thought she was the most beautiful woman in the country. He didn't even know her name. He knew from the books she carried that she was a first-year student in the English language department at university, and for her sake he went to the British Council to improve his English. His passion for her was insane. When I saw her later I realised that she wasn't that beautiful. She was beautiful in an ordinary way: short with a fairly dark complexion, a small arched nose and a little mole on the curve of her chin. Talking about her later, he told me she radiated a femininity that was overpowering and irresistible. But I think he projected onto her an idea of an ideal woman that existed only in his head.

That day in the bus he decided to carry out his first move. He sat down, slightly apprehensive, without saying a word. When the bus moved off, he opened his sketchbook and began drawing in order to attract her attention, but she just looked out of the window and showed no interest in him. When the bus was close to Baquba he spoke to her in a soft voice: "For an hour I've been drawing in this damn sketchbook in the hope of impressing you, and all you do is look at those boring scenes outside that you've seen a thousand times." The woman was speechless and had to suppress a laugh. "Look, look at my drawings," he continued, and started to turn the pages of his sketchbook to show her his designs. "I had this idea that if you saw what I was doing," he added in a grating tone, "you would slip, I mean you would fall into the well, I mean in love, in love with me. But you're not interested. You find them silly, don't you?" She wanted to be angry with him but in the end her sense of humour proved more powerful. "That is the stupidest way to try to attract a woman," she said with a broadening smile. "I know, he replied, "It was very stupid. You're quite right. But I couldn't think of any other way. You see, it's the way people do it when they have a screw loose. Now, what do you say?" "About what?" she said, feigning ignorance of his intent. He waved his hand dismissively and said: "You ask me what, when I've been explaining to you all along . . . Listen, I'm deeply, deeply . . . I'm Mahmoud al-Marzouq, an artist, I swear, a painter. It's true I'm a bit of a jackass, but I . . ."

He noticed that the bus was stopping. He stayed in his seat till the last passenger had got off, and then she was trapped in the window seat, waiting for him to make way for her. He didn't do so. "Excuse me," she said, standing up.

He stood up and moved from his seat to the aisle and gestured to her to go past, putting out his hand and making a slight bow. She walked past and he walked behind her to the back of the bus.

As she was about to get off, without looking back, she said: "I'm Ghada."

(This wasn't her real name. I have used the name by which I referred to her in the session of the Writers' Union at the end of the 1990s.)

He was from a middle-class Baquba family, and Baquba was a town that had not completely rid itself of its rural features. It was a big family with many branches that made its living in the cloth trade and owned orchards. She was from an old Baghdad family, a branch of which had recently settled in Baquba because it had come down in the world after the 1958 revolution. Her father was a lawyer and associate of the royal family and had once been tipped for a ministerial position.

Over the remaining part of the academic year they wove an extraordinary love story together. He convinced her that marrying now would make their life dull and meaningless, and so they should continue with the relationship until she graduated. "By then I will have established my name in the world of art and saved up some money and you will be ready to come to Paris with me. Paris, the city of lights, the city of creativity and beauty. There I will achieve glory, with you as my partner. You will be my Simone de Beauvoir." He didn't believe in marriage. He wanted it to be an open relationship, at least for some years. You would say with a laugh: "We have to have our own adventures and memories. There's no harm in a few manageable problems." But the conservative society around them wasn't prepared to accept such a leap. She believed in him and for his sake she accepted the risk. The first problem arose when one of her relatives saw them in the Roxy Cinema in Baghdad watching an Egyptian film. Her father almost forced her to abandon her education although she was already in the third year. To deal with the crisis Mahmoud went to see her father in his office and asked to marry her. He went alone. The eminent and sophisticated lawyer looked at him with disdain and said: "And where are your family? You come alone to ask for my daughter's hand, here in my place of work? Are you crazy?" Stammering, or pretending to stammer, he replied: "You're right, sir. I am a little crazy, it's true. And you'll find out why later. I'll tell you frankly why I came alone." "Why?" "Because I don't have confidence in their ability to convince you. I was worried one of them might unintentionally say something rude, just because he's stupid, and you'd kick us out into the street." The man looked at him, unable to believe his ears and trying to conceal a smile. "And you?" he said. "Can you convince me?" Mahmoud shook his head. "I don't know. You're a frightening man," he said. "Frightening?" " I mean formidable. You're a formidable man. I'd prepared hundreds of things to say to you but I've forgotten them all. You're a lawyer and very intelligent so you can guess what I wanted to say in such a situation." The lawyer waved his finger close to Mahmoud's nose and said sharply: "I do not give my consent." "Why not?" "Because you're certifiably insane and I never want it to be said of my daughter that her husband is in the lunatic asylum." "That I'll never do. I won't go to any lunatic asylum. I'm an artist, so my craziness is within the permissible margin." The father let out a loud guffaw and said: "You're the strangest person I have ever met. Go and fetch your family. I have nothing else to say." Maybe he thought the Marzouq family objected to this engagement and hence Mahmoud had come alone. So this would be the end of the matter.

But it wasn't the end of the matter. On the evening of February 7, which was the thirteenth day of Ramadan, after the meal to break the fast, some of Mahmoud's female relatives came to arrange an engagement between him and Ghada. He stipulated that they should remain engaged until she graduated in a year and a few months. The women celebrated in the lawyer's house that night. The custom was that the men went with the women the next day to finish off the agreement over aspects of the dowry and how much should be paid in advance and the other traditional details of the marriage contract. Then they read the first chapter of the Qur'an and the couple put rings on each other's fingers.

The next day, February 8 or the fourteenth day of Ramadan, people woke up to news of a military coup, broadcast on the radio. Much blood was shed and the country was in turmoil. President Abdel Karim Qasim was executed and thousands of communists were herded into prisons. Mahmoud was a Marxist unattached to any group but he was at the top of the new government's list of wanted people. They didn't put him in Baquba prison but took him to the Qasr al-Nihaya detention camp in Baghdad in the belief that he was the most dangerous leader in communist circles in the province. That was based on false information that someone in the National Guard called Shafiq Nouna gave them for some purely personal reason. But to be fair to Shafiq Nouna I want to emphasise that he also sent his communist cousin, Sattar Nouna, into detention, so he was consistent in his political loyalties. There's talk, or a rumour, that a woman had killed herself in the home of Mahmoud's uncle and there was an argument and some shooting in a bar between the three of them – I mean the two from the Nouna family and Mahmoud al-Marzouq. I'm not sure of the details since it happened when I was a child, years before I met Mahmoud. In the detention camp Mahmoud was severely tortured. Two months later hundreds of detainees found themselves crammed into railway carriages with doors and windows sealed so tight that not a single air molecule could enter. That was the train known in books on contemporary political history as "the death train" and one of the passengers was Mahmoud al-Marzouq.

The train rolled south, bound for Nagrat al-Salman prison in the desert near al-Samawa. The plan was that as many as possible should die on the way but the driver realised what kind of cargo the train was carrying. The piles of humans in danger of perishing started banging on the sides of the carriages and tried in vain to knock out the windows. The driver was shocked but all he could do was set off as fast as he could in order to reach al-Samawa station before disaster struck or too much damage was done. After some uncomfortable hours he stopped the train there and the people of al-Samawa, who had somehow received the news, were waiting. They smashed down the doors of the carriages and took out the men who were about to suffocate. There were some dead, and some who were as good as dead, including Mahmoud al-Marzouq, who did however survive.

If Ghada's father hadn't had connections among the Arab nation-
alists they would have arrested her too, since she was the friend of a
communist renegade and he must have affected her with his ideas.
Ghada's father was not a party member either. He had never joined
the Nasserists or the Baathists. His inclinations were closest to those
of the bourgeois nationalists who dreamed of an Iraqi state on the
liberal Western model. Even so, he was interrogated a few months
later, not because of his daughter but because he was associated with
the men who had been in power in the days of the monarchy. Two
hours after he was detained in a National Guard tent some influential
friends intervened and he was released.

Mahmoud went into Nagrat al-Salman prison at the age of twenty-
five and came out when he was thirty. During this miserable and
neglected gap in his life he lost three things: first, his complete faith
in love after his beloved Ghada married, or was forced to marry, a
rich cousin of hers who would become seriously important after the
coup of 1968; second, three quarters of his faith in his talent as an
artist who could pursue his private project with success; and third,
half of his faith in the left as an idea and in leftist organisations.

In Prague he would regain his faith in love when he fell in love with
a white Russian woman. He would preserve the remaining quarter
of his faith in his talent and would lose the other part of his faith in
the existing leftist organisations, in return for a radical and critical
rethinking of leftist thought, in the wake of which some orthodox
Marxists would denounce him as a revisionist.

At the beginning of the 1970s he cast doubt on the National Front
project, and when they told him, "You're not one of us and you don't
understand politics," he said, "You're right. I'm not a political animal
like you. I'm an animal that knows how to draw." What prevented
Mahmoud al-Marzouq from becoming famous in artistic and cultural
circles was his lack of self-confidence. He didn't have enough faith
in his own talent or maybe in the value of art in general. The lazy ni-
hilism behind the way he behaved often got on my nerves. I often
lost my temper with him, although I was his friend and in a sense his
disciple in the world of ideas and art. I could see the flame that
burned inside him and that he hid under a layer of cold ashes: the
flame I could sense whenever I saw one of his preliminary sketches,
an unfinished painting or even a crazy scribbling on a piece of paper

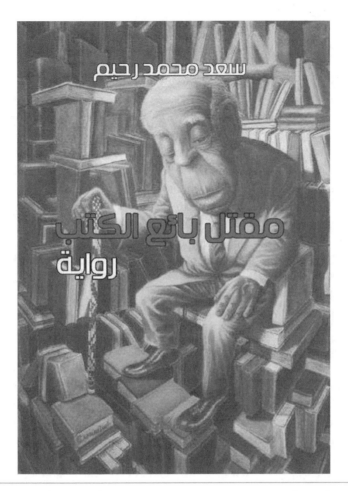

The Bookseller's Murder *follows Magid Baghdadi, an experienced journalist, who arrives in Baquba, 60 km north of Baghdad, to conduct a two-month investigation commissioned by a rich and influential anonymous person. He must write a book about the life and mysterious death of 70-year-old Mahmoud al-Marzouq, a bookseller and artist. Magid forms relationships with friends and acquaintances of the deceased and comes across a notebook containing some of his diaries. These record his life in the city since the first day of the US occupation. He also discovers letters between al-Marzouq and Jeanette, a Frenchwoman who worked as a model for artists, with whom al-Marzouq had had a relationship when he was a refugee in Paris. From these and other sources, the personality of al-Marzouq comes to life and various chapters of his interesting and complex life are revealed. What will remain obscure is the reason for his death.*

Published by Dar wa Maktabat Sutur, Baghdad, Iraq, May 2016 he had left on his table. I would say: "Mahmoud, it's a shame that all this energy should go to waste." "Hey, energy-man," he would reply, "don't make me dizzy with your philosophy. I got on the wrong train thirty years ago and I don't talk politics." When I laughed in pain, he would add: "The station's in ruins, the track has rusted and all you can hear is the wind howling." That was after he left Europe, came back to Baquba and opened a large bookshop in the belief that it would be useful and profitable, culturally and financially. At the time he said: "Listen, Sami, I've grown up and I've washed my hands of art. What I earn from this business I'll spend on culture. I'll turn the bookshop some day soon into a publishing house and I'll finance artistic workshops and bring the theatre back to life in this city."

"You're like the sleepers of Ephesus when they woke up in another age," I said. "You'll find that your old currency is now worthless. The book trade is dead. It's wonderful of you to open a bookshop here but don't expect to make a profit."

He wasn't convinced. He didn't believe that after all the wars had worn them down people had given up reading, and that then sanctions would come and people would no longer go to theatres, cinemas or art exhibitions. One day I said to him: "Take bread and theatre. Bread is now so rare that people can hardly find any, so who would think about theatre or art?" I suggested he go into seclusion and take up drawing again. No harm in having a small bookshop to pass the time. "All a writer needs is a pen and some paper and that doesn't cost much," I said. "But painting needs money, to buy paint, brushes, canvas, frames and other equipment. And you invest some of the money you have in your artistic production." "If people no longer need books," he said: "why would they need my paintings?" I explained that there was a wealthy class that bought paintings and hung them in their fancy living rooms, as well as foreigners who went to the galleries in Baghdad and bought good paintings at reasonable prices.

"I'll think about it," he said, but he didn't do it. He opened a large bookshop and lost money. He closed it down and moved his books to the basement of the building that his uncle owned. I think you know the rest of the story.

ASHUR ETWEBI

Yahya al-Sheikh's Objectives

There's nothing that doesn't stand on something else, however big or small. Mud carried by water turns into plants, insects, mammals and then humans. Air in its various forms breathes life into creatures. It breathes life into both fresh water and salt water. In vestal garb life swam through the water to reach the dry land, and forms of life as numerous as the pebbles in the universe emerged. Then creatures with eyes looked up at the sky. New lungs filled with air. Some forms of life flew through the boundless air and some landed on the branches of trees, some stretched their legs and ran as fast as they could, some dug tunnels deep in the ground, others stood upright on the ground and had a good look at the sky. "Am I from there?" some of them asked. "Where are those who live in the sky?" They burst with questions. "Where from? Where to? Why is there all this similarity, and why all this divergence? Why do creatures die?" This is what the unusual creatures ask. Ever since they learnt to write things down. Ever since they

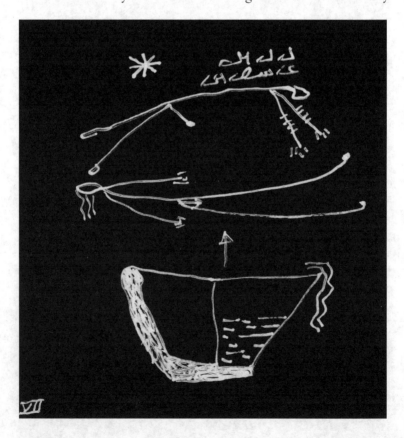

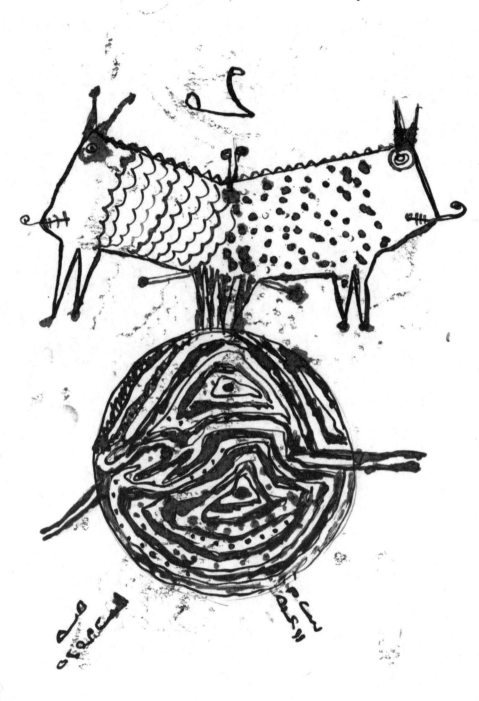

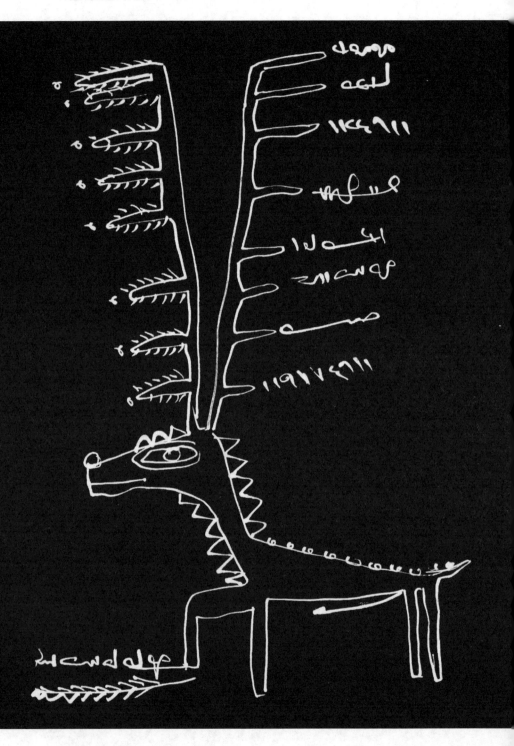

learnt to speak. Ever since they learnt that the sun comes from the east and goes to a place beyond the west, dragging night behind it. Night with its own creatures, sounds and spirits, with its cold and its fear.

Just as words live on people's tongues, lines and circles live in the features of rocks. Just as the waves of the sea are driven by the wind to a place where they can come to rest, the heart and the emotions have been pushing questions to a place where there is no rest, ever since humans sat in some cave on some mountain, or in a hole under some stretch of plain, or on top of some tree in some forest. In front of them stretches a desert with its dunes or a wasteland leading to another wasteland or a vast sea of which only the thin blue line of the horizon is visible, where the upper and the lower meet, the air and the water, sky and earth. They reached out their hands and drew shapes on the rock. These shapes and designs expressed the raw sensory impressions preserved in their memories, what they had learned and what they had forgotten when they were running after a prey or away from a predator. They tried to depict the one who controls everything: one that is mighty, compassionate and omnipotent and that hears everything, and since they didn't have the means to see any such beings, they created out of their imaginations shapes to which they gave names and to which they granted whatever powers and abilities they chose. They knew that they lived there in the highest, in the place they call the sky, and they knew that good existed. Then they placed similar beings in the darkest corners of the Earth, and they knew that evil existed. Then they saw around them creatures dying; that made them think of death and they longed for eternity. Then they realized that there was no escape from passing to the other side. Certainty was a guide to those making that passage. They learned that this world is where the good powers on high converge with the evil powers below. How could they obtain the sympathy and compassion of the powers on high, and how could they avert the evil and hostility of the powers below?

A boat made of water and mud. That is the equipment of the being that makes words. On every mountain there's an upward slope that the man with tears in his eyes is climbing. On every plain there's a downward slope down which comes the man that everyone is now talking about. The unusual beings search the horizons for a path that will take them to the place where the enthroned one sits on the waters, with all of creation around Him.

In the mirror of which the Sufis speak they say: "Ascent is descent, to go down is to go up. Choose who you are to be: inside the mirror or outside it." The unusual being says: "I'm in limbo, so there is no ascent and no descent. I wasn't frightened when I saw myself as a bird holding an arrow in its beak and a bow with its feet. I looked down and knew I was high up. The towering mountains were like ripe grains of corn with their domes shining in the light of a sun that had a white eye, a red eye and a veil. The houses were like the pebbles in some remote wasteland. The seas were like cats' eyes by night. What would I do with a bow and arrows? I have to go high, high, high . . ."

Stone is a being that pulses, a being that has lost its tongue, a being that has lost its sight, a being that hears the beating of the drums in the jungle and the croaking sound of souls in limbo. A being whose sole concern is to live forever in peace without a name and without a voice. Stone is the bird's companion. Birds always land on stones, even if they are hidden.

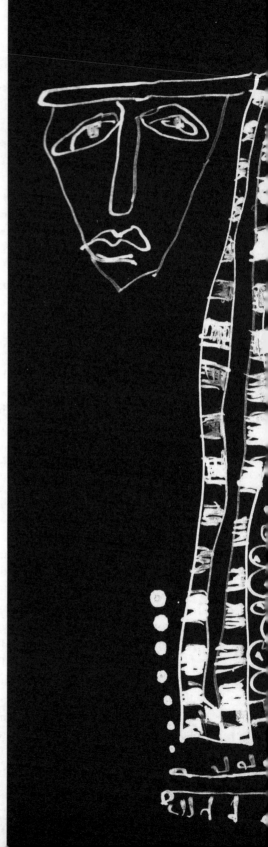

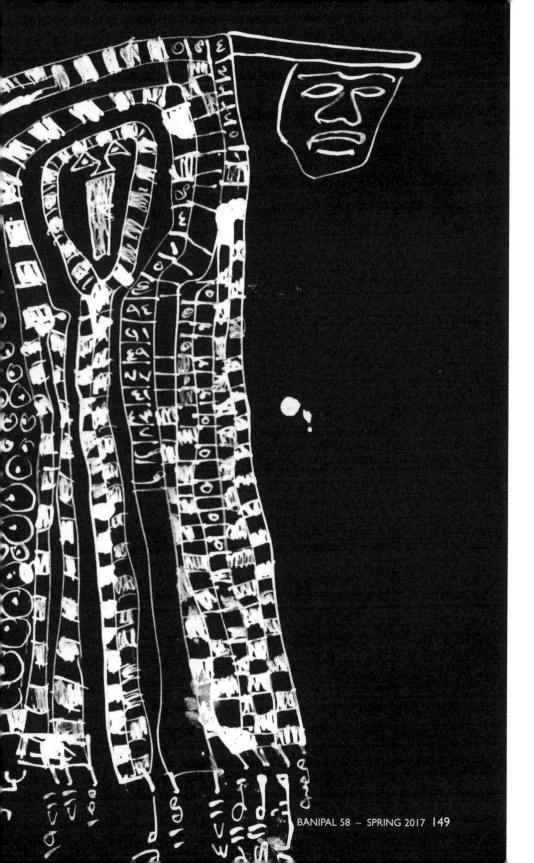

Whenever the sweat of the unusual being's brow lands on the ground, there grows from it a created world, some of which resembles him and some of which does not.

Whenever the being's sighs reach the ground they give rise to tongues that speak every language.

Whenever the being's dreams land on the ground they give rise to uncertainties and convolutions.

Whenever the being's voices land on the ground, they give rise to songs and melodies.

Yahya al-Sheikh is skilled at picking the primitive line. He may be the one who picked up the rock and lay down the lines. In his sky the circles rise from the constellations. He suspends the sky between the horns of a bull. Doesn't everything start from a point and end in a point?

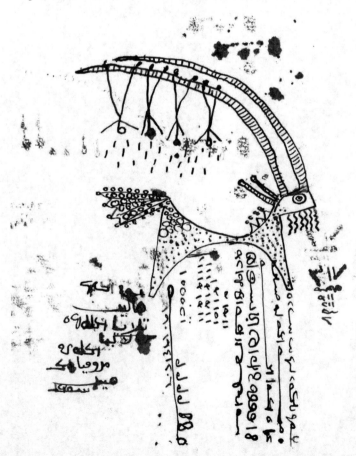

Maybe he's the one who chose to be created in the likeness of be-
ings. He seats magicians in the sky. In their hands they have pens.
Their breath is cold and their eyes throw sparks. On their chests
hang chains of precious stones that emit a light that can be seen from
afar. In the water the priests intone sacred anthems. As soon as sun-
light rises on the surface, a phallus emerges from the sea and spills
its semen onto the thirsty land, and the land is impregnated. There
is land above and land below. The imagination of the unusual being
infiltrates the soil and at every step a spring of water bursts forth
and if the soul of any being is washed in the spring water it becomes
immortal. But where does the fire of creation comes from?

It comes from the fingers of the unusual being.

Yahya al-Sheikh is skilled at plucking the eternal melody. Maybe
he's the one who blew the fire of eternity into the poignant tune.

How does he hold the bull? By the horns, with his steady hands.
There, not far off stands the spotted bull, with blood dripping from

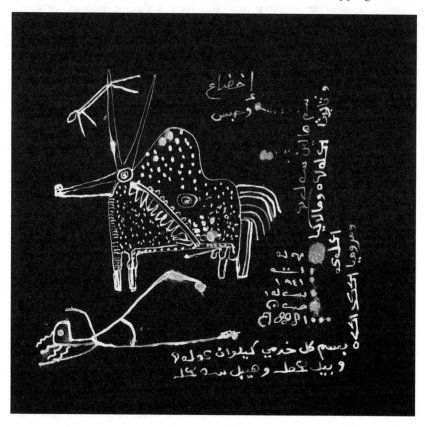

its body. There, not far off, lies a man, breathing his last. There, not far off, a star shines in the highest. There horses neigh on the steppe, a man becomes one with his wife. A plain bursts into flower, and a mountain exudes forests. There a river runs after a mysterious dream.

Yahya al-Sheikh came from the eternal memory of water and mud. He came from mighty Iraq. He came from a rare and ancient purity.

He underwent major transformations in the cocoon of the elements. With the experience of a skilled craftsman, he knew how to patch up the cloak of the gods. He knew how to light the fire of the question in the furnace of the idea. He knew that replying is sterile and that the path to the unusual being starts from a pebble thrown in the wasteland.

Yahya achieved his own objectives after scattering the objectives of the beings in the wilderness. His objectives drowned him and took him to their valleys. They took him to their forests, they took him to their plains and their mountains. They took him to great uncertainty. They took him to long and bitter lamentation. They took him to incessant laughter. They took him to a turbulent spirit. They took him to the unusual being by day and by night.

In this great intellectual and artistic achievement Yahya al-Sheikh places his objectives in front of us through an extraordinary dyad:

One diurnal, with white land and brown soil, throwing off its anxiety, its disease, its fear, its poverty, its longing, its love, its hatred. It is unable to act and it safeguards its house with sacred words, fending off its fears with countless amulets.

The other nocturnal: secrecy, darkness, blindness, a night in which the guard is the treasure, the sea is the ship, the water is the tree, the mountain is the oven, the desert is the beetle, the horse is the rider, the hunter is the prey, in which everything is nothing, in which the created is the god of words.

The objectives of Yahya al-Sheikh: the objectives of the unusual being.

Translated by Jonathan Wright

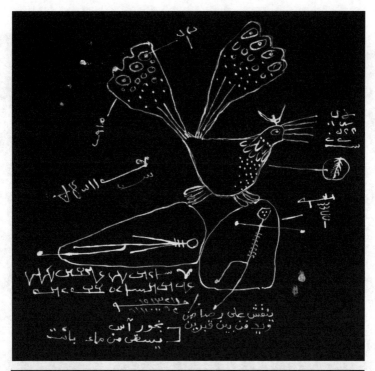

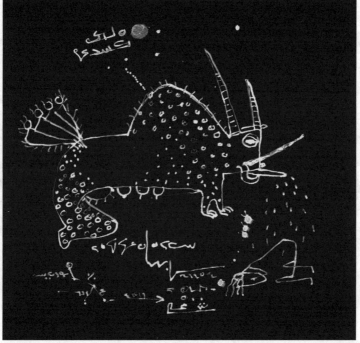

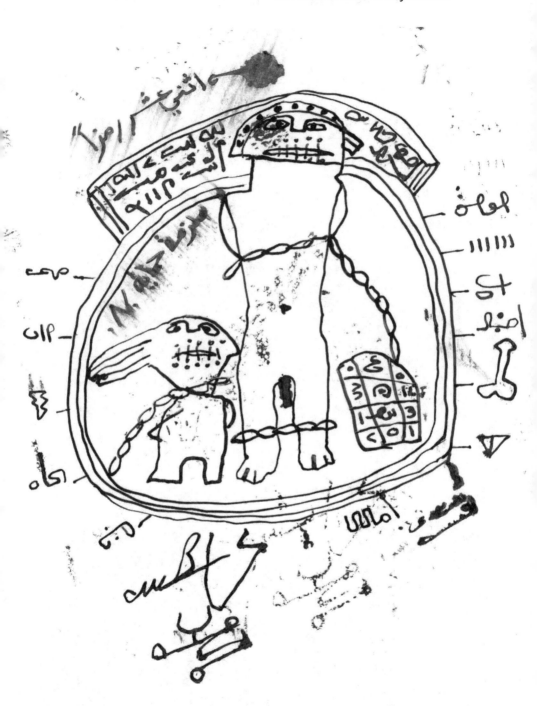

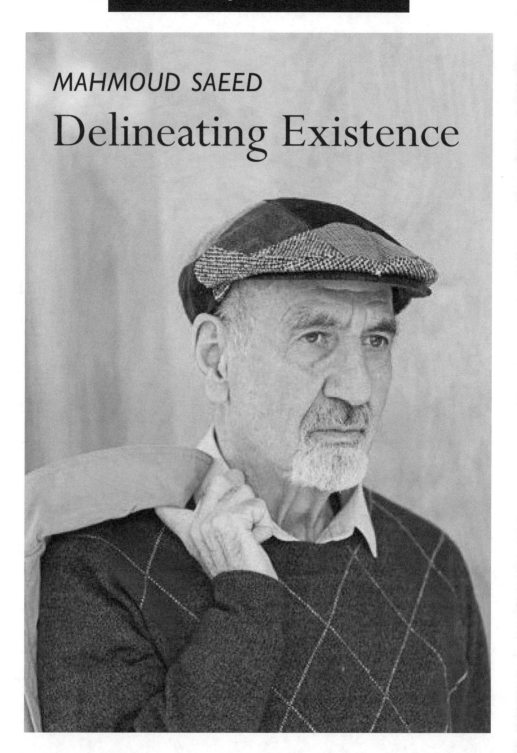

MAHMOUD SAEED

Delineating Existence

Banipal regularly invites a prominent Arab author to write about the books and authors that have had an influential impact on their life and work.

Iraqi author Mahmoud Saeed, with more than 20 novels and collections of short stories to his name, recounts his journey through literature.

My formal education began when I was two and a half; my family placed me in a Qur'an school in the Shaykh Muhammad Mosque in Mosul. Our house adjoined this mosque, and my father offered his sunset and evening prayers there. Mullah Abd al-Hamid taught us just the Qur'an. All I remember from those years is reciting verses while the mullah's dread stick hovered over our heads – hunting for idlers, slackers, and dunces.

Although this mullah alienated us by making us repeat verses we did not understand at all and by threatening us with his stick, our presence in the mosque also brought us happiness and contentment, because, in the morning, we enjoyed two long recesses that we spent clustered around Shaykh Shuhdi. He was a blind man who was more than 127 years old, according to Mullah Abd al-Hamid, and 120 according to his own reckoning which he never updated during more than ten years before I left for Baghdad. Shaykh Shuhdi was from a long-lived family, and his father had survived to about 130. He had been a young man at the time Nader Shah attacked Mosul with 350,000 men, the largest army in the region's history, as an ally of Russia and Germany, opposing the Ottoman Empire.

Shuhdi was an eloquent person and won all our hearts when he described how people had defended the city, or recounted miracles accomplished by Muslim holy men and Christian saints who had polished off oppressors and tyrants. We especially liked the story of Saint George killing the dragon.

Once I turned five, I would run about a kilometre to sit in my father's store while he prayed for "five minutes" in the mosque. My return home was like watching a film, because I typically saw a collage of dervishes, singers, vendors hawking their wares, Gypsy troupes, and displays of goods for sale.

Before I began public school, a friend of my older brother presented me with a copy of the Arabic version of the *Reader's Digest*.

Mosul

He asked me to read the first word of the title, but I couldn't. I knew all the letters in the word but could not link them together to pronounce them as a single word. My first day in school, however, I was able to read the entire alphabet book (*al-Qira'a al-Khalduniya*) in five minutes. How did that happen? I have no explanation for it. So I began to read whatever I saw. Soon I was reading other books – up to a hundred pages a day when I was in second grade. In third grade I went to the public library to satisfy my hunger for reading. By the time I finished elementary school I was familiar with important works of our cultural heritage like *The Thousand and One Nights* and the sagas of 'Antara and Sayf Ibn Dhi Yazan.

I was also reading all the translated works I could find in the Mosul Public Library by the giants of world literature. I began with the detective stories of Agatha Christie like *Murder in Mesopotami*a and *They Came to Baghdad* and something by Edgar Allan Poe – I don't remember what. Chekhov's short stories made an impact on me then; I still remember one: "Vanka", the letter of a child to his grandfather. From Dostoyevsky I read *Crime and Punishment*, *The Brothers Karamazov*, *The Gambler*, and *The House of the Dead*. The last of these would have a special impact on me, because I remembered it every time I was hauled off to a police station or prison. It also provided me with a major lesson in narration, since it avoided tedious repetitions and monotonous descriptions. I kept this in mind when I was writing *Ana Alladhi Ra'a* (I am the one who saw), which was published in English

Chekhov

as *Saddam City*. I read *Mother* by Maxim Gorky and started reading Tolstoy's *War and Peace*, which I could not finish because I found it too monotonous and too full of description. On the other hand, I thoroughly enjoyed *Anna Karenina* and to a lesser extent his *Hadji Murat*. Émile Zola's novels *L'Inondation* and *Le Roman Experimental* did not attract me at all, so I did not finish them. I liked many of the short stories by Guy de Maupassant as much as those of Chekhov, although their approaches differed. I wrote an essay about three novels by Turgenev – the first of these was *Fathers and Sons*, and the woman who taught us English helped me translate a short excerpt from it. I used this essay when I applied for admission to Harvard University, but, as it was 1963, instead of enrolling in a university I was incarcerated. Back then, Iraq still provided students with a solid education.

Naturally I read *A Tale of Two Cities* by Dickens, *Les Misérables* by Hugo, poetry by Pushkin, *Madame Bovary* by Flaubert, *The Red Lily* by Anatole France, and many of Shakespeare's plays. The most translated European author then was Alexandre Dumas, père, especially his novel *The Three Musketeers*. I could barely read ten pages of Dante, although I enjoyed reading *Don Quixote* by Cervantes and many novels by Honoré de Balzac. The Mosul library contained four books by the Turkish author Aziz Nesin and a short story collection by Sadegh Hedayat – so I read those works as well.

My perusal of Arabic literature and those translated works of world literature in Mosul Public Library was balanced by my love of nature – especially during fall and spring when the weather was temperate. Because I spent a lot of time outdoors, I stood on firm ground when I began to write. A person is inevitably astonished by nature's beauty in the spring, whether in the villages around Mosul or in the surrounding countryside, the place where the earth becomes a green carpet dotted with gorgeous flowers – especially anemones, which proliferate in an amazing way and spread for tens of metres.

Standing on the iron bridge to observe fishermen cast their white nets into the sky and watching them fall into the water offered a splendid sight that imbued a small child with a love of nature and encouraged him to harmonize with it.

Our neighbours in the market were Jewish, and the seamstress was a Christian who sewed clothes for men and women from the surrounding villages. So I became a member of two other families – one Jewish and one Christian. I spent most of my free time with my friend Sami, who was Jewish, and frequently took cloth from my father's store to the house of Mary the seamstress. Those friendships broadened my horizon, and I realized that our society was a collective of complementary ethnicities. When I started writing, I profited from this stock of acquaintances, views, and diversity.

I began to think about the detective story for the first time when I was thirteen. Why? I don't know. I laid hands on a short story about Arsène Lupin and read it. I loved it and then read one by Agatha Christie. I suddenly found myself brooding about this genre for days, without knowing what was prompting me to write a detective story.

When I sat down to write, I discovered that this desire was one thing and its execution quite something else. After a number of attempts to write a detective story, I gave up entirely even though the desire remained latent in me as a goal I aspired to.

All schools around the world – including those in Iraq – offer composition classes. Back then, the bureaucrats in charge of setting our centralized curriculum, and our teachers as well, lacked an outlook broad enough to provide a successful composition programme that would prepare anyone to be a writer. The Arabic language instructor would give us an oral prompt or write a topic on the blackboard. He would force us to stick to the subject but would not teach us how to write or express ourselves. He would not even specify the number of words or pages.

The teacher's topics were traditional and were the same almost every year. After summer vacation we had to write about the holiday and how we had spent it. Similarly, after our mid-term break, the major and minor Eids, and all other notable points in the calendar, like the Prophet's birthday, we were supposed to write about the holiday and what we had done. At the start of a new year, we were asked to record what we anticipated from it. Some students wrote excellent compositions and received the highest mark – a thirty or a twenty-nine. Others, like me, always failed at composition. My

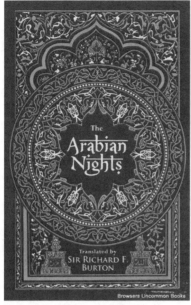

lack of conviction about the topic was the major reason that I flunked writing.

Then I had an astonishing idea. It was to write a summary of one of the books I had read during the week. So I sat down to do this but encountered another difficult problem that was worse than the original one. The books I read typically contained between 150 and 300 pages. When I began to summarize each chapter in turn, I encountered severe difficulties, and it took me two days to write three lines. Then I realized that it would be impossible for me to summarize an entire book this way in a page and a half or two pages. So I wasted two days and gave up. I could do my homework for algebra, physics, chemistry, and plane geometry in a quarter of an hour each but could not write a composition or summarize the book I was reading. I procrastinated for two more days and brooded about this. Then I asked my plane geometry teacher, whose respect I had earned because I was the best student in his class, if he could give me some pointers on summarizing. He asked me: "Have you seen the film Tarzan?" I laughed and replied: "Yes." He looked me straight in the eye and said: "Go home and think how to summarize the film in fewer than ten lines." When I wanted to ask him for more clarification, he put his forefinger to his lips. "Not another word. Go." Walking home I was

Aziz Nesin

able to summarize the plot of the film Tarzan not only in fewer than ten lines but in only a few words: "A child lost his family in the jungle and grew up among wild animals. So he was able to communicate with them as if he were one of them." I reflected on the method I had followed and discovered that I had suppressed all the minor details and had overlooked inessential events. Then I was overjoyed, because I had discovered my own way to summarize.

Despite my intense effort, my grade in composition was still zero, because I ignored the set topic. So throughout middle and secondary school my average in composition remained below passing, and everyone thought I was the weakest in the Arabic language class. All the same, I continued to summarize whatever book I was reading the way I had summarized Tarzan.

During my final year in secondary school, the renowned Mosul poet Shadhil Taqa was named to be our Arabic language instructor. He wrote on the blackboard a number of topics, and we were supposed to choose one to write on during class. Since, as usual, I did not like any of the proposed topics, I proceeded to summarize a book I had read – one about Mustafa Kemal Ataturk, the founder of modern Turkey. At the end of the class period, he collected all our copybooks.

The next week he distributed all our corrected essays, except for three that he retained on his desk. From two of these copybooks he selected a few sentences that he wrote on the blackboard and asked us to correct, because they contained serious but common errors. Since he had held back mine too, I was holding my hand over my heart the whole time. I could only imagine how savagely he would attack me, drawing attention to my failings. When he did open my copybook, he told the students: "This is the best composition I have seen from any student." He gave me a grade I had never dreamed of: 28 out of a possible 30 points. He also said he would allow me to

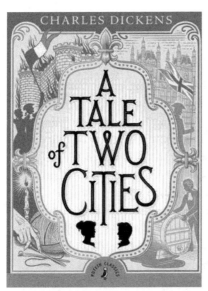

ignore the set topic in the future and to write whatever I wanted.

The next year I won first prize in a short story competition sponsored by the newspaper *Iraqi Youth*. This was the most important literary prize at that time, and young people were eager to compete for it. For me, this award was an incentive and encouragement. I continued writing and published my first short story collection, *Port Said and Other Stories* in 1957. The prize, though, also heralded the beginning of a period of ferocious and relentless hostility directed at me. A few individuals sought me out and whispered that I should write (or help them write) a story they would submit to the newspaper under their name. I explained to each person in turn that this was out of the question but offered to do my best to revise a manuscript that any of them wrote – even though I was a novice with no expertise in writing. A group of them accepted my explanations, but most became my bitter enemies, especially one fellow who became a police informant and continued to file reports denouncing me until the Saddam regime fell.

Our generation had the excellent fortune to learn for free from the finest, most eloquent Arabic language teachers, and we listened to them every day. I am referring to the singers Umm Kulthum, Mohammed Abdel Wahab, Nazem al-Ghazali, and Mohammed al-Qubanchi. Soon Fairuz appeared on the scene with the Rahbani Brothers and so did Abdel Halim Hafez. These great artists selected the most beautiful poems from Arabic literature to sing with lovely melodies that enchanted everyone and forced us youngsters to sing along with them, willingly or not.

Books by creative geniuses – like Naguib Mahfouz, Ahmad Shawqi, and Tawfiq al-Hakim – were readily available for every reader, both for sale at cheap prices and in public libraries. The Gold Club, the Silver Club, and the Egyptian Short Story Club also distributed books. At this time, when the lyrics to Arabic songs attracted me and focused me on their content, I attempted to understand and study modern Iraqi poetry. I was, however, repelled by its distance from the spirit of our age, petrification, rigidity, and failure to achieve its goals.

At the behest of some friends, I began reading literary magazines, the most important of which were from Beirut: *al-Adib* and *al-Adab*. I enjoyed the articles published in them but had no taste for the literary battles that divided authors in those days into two factions – whether art should be for art's sake or for the sake of the people and whether style is more important than content or vice versa.

After winning that prize, I started thinking about writing a novel. I was further motivated to do this by an important political event that profoundly influenced me. In 1956, butchers in Mosul went on strike, and this action lasted seven full days. It achieved its objectives, and the municipality abolished the extra taxes on animal slaughter. Since I was close to the site of the events, I decided to write a novel about it. But I was confronted with no end of difficulties in writing. I could write short stories without much reflection. I would just start writing as the thought percolated and then the story's complete details would appear in my mind. The situation with a novel, however, proved different, and I found myself faced by huge roadblocks I could not surmount.

The first was that a novel needs links between its parts so it won't seem disjointed. The second was that I frequently found that I had failed to express what I longed to say. The third was that I discovered that I failed to describe beauty adequately. I would write: 'a beautiful, fiery red rose' and then realize that what I had written was simplistic and superficial. The fourth was that I was totally incapable of creating new, inspirational ways of expressing something. My own writing copied styles I had studied or had encountered in my wide-ranging reading.

So I stopped writing that novel and brooded for a long time about how to overcome these hurdles. Even so I continued reading all the Arabic and translated novels I saw, and some questions imposed themselves on me. Why could the typical Western writer describe human emotions more accurately than most Arab authors? Why did Western novels draw me in more forcefully than Arab ones? Why did the Western novel plentifully supply the excitement that most Arab novels lacked? Why did Western novels seem more authentic

"I had no taste for the literary battles that divided authors in those days into two factions – whether art should be for art's sake or for the sake of the people"

and saturated with life than Arab ones?

Eventually my brooding led me to three important principles that Arab critics appeared to have ignored: (A) the human content being far removed from ethnic chauvinism, anger, or xenophobia; (B) original plots and plot treatments; and (C) clarity and simplicity of style, and straightforward structures.

I realized then that these points were relevant to the immortality of some literary works and their triumph over time – works by Chekhov, Dostoyevsky, Tolstoy, Guy de Maupassant, and Hemingway, for example.

In the autumn of 1959, when I finished writing *Idhrab al-Qassabeen* (*The Butchers' Strike*) I did not feel satisfied, because how could I be sure my work wasn't idle chatter? I was also a Leftist, and political conditions soon changed: a vicious assault on the Left began, especially against Communists. It was impossible for me to remain in Mosul, and I was compelled to hide in al-Shirqat in the home of a relative. I was a nervous wreck all this time, because the entire region was controlled by Nationalists who killed Leftists as nonchalantly as if swatting a fly. I spent a long time hunkered down in a small room that was tantamount to a prison cell. I did not move from there or walk anywhere, and there was no one who visited me or whom I could visit.

I next sought refuge in Baghdad with my friend Fouad Ala' al-Din, who subsequently died in the custody of the security services. Fouad helped me publish my *Port Said* short story collection and gave the manuscript of my novel to a famous journalist, whom I met a week later. Then he praised my novel but confessed that he knew nothing about literature. He introduced me to a member of the Iraqi Writers Union. Three days later this man told me: "The novel is excellent, but during these critical times we do not recommend publishing a novel about a contentious topic." In any event, I became a member of the Iraqi Writers Union, and membership entitled me to place the manuscript in their vault. If I had left it at home, it would have

"He showed me – on a top shelf – the files of Communists who were collaborating with the Ba'ath Party. 'Look!' he said. 'All of them are cooperating with us. Why don't you?' "

been destroyed and I would have been prosecuted. Even members of my own family were openly hostile to Leftists, including me. After I was imprisoned in 1980, I learned that a nephew and a brother-in-law had reported me to the Ba'ath Party.

Many Leftists of different stripes fled Mosul and Kirkuk and moved to New Baghdad. I wrote about their migration in a novel of about 150 pages. When my contact at the Iraqi Writers Union read it, he liked it a lot and offered to publish it there. They requested financial support from me, and for that reason I would have preferred to send it to Dar al-Adab in Beirut. At the time I was supporting the large family my father had left me. But I agreed to have this novel published in Iraq when he said it would be the first novel they published after the 1958 Revolution. This proved to be the most atrocious error of my entire life.

The manuscript rotted for years at Military Intelligence. Finally, in the autumn of 1962, they authorized its publication; it was re-leased on February 1, 1963, but because of the coup d'état that oc-curred exactly a week later all copies of this novel were destroyed, together with the manuscript of my earlier novel *The Butchers' Strike*. So I went to prison for a second time and spent a year and a day there. After that I was banned from working for three years. During this period I wrote the novel *al-Iqa' wa-l-Hajis* (The Rhythm and the Premonition) about the suffering that victims of this coup had en-dured. In 1968, the censor refused permission for its publication un-less I changed many sections. Then in 1970 I offered my novel *Ben Barka Lane* to the censors, who again refused me permission to pub-lish.

My greatest problem was safeguarding my manuscripts, since the security officers who raided my home were illiterate and feared the written word, which they interpreted according to the dictates of their imagination. I lost the manuscripts of three more novels in this manner.

In 1970, an award-winning author visited Basra, where I was living then, and I invited him and his wife to the Port Club. I was not surprised to hear that he was working for a top Ba'ath party official. He hinted that he was on an important mission to the Gulf nations. Once he returned to Baghdad, he invited me to visit his office, where he showed me – on a top shelf – the files of Communists who were collaborating with the Ba'ath Party. "Look!" he said. "All of them are cooperating with us. Why don't you?" I had hoped he would help me publish but found myself offered a choice between collaborating with people whose principles I rejected or remaining true to my principles and unpublished. All my manuscripts were then denied publication until the fall of the Baath regime in 2003. Even after that, the new regime banned two of my novels, in 2006 and 2008 respectively.

At the middle school where I taught Arabic, some of my colleagues and students eagerly volunteered to convey any of my comments – along with their own insidious glosses – to the authorities. Perhaps I helped them by refusing to join the Party. Thus I was continually being interrogated and arrested for periods of a few days or a week. I served time in Abu Ghraib prison and in other detention facilities in Basra, Baghdad, and Mosul.

For three months in 1961 I had stays of different durations in various jails. Mosul was especially troubling because they had taken me more than a thousand kilometres from my wife and children, and I did not know what would become of me. From one day to the next I expected to be interrogated; but I was imprisoned and finally released without any explanation ever being provided or any charge brought against me.

The terrifying atmosphere of imprisonment inspired me to write the novel *I am the one who saw* about my incarceration – before forgetfulness could erase those memories. I never felt safe, though, because I lived in Basra during the years of the Iran-Iraq War, and Basra was a battleground. Lethal bombs fell on civilians daily with no rhyme or reason and harvested the spirits of innocent people of all ages – not to mention those who died as martyrs on the battlefields. Thus I lived in constant fear for the welfare of my family and hoped that the outside world would notice what was happening in Iraq.

When I had a chance to travel to Jordan, I offered this novel to a publisher, who replied so softly he might as well have been whispering: "You can publish this book in Syria without any obstacles." Nod-

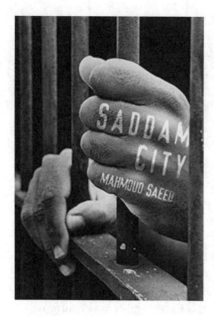

ding and shaking his head, he declared: "You cannot publish it here through any government outlet!"

I felt he was offering me sincere advice, and so travelled to Syria. Unfortunately, I was unlucky in Damascus too. The expert in charge of reading novels offered to the Arab Writers Union asked me to delete two chapters from the novel. The first described homosexual conduct in prison and the second discussed the strong ties between the families of Saddam and al-Assad – even though everyone believed they hated each other. My second greatest mistake of my whole life was to agree to suppress those two chapters, but it would have been my first opportunity to publish in two decades. Two days later, the expert reader added a new condition; they would not publish the novel unless I consented to become a spy for the Syrian regime. Since that was out of the question, he returned my manuscript – minus those two chapters. So I was obliged to return to Iraq with the truncated manuscript.

In 1992 *Ben Barka Lane* was published in Jordan – a quarter of a century after it was written – and the publisher distributed many copies of it in Baghdad. A lot of articles were written about it, and I was asked to submit it to a competition organized by the Ministry of Information. A few months later it won the first prize for best novel, but when the officials learned that it had been banned in Iraq, they withheld the prize. Three months later, the prize was released, but I declined it then.

I published my novels and short story collections outside of Iraq. My attempts to publish in my homeland were destined to failure. Perhaps for this reason I eventually headed to the United States where I hoped to continue writing and to have my works translated.

During my first year in Chicago I spoke at a conference at the University of Chicago and met a scholar who expressed an interest in seeing some of my works. When he eventually requested permission to translate *Ana alladhi Ra'a*, I objected at first, however, because this novel had been amputated and deformed when the Syrian censor removed two chapters. Finally I agreed, and it was published in London as *Saddam City* in 2003. Two years later an Italian translation was published. The novel was listed in 2008 on the website LibraryThing as one of the best novels in the world and

then was mentioned favourably in 2010 in an article in *The New Yorker*.

English translations of my short stories have appeared in *Banipal*, *World Literature Today*, *The Brooklyn Rail*, on the website Words Without Borders, and in Amnesty International's anthology: *Freedom: Short Stories Celebrating the Universal Declaration of Human Rights*, 2011. My novel *A Portal in Space* was published in English in January 2016, and several of my other novels have already been published in English translation: *Saddam City*, *Two Lost Souls, Ben Barka Lane* and *The World Through the Eyes of Angels*. In 2014 I was appointed the first writer-in-residence at the American University of Iraq, Sulaymaniyah, where I taught calligraphy.

Translated by William M Hutchins

• *A Portal in Space* was reviewed in *Banipal 55 — Sudanese Literature today*
• *Ben Barka Lane* and *The World Through the Eyes of Angels* were reviewed in *Banipal 48 — Narrating Marrakech,* and are available to read online at http://www.banipal.co.uk/book_reviews/111/2-novels-by-mahmoud-saeed/.
• The short story "The Sound of Footsteps", translated by Sophia Vasalou, was published in *Banipal 49 — A Cornucopia of Short Stories*

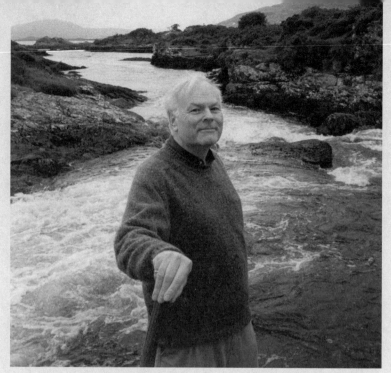

Remembering
Herbert Mason
(1932–2017)

Herbert Warren Mason II (1932-2017), eminent American scholar, translator, writer and poet, died suddenly on New Year's Day in Newbury, MA, USA. He was Professor Emeritus and the William Goodwin Aurelio Professor of History and Religious Thought and past President of the Association des Amis de Louis Massignon, Paris. He was for a number of years a consulting editor and contributor to *Banipal* magazine.

He was the translator into English of Louis Massignon's four volume *The Passion of al-Hallaj: Mystic and Martyr of Islam,* devoting thirteen years to translating and editing Massignon's magnum opus. The eminent historian of religions Huston Smith wrote: "The French original of this work has stood for most of this century as a model of the way Western scholarship can illuminate a foreign culture, not patronize or denature it. This translation climaxes one of the most focused projects of humanistic scholarship this century has seen."

Herbert Mason also produced an abridged Volume 1 which was popularly received. He went on to translate selected critical essays of Massignon in *Testimonies and Reflections of Louis Massignon*. His *Memoir of a Friend: Louis Massignon* makes the thought of Massignon better known to the English-speaking world. His dramatic narrative *The Death of al-Hallaj* has been adopted in college courses in the US and performed publicly, bringing us closer to the 10th-Century Muslim mystic.

Herbert Mason lived for long periods of time in France and Ireland, and has travelled extensively in Europe, North Africa, the Middle East and Japan. His books, including poetry and fiction in addition to scholarly works have been translated into numerous foreign languages, including French, German, Spanish, Arabic, Persian, Urdu, and Japanese, and his novel *Where the Rivers Meet* was reviewed in *Banipal 19* (Summer 2004).

His verse narrative *Gilgamesh*, an interpretation of the ancient Sumerian epic poem transcends boundaries of age, language, religion, and time. His friendship with the Italian painter Dino Cavallari and their shared interest in this ancient Near Eastern story led to Cavallari's creation of 70 illustrations and Mason's publication of his poetic retelling with Gilgamesh's journey on the river of death as the cover art. The paintings were exhibited in Galerie Lee, Paris, in 2011. Mason's book was a finalist for the National Book Award in 1971 and continues to be a best seller in America.

He is survived by his wife, Jeanine Young-Mason, his children Cathleen Mason, Paul Mason, Sarah Mason and their families and his step-sons Scott Angell, Gregg Angell, and Glenn Angell and their families. He is also survived by his sister, Sarah Nelson and her family.

He is interred at Mt. Auburn Cemetery in Cambridge, MA. His life and works will be celebrated in a memorial service in April. The family, friends, and colleagues are establishing an International Writing Prize in his name.

• His works for *Banipal* included the review of *The Journals of Sarab Affan* by Jabra Ibrahim Jabra, whom he had met on many occasions. See *Banipal 33* (Autumn/Winter 2008): http://www.banipal.co.uk/book_reviews/52/the-journals-of-sarab-affan-by-jabra-ibrahim-jabra/; and, in *Banipal 46 – 80 New Poems* (2013), an article about his friendship with Lorand Gaspar, in the issue's feature on the poet surgeon.

Fadia Faqir reviews
Al-Khaima al-Baidha' (The White Tent) by Liana Badr
Published by Hachette Antoine S.A.L.,
Beirut 2016
ISBN: 978-614-438-617-0

An ode to Palestine

In her many works the writer and filmmaker Liana Badr documents the different stages of Palestinian national struggle against occupation and chronicles the Palestinian diaspora experience, including the Nakba of 1948. From her first novel, *A Compass for Sunflower*, which follows the life of a young woman working in refugee camps in Amman and Beirut, to *A Balcony over the Fakihani*, three novellas set against the departure from Jordan in 1970 and Israeli airstrikes during the 1982 invasion of Lebanon, to *Stars of Jericho*, set in Jericho pre-1967 war and then revisited post the first Gulf War, to *The Eye of the Mirror*, which I commissioned as part of the Arab Women Writers Series, her narrative, as Therese Saliba wrote, is : "suffused by nationalist consciousness and critical of masculinist conceptions of nationalism".

In my introduction in *The Eye of the Mirror*, I wrote: "The novel is not merely historical or documentary. It transcends what took place to create a mosaic of eye-witness accounts, documents and fictitious testimonies. Liana Badr tries to place Tel-al-Zaatar at the heart of Palestinian consecutive tragedies." This applies to her latest novel, *The White Tent*, though her writing has matured and reached new heights.

The novel, which can be considered an ode to Palestine, is set in Ramallah, where the main character, Nashid, lives. Being a filmmaker Badr writes as if she is holding a camera to Ramallah today, and its landmarks: al-Manara Square, the Clock Tower and Water roundabouts, the so-called "Alhambra Palace", streets, shops and people, and that dark cloud that hangs above it: the Israeli settler colonial state, which manifests itself in the fortified settlements and the tanks surrounding a city constantly under siege. But other towns and cities like Nablus, Jerusalem, Acre, Jaffa and Gaza are also described and their history recounted to commit them to collective memory and assert Palestinian ownership over them.

Cover of *Al-Khaima Al-Baidha'/The White Tent*

Like Virginia Woolf in *Mrs Dalloway* and Michael Cunningham in *The Hours*, Badr places the action within a single day. The narrative moves swiftly and seamlessly between the external environment, and inside heads of characters. The interior monologue used is punctuated by flashbacks, vignettes and sub stories. Badr layers the voices within the narrative discourse, which allows her to present a rich diversity of Palestinian voices and ideologies and to collect them into a resounding political and social protests against a merciless occupier and a misogynist society.

The first narrative line is from Nashid's perspective. She is an activist and an observer who constantly documents her life and that of others and her surroundings and ponders the significance of events unfolding quickly. In the twenty-four hours of this novel the reader is offered a glimpse of Nashid's life, her work at an NGO, her struggle against occupation, and her fear for her son and other youths in a volatile environment where civilians are targeted by the Israeli army and/or collaborators. She is on a mission to save Hajar, who is unmarried, from a possible honour crime.

The second narrative line is from the point of view of the about-to-retire "fidayee, fighter, journalist, revolutionary" Asi, who after fighting for years has becomes a pariah because of his constant criticism of his organisation and its leadership. He feels lonely and un-appreciated by a society corrupted by a prolonged occupation. In a divided community and amidst the rise of a new class of mercenaries who are after instant profit at any price: selling their land, building skyscrapers, or exporting Palestinian labour to Israel, he feels alien-ated. This new class of profiteers has no allegiance or any respect for the past: the long national struggle, the first and second Intifadas, and the war of attrition launched on a daily basis against Palestinians.

His wife, Lamis, whom he had abandoned years before when the national struggle took him from one country to another, has decided to lead her own life. Unlike most, she has a Jerusalem ID and uses it to visit her mother and take care of their old house. She shows re-markable endurance as she crosses the many permanent road blocks and checkpoints maned by the Israeli Military or Border Police every day to assert her right to her Jerusalemite house, which was built hundreds of years ago and was handed down from one generation to another. "Asi imagines her watering the plant pots, clipping the plumosa fern, so it won't wind itself around the window's metal grill, obstructing the magnificent view of the Dome of the Rock, tops of houses and vaults of historical churches . . . She takes care of her mother and prepares her food as settlers, who had become com-pulsory neighbours, throw water and garbage at them." (page 64)

Like Lamis, Nashid has to cross a checkpoint to arrive in Jerusalem and with the help of other women save Hajar from imminent death. In a vivid scene, one you would rarely see in the western media's coverage of Palestine, Badr describes the despair and impotence of Palestinians degraded, humiliated and abused at the barrier. "The mere thought of crossing that checkpoint fills her with dread and she shudders. She will stand in the queue again in that checkpoint's corridor made of wrought iron, her body, damp with the sweat of annoyance and hidden fear, shoulder to shoulder with others, as the occupier raises his rifle against them for no reason and without any justification. That hellish barrier there." (page 72)

The novel also shows what has become of Palestinians after years of arbitrary arrests, deportations and the Israeli West Bank Wall, which divides farming communities and strangles towns and villages. Due to poverty and a lack of job opportunity or economic prospects, many ended up as construction workers and garbage collectors in the prosperous neighbouring settlements. Slowly corruption spreads and entrenches itself in a society constantly under siege. Love and its symbols, like "red roses", becomes irrelevant in an environment where the individual has no control over his/her surroundings.

The novel is polyphonous and the two main narratives lines are dotted with vignettes about life under occupation. For example, the description of Sit Jawaher's mysterious death exposes how colonialism and patriarchy are intertwined and sometimes in collusion with each other. Sit Jawaher allows into her house a relative, who attacks her, ties

Liana Badr

her to the bedframe, and subjects her to a violent interrogation. She subsequently dies of a heart attack. Nashid wonders whether the assailant was after the deeds of her family's large plot of land and wanted to force her to transfer ownership to her male relatives. Was he a secret agent sent to steal the deeds because the settlement next to their land has its sights on it and wanted to forge the documents to conceal the fact from any future enquiries that it had acquired by force? Or in this patriarchal culture could it be a male relative bent on cleansing his honour?

The Palestinian issue is central to this narrative, but equally so is the "other issue", namely that of women's position in society and their bid for freedom. In the past the leadership has prioritised the national struggle over gender equality, but for Badr the two liberations go hand in hand. Throughout the novel, which can easily be classified as feminist literature, there is an attempt to explore, bring to the foreground and validate women's experiences and subculture.

The presence of women in this novel is strong: Nashid, Lamis, Bisan, Nada, Hajar, Sit Jawaher and other unnamed characters, such as Nashid's mother, are all active members of the Palestinian resistance, but each in her own way. The young have found new ways of fighting occupation using social networks and other means of communication. Bisan, for example, sees the way out through rap music.

The writing sometimes rises from prose to poetic fiction. There are many examples of that and here is my translation of two such sections: "He went to Acre, whose famous walls protected the city from Napoleon and his army. He listened to the gentle hissing of waves as they flirted with the beach, and the quivering and shudders of the silver foam. The children, who leapt into the water and turned into fish twisting this way and that, gleamed like gold." (page 157) And the following is a description of Palestinian embroidery and its symbols, which can be traced to consecutive civilizations: "The embroidery represents light, that of Venus in its zenith, of the pulsating sun, of the splendid moon in the middle of an indigo sky. You will find the cross stitch which the crusaders brought with them from Europe's monasteries . . . As for the small keys in the middle of the pine and acacia gardens, it either appeared or disappeared depending on the region where the dress was embroidered." (page 160)

The two narrative lines are in parallel with each other and here lies a weakness or a missed opportunity. If the two main characters had met, exchanged views on issues raised in the novel, or even contemplated being together, this would have provided tension and an opportunity with both protagonists for transformation or transcendence. It probably would have been difficult to achieve within the constraints of the twenty-four-hour timescale, but a crisis or a challenge could have forced the characters to question their choices and would have enriched the novel.

In his collected of essays *The Small Voices of History* Ranajit Guha urges us to attend to the small voices of history and stresses the power they may have in challenging the master narrative, "interrupting the telling in the dominate version, breaking up its storyline and making a mess of its plot." *The White Tent* does exactly that and is a triumph against acts of erasure of Palestinian history, geography and culture.

Clare Roberts reviews
Hend and the Soldiers
by Badriah Albeshr
Translated by Sanna Dhahir
Centre for Middle East Studies, University of
Texas Press, USA, May 2017
ISBN 978-1477313060. Pbk, 155pp, $21.95

Shaking off the chains of bondage

L ike a growing number of works by women writers from the Gulf to have presented damning condemnations of societal norms, Badriah Albeshr's *Hend and the Soldiers* has not been without controversy. Although the novel itself has not been banned in the author's home country of Saudi Arabia, comparisons have been made with Rajaa Alsanea's 2005 novel *Girls of Riyadh*, which was immediately banned in the country upon publication but hugely popular and easily accessible elsewhere. Sanna Dhahir's sensitive and thoughtful translation of *Hend and the Soldiers*, ten years after the novel's original publication in Arabic, will be welcomed by English-speaking readers seeking to make sense of such a seemingly impenetrable society.

A PhD graduate and award-winning columnist and novelist, Albeshr studied at the American University of Beirut and King Saud University. Her outspoken social critique columns in *Al-Hayat* and *Al-Arabiya* newspapers cover issues ranging from religious fatwas to domestic violence against women in Saudi society. This daringness is carried over to the protagonist of her first novel, *Hend and the Soldiers*, who, in many ways, resembles the author herself. Hend is also an educated career woman and single mother who writes for a local column, reads provocatively titled books in public, and craves personal freedom over everything else.

As a young girl growing up under the tight-fisted control of her

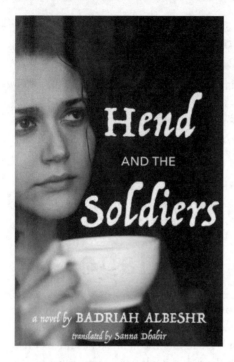

a novel by **BADRIAH ALBESHR**
translated by Sanna Dhahir

conservative and emotionally detached mother, Hend turns to writing for refuge and solace, but most importantly to have a voice of her own. As a grown woman, her writing provokes outrage when she sends it to local columns under a pseudonym. Hend goes to considerable lengths to achieve even a flicker of personal freedom. Yet her fear of being reprimanded is never far from the surface, crippling not only her writing but also the very fundamentals of her daily life. Through her problematic relationship with her mother, and later her husband, her hatred towards the religious police, and her criticism of the way courtship, marriage and love play out in her society, she constantly seeks to defy those around her. They – not least her army officer husband – seek to control her in an almost militant way. The shackles created by the traditional values that envelop her family create for Hend a constant feeling of entrapment. We quickly learn, however, that women are not the only victims in this patriarchal environment: even the protagonist's brothers seek escape from it, sometimes in extreme ways.

For readers familiar with these aspects of Saudi society and the challenges such a militantly patriarchal society can bring, few of the

novel's themes will come as a huge surprise. This novel is most insightful, however, in its spanning of several decades of Saudi history. It retells the story of women from the family over three generations, beginning with King Faisal's abolition of slavery in the 1960s. Throughout the novel the reader is invited to view the situation of Saudi women as one of slavery. Just as it takes former slaves a long time to comprehend the full meaning of their freedom, to shake off "the chains of bondage when other people continue to perpetuate them", accepting the increasing freedom of women in society is no easy feat. Even for women themselves it is no quick or easy feat to embrace the new freedoms being afforded to

Badriah Albeshr

them. The novel traces gradual changes in societal attitudes over recent decades, such as the increasing acceptance by society of women postponing marriage in order to pursue their studies. In the mid-1970s, the physical landscape of Riyadh also starts to change, with families, including Hend's, moving out to larger mansions, the glittering lights of the expanding city symbolic of its new-found wealth. The city changes quickly, but whether traditions can maintain their foothold in society is a complex, more toxic question.

Albeshr clearly believes in change. Through her protagonist, as in reality, she does not shy away from criticising traditions she believes are in need of an overhaul. Although *Hend and the Soldiers* is not alone in its indictment of many aspects of Saudi society, it will nonetheless stand out as an enduring record of a society on the brink of momentous change, and the fitful struggle between old and new.

• *Banipal 54 – ECHOES* published two excerpts, translated by Sally Gomaa, from her novel *Love Stories from al-A'sha Street* which was longlisted for the 2014 International Prize for Arabic Fiction

Olivia Snaije reviews
The Shell: Memoirs of a Hidden Observer
by Mustafa Khalifa
Translated by Paul Starkey
Interlink Publishing, 2017
ISBN 978-1566560221. Pbk, 252pp,
USD15, £12.00

The challenge of translation

The long-awaited English translation of Mustafa Khalifa's *The Shell* has finally become a reality. First published in French translation by Actes Sud in 2007, then published in the original Arabic a year later by Dar-al-Adab, the semi-autobiographical novel about 13 years spent in a Syrian prison during Hafez-al-Assad's reign has been a continuous bestseller among Syrian exiles. Now the entire novel is available, translated by Paul Starkey, winner of the 2015 Saif Ghobash Banipal Prize for Arabic Literary Translation, and published by Interlink Publishing.

Mustafa Khalifa, born in Syria in 1948, studied law and was a member of a far left wing opposition group until his arrest in 1979. He had always dreamed of writing, Khalifa said in an interview in 2014 in Paris, where he lives in exile, but he first focussed on his political activities and then his long imprisonment further delayed writing. *The Shell*, in journal form, is his first novel, and is written in a stark, simple form. Khalifa, in fact, more or less used a method he describes in *The Shell*, in which his character keeps a journal in his head during all his years in prison, a method developed by Islamists to recite suras from the Koran, and then as a way to remember details about their incarceration. Khalifa based the background of his narrator, a Christian and an atheist, on that of a personal friend of his, adding his intimate feelings to the account. His character describes the infamous Tadmur prison's brutal conditions, which include torture, dehumanization and executions, and his absolute isolation from the other prisoners, most of whom are devout Muslims who reject him because he is an atheist, despite living one on top of the other. Khalifa's character hence creates a protective shell about himself.

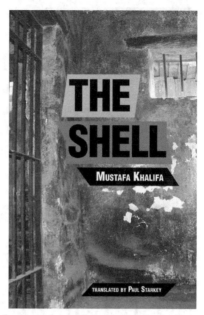

Neither Paul Starkey nor the French translator Stéphanie Dujols had any contact with Khalifa during the time they were translating *The Shell*. Starkey said he had not translated a full-length prison novel before, "though I have read and dealt with similar material, such as in my book [*Rebel with a Pen*] on Sonallah Ibrahim, published last year".

Of the Arabic language, Starkey said it was "reasonably manageable" and agreed with Dujols, who had said the translation had not been difficult linguistically rather psychologically; the translation seeming at times a physical challenge . . . "There were one or two passages in the book that made me feel physically sick."

Despite the wear and tear on the translators, Starkey's English version is seamless, with Khalifa's terrible and compulsive narration rhythmic and powerful. The author, although released from prison in 1994, said that upon awakening he sometimes still thinks he is in prison. Of his motivation to write *The Shell* he said there were two reasons: "the first was personal; I wanted to download my emotions. The second was more general and was tied to the country and being a human being. I wanted the book to be a rock of freedom, a condemnation against all violence against humanity, wherever one is and whatever the violence is."

• Go to *Banipal 50 – PrisonWriting* for a full review by Olivia Snaije of the French edition *La Coquille – Prisonnier politique en Syrie,* also online on the Banipal website at http://www.banipal.co.uk/book_reviews/137/la-coquille-prisonnier-politique-en-syrie/

Abdo Wazen reviews

Sulaf Baghdad

(Sulaf Tavern of Baghdad)

by Muhsin al-Musawi

Published by al-Markaz al-Thaqafi al-Arabi,

2017, Casablanca, Morocco

ISBN: 978-9953-68-819-0

Musawi's Baghdad overflows with nostalgia and tragedy

For his new novel, Muhsin al-Musawi has chosen a polysemic title, *Sulaf of Baghdad*, which brings together the rich Arabic vocabulary of wine with the history of Baghdad's bars that were at their peak in the 1950s as meeting places for writers and "strange happenings", as one of the two narrators calls them, as well as being part of the turbulent reality Baghdad has witnessed in its recent history of one catastrophe after another. While the tavern called Sulaf seems itself to be the metaphorical protagonist of the novel, the city of Baghdad also shows itself as another protagonist. Together, they form the backgrounds for the novel's many characters. Through this duality, it becomes clear why al-Musawi chose not to call his novel something like "The Sulaf Tavern", for the novel is in fact several novels enacted simultaneously: a novel of Baghdad; a novel of the Sulaf tavern with its regulars and its goings-on; a novel of its first narrator, a woman named Samira Muhammad Tawfiq who is a geography teacher in a girls' high school; and finally a novel of the second narrator, Hamdi al-Sammak, who is the author of a manuscript entitled "Sulaf Notes", which Samira chances upon, and in which he writes about the bar and Baghdad and recounts tales that mix fact and fiction.

Musawi opens the novel with the voice of Samira, the first narrator, who paves the way for introducing the second narrator (Hamdi), who is a well-known poet and novelist and regular at the Sulaf, but whose name remains undisclosed and a source of confusion until the novel's finale. His manuscript is posted by his friend Bahnam, together with a letter by Hamdi, to Najm, the owner of the Chakmakji Record Store located opposite the tavern. This strange manuscript is an unauthenticated document that contains implausible stories

Cover of Sulaf Baghdad

and anecdotes from the heart of 1990s Iraq that was reeling under sanctions and occupation. Another central character of the book is Najm, whom Samira visits to repair her crashed computer, and who opens up for her a filing cabinet belonging to his father, who used to store in it manuscripts that novelists and poets gave him for safekeeping from being lost or destroyed. In Samira, Najm finally finds someone to whom he can show these hidden-away texts, including one called "Sulaf Notes", which has no name to it.

"Sulaf Notes" includes a map of Baghdad, which in the 1990s had become "a total maze". Al-Musawi has created this map by integrating the geographical with the cultural, the real with the imaginary, and the tragic with the bizarre. Everything in the novel takes place in the real city of Baghdad, but with Sulaf as the guiding compass from the start to the endpoint of the narrative. The "bar" is the space in which images of the city, of shattered dreams and frustrations reveal themselves clearly. Baghdad is a city of poets and novelists, of the oppressed and defeated, or as Hamdi recounts in the manuscript, a city of a generation of major ideologies and concepts that are in danger of disappearing. What remains of this generation "has become like Don Quixote's broken sword, after dictatorship and one-party rule broke its will, whether by force or willingly".

In spite of the lament for Baghdad that is implicit or openly described, al-Musawi's novel is not devoid of nostalgia for the city. Nostalgia for the Baghdad of the Sulaf tavern and other landmarks that were wiped out by sanctions and occupation. Anyone who knows Baghdad well can appreciate why the author would reminisce over its streets, squares, cafés, bookstores, and its actual people, who became phantoms or left: Rashid Street, Rusafi Square, the Uruzdibak bookstore, Café Suisse, al-Khayyam Street, Abu Nuwas Street, Sa'dun Street, the Kubbet Irbil restaurant, et. al., but at the forefront was always the Sulaf tavern, the watering hole for poets and novelists of any status, age, or mood: Kadhim Jawad, Husayn Mardan, Rushdi al-'Amil, Buland al-Haydari, along with all the bohemians such as Abd al-Rahman Tuhmazi, Salah Faik, and others, in addition to Hamdi al-Sammak, author of the manuscript and the writer who "was terrified of himself, of the Americans, of Saddam, and everyone else . . ."

The novel has a predominantly eulogizing feel to it, as well as an overflowing nostalgia. The 1990s were the harshest and most miserable period, not just for Baghdad but for all of Iraq, so perhaps eulogy, along with tears and wailing, befits it the most. The period was a combination of a collapsing dictatorship and the rise of a new power, the American occupation, which put the country in a state of total unrest. As one narrator says, "Baghdad became an all-purpose scrap yard with piles and piles of anything and everything." Kidnapping, murder, abject poverty, bombs and rockets, cold and hunger, terror, nightmares, and corpses; streets crammed with madmen, homeless people, thieves, soldiers, and armed groups; houses emptied of their furniture; and the dinar's value plummeting even further. Then we read from Samira: "The culture of the occupation brought us veils to fasten around our heads and abayas to wrap around our bodies." Meanwhile, Hamdi likens the ravaging of Baghdad by mice and locusts to the horrifying scenes described by Albert Camus in his novel *The Plague*. And there is nothing wrong with returning to medieval chronicles like the *Kitab al-Hawadith* of Ibn al-Futi to examine Baghdad's ongoing disaster in the light of disasters of the past.

Muhsin al-Musawi is well known as an academic and literary critic, and some of his most important work has been on *The Thousand and*

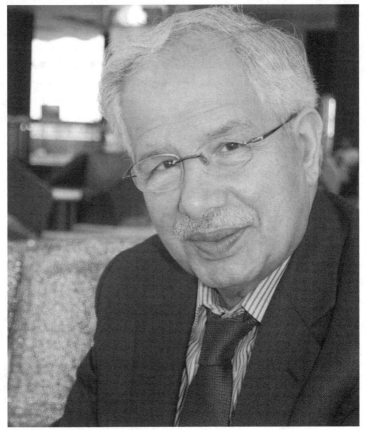

Muhsin al-Musawi

One Nights, with several studies in this field in both Arabic and English, the most recent of which is his monumental work *al-Dhakira al-Sha biyya li-Mujtama at Alf Layla wa Layla* (The Popular Memory of the Societies of the 1001 Nights, published by al-Markaz al-Thaqafi al-Arabi). *Sulaf of Baghdad* is al-Musawi's fifth novel, and he has figured out how to wear both hats in a balanced way – between his work as a serious academic critic immersed in theories and techniques of narrative, and that of being an artistic creator as a novelist. He seems to have made great use in this novel of the ambience of *The Thousand and One Nights*. This is not to imply that he has directly adapted or transposed from the tales, especially when having to do with style or technique, yet the Baghdad as narrated by al-Musawi is not dissimilar from the fantastical quality of Baghdad in *The Nights*, even if the tragic events of the novel are based in history.

For example, there is the intriguing character of Hannun, who seems akin to a character from *The Nights* because of his amusing nature, which has a strong element of anguish after witnessing the massacre that killed his family and afflicted him with a kind of dementia. He is described as "the crazy man who wanders through Baghdad day and night", and is the one who opens semi-secret doors for the narrator Hamdi, which resemble the doors of *The Nights*, and open into labyrinths that lead to an unexpected world, albeit one that seems real on the surface. Hannun leads Hamdi to the shelter of the scientist Yohanna the Assyrian, also one of Sulaf's regulars; he takes him through a hidden door in the back of a crumbling building, then opens another door that leads to a hall, then a narrow passageway and then along an underground tunnel, where he finally finds Yohanna, who has sent for him to alert him first that Sulaf is in danger of being bombed, and then to introduce him to his daughter Colette, who is addicted to reading his books and attracted to him. He hopes that meeting Hamdi will bring his daughter out of the psychological crisis she has been confronting ever since she watched a corpse in the street being ripped to shreds by dogs, which has become recur-

ring nightmare for her. In this shelter, where Yohanna has taken refuge out of fear of the assassinations of scholars in Iraq at that time, he lives his entire life. One of the halls is taken up by a telescope that Yohanna and Colette use to gaze at the planets and celestial bodies. Hamdi ends up falling in love with Colette. They kiss and embrace, and this strange relationship results in marriage. The ceremony is conducted by a sheikh named Issa who allows Colette to remain a Christian.

Just as Hannun took Hamdi to the hideout through a secret door, he also takes him into another hideout through the door of the restaurant called Kubbet Irbil, during a night-time tour of Baghdad. Here they enter a long, empty alleyway and find themselves facing a secret door that opens up and leads them to another door, which in turn leads them to a hall with a strange table and bodies dangling from the ceiling. . .

The novel's atmosphere is truly surreal but does not become excessively bizarre, rather it stays close to reality. We cannot forget the strange journey made by Hannun and Hamdi to the town of Ba shiqa (in the Mosul district), where Yohanna's brother Bahnam lives. They travel there on two donkeys, on Hannun's insistence as he believes donkeys cannot be booby-trapped or explode. The donkeys are then replaced by mules in the elevated rocky regions. There too is an underground passageway and guarded cave. The journey ends in the monastery of Mar Iliyya where the narrator discovers the poems of Abu Nuwas scrawled on the walls by a priest who was a fan of the poet. And in the first place it has to be said that poetry is omnipresent in the novel as an extension of its atmosphere and characters.

Sulaf of Baghdad is a novel of 1990s Baghdad, Baghdad of the past, and perhaps also of the unknown future. And we must learn how to write this future, to which all the tragic aspects of the nineties are relevant.

Perhaps the question posed by Hamdi al-Sammak about the writer's block he suffers from is the central question posed by the novel: "Don't we all suffer from an incapacity?" And then he adds: "There is some defect afflicting our psyches."

Translated by Suneela Mubayi

Susannah Tarbush reviews

Two novels by Youssef Fadel

A Rare Blue Bird Flies with Me
Translated by Jonathan Smolin
Published by Hoopoe Fiction (AUC Press),
2016. ISBN: 978 977 416 754 6,
Pbk, 248pp, $16.95

A Beautiful White Cat Walks with Me
Translated by Alexander E. Elinson
Published by Hoopoe Fiction (AUC Press, 2016)
ISBN: 978 977 416 776 8, Pbk, 232pp, $16.95

Networks of power, corruption and abuse

In these two novels the Moroccan author and screenwriter Youssef Fadel tackles facets of Morocco's grim "Years of Lead" in the 1970s and 1980s. Attempted coups in 1971 and 1972 were followed by a clampdown on all forms of dissent, with widespread imprisonments, torture, and violations of human rights.

Fadel was himself incarcerated as a political prisoner in the notorious Derb Moulay Chérif prison in 1974-75. He dedicates *A Rare Blue Bird Flies with Me* to "the martyrs of the extermination prison camps in Tazmamart, Agdz, Kalaat, M'Gouna, Skoura, Moulay Chérif, Kourbis, the Complex, and Dar Moqri; those among them who are living and those who are dead."

The Arabic originals of both novels were published by Dar al-Adab of Beirut. *A Beautiful White Cat Walks with Me* appeared in 2011. *A Rare Blue Bird Flies with Me*, published two years later, was shortlisted for the 2014 International Prize for Arabic Fiction (IPAF).

The translators have produced lively renderings of the novels in English. Alexander E. Elinson, translator of *A Beautiful White Cat Walks with Me* , is Associate Professor of Arabic at Hunter College of

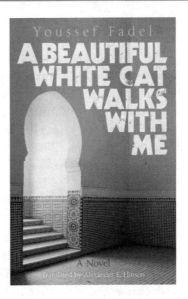

the City University of New York, and director of Hunter College Summer Arabic Program. He has been working on a book project on language change and ideology in Morocco, particularly the use of Moroccan colloquial Arabic in novels, short stories, poetry, translation, journalism and education.

Professor Jonathan Smolin, translator of *A Rare Blue Bird*, is Department Chair and Associate Professor (Arabic) in the Department of Asian and Middle Eastern Languages and Literature at Dartmouth College, New Hampshire. He is the author of the prizewinning *Moroccan Noir: Police, Crime, and Politics in Popular Culture* (Indiana University Press, 2013). His translation of Moroccan detective novel writer Abdelilah Hamdouchi's *Whitefly* (Hoopoe Fiction, 2016) was reviewed in *Banipal 56*.

Each translator provides a helpful foreword to the novel he has translated, explaining the work's political context. These introductions might have benefited from the addition of some observations on the language Fadel uses and on their translation processes.

The novels portray the elite around the king, and the network of power, corruption and abuse that percolates through society. Fadel has a gift for combining humour and tragedy, and the humanity of his writing and its forays into magical realism relieve the darkness of the subject matter. He introduces numerous memorable characters as he explores the struggles of ordinary people to survive. For women, marriage or prostitution may seem the only way out of poverty.

A Rare Blue Bird Flies with Me begins in 1990. Former military pilot Aziz has been in prison for 18 years for his part in the 16 August 1972 failed coup attempt in which pilots attacked King Hassan II's Boeing en route to Rabat. The previous day Aziz had married 16-year-old Zina after saving her from a pimp who was trying to force her into prostitution. Zina has searched for Aziz ever since his disappearance, but still has no idea where he is.

A stranger in the Stork Bar in Azrou, where Zina works, passes her a handwritten note and whispers that she has time to catch the nine o'clock bus from Fes. She decides to follow this lead and sets off in search of her husband, supposedly held in a secret prison in the old casbah of Pasha Thami El Glaoui in the Atlas Mountains.

Each chapter of *A Rare Blue Bird Flies with Me* is narrated by one of six characters. In addition to Aziz and Sina, they are: Zina's highly protective older sister Khatima (a former prostitute who inherited the Stork Bar from a Frenchwoman); two guards in the casbah prison, and the quick-witted prison dog Hinda who plays a key role in the story.

While Zina travels on the bus she hopes will take her to Aziz, he is lying near death in his solitary cell, suffering from an infected rat bite. Aziz is the sole surviving prisoner in the casbah. The two prison guards, Bab Ali and Benghazi, play checkers and wait for him to die so they can bury him in the courtyard. "We've been burying them for twenty years. One on top of another. Dead on top of dead," thinks the nervy Bab Ali.

As the novel's title suggests, one of its major motifs is Aziz's passion for flying, with its connotations of escape and freedom. Birds often occur in the novel, and in his prison cell Aziz muses that he "can read the mind of every flying being and I'm good at listening to them. All living things that fly: butterflies, cockroaches, and bats. But not human beings because they don't fly." The novel's flashbacks to 1972 take us back to his days as a pilot at the airbase and his ecstatic experiences while flying. Captain Hammouda tells him: "One day, Aziz, you'll fly off and you won't come back." We trace his transformation from being a supporter of the regime to willingly participating in the Air Force's coup attempt.

In *A Beautiful White Cat Walks with Me* two narrators tell their sto-

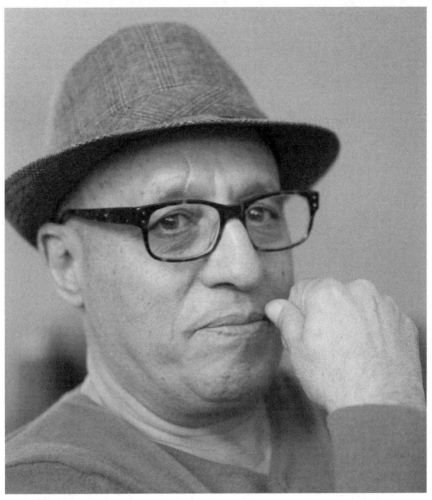

Youssef Fadel

ries in alternate chapters. They are 60-year-old court jester Balloute and his son Hassan whom Balloute abandoned years earlier when he walked out on his first wife and his family. Balloute now lives with his 24-year-old third wife Aziza: she and her mother are clearly determined to gain all they can from his privileged position in the royal court.

Whereas Balloute specialises in buffoonery and jokes revolving around sex and bodily functions, 27-year-old Hassan has become a writer and performer of sketches satirising the political elite. His sketches "always resonated with large numbers of people, and the press wrote about their boldness, considering them politically committed works, just as some considered me a leftist"

But Hassan is suddenly summoned to do compulsory military service in the Western Sahara, and he vividly recounts the horrors to which he and three of his fellow conscripts are subjected in a desert war which they understand little and for which they are ill-prepared.

While Hassan and his comrades pay a heavy price for the royal court's Western Sahara war policy, Balloute gives an appalling yet comic portrayal of life within that court. "All sorts of people flock to the palace – high-ranking officers, professional politicians, ministers, honoured guests – and they all resemble one another to a great degree." They are "nothing more than a bunch of creeps who spend their time trying to ingratiate themselves with the king. Oh, how I hate them." But after 15 years as a jester he feels under pressure to be constantly entertaining, and dreads falling out of favour.

Balloute's enemy and competitor in the court is the hunchback Zerwal. He is alarmed when Zerwal asks him whether he has a son named Hassan, and "does he still perform sketches insulting the government of His Majesty the king?" Balloute tries to get rid of his rival by arranging for him to have sex with a young prostitute infected with syphilis.

Hassan could hardly be more different from his father. He is devoted to his wife Zineb and worries about having left her for the Western Sahara war while she was unwell. He is idealistic, romantic and perhaps too trusting. Alas, he will discover that his wife is not quite what he thought. And he is set on a collision course with his father who blames Hassan's political sketches for his downfall at court.

A Rare Blue Bird Flies with Me and *A Beautiful White Cat Walks with Me* are the first of Youssef Fadel's novels to appear in English translation. Hoopoe Fiction notes that they are part of his modern Morocco series. It is to be hoped that further works by this compelling author will at some point be available to an English-reading audience.

Follow us on twitter @BanipalMagazine
https://www.twitter.com/BanipalMagazine

Adil Babikir reviews

Saba't Gurabaa' fil-Madina (Seven Strangers in Town) by Ahmad Al Malik

published by Awraaq Publishing & Distribution, Cairo.
March 2014, ISBN 978-977-5163-96-7

The Sergeant's predicament

"Sergeant Abdel Hai's job was to keep an eye all night on the insurgents held in custody at the military garrison, and hand them over at dawn to the firing squad. He would keep himself vigilant with the help of sips from the poor quality arak he procured daily from the local *endaya* at the outskirts of the border town. But he never bothered to chat with any of his prisoners or offer them a drink. One particular night, however, the arak was unusually strong, and he found himself warming to the only prisoner he happened to have in custody. He offered him many shots and they spent the night chatting and singing. But when he opened his eyes before dawn, the cell door was open and his guest had vanished into thin air."

With this prologue, Sudanese novelist Ahmad Al Malik introduces us to the predicament of Sergeant Abdel Hai, who has to lay hands on the fugitive or find a replacement to face the firing squad in less than three hours if he cares for his life. The best scenario for the sergeant is to catch one of the seven strangers he saw the previous night in al-Naseem's *endaya*, a bar that sold locally made liquor. But it would be a disaster if he caught a local because the matter it be discovered sooner than later. As he lurks in a bushy ditch near the bar in wait for someone to come out, the inner world of the bar starts to unfold. The bar serves as the central terminal from which the reader is taken on a series of flashback rides into the lives of the clients: strangers dislocated by the

Cover Saba't Gurabaa' fil-Madina/Seven Strangers in Town

endless wars raving across the country, young men running for their lives, and brokers offering their service to help those desperate souls sneak through the borders. Among the guests that night was a VIP: a deposed military ruler who was dreaming of recapturing power with the help of the government of a neighbouring country.

This part of the narrative is intercepted by gripping snapshots from the "backyard" of the house: the service girls and their tacit war to win the heart of the only male servant, Sulaiman al-Askari, the pleasant-looking, enigmatic young man. And there is the woman in charge, al-Naseem, a strong personality and an outspoken political critic. In one of her political tirades, she tells Sergeant Abdel Hai:

"People are starving to death and children can't go to school, and still there are some who want to convince us that we do have a government. What we have is no more than a gang that lives off the sweat of the disadvantaged. When they run out of money, they crack down on us and on poor merchants, looting our money in the name of taxes, *zakat*, or fines. It's a kind of armed robbery similar to that of the *shifta* bandits [gangs who operate across the border areas of Sudan, Eritrea and Ethiopia]. The only difference is that the gangs live in mountainous caves while the government lives in the palace."

Occasionally, Sergeant Abdel Hai, a bona fide client of al-Naseem, would sit alone to sip from the free *mareesa* beer that the girls kept in the courtyard for those who could not afford it, or for promotion

Ahmad Al Malik. Photo Margot Rood

purposes. When liquor turned his head, he would lose his reservations and tell al-Naseem some of his past glories in the army. He would credit himself with fake heroic acts. There was always someone else, other than him, who made a mistake and, as a result, the coup attempt was foiled! Al-Naseem would burst into laughter and say:

"If the attempt was foiled, how come you are still alive? Did they run out of bullets when it was your turn?"

"I was granted clemency by the President on the Revolution Day," he finally said. Rubbing her henna-tinted plaits, al-Naseem asked him: "Which revolution are you talking about?" Pointing to an old, drab radio set, she added: "Many revolutions have we heard about through this radio set, but we haven't seen any improvement at all. Every newcomer starts by blaming their predecessor. Thus, the spin goes on and we alone are the losers. We never take part in this game of musical chairs and yet we have to pay our share of the cost along with the others!"

Weaving all these threads together, Al Malik has managed to build a compelling narrative, full of satire and humour but also of deep frustration and aborted dreams.

Quoted text translated by the reviewer

Laura Ferreri reviews

Otared
by Mohammad Rabie

Translated by Robin Moger

Published by Hoopoe Fiction, Cairo, October 2016

ISBN: 9789774167843, pbk, 352pp, $17.95 / £9.99
/ LE120

A Hell on Earth

From its very first pages, *Otared* hits the reader with its graphic scenes and relentless violence. It is the year 2025 and Cairo is under the occupation of the Knights of Malta. The protagonist of the story, Otared, once a police officer, is now a sniper of the resistance. After spending two years on top of the Cairo Tower killing anyone he was ordered to, the time has come for him to leave the tower and take part in the ultimate mission to defeat the oppressor. Back in the streets of Cairo, Otared has to face a reality he had only observed from a detached point of view, a reality much harder to accept than just the occupation of the Knights. Cairo is a city where prostitution has been legalized, people are so afraid to be recognized that they cover their faces with masks or newspapers whenever they leave their houses, and the quality of life is so low that the only way to get through the day is to use drugs.

The plan the resistance has laid out to overthrow the Knights of Malta is inspired by the tactic used by the police during the last days of Mubarak's regime, shooting random people in the streets. Remembering the events of 2011, Otared is not convinced of the effectiveness of the mission, but decides to take part in it, hoping to bring some relief to his country, which has sunk into despair. The mission succeeds and the Knights leave Egypt, however, as we venture into Cairo with Otared, the truth slowly unveils before our eyes. Cairo is hell on earth and its people are doomed to suffer. There is no hope except, perhaps, that of finding relief in death. After this epiphany, Otared finally becomes aware of his role: deliver as many people as possible to a better life.

Otared is Mohammad Rabie's third novel and it was shortlisted for the International Prize for Arabic Fiction in 2016. This novel, as well as Rabie's previous two, has a strong connection to his country, Egypt, and its current situation. The author creates a dystopic future to show his disappointment in the results of the uprisings of 2011 and 2012, which have failed to bring an honest ruling class to power and have left the country in a state of decay. He exacerbates his feeling of hopelessness and transforms Egypt into a hell on earth, a place where brutality has almost become desirable, where violence and death are the only hopes to find an escape.

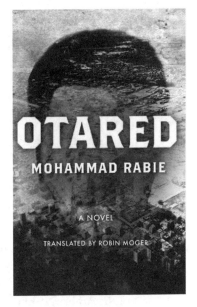

Otared cannot certainly be considered an easy reading; on the one hand the narration flows extremely well, and the reader almost feels like they are watching an action movie. On the other hand, the novel indulges too much in scenes so violent and disturbing that the reader has to make an effort to keep reading. It goes without saying that the author has deliberately chosen to shock his readers and in this way he succeeds in making them feel the same desperation and frustration he feels for the state of his country and his people. The underlying criticism towards Egyptian politics, however, does not seem fully developed in the story, and the reader gets the feeling that the events Rabie wants to discuss are still too fresh and painful for him to be able to express his thoughts clearly.

It is worth mentioning the excellent translation done by Robin Moger. I particularly appreciated the work he did with punctuation; he gives the novel a rhythm that I can imagine, knowing Arabic, differs from the original and gives the narration a Western style. It is thanks to the fact that the story flows so smoothly that I kept on reading the novel despite the brutality of its scenes.

In conclusion, even though I found the novel too extreme for my tastes, I have to recognise its originality and its contribution to a genre, dystopian literature, that is still very young in Arabic fiction and that has the potential to attract more readers to explore Arabic literature.

Becki Maddock reviews two novels

The Holy Sail
by Abdulaziz al-Mahmoud
Translated by Karim Traboulsi
published by BQFP, January 2016, ISBN 978-
9927101670. Pbk, 448pp, £8.9

A gripping yarn

This second historical novel by Qatari author and journalist Abdulaziz al-Mahmoud, *The Holy Sail*, is another entertaining page-turner. Once again, he focuses on the naval history of the Arabian Peninsula. The Holy Sail of the title refers to the sails of Portuguese ships, emblazoned with the Christian cross. It is 1486 and the Portuguese want to take control of Gulf ports in order to control the spice trade and spread Christianity. Meanwhile, the Ottoman Empire is gaining power, at the expense of the Mamluk sultanate in Egypt. All this occurs alongside power struggles between and within the many territories and cities of the Gulf region. In his introduction to the novel, the author says he has long been interested in this pivotal moment of history in the balance of power between Europe and the Near East. He also tells us that he has used Western and Arab references in his attempt to link together events, and notes the obscurity and inaccuracy of some of the Arab sources.

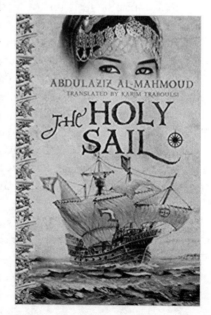

Al-Mahmoud's effort to present a complex historical period encompasses many characters and the action ranges from Portugal to India and East Africa, via Cairo, Bahrain,

Hormuz and several places in between. The author incorporates real historical figures into the narrative: the brutal Portuguese general Afonso de Albuquerque; Mamluk Amir, Hussein al-Kurdi; Jabrid Sultan Muqrin bin Zamel. The ambitious scope of the novel, with its multitude of interlinked plot lines and abundance of characters unfortunately does not allow any of the characters to be explored in depth. As a result, the novel's protagonists are somewhat two-dimensional, almost verging on stereotypes. Al-Mahmoud's effort to retell these events through Arab eyes is laudable. However, there is a distinct lack of ambiguity in his black and white portrayal of the protagonists, who are either good (the brave and honourable Arabs) or bad (the brutal Portuguese). The stock subjects of traditional Arab storytelling are all present; love, honour, nobility, betrayal. The romance is provided by Halima, the beautiful, chaste and wise heroine, who is very much in the mould of a traditional fairy tale heroine.

Nevertheless, *The Holy Sail* is an entertaining and enjoyable read. Abdulaziz Al-Mahmoud has given us another gripping yarn about an interesting and significant period in the region's history.

The Weight of Paradise
by Iman Humaydan
Translated by Michelle Hartman
Published by Interlink Publishing, April 2016,
ISBN 978-1566560559. Pbk, 240pp, £12.15, $15.00

Reconstructing Beirut

Lebanese novelist Iman Humaydan's fourth novel, *The Weight of Paradise*, was translated by Michelle Hartman in close collaboration with the author. Maya has returned to Beirut from Paris. While working on a film about the city's reconstruction, she finds a suitcase full of old papers. Researching the suitcase's contents is cathartic for Maya, who has recently lost her husband. The suitcase belongs to Noura, whose death in 1978 is described in the first chapter. Through its contents, Humaydan employs multiple voices to weave together the stories of Noura, her Turkish lover

Kemal, Noura's friend Sabah and her sister Henaa, with the story of Beirut itself, which in turn speaks to Maya's situation. Self-contained stories are linked though the device of the suitcase, with entire chapters devoted to the letters and diaries it contains.

Tying Beirut's past to its present, Humaydan explores memory and forgetfulness. The Armenian cobbler describes how in post-war Beirut the East-West division of the city lives on inside people's heads. Lonely Sabah's memories come tumbling out when prompted by Maya's discovery. The author problematizes the process of Beirut's reconstruction, contrasting people's long memories with the efforts of the bulldozers to erase the scars of war. Sabah remarks: "Maybe they want to build and construct so that people will forget." While Maya "didn't understand why the [reconstruction] company had asked her to document the memory of these places, without noticing that it was in fact completely erasing this memory." These comments are examples of a recurring device employed by the author whereby she has her characters give voice to what she wants to tell the reader.

This novel's interwoven themes exemplify Humaydan's statement that "The modern Lebanese novel is a product of the war." Themes such as love and loss (Maya's love for her son and husband; Sabah's

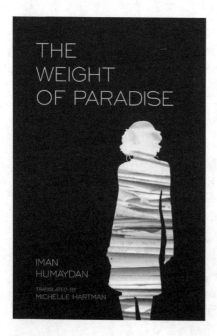

love for her disappeared husband, Ahmad and boyfriend Ahmad); and exile and home. As in Humaydan's earlier novel, *B for Beirut*, emigration is a key theme. Beirut draws emigrants from rural areas and adjacent countries, just as the civil war scattered the city's inhabitants across the globe. Armenians, Kurds, the Arabs of Antakia and the Jews of Beirut all feature in *The Weight of Paradise*. The novel also attempts to address the importance of identity, in the history of Beirut and that of Humaydan's characters. Examples include Maya's marrying "outside our community"; Kemal's description of how, after the First World War, the residents of Antakia "became Turks overnight"; and the village shaykhs' refusal to perform funeral prayers for Noura's grandma because "there was no mercy for a woman whose origins at birth were so distant from their sect". In the story of Beirut, "Everything is connected to everything else", as a man in one of the city's cafés remarks.

SAMUEL SHIMON

AN IRAQI IN PARIS

A fully revised third edition in translation of this best-selling 'gem of autobiographical writing' in the Arab world, by an author who has been called 'a relentless raconteur', 'a modern Odysseus', 'the Iraqi Don Quixote'

"It is a wonderful text. Full of life and art. An autobiography full of humour, irony, noblesse and sadness. It reminds me of George Orwell's great book *Down and Out in Paris and London*" **Alaa Al Aswany**, author of *The Yacoubian Building*

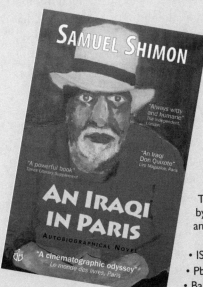

"Gripping autobiographical novel" **Carlo Strenger**, *Neue Zürcher Zeitung, Zurich*

"It's an Arabic answer to Miller's *Tropic of Cancer* – occasionally shocking; always witty and humane. Also included is his delightful memoir of an Iraqi childhood." **Boyd Tonkin**, *The Independent, London*

Translated from the Arabic by Christina Phillips and Piers Amodia with the author

- ISBN: 9780957442481
- Pbk • 282pp • £9.99 / $15.00
- Banipal Books, November 2016

STEFAN WEIDNER

A marshlander has left us

TRIBUTE TO HUSSAIN AL-MOZANY

The Iraqi-German author Hussain al-Mozany, winner of the 2002 Adelbert von Chamisso Prize, died unexpectedly on 5th December 2016 at the age of 62. The translator and scholar of Islam Stefan Weidner, who knew the author well, pays tribute to him in this obituary.

It is seldom the case that the death of an author is a painful loss for two entirely different linguistic and cultural realms; that someone moves through both like a fish in water and leaves a lasting legacy in two languages. Perhaps one could only say the same of Vladimir Nabokov or Joseph Brodsky. The vast majority of authors who switch languages, who do not write in their mother tongue and who lay claim to multiple origins and identities, eventually settle on one of the two sides. The fact that Hussain al-Mozany could not, or would not, settle may have been part of the reason why greater fame eluded him. It also makes him an exception among the Chamisso Prize-winning authors. This man, who created the authoritative Arabic translation of Günter Grass's *Tin Drum*, was not just – as is so often said of so many – a mediator or bridge-builder: he himself was the centre that was pulled in two directions, in danger of tearing apart. He was one of the few with a foot on each bank, and thus never wholly in one place or the other; who was, in a strange way, caught between two stools. Hussain al-Mozany's true home was the in-between, and he certainly did not see it as incum-

photo by Samuel Shimon

bent upon him to diminish this in-between, to iron out the differences. Rather, they were his element; he emphasised them, allowed them to take effect. His novels are suffused with a Rabelaisian spirit; they are simultaneously provocative, surprising, uncompromising, effervescent, thoughtful and ridiculously amiable, just like the man himself, regardless of whether he was speaking in German or Arabic.

Born in southern Iraq in 1954, Hussain al-Mozany came to Germany with the first big wave of refugees from the Middle East – which at the time, of course, was barely registered by the public. It was primarily Iraqis and Iranians who fled to the West, either to escape repression – by Saddam Hussein in Iraq and the Khomeini dictatorship in Iran – or to avoid conscription to one of the fronts in the Iran-Iraq war. This wave of refugees brought a number of significant Arab authors to Germany: as well as Hussain al-Mozany, these included the poet Khalid al-Maaly, who later became al-Mozany's Arabic publisher, and Najem Wali. Al-Mozany arrived via East Germany and Checkpoint Charlie. At the time, anyone who entered West Germany via this border and requested asylum could not be turned down. Al-Mozany worked as a journalist in Beirut for left-wing Palestinian groups in the late 1970s, which was why he was able to get a visa for the Eastern Bloc countries.

After his asylum application was accepted, he studied German and Islamic Studies in Münster, married, took German citizenship, wrote and translated. I had already heard a great deal about him from my Iraqi friends when I finally met him in 1998. He had just moved to Cologne with his wife and children. There followed a period of fruitful collaboration and friendship until, in 2006, he moved to Berlin to work for Deutsche Welle's Arabic Service.

The novels that secured his reputation in Germany were published during his time in Cologne: *Der Marschländer* [The Marshlander] in 1999, and *Mansur oder der Duft des Abendlandes* [Mansur or the scent of the West] in 2002. Their publication just before and just after the attacks of 11 September 2001 and the subsequent Iraq War coincided with the years of sudden, manifest confrontation with the Islamic world. Political events ensured that the books received the attention they deserved, but also reduced them to their political dimension. Many authors from the Arab world encountered this problem: previously marginalised and little known, suddenly they were constantly

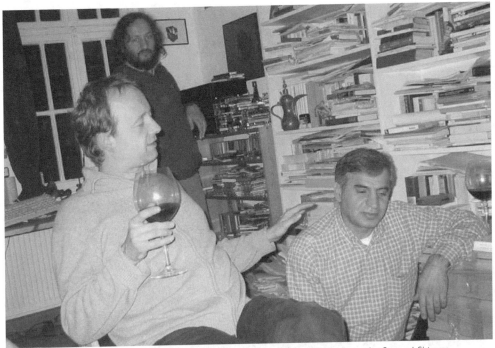

Stefan Weidner, Khalid al-Maaly and Hussain al-Mozany, Köln 2004, photos by Samuel Shimon

Hussain Al-Mozany and Sargon Boulus, Frankfurt Book Fair, 2004

Shukri Mabkhout, Hussain al-Mozany, Fadhil al-Azzawi and Gunther Orth, Berlin International Literature Festival 2015. Photo Samuel Shimon

Hussain al-Mozany was pleased to meet Salman Rushdie at the Berlin International Literature Festival in 2015.
Photo Ali Ghandtschi

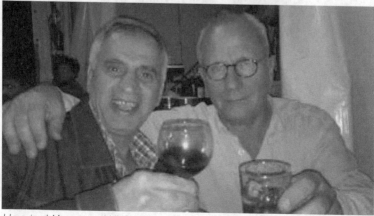

Hussain al-Mozany and Uli Schreiber, director of Berlin Literature Festival 2016

being asked for their opinion on everything along with every political escalation, until public attention focussed on another subject. Hussain al-Mozany was, rightly, affronted by this misuse of literature and the author by the media. At the same time, it both warned him against and saved him from deciding wholly in favour of his German side, as many authors do once they become successful here. For Hussain al-Mozany, it was not only Germany that offered asylum from the Arab world – the Arab world also offered asylum from Germany, even if only intellectually, and on visits. He didn't want to idealise either side.

The novel *Mansur oder der Duft des Abendlandes* is a subtle satire on German citizenship law, which prefers to recognise as Germans those who have German blood in their veins. Why should something ethnic Germans from Russia are entitled to not also be granted to the Arab descendents of German crusaders? Mansur, a young Iraqi soldier, avails himself of this circumstance in a bid to escape the poison gas of the Iran-Iraq War. In a history book he reads about a medieval monk, Peter of Cologne, who came to Iraq with the crusaders' entourage and fathered children with an Iraqi woman. One of Mansur's acquaintances confides to him that he looks German, whereupon he flees to Cologne, declares himself a descendent of Peter, and applies for German citizenship.

Hussain al-Mozany and Samuel Shimon, Berlin International Literature Festival 2015.

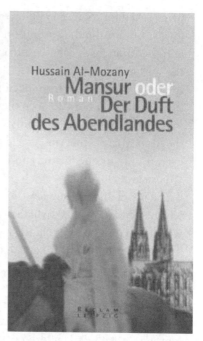

But this is just the background story. With the same wit he uses to construct this fantastical tale, al-Mozany also describes the life of asylum seekers in Germany and dubious moral standards – both theirs, and those of the German authorities. The subject is once again highly topical today. Passages of highly poetical description alternate with graphic depictions of asylum seekers' drunken parties. The Cologne Carnival features in the novel as a great festival of fraternisation, though one that is also, of course, utterly bewildering. The author manages to incorporate numerous stylistic elements from Arabic literature into the story, as well as grotesque humour, a central characteristic of all Hussain al-Mozany's novels.

The new generation of Arab immigrants can learn from Hussain al-Mozany not to jettison the connection with their origins, even if they obtain German citizenship and become great lovers of Germany. It is good to know that neither flight, nor the disasters of the contemporary Arab world, nor half a century of Germany were able to erase this author's cultural memory. In his country of origin, it is this that roots its people more deeply in their language and culture than is conceivable in Germany, particularly after the cultural caesura of the Nazi era – another great preoccupation of al-Mozany's. The

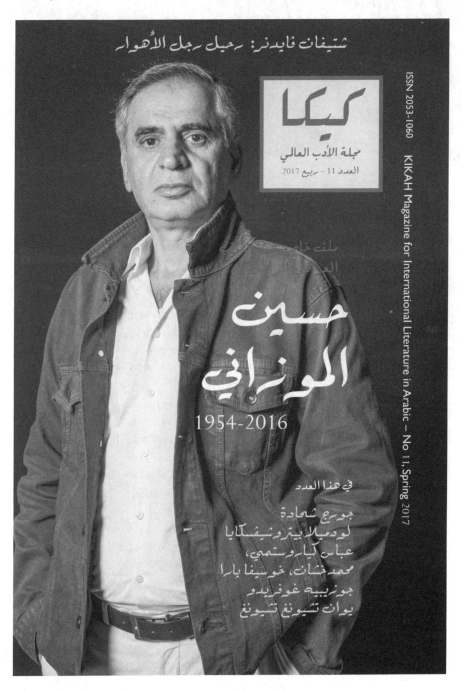

Front cover of Kikah magazine for International LIterature, No 11, Spring 2017

Felicitas von Lovenberg, former literary editor of the Frankfurter Allgemeine Zeitung interviewing Hussain al-Mozany at the Frankfurt Book Fair, 2011

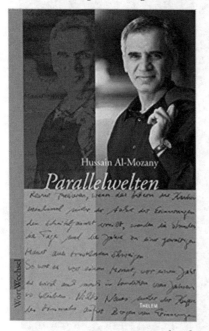

oldest elements of this cultural continuity stretch back four thousand years. The marshland in southern Iraq – the home region of the "marshlander" of al-Mozany's first German novel – is one of the oldest cultural landscapes in human history. For al-Mozany, the German word – Marschländer – also has literal significance, describing what the author himself was: one who marches across lands.

The flat boats Hussain al-Mozany saw the marshlanders use to punt themselves across the marshes will have looked exactly the same as the boats of 4,000 years ago, depicted in clay models found by archaeologists. The author regarded his language as part of a similar, ancient continuity – be that Arabic, or Arabic-enriched German. The Arabic expressions and anecdotes that pepper Hussain al-Mozany's German books, which German readers may only pick up on in passing, were originally formulated in a language that is much the same now, as it is spoken and written today, as it was 1,500 years ago.

We can only hope that the future literary figures among the Arab refugees newly arrived in Germany will also consider their origins and keep them in mind, as Hussain al-Mozany did. They will rediscover him as one of those who paved the way for them, who experienced and gave expression to many of their problems. I recommend to them – and to all others – not only the books already

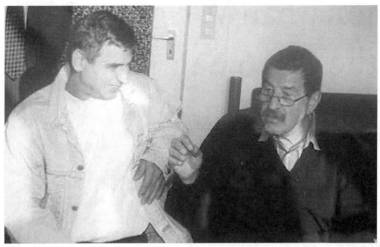

Hussain al-Mozany with Günter Grass

Arabic edition of Günter Grass's Tin Drum, translated by Hussain Al-Mozany

mentioned above, but also al-Mozany's first novel in Arabic, "The Meat Merchant", a revised German edition of which was published in 2007 in the author's own translation, as *Der Fleischhändler*. This novel provides an interesting contrast to the author's works originally written in German: it is set predominantly in Egypt, and its subject matter is an Arab, a naturalized German, who is alienated from his own culture. Finally, I also recommend al-Mozany's Chamisso Poetry Lectureship at the University of Dresden: his essay was published in 2011 under the title *Parallelwelten* [Parallel Worlds], accompanied by a detailed biography.

Translated from the German by Charlotte Collins

• Hussain al-Mozany's essay on language and identity, entitled *Mother, Mother Tongue, and Fatherland,* is available online from *Banipal 54 — ECHOES* at http://www.banipal.co.uk/selections/92/318/hussain-al-mozany/

Jonathan Wright wins the 2016 Saif Ghobash Banipal Prize

The 2016 Saif Ghobash Banipal Prize for Arabic Literary Translation has been awarded to Jonathan Wright for his translation of the novel *The Bamboo Stalk* by Saud Alsanousi, published by Bloomsbury Qatar Foundation Publishing (now HBKU Press), Qatar.

The four-member judging panel comprised Paul Starkey (Chair), Emeritus Professor of Arabic, University of Durham, and literary translator; Lucy Popescu, author and journalist; Zahia Smail Salhi, Professor of Arabic and translator, and Bill Swainson, editor and literary consultant. They made their decision in November 2016 at a meeting at the offices of the Society of Authors convened by Paula Johnson, the Administrator of the Translation Prizes, as reported below:

"The judges were unanimous in deciding to award this year's prize to Jonathan Wright for his translation of Saud Alsanousi's *The Bamboo Stalk*.

"Originally published in Arabic in 2012, *The Bamboo Stalk* is a daring work which takes a critical but objective look at the phenomenon of foreign workers in the Arab countries of the Gulf. The novel examines problems of race, religion and identity through the life of a half-Filipino, half-Kuwaiti young man, who moves from an impoverished life in the Philippines to return to his father's Kuwait – a 'paradise', as his Filipina mother has described it to him since he was a child. In its Arabic original, the work had already won the author the 2013 International Prize for Arabic Fiction, and the judges found

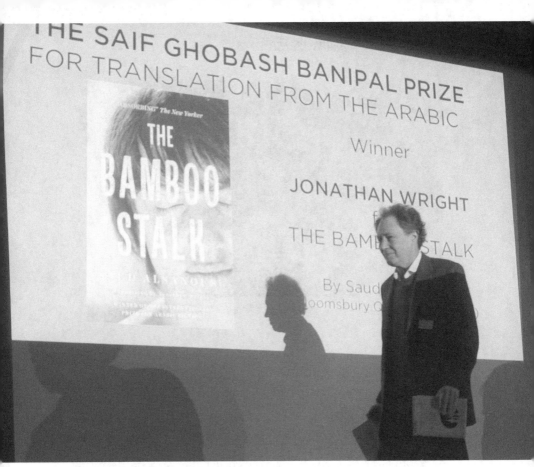

The Award Ceremony of the 2016 translation prizes, organised and hosted by the Society of Authors, took place on 22 February 2017, and for the first time at the British Library's spacious Knowledge Centre. This year, six prizes were awarded – for translation from Arabic, Italian, Hebrew, German, French and Spanish. Jonathan Wright, together and his author Saud Alsanousi, read short passages in English and Arabic from the winning work The Bamboo Stalk *after receiving his award.*

in the book the same qualities that had commended it to the IPAF jury. It combines a daring choice of subject with a tight but subtle literary structure and an approach to a highly charged and emotional subject matter that is both sensitive and measured.

"The judges questioned the omission, in the English publication, of the Arabic edition's 'second title page' – which had added an additional structural twist to the original work – but this was not felt to detract from the quality of the translation itself. Jonathan Wright's seamless English rendering does full justice to the original, exhibiting a sureness of touch that fully captures the spirit of the Arabic version. Although the particular cultural context of the work will be unfamiliar to many English-speaking readers, Wright's 'page-turner'

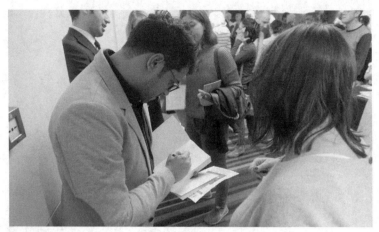

The reception following the Awards was a chance for signing copies and meeting readers and colleagues from the other prizes

translation has a universal appeal, and it is difficult not to be moved by the predicament of the narrator, with his dual identity of Isa and José, as he comes to terms with the reality of life in Kuwait.

"The judges discussed at length a number of other entries – including some by younger translators – with a view to naming a runner-up, but after extensive discussion decided not to do so on this occasion. The translators had tackled challenging works with equally impressive results, and but none came close to matching the broad appeal that the judges discerned in *The Bamboo Stalk*, and in these circumstances it was felt inappropriate to single out any particular work to be named as runner-up."

"A leap of imagination across cultures"

Translator **Jonathan Wright** said: "I'm delighted by the award, not just for myself but because the novel is a brave – and as far as I know unprecedented – attempt to address through literature two important aspects of Gulf and Kuwaiti society: firstly, the ambiguous status of a vast army of foreign workers who have few rights and are not expected to integrate or interact as equals with the host community, and secondly the denial of Kuwaiti citizenship to the 'bidoun' community, although many bidoun families have lived in the country for generations. Saud Alsanousi presents these injustices through the stories of credible people, without polemics or preaching. For Saud to create and fill out the main character and narrator, the half-Filipino half-Kuwaiti Jose, required a leap of imagination across cultures that strikes me as unusually successful for contemporary Arabic fiction. The book is written in an admirably direct and unpretentious style, relying mainly on the power of the narrative for its powerful emotional effect."

Author **Saud Alsanousi** said: "I was pleased to hear that *The Bamboo Stalk* has won the Saif Ghobash Banipal Prize for Arabic Literary Translation. This will give the novel a chance to be more widely known. Credit must go to the translator, Jonathan Wright, who not only translated the novel but also played a role in editing it, based on what he thought would be appropriate for the Western reader. Jonathan Wright has been a gain for me and for the novel."

Publisher **Rodolphe Abou-Ghaba**, Acting Executive Director of Hamad Bin Khalifa University Press (formerly BQFP), Qatar, said, on hearing the news: "HBKU Press is honoured that one of our published translations has received the 2016 Saif Ghobash Banipal Prize. Receiving this award is yet another milestone for HBKU Press and it is a testament to the high quality literary translations that we produce at HBKU Press. The success of Jonathan Wright's translation will further contribute to raising the profile of contemporary Arabic literature and of emerging Arab writers to the attention of the wider world and will enhance the cross-cultural understanding between the East and the West."

About the translator and the author

Jonathan Wright studied Arabic, Turkish and Islamic History at St. John's College, Oxford University. Between 1980 and 2009 he worked for Reuters news agency, mainly in the Middle East.

His latest literary translations include: *The Longing of the Dervish* by Sudanese author Hamour Ziada, which won the Naguib Mahfouz Medal for Literature; *The Televangelist* by Ibrahim Essa (Hoopoe Fiction, Egypt/USA), one of this year's entries and whose original was shortlisted for the International Prize for Arabic Fiction; and *Land of No Rain* by Amjad Nasser (BQFP, 2014), which was commended for the 2015 Saif Ghobash Banipal Prize.

He was joint winner of the 2013 Saif Ghobash Banipal Prize for his translation of the novel *Azazeel* by Youssef Ziedan (Atlantic Books,

2012) whose original Arabic edition won the 2009 International Prize for Arabic Fiction and in 2014 he won the Independent Foreign Fiction Prize for his translation of *The Iraqi Christ* by Hassan Blasim (Comma Press, 2013). He was a judge of the 2014 Saif Ghobash Banipal Prize.

His first literary translation – from colloquial Egyptian – was *Taxi* by Khaled al-Khamissi (Aflame Books, 2008, Bloomsbury Qatar Foundation Publishing, 2012). Further literary translations include Hassan Blasim's *The Madman of Freedom Square* (Comma Press, 2009); *Judgment Day* by Rasha al-Ameer. *Life on Hold* by Fahd al-Atiq (AUC Press, 2012); and Bahaa Abdelmegid's *Temple Bar* (AUC Press, 2014). His non-fiction translations include *On the State of Egypt:What Caused the Revolution* by Alaa Al-Aswany (Canongate, 2011) and *Whatever Happened to the Egyptian Revolution?* by Galal Amin (AUC Press, 2013).

With Reuters, Jonathan Wright was based in Egypt, Lebanon, Sudan, Oman, Kenya, Tunisia, Cyprus, London and Washington DC. For six years he was U.S. State Department correspondent for Reuters, travelling the world with Secretaries of State Madeleine Albright and Colin Powell. He covered several major events, including the Israeli invasion of Lebanon and the siege of West Beirut in 1982, the war over Kuwait in 1991, the Yemeni civil war in 1994 and the Egyptian revolution of 2011.

Saud Alsanousi is a Kuwaiti novelist and journalist, born in 1981. His first novel *Sijeen al-Maraya* (Prisoner of Mirrors) was published in 2010 and in the same year won the fourth Leila Othman Prize, awarded for novels and short stories by young writers.

What a wonderful venue for celebrating Arabic literature in English translation – the International Anthony Burgess Foundation in Manchester. We arrived late from London, that is Jonathan Wright, Saud Alsanousi, Margaret Obank and me, Samuel Shimon, after Storm Doris cancelled all the trains and we had to drive there. But after a quick preparation, we got going: Author Melvin Burgess introduced the evening brilliantly, and journalist Ben East inspired the translator and his author with probing questions. A very interesting discussion with readings, and lots of questions from the audience. Photo: Samuel Shimon

Melvin Burgess and Jonathan Wright conferring at the reception afterwards

In the "Stories of the Air" competition, organised in July 2011 by Kuwait's *Al-Arabi* magazine with BBC Arabic, he won first place for his story "The Bonsai and the Old Man".

His second novel, *Saq al-Bamboo* (*The Bamboo Stalk*), won the Kuwait State Prize for Letters in 2012 and the 2013 International Prize for Arabic Fiction and its translation has now won the Saif Ghobash Banipal Prize. His third novel, *Mama Hissa's Mice*, was long-listed for the current 2016/17 cycle of the Sheikh Zayed Book Award. His work has appeared in a number of Kuwaiti publications.

Zahia Smail Salhi, who is Professor of Arabic at Manchester University, surprised the audience when she said that she had had the rare opportunity of twice being a judge of Saud Alsanousi's novel – for its Arabic version when it won the 2013 IPAF, and by chance also for its English translation.

Banipal 57 – Syria in the Heart at Waterstones Piccadilly

Margaret Obank, with Nouri al-Jarrah, Charlotte Van den Broeck, Muhsin al-Ramli, Paul Blezard

The evening at Waterstones Piccadilly for *Banipal 57 – Syria in the Heart* on 17 January was a great and positive start to 2017.

Charlotte Van den Broeck

Muhsin al-Ramli

Iraqi author Muhsin al-Ramli, whose forthcoming novel *The President's Gardens* was excerpted in the issue, travelled from Spain. Charlotte Van den Broeck, with poems in the Guest Literature from Flanders feature, came from Belgium. Nouri al-Jarrah, the Syrian poet whose work was in both Banipal 56 and 57, is based in London.

Banipal's publisher Margaret

Nouri al-Jarrah

GUEST LITERATURE FROM FLANDERS

BANIPAL 57
Magazine of Modern Arab Literature

Syria in the Heart

NOURI AL-JARRAH, RASHA OMRAN,
KHALED KHALIFA, DIMA WANNOUS,
MAHA HASSAN, HALA MOHAMMAD
NADA MENZALJI, MONIR ALMAJID,
FAWAZ KADERI, HAITHAM HUSSEIN,
MOHAMAD ALAAEDIN ABDUL MOULA,
ROSA YASSIN HASSAN

PLUS Liana Badr and Muhsin al-Ramli

Obank opened the evening, announcing to the packed audience in Waterstones dedicated event space the exciting news of the launch of the complete digital archive of Banipal issues at the end of the month before introducing the authors. Muhsin al-Ramli has lived in Madrid since 1995, has published more than twenty books as well as many translations into Arabic of Spanish literature, his major work being *Don Quixote*. Charlotte Van den Broeck is a household name in her coun-

Charlotte Van den Broeck, Nouri al-Jarrah and Muhsin al-Ramli relaxing after the event. Photo: Salam Sarhan

Wen-chin Ouyang, and Paul Blezard

try Belgium as a performance poet and has toured Belgium and the Netherlands with her debut volume *Kameleon* (Chameleon). Nouri al-Jarrah has published over 14 collections of poetry, with his most recent (*A Boat to Lesbos*) dedicated to the thousands of refugees fleeing war across the Mediterranean, with parts translated in Banipal 57 and which Banipal Books will publish in full.

Chair Paul Blezard and Prof Wen-chin Ouyang, who provided brilliant interpretation for Muhsin, created a wonderful atmosphere in which the authors spoke about how they wrote about difficult issues, and what inspired them, and poems and texts were read in Arabic, Dutch and English, followed by many questions from the audience.

Fatma Alboudy is the publisher of Dar al-Ain, in Cairo, which she founded in 2000.

Ashur Etwebi was born in Tripoli in 1952, is a well-known Libyan author. He was professor of medicine at the university of Zawia, in Libya. He lives now in Norway. He has published six books of poetry.

Ibrahim Farghali is an author and journalist, born in 1967 in Mansourah, Egypt and spent a good part of his childhood in Oman. He is currently with Al-Ahram newspaper. He has two short story collections and two novels. His short story "Body Map", translated by Thomas Aplin, was published in *Banipal 49 – A Cornucopia of Short Stories*.

Elias Farkouh is a Jordanian author and publisher, born in Amman in 1948, with six short story collections and three novels, of which *Land of Limbo* was shortlisted for the 2008 International Prize for Arabic Fiction. An excerpt from his first novel *Columns of Dust* (1987), which is on the list of best 100 Arab novels of the twentieth century, was published in *Banipal 13*, which featured the literature of Jordan.

Fadia Faqir is a dual citizen of Britain and Jordan. Her work has been published in eighteen countries and translated into fourteen languages. She has five novels: Nisanit (1990), Pillars of Salt (1996) My Name is Salma (2007), Willow Trees Don't Weep (2014), and In Petra Mon Amour (In progress). She is an Honorary Fellow of St Mary's College and a Writing Fellow at St Aidan's College, Durham University, where she teaches creative writing.

Ismail Ghazali is a Moroccan novelist and short story writer, born in the Amazigh village of M'Rirt, Morocco, in 1977. He has a BA in Arabic literature and works in the media. His novel *The Season of Pike Fishing* (2013) was longlisted for the 2014 International Prize for Arabic Fiction.

Alaa Khaled See page 11

Muhammad Khudayyir is a major Iraqi author, born in 1942 in Basra, Iraq, where he still lives. He was for many years a teacher, publishing novels and short stories since he was 20. His work was feaetured in Banipal 14 (2002, translated by Shakir Mustafa), his novel *Basriyatha* (1996) published in 2008 translated by William M Hutchins, and a collection of short stories translated into French Le Royaume Noir (2000).

Naguib Mahfouz (1911-2006) is the renowned Egyptian novelist who was awarded the Nobel Prize for Literature in 1988.

Chip Rossetti has translated several works of Arabic fiction, including Beirut, Beirut by Sonallah Ibrahim, Utopia by Ahmed Khaled Towfik, and the graphic novel Metro by Magdy El Shafee. He is Editorial Director of the Library of Arabic Literature book series at NYU Press. He has a doctorate in Arabic literature from the University of Pennsylvania.

Mahmoud Saeed was born in Mosul, Iraq, and settled in the USA in 1999. He has written over 20 novels and short story collections. Several of his novels have been published in English translation, including Saddam City, The World through the Eyes of Angels and Ben Barka Lane.

Yahya Al-Sheikh is a Iraqi-Norwegian artist, born in Qalat Salih, Iraq, in 1945. He has a BA (Baghdad 1966), an MA (Ljubljana 1970), and a PhD (Moscow 1984). He has worked as a designer, illustrator and professor of fine art since 1970, and has works in both private and public collections worldwide. He has received numerous awards, and has held solo exhibitions in many capital cities.

Khalil Suweileh was born in Syria in 1959. He has three collections of poetry, and since 2002 five novels. He writes for the Lebanese newspaper *Al-Akhbar* and Radio Monte Carlo. He lives in Damascus. In 2009 his book *Warraq al-Hubb* won the Naguib Mahfouz Medal for Literature.

Shahla Ujayli is a Syrian-Jordanian writer, born in 1976. She teaches Modern Arabic Literature and has one short story collection and three novels. Her third, *A Sky Close to Our House*, was shortlisted for the 2016 IPAF.

Abdo Wazen is a well-known poet and translator of French poetry into Arabic. He is cultural editor of the daily *Al-Hayat* newspaper, Beirut.

Stefan Weidner (b. 1967, Cologne, Germany), is a literary translator from Arabic to German, a writer, editor and critic, and was editor of the journal *Fikrun wa Fann* until its recent demise. He studied Islamic Studies, German language and literature, and philosophy at the universities of Göttingen, Damascus, Berkeley, and Bonn, concluding his degree with a thesis on the Lebanese poet Adonis.

Hassan Yaghi is a well-known publisher from Lebanon, currently with Dar al-Tanweer, Beirut.

Ahmad Yamani is an Egyptian poet and literary translator from Spanish to Arabic. He was born in Cairo in 1970, and lives in Madrid.

THE 2017 INTERNATIONAL PRIZE
FOR ARABIC FICTION
– SHORTLISTED AUTHORS

Mohammed Abdel Nabi is an Egyptian writer, born in 1977. He obtained a BA in Languages and Translation from the English and Simultaneous Translation Department of Al-Azhar University and currently works as a freelance translator. He has published five short story collections, a novella titled *Imprisoned Phantoms* (2000) and two novels: *The Return of the Sheikh* (2011), which was longlisted for the 2013 International Prize for Arabic Fiction, and *In the Spider's Room* (2016). In 2010, his short story collection, *The Ghost of Anton Chekhov*, won the Sawiris Literature Prize, and his latest collection, *As the Flood Passes the Sleeping Village*, won the prize for best short story collection at the 2015 Cairo Book Fair. He publishes creative writing, criticism and translations in a number of newspapers and websites, and since 2009 he has taught creative writing in a workshop called The Story and What Is In It.

Mohammed Hasan Alwan is a Saudi Arabian novelist, born in Riyadh, Saudi Arabia in 1979. He graduated with a doctorate in International Marketing from the University of Carleton, Canada. Alwan has published five novels to date as well as a non-fiction work. His work has appeared in translation in *Banipal* (Blonde Grass and Statistics, translated by Ali Azeriah), in *The Guardian* (Oil Field, translated by Peter Clark), and in Words Without Borders (Mukhtar translated by William M. Hutchins). In 2009-10, Alwan was chosen as one of the 39 best Arab authors under the age of 40 by the Beirut39 project and his work was published in the Beirut39 anthology. He was also a participant in the first IPAF Nadwa in 2009 and a mentor on the Nadwa in 2016. In 2013, The Beaver was shortlisted for the International Prize for Arabic Fiction and in 2015, its French edition (translated by Stéphanie Dujols) won the Prix de la Littérature Arabe awarded in Paris for the best Arabic novel translated into French for that year.

Najwa Binshatwan is a Libyan academic and novelist, born in 1970. She is the author of two novels: The Horses' Hair (2007) and Orange Content (2008), three collections of short stories and a play. In 2005, The Horses' Hair won the inaugural Sudanese al-Begrawiya Festival prize, in the same year that Sudan was Capital of Arab Culture. She was chosen as one of the 39 best Arab authors under the age of 40 by the Beirut39 project and her story "The Pool and the Piano" was included in its anthology.

Ismail Fahd Ismail is a Kuwaiti writer and novelist. Born in 1940, he has worked as a full-time writer since 1985. He graduated with a BA in Literature and Criticism from the Higher Institute for Dramatic Arts, Kuwait, and has worked as both a teacher and in the administration of educational resources. He also managed an artistic production company. Ismail is regarded as the founder of the art of the novel in Kuwait. Since the appearance of his first novel, The Sky Was Blue, in 1970, he has published 27 novels as well as three short story collections, two plays and several critical studies. His novel The Phoenix and the Faithful Friend (2012) was longlisted for the International Prize for Arabic Fiction in 2014. His support for a large number of short story writers and novelists and his encouragement of new creative talent had a significant impact on the Kuwaiti and Arab literary scene.

Elias Khoury was born in Beirut in 1948. He worked as an assistant editor on Palestinian Affairs magazine (1975-1997) and was editor of the cultural section of As-Safir newspaper (1981-1991), Al-Karmel magazine (1981-83) and the literary supplement of An-Nahar newspaper (1992-2008). Since 2001, he has edited Palestinian Studies magazine. He has previously been a visiting professor at Columbia University, New York (1980-82), global distinguished professor at the University of New York (2001-2014) and visiting professor at the Lebanese American University (2015). He is the author of 13 novels including Little Mountain (1977), The Journey of Little Ghandi (1989) and Sinalkul (2012), which was longlisted for the International Prize for Arabic Fiction, as well as three plays and four critical works on the theatre. His work has been translated into 15 languages.

Saad Mohammed Raheem is an Iraqi writer, born in Diyala province, Eastern Iraq in 1957. He has worked as a teacher and journalist and his articles have been published in Iraqi and Arab newspapers and periodicals. He is the author of six collections of short stories, a number of political and literary studies and three novels: *Twilight of the Wader* (2000), which won the 2000 Iraqi Creativity Award for Fiction, *The Song of a Woman, Twilight of the Sea* (2012) and *The Bookseller's Murder* (2016). In 2005, he won the Iraqi Award for Best Investigative Journalism for that year, and was also awarded the 2010 Creativity Prize for the Short Story, for his collection *Almond Blossom* (2009).

CONTRIBUTORS

TRANSLATORS AND REVIEWERS

Hagar Hesham Ahmed is an Assistant Lecturer at Ain Shams University where she is pursuing a Ph.D. in Drama. In 2013/14, she was a Visiting Fulbright Scholar at Northern Michigan University.

Adil Babikir is a Sudanese translator into and out of English and Arabic, living in Abu Dhabi. He has translated two novels by Abdelaziz Baraka Sakin. and two anthologies – of poetry and short stories.

Raphael Cohen is a translator based in Cairo and a contributing editor of *Banipal*. Recent Arab fiction translations include Mona Prince's *So You May See* (2011) & *Status: Emo* by Eslam Mosbah.

Charlotte Collins is a literary translator from the German. Her work includes *A Whole Life* by Austrian writer Robert Seethaler, shortlisted for the Man Booker International 2016.

Humphrey Davies is a prizewinning translator of contemporary Arabic literature, including *The Gate of the Sun*, *Yalo*, and *As Though She Were Sleeping*, all by Elias Khoury, and four volumes of Ahmed Faris al-Shidyaq's *Leg over Leg* (NYU Press).

Ayane Ezaki was born in Japan and raised in Singapore. She graduated from Brown University with a degree in Development Studies and is now based in Amman, Jordan.

Laura Ferreri has a BA in interpreting and translation (Trieste University, Italy) and an MA in Arabic Translation (Edinburgh Univ. CASAW).

Sally Gomaa was born and raised in Alexandria, Egypt. She has a BA in English Literature and a PhD in Rhetoric and Composition. She is currently an Associate Professor of English at Salve Regina University, USA. Her publications include an English translation of Amina Zaydan's *Red Wine* (AUC Press, 2010).

Nathaniel Greenberg is Assistant Professor of Arabic at George Mason University and author of *The Aesthetic of Revolution in the Film and Literature of Naguib Mahfouz* (Lexington, 2014), and *Narrative Dimensions of the Arab Uprisings: Form, Ideology, and Aesthetics in an Age of Revolution* (Rowman & Littlefield, Forthcoming). He is book reviews editor for the *Journal of Arabic Literature*.

William Maynard Hutchins is a prizewinning and prolic translator of contemporary Arab authors, including Naguib Mahfouz (*Cairo Trilogy*), Muhammad Khuddayir, Fadhil al-Azzawi, Amir Tag Elsir, Ibrahim al-Koni and Wajdi al-Ahdal. He is a contributing editor of *Banipal*.

Becki Maddock is a translator and researcher living in London. She translates from Arabic, Persian and Spanish into English. She has a first class BA in Arabic and Spanish (Exeter University) and an MA in Near and Middle Eastern Studies from SOAS, University of London. She is now taking Kurdish language classes, also at SOAS.

Suneela Mubayi is a graduate student in Arabic literature at the Department of Middle Eastern and Islamic Studies at New York University.

Clare Roberts has a BA in Arabic and Islamic Studies (Oxford University) and an MA in Arabic Poetry and Turkish Politics (SOAS, London). She works at a charity, and reviews for *Banipal*.

Olivia Snaije is a journalist and has covered the Middle East for the past twenty years. She writes for *Publishing Perspectives*, bookwitty.com and reviews for *Banipal*.

Paul Starkey is Emeritus Professor of Arabic at Durham University and Vice-President of BRISMES. He has translated many works by contemporary Arab authors, and won the 2015 Saif Ghobash Banipal Prize for Youssef Rakha's *The Book of the Sultan's Seal* (Interlink, 2014). He is a contributing editor of *Banipal* and chair of the Banipal Trust.

William Tamplin is a third-year PhD candidate in Comparative Literature at Harvard University. After graduating from Georgetown University in 2012, he taught English in Alexandria, Egypt and later won a Fulbright to Jordan, where he translated the political poetry of Bedouin poet Muhammad Fanatil al-Hajaya.

Susannah Tarbush is a freelance journalist specialising in cultural affairs in the Middle East. She writes the Tanjara blog, and is a consulting editor of *Banipal* and regular reviewer.

Valentina Viene is Italian by birth, now settled in the UK. She has a BA in Arabic and English from the University of Naples L'Orientale, and an MA in the Theory and Practice of Arabic Translation.

Jonathan Wright is a prizewinning translator who worked for many years as a journalist in the Arab world. His translations include three IPAF winners, Raja Alem's *The Dove's Necklace* (2011), Saud Alsanousi's *The Bamboo Stalk* (IPAF 2013 & 2016 Saif Ghobash Banipal Prize), and Youssef Ziedan's *Azazeel* (IPAF 2009 & 2013 Saif Ghobash Banipal Prize), and Hassan Blasim's *The Iraqi Christ* (2014 Independent Foreign Fiction Prize).

THE DIALOGUE OF THE SERAPHIC VIRGIN CATHERINE OF SIENA

Dictated By Her, While In A State Of Ecstasy,
To Her Secretaries, And Completed
In The Year Of Our Lord 1370

together with

An Account Of Her Death By An Eye-Witness
Translated From The Original Italian,

and preceded by

An Introduction On The Life And Times Of The Saint,
by Algar Thorold

British Library Cataloguing in Publication Data

A catalogue record for this book is available from the British Library

ISBN-13: 978-1-908388-85-8

Printed and bound in Great Britain by Lightning Souce UK Ltd., 6
Precedent Drive, Rooksley, Milton Keynes MK13 8PR.

Cover Illustration: St. Catherine of Siena Receiving the Stigmata.
Giovanni di Paolo (Circa 1461)

Then the virgin sent for me and said quietly, "You must know, Father, that by the mercy of the Lord Jesus I now bear in my body His stigmata." I replied that while I had been watching the movements of her body when she was in ecstasy I had suspected something of the sort; I asked her how the Lord had done all this. She said, "I saw the Lord fixed to the cross coming towards me in a great light, and such was the impulse of my soul to go and meet its Creator that it forced the body to rise up. Then from the scars of His most sacred wounds I saw five rays of blood coming down towards me, to my hands, my feet and my heart. Realizing what was to happen, I exclaimed, 'O Lord God, I beg you - do not let these scars show on the outside of my body!' As I said this, before the rays reached me their colour changed from blood red to the colour of light, and in the form of pure light they arrived at the five points of my body, hands, feet and heart." "So then," I said, no ray reached your right side?" "No," she replied, "it came straight to my left side, over my heart; because that line of light from Jesus's right side struck me directly, not aslant."

from Raymond of Capua's *Life of St. Catherine of Siena* (Lamb's transalation)

CONTENTS

INTRODUCTION

It would be hard to say whether the Age of the Saints, *le moyen âge énorme et délicat,* has suffered more at the hands of friends or foes. It is at least certain that the medieval period affects those who approach it in the manner of a powerful personality who may awaken love or hatred, but cannot be passed over with indifference. When the contempt of the eighteenth century for the subject, the result of that century's lack of historic imagination, was thawed by the somewhat rhetorical enthusiasm of Chateaubriand and of the Romanticists beyond the Rhine, hostility gave place to an undiscriminating admiration. The shadows fell out of the picture; the medieval time became a golden age when heaven and earth visibly mingled, when Christian society reached the zenith of perfection which constituted it a model for all succeeding ages. Then came the German professors with all the paraphernalia of scientific history, and, looking through their instruments, we, who are not Germans, have come to take a more critical and, perhaps, a juster view of the matter. The Germans, too, have had disciples of other nations, and though conclusions on special points may differ, in every country now at a certain level of education, the same views prevail as to the principles on which historical investigation should be conducted. And yet, while no one with a reputation to lose would venture on any personal heresy as to the standards of legitimate evidence, the same facts still seem to lead different minds to differing appreciations. For history, written solely ad narrandum, is not history; the historian's task is not over when he has disinterred facts and established dates: it is then that the most delicate part of his work begins. History, to be worthy of the name, must produce the illusion of living men and women, and, in order to do this successfully, must be based, not only upon insight into human nature in general, but also upon personal appreciation of the particular men and women engaged in the episodes with which it deals. With facts as such, there can indeed be no tampering; but for the determination of their significance, of their value, as illustrative of a course of policy or of the character of those who were responsible for their occurrence, we have to depend in great measure on the personality of the historian. It is evident that a man who lacks the sympathetic power to enter into the character that he attempts to delineate, will hardly be able to make that character live for us. For in Art as well as Life, sympathy is power.

Now, while this is true of all history whatever, it is perhaps truer of the history of the middle ages than of that of any more recent period, nor is the reason of this far to seek. The middle ages were a period fruitful in great individuals who molded society, to an extent that perhaps no succeeding period has been. In modern times the formula, an abstraction such as "Capital" or the "Rights of Man" has largely taken the place of the individual as a plastic force. The one great Tyrant of the nineteenth century found his opportunity in the anarchy which

5

followed the French Revolution. The spoil was then necessarily to the strong. But even Napoleon was conquered at last rather by a conspiracy of the slowly developing anonymous forces of his time than by the superior skill or strength of an individual rival. The lion could hardly have been caught in such meshes in the trecento. Then, the fate of populations was bound up with the animosities of princes, and, in order to understand the state of Europe at any particular moment of that period, it is necessary to understand the state of soul of the individuals who happened, at the time, to be the political stakeholders.

It must not be thought, however, that the personality of the prince was the only power in the medieval state, for the prince himself was held to be ultimately amenable to an idea, which so infinitely transcended earthly distinctions as to level them all in relation to itself. Religion was in those days a mental and social force which we, in spite of the petulant acerbity of modern theological controversies, have difficulty in realizing. Prince and serf would one day appear as suppliants before the Judgment-seat of Christ, and the theory of medieval Christianity was considerably in favor of the serf. The Father of Christendom, at once Priest and King, anointed and consecrated as the social exponent of the Divine Justice, could not, in his own person, escape its rigors, but must, one day, render an account of his stewardship. Nor did the medieval mind, distinguishing between the office and the individual, by any means shrink from contemplating the fate of the faithless steward. In a "Last Judgment" by Angelico at Florence, the ministers of justice seem to have a special joy in hurrying off to the pit popes and cardinals and other ecclesiastics.

For it is an insufficient criticism that has led some to suppose that the medieval Church weighed on the conscience of Christendom solely, or even primarily, as an arbitrary fact: that the priesthood, aided by the ignorance of the people, succeeded in establishing a monstrous claim to control the destinies of the soul by quasi-magical agencies and the powers of excommunication. Nothing can be further from the truth. Probably at no period has the Christian conscience realized more profoundly that the whole external fabric of Catholicism, its sacraments, its priesthood, its discipline, was but the phenomenal expression, necessary and sacred in its place, of the Idea of Christianity, that the vitality of that Idea was the life by which the Church lived, and that by that Idea all Christians, priests as well as laymen, rulers as well as subjects, would at the last be judged. When Savonarola replied to the Papal Legate, who, in his confusion, committed the blunder of adding to the formula of excommunication from the Church Militant, a sentence of exclusion from the Church Triumphant, "You cannot do it," he was in the tradition of medieval orthodoxy. Moreover, even though the strict logic of her theory might have required it, the hierarchical Church was not considered as the sole manifestation of the Divine Will to Christendom. The unanimity with which the Christian idea was accepted in those times made the saint a well-known type of human character just as nowadays we have the millionaire or the philanthropist. Now the saint, although under the same ecclesiastical dispensation as other Christians, was conceived to have his own special relations with God, which amounted almost to a personal revelation. In particular he was held to be exempt from many of the limitations of fallen humanity. His prayers were of certain efficacy; the customary uniformities of experience were thought to be constantly transcended by the power that dwelt within him; he was often accepted by the people as the bearer to Christendom of a Divine message over and above the revelation of which the hierarchy was the legitimate guardian. Not infrequently indeed that message was one of warning or correction to the hierarchy. Sabatier points out truly that the medieval saints occupied much the same relation to the ecclesiastical system as the Prophets of Israel had done, under the older dispensation, to the Jewish Priesthood. They came out of their hermitages or cloisters, and with lips touched by coal from the altar denounced iniquity wherever they found it, even in the highest places. It is needless to say that they were not revolutionaries - had they been so indeed the state of Europe might have been very different today; for them, as for other Christians, the organization of the Church was Divine; it was by the sacred responsibilities of his office that they judged the unworthy pastor.

An apt illustration of this attitude occurs in the life of the Blessed Colomba of Rieti. Colomba, who was a simple peasant, was called to the unusual vocation of preaching. The local representatives of the Holy Office, alarmed at the novelty, imprisoned her and took the opportunity of a visit of Alexander VI. to the neighboring town of Perugia to bring her before his Holiness for examination. When the saint was brought into the Pope's presence, she reverently kissed the hem of his garment, and, being overcome with devotion at the sight of the Vicar of Christ, fell into an ecstasy, during which she invoked the Divine judgment on the sins of Rodrigo Borgia. It was useless to attempt to stop her; she was beyond the control of inquisitor or guards; the Pope had to hear her out. He did so; proclaimed her complete orthodoxy, and set her free with every mark of reverence. In this highly characteristic episode scholastic logic appears, for once, to have been justified, at perilous odds, of her children. . . .

* * *

Midway between sky and earth hangs a City Beautiful: Siena, Vetus Civitas Virginis. The town seems to have descended as a bride from airy regions, and lightly settled on the summits of three hills which it crowns with domes and clustering towers. As seen from the vineyards which clothe the slopes of the hills or with its crenellated wall and slender-necked Campanile silhouetted against the evening sky from the neighboring heights of Belcaro, the city is familiar to students of the early Italian painters. It forms the fantastic and solemn background of many a masterpiece of the trecentisti, and seems the only possible home, if home they can have on earth, of the glorified persons who occupy the foreground. It would create no surprise to come, while walking round the ancient walls, suddenly, at a turn in the road, on one of the sacred groups so familiarly recurrent to the memory in such an environment: often indeed one experiences a curious illusion when a passing friar happens for a moment to "compose" with cypress and crumbling archway.

Siena, once the successful rival of Florence in commerce, war, and politics, has, fortunately for the more vital interests which it represents, long desisted from such minor matters. Its worldly ruin has been complete for more than five hundred years; in truth the town has never recovered from the plague which, in the far-off days of 1348, carried off 80,000 of its population. Grassy mounds within the city walls mark the shrinking of the town since the date of their erection, and Mr. Murray gives its present population at less than 23,000. The free Ghibelline Republic which, on that memorable 4th of September 1260, defeated, with the help of Pisa, at Monte Aperto, the combined forces of the Guelf party in Tuscany, has now, after centuries of servitude to Spaniard and Austrian, to be content with the somewhat pinchbeck dignity of an Italian Prefettura. At least the architectural degradation which has overtaken Florence at the hands of her modern rulers has been as yet, in great measure, spared to Siena. Even the railway has had the grace to conceal its presence in the folds of olive which enwrap the base of the hill on which the city is set.

Once inside the rose-colored walls, as we pass up the narrow, roughly paved streets between lines of palaces, some grim and massive like Casa Tolomei, built in 1205, others delicate specimens of Italian Gothic like the Palazzo Saracini, others again illustrating the combination of grace and strength which marked the domestic architecture of the Renaissance at its prime, like the Palazzo Piccolomini, we find ourselves in a world very remote indeed from anything with which the experience of our own utilitarian century makes us familiar. And yet, as we rub our eyes, unmistakably a world of facts, though of facts, as it were, visibly interpreted by the deeper truth of an art whose insistent presence is on all sides of us. Here is Casa Tolomei, a huge cube of rough-hewn stone stained to the color of tarnished silver with age, once the home of that Madonna Pia whose story lives forever in the verse of Dante. Who shall distinguish between her actual tale of days and the immortal life given her by the poet? In her moment of suffering at least she has been made eternal. And not far from that ancient fortress-home, in a winding alley that can hardly be called a street, is another house of medieval Siena - no palace this time, but a small tradesman's dwelling. In the fourteenth century it belonged to Set Giacomo Benincasa, a dyer. Part of it has now been converted into a chapel, over the door of which are inscribed the words: Sponsae Xti Katerinae Domus. Here, on March 5, 1347, being Palm Sunday, was born Giacomo's daughter Caterina, who still lives one of the purest glories of the Christian Church under the name of St. Catherine of Siena. More than 500 years have passed since the daughter of the Siennese dyer entered into the rest of that sublime and touching symbolism under which the Church half veils and half reveals her teaching as to the destiny of man. Another case, but how profoundly more significant than that of poor Madonna Pia, of the intertwining of the world of fact with the deeper truth of art.

St. Catherine was born at the same time as a twin-sister, who did not survive. Her parents, Giacomo and Lapa Benincasa, were simple townspeople, prosperous, and apparently deserving their reputation for piety. Lapa, the daughter of one Mucio Piagenti, a now wholly forgotten poet, bore twenty-five children to her husband, of whom thirteen only appear to have grown up. This large family lived together in the manner still obtaining in Italy, in the little house, till the death of Giacomo in 1368.

There are stirring pages enough in Christian hagiology. Who can read unmoved of the struggles towards his ideal of an Augustine or a Loyola, or of the heroic courage of a Theresa, affirming against all human odds the divinity of her mission, and justifying, after years of labor, her incredible assertions by the steadfastness of her will? There are other pages in the lives of the saints, less dramatic, it may be, but breathing, nevertheless, a naïve grace and poetry all their own: the childhood of those servants of Christ who have borne His yoke from the dawn of their days forms their charming theme. Here the blasting illuminations of the Revelation are toned down to a soft and tender glow, in which the curves and lines of natural humanity do but seem more pathetically human. The hymn at Lauds for the Feast of the Holy Innocents represents those unconscious martyrs as playing with their palms and crowns under the very altar of Heaven :-

> "Vos prima Christi victima
> Grex immolatorum tener
> Aram sub ipsam simplices
> Palma et coronis luditis!"

And so these other saintly babies play at hermits or monasteries instead of the soldiers and housekeeping beloved of more secular-minded infants. Heaven condescends to their pious revels: we are told of the Blessed Hermann Joseph, the Premonstratensian, that his infantile sports were joyously shared by the Divine Child Himself. He would be a morose pedant indeed who should wish to rationalize this white mythology. The tiny Catherine was no exception to the rest of her canonized brothers and sisters. At the age of five it was her custom on the staircase to kneel and repeat a "Hail Mary" at each step, a devotion so pleasing to the angels, that they would frequently carry her up or down without letting her feet touch the ground, much to the alarm of her mother, who confided to Father Raymond of Capua, the Dominican confessor of the family, her fears of an accident. Nor were these phenomena the only reward of her infant piety. From the day that she could walk she became very popular among her numerous relatives and her parents' friends, who gave her the pet name of Euphrosyne, to signify the grief-dispelling effect of her conversation, and who were constantly inviting her to their houses on some pretext or other. Sent one morning on an errand to the house of her married sister Bonaventura, she was favored with a beautiful vision which, as it has an important symbolical bearing on the great task of her after-life, I will relate in Father Raymond's words, slightly abridging their prolixity.

"So it happened that Catherine, being arrived at the age of six, went one day with her brother Stephen, who was a little older than herself, to the house of their sister Bonaventura, who was married to one Niccol˜, as has been mentioned above, in order to carry something or give some message from their mother Lapa. Their mother's errand accomplished, while they were on the way back from their sister's house to their own and were passing along a certain valley, called by the people Valle Piatta, the holy child, lifting her eyes, saw on the opposite side above the Church of the Preaching Friars a most beautiful room, adorned with regal magnificence, in which was seated, on an imperial throne, Jesus Christ, the Savior of the world, clothed in pontifical vestments, and wearing on His head a papal tiara; with Him were the princes of the Apostles, Peter and Paul, and the holy evangelist John. Astounded at such a sight, Catherine stood still, and with fixed and immovable look, gazed, full of love, on her Savior, who, appearing in so marvelous a manner, in order sweetly to gain her love to Himself, fixed on her the eyes of His Majesty, and, with a tender smile, lifted over her His right hand, and, making the sign of the Holy Cross in the manner of a bishop, left with her the gift of His eternal benediction. The grace of this gift was so efficacious, that Catherine, beside herself, and transformed into Him upon whom she gazed with such love, forgetting not only the road she was on, but also herself, although naturally a timid child, stood still for a space with lifted and immovable eyes in the public road, where men and beasts were continually passing, and would certainly have continued to stand there as long as the vision lasted, had she not been violently diverted by others. But while the Lord was working these marvels, the child Stephen, leaving her standing still, continued his way down hill, thinking that she was following, but, seeing her immovable in the distance and paying no heed to his calls, he returned and pulled her with his hands, saying: 'What are you doing here? why do you not come?' Then Catherine, as if waking from a heavy sleep, lowered her eyes and said: 'Oh, if you had seen what I see, you would not distract me from so sweet a vision!' and lifted her eyes again on high; but the vision had entirely disappeared, according to the will of Him who had granted it, and she, not being able to endure this without pain, began with tears to reproach herself for having turned her eyes to earth." Such was the "call" of St. Catherine of Siena, and, to a mind intent on mystical significance, the appearance of Christ, in the semblance of His Vicar, may fitly appear to symbolize the great mission of her after-life to the Holy See.

* * *

Much might be said of the action of Catherine on her generation. Few individuals perhaps have ever led so active a life or have succeeded in leaving so remarkable an imprint of their personality on the events of their time. Catherine the Peacemaker reconciles warring factions of her native city and heals an international feud between Florence and the Holy See. Catherine the Consoler pours the balm of her gentle spirit into the lacerated souls of the suffering wherever she finds them, in the condemned cell or in the hospital ward. She is one of the most voluminous of letter-writers, keeping up a constant correspondence with a band of disciples, male and female, all over Italy, and last, but not least, with the distant Pope at Avignon.

Her lot was cast on evil days for the Church and the Peninsula. The trecento, the apogee of the middle ages was over. Francis and Dominic had come and gone, and though Franciscans and Dominicans remained and numbered saints among their ranks, still the first fervor of the original inspiration was a brightness that had fled. The moral state of the secular clergy was, according to Catherine herself, too often one of the deepest degradation, while, in the absence of the Pontiff, the States of the Church were governed by papal legates, mostly men of blood and lust, who ground the starving people under their heel. Assuredly it was not from Christian bishops who would have disgraced Islam that their subjects could learn the path of peace. The Pope's residence at Avignon, the Babylonish Captivity, as it was called, may have seemed, at the time when his departure from Rome was resolved upon, a wise measure of temporary retreat before the anarchy which was raging round the city of St. Peter. But not many years passed before it became evident that Philip the Fair, the astute adviser to whose counsel - and possibly more than counsel - Clement had submitted in leaving Rome, was the only one who profited by the exile of the Pope. Whatever the truth may be about the details of Clement's election, so far as his subservience to the French king went, he might have remained Archbishop of Bordeaux to the end of his days. He accepted for his relations costly presents from Philip; he placed the papal authority at his service in the gravely suspicious matter of the suppression of the Templars. Gradually the Holy See in exile lost its ecumenical character and became more and more the vassal of the French crown. Such a decline in its position could not fail to affect even its doctrinal prestige. It was well enough in theory to apply to the situation such maxims as Ubi Petrus ibi Ecclesia, or, as the Avignonese doctors paraphrased it, Ubi Papa ibi Roma; but, in practice, Christendom grew shy of a French Pope, living under the eye and power of the French king. The Romans, who had always treated the Pope badly, were furious when at last they had driven him away, and gratified their spite by insulting their exiled rulers. Nothing could exceed their contempt for the Popes of Avignon, who, as a matter of fact, though weak and compliant, were in their personal characters worthy ecclesiastics. They gave no credit to John XXII. for his genuine zeal in the cause of learning, or the energy with which he restored ecclesiastical studies in the Western Schools. For Benedict XII., a retiring and abstemious student, they invented the phrase: bibere papaliter - to drink like the Pope. Clement VI. they called poco religioso, forgetting his noble charity at the time of the plague, and also the fact that Rome herself had produced not a few popes whose lives furnished a singular commentary on the ethics of the Gospel.

The real danger ahead to Christendom was the possibility of an Italian anti-Pope who should fortify his position by recourse to the heretical elements scattered through the peninsula. Those elements were grave and numerous. The Fraticelli or Spiritual Franciscans, although crushed for the time by the iron hand of Pope Boniface, rather flourished than otherwise under persecution. These dangerous heretics had inherited a garbled version of the mysticism of Joachim of Flora, which constituted a doctrine perhaps more radically revolutionary than that of any heretics before or since. It amounted to belief in a new revelation of the Spirit, which was to supersede the dispensation of the Son as that had taken the place of the dispensation of the Father. According to the Eternal Gospel of Gerard of San Domino, who had derived it, not without much adroit manipulation, from the writings of Abbot Joachim, the Roman Church was on the eve of destruction, and it was the duty of the Spirituali, the saints who had received the new dispensation, to fly from the contamination of her communion. An anti-Pope who should have rallied to his allegiance these elements of schism would have been a dangerous rival to a French Pope residing in distant Avignon, however legitimate his title. Nor was there wanting outside Italy matter for grave anxiety. Germs of heresy were fermenting north of the Alps; the preaching of Wycliffe, the semi-Islamism of the Hungarian Beghards, the Theism of the Patarini of Dalmatia, the erotic mysticism of the Adamites of Paris, indicated a widespread anarchy in the minds of Christians. Moreover, the spiritual difficulties of the Pope were complicated by his temporal preoccupations. For good or ill, it had come to be essential to the action of the Holy See that the successor of the penniless fisherman should have his place among the princes of the earth.

The papal monarchy had come about, as most things come about in this world, by what seems to have been the inevitable force of circumstances. The decay of the Imperial power in Italy due to the practical abandonment of the Western Empire - for the ruler of Constantinople lived at too great a distance to be an effective Emperor of the West - had resulted in a natural increase of secular importance to the See of Rome. To the genius of Pope Gregory I., one of the few men whom their fellows have named both Saint and Great, was due the development of the political situation thus created in Italy.

Chief and greatest of bishops in his day was St. Gregory the Great. Seldom, if ever, has the papal dignity been sustained with such lofty enthusiasm, such sagacious political insight. Himself a Roman of Rome, Romano di Roma, as those who possess that privilege still call themselves today, the instinct of government was his by hereditary right. He had the defects as well as the qualities of the statesman. His theological writings, which are voluminous and verbose, are marked rather by a sort of canonized common sense than by exalted flights of spirituality. His missionary enterprise was characterized by a shrewd and gracious condescension to the limitations of human nature. Thus he counsels St. Augustine, who had consulted him as to the best means of extirpating the pagan customs of our English forefathers, to deal gently with these ancient survivals. He ruled that the celebration of the Festivals of the Sabots should if possible be held at the times and places at which the people had been in the habit of meeting together to worship the gods. They would thus come to associate the new religion with their traditional merry-makings, and their conversion would be gradually, and as it were unconsciously, effected. It was a kindly and statesmanlike thought. In this way Gregory may truly be looked upon as the founder of popular Catholicism, that "pensive use and wont religion," not assuredly in the entirety of its details Christian, but at least profoundly Catholic, as weaving together in the web of its own secular experience of man so large a proportion of the many-colored threads that have at any time attached his hopes and fears to the mysterious unknown which surrounds him. No miracle is needed to explain the political ascendancy which such a man inevitably came to acquire in an Italy deserted by the Empire, and, but for him and the organization which depended on him, at the mercy of the invading Lombard. More and more, people came to look on the Pope as their temporal ruler no less than as their spiritual father. In many cases, indeed, his was the only government they knew. Kings and nobles had conferred much property on the Roman Church. By the end of the sixth century the Bishop of Rome held, by the right of such donations to his See, large tracts of country, not only in Italy, but also in Sicily, Corsica, Gaul, and even Asia and Africa. Gregory successfully defended his Italian property against the invaders, and came to the relief of the starving population with corn from Sicily and Africa, thus laying deep in the hearts of the people the foundations of the secular power of the Papacy.

It would be an unnecessary digression from our subject to work out in detail the stages by which the Pope came to take his place first as the Italian vicar of a distant emperor, and at length, as the result of astute statecraft and the necessities of the case, among the princes of Europe, as their chief and arbiter. So much as has been said was, however, necessary for the comprehension of the task with which Catherine measured, for the time, successfully her strength. It was given to the Popolana of Siena, by the effect of her eloquence in persuading the wavering will of the Pope to return to his See, to bring about what was, for the moment, the only possible solution of that Roman question, which, hanging perpetually round the skirts of the Bride of Christ, seems at every step to impede her victorious advance.

* * *

Nevertheless, it is neither the intrinsic importance nor the social consequences of her actions that constitute the true greatness of St. Catherine. Great ends may be pursued by essentially small means, in an aridity and narrowness of temper that goes far to discount their actual achievement. History, and in particular the history of the Church, is not wanting in such instances. Savonarola set great ends before himself - the freedom of his country and the regeneration of the state; but the spirit in which he pursued them excludes him from that Pantheon of gracious souls in which humanity enshrines its true benefactors. "Soul, as a quality of style, is a fact," and the soul of St. Catherine's gesta expressed itself in a "style" so winning, so sweetly reasonable, as to make her the dearest of friends to all who had the privilege of intimate association with her, and a permanent source of refreshment to the human spirit. She intuitively perceived life under the highest possible forms, the forms of Beauty and Love. Truth and Goodness were, she thought, means for the achievement of those two supreme ends. The sheer beauty of the soul "in a state of Grace" is a point on which she constantly dwells, hanging it as a bait before those whom she would induce to turn from evil. Similarly the ugliness of sin, as much as its wickedness, should warn us of its true nature. Love, that love of man for man which, in deepest truth, is, in the words of the writer of the First Epistle of St. John, God Himself, is, at once, the highest achievement of man and his supreme and satisfying beatitude. The Symbols of Catholic theology were to her the necessary and fitting means of transit, so to speak. See, in the following pages, the fine allegory of the Bridge of the Sacred Humanity, of the soul in vi‰ on its dusty pilgrimage towards those gleaming heights of vision. "Truth" was to her the handmaid of the spiritualized imagination, not, as too often in these days of the twilight of the soul, its tyrant and its gaoler. Many of those who pass lives of unremitting preoccupation with the problems of truth and goodness are wearied and cumbered with much serving. We honor them, and rightly; but if they have nothing but this to offer us, our hearts do not run to meet them, as they fly to the embrace of those rare souls who inhabit a serener, more pellucid atmosphere. Among these spirits of the air, St. Catherine has taken a permanent and foremost place. She is among the few guides of humanity who have the perfect manner, the irresistible attractiveness, of that positive purity of heart, which not only sees God, but diffuses Him, as by some natural law of refraction, over the hearts of men. The Divine nuptials, about which the mystics tell us so much, have been accomplished in her, Nature and Grace have lain down together, and the mysteries of her religion seem but the natural expression of a perfectly balanced character, an unquenchable love and a deathless will.

* * *

The Dialogue of St. Catherine of Siena was dictated to her secretaries by the Saint in ecstasy. Apart from the extraordinary circumstances of its production, this work has a special interest.

The composition of the Siennese dyer's daughter, whose will, purified and sublimated by prayer, imposed itself on popes and princes, is an almost unique specimen of what may be called "ecclesiastical" mysticism; for its special value lies in the fact that from first to last it is nothing more than a mystical exposition of the creeds taught to every child in the Catholic poor-schools. Her insight is sometimes very wonderful. How subtle, for instance, is the analysis of the state of the "worldly man" who loves God for his own pleasure or profit! The special snares of the devout are cut through by the keen logic of one who has experienced and triumphed over them. Terrible, again, is the retribution prophesied to the "unworthy ministers of the Blood."

And so every well-known form of Christian life, healthy or parasitic, is treated of, detailed, analyzed incisively, remorselessly, and then subsumed under the general conception of God's infinite loving-kindness and mercy.

The great mystics have usually taken as their starting-point what, to most, is the goal hardly to be reached; their own treatment of the preliminary stages of spirituality is frequently conventional and jejune. Compare, for instance, the first book with the two succeeding ones, of Ruysbrock's Ornement des Noces spirituelles, that unique breviary of the Christian Platonician. Another result of their having done so is that, with certain noble exceptions, the literature of this subject has fallen into the hands of a class of writers, or rather purveyors, well-intentioned no doubt, but not endowed with the higher spiritual and mental faculties, whom it is not unfair to describe as the feuilletonistes of piety. Such works, brightly bound, are appropriately exposed for sale in the Roman shop-windows, among the gaudy objets de religion they so much resemble. To keep healthy and raise the tone of devotional literature is surely an eighth spiritual work of mercy. St. Philip Neri's advice in the matter was to prefer those writers whose names were preceded by the title of Saint. In the Dialogo we have a great saint, one of the most extraordinary women who ever lived, treating, in a manner so simple and familiar as at times to become almost colloquial, of the elements of practical Christianity. Passages occur frequently of lofty eloquence, and also of such literary perfection that this book is held by critics to be one of the classics of the age and land which produced Boccaccio and Petrarch. To-day, in the streets of Siena, the same Tuscan idiom can be heard, hardly altered since the days of St. Catherine.

One word as to the translation. I have almost always followed the text of Gigli, a learned Siennese ecclesiastic, who edited the complete works of St. Catherine in the last century. His is the latest edition printed of the Dialogo. Once or twice I have preferred the cinquecento Venetian editor. My aim has been to translate as literally as possible, and at the same time to preserve the characteristic rhythm of the sentences, so suggestive in its way of the sing-song articulation of the Siennese of today. St. Catherine has no style as such; she introduces a metaphor and forgets it; the sea, a vine, and a plough will often appear in the same sentence, sometimes in the same phrase. In such cases I have occasionally taken the liberty of adhering to the first simile when the confusion of metaphor in the original involves hopeless obscurity of expression.

Viareggio, September 1906.

A TREATISE OF DIVINE PROVIDENCE

How a soul, elevated by desire of the honor of God, and of the salvation of her neighbors, exercising herself in humble prayer, after she had seen the union of the soul, through love, with God, asked of God four requests.

The soul, who is lifted by a very great and yearning desire for the honor of God and the salvation of souls, begins by exercising herself, for a certain space of time, in the ordinary virtues, remaining in the cell of self-knowledge, in order to know better the goodness of God towards her. This she does because knowledge must precede love, and only when she has attained love, can she strive to follow and to clothe herself with the truth. But, in no way, does the creature receive such a taste of the truth, or so brilliant a light therefrom, as by means of humble and continuous prayer, founded on knowledge of herself and of God; because prayer, exercising her in the above way, unites with God the soul that follows the footprints of Christ Crucified, and thus, by desire and affection, and union of love, makes her another Himself. Christ would seem to have meant this, when He said: To him who will love Me and will observe My commandment, will I manifest Myself; and he shall be one thing with Me and I with him. In several places we find similar words, by which we can see that it is, indeed, through the effect of love, that the soul becomes another Himself. That this may be seen more clearly, I will mention what I remember having heard from a handmaid of God, namely, that, when she was lifted up in prayer, with great elevation of mind, God was not wont to conceal, from the eye of her intellect, the love which He had for His servants, but rather to manifest it; and, that among other things, He used to say: "Open the eye of your intellect, and gaze into Me, and you shall see the beauty of My rational creature. And look at those creatures who, among the beauties which I have given to the soul, creating her in My image and similitude, are clothed with the nuptial garment (that is, the garment of love), adorned with many virtues, by which they are united with Me through love. And yet I tell you, if you should ask Me, who these are, I should reply" (said the sweet and amorous Word of God) "they are another Myself, inasmuch as they have lost and denied their own will, and are clothed with Mine, are united to Mine, are conformed to Mine." It is therefore true, indeed, that the soul unites herself with God by the affection of love.

So, that soul, wishing to know and follow the truth more manfully, and lifting her desires first for herself - for she considered that a soul could not be of use, whether in doctrine, example, or prayer, to her neighbor, if she did not first profit herself, that is, if she did not acquire virtue in herself - addressed four requests to the Supreme and Eternal Father. The first was for herself; the second for the reformation of the Holy Church; the third a general prayer for the whole world, and in particular for the peace of Christians who rebel, with much lewdness and persecution, against the Holy Church; in the fourth and last, she besought the Divine Providence to provide for things in general, and in particular, for a certain case with which she was concerned.

How the desire of this soul grew when God showed her the neediness of the world.

This desire was great and continuous, but grew much more, when the First Truth showed her the neediness of the world, and in what a tempest of offense against God it lay. And she had understood this the better from a letter, which she had received from the spiritual Father of her soul, in which he explained to her the penalties and intolerable dolor caused by offenses against God, and the loss of souls, and the persecutions of Holy Church.

All this lighted the fire of her holy desire with grief for the offenses, and with the joy of the lively hope, with which she waited for God to provide against such great evils. And, since the soul seems, in such communion, sweetly to bind herself fast within herself and with God, and knows better His truth, inasmuch as the soul is then in God, and God in the soul, as the fish is in the sea, and the sea in the fish, she desired the arrival of the morning (for the morrow was a feast of Mary) in order to hear Mass. And, when the morning came, and the hour of the Mass, she sought with anxious desire her accustomed place; and, with a great knowledge of herself, being ashamed of her own imperfection, appearing to herself to be the cause of all the evil that was happening throughout the world, conceiving a hatred and displeasure against herself, and a feeling of holy justice, with which knowledge, hatred, and justice, she purified the stains which seemed to her to cover her guilty soul, she said: "O Eternal Father, I accuse myself before You, in order that You may punish me for my sins in this finite life, and, inasmuch as my sins are the cause of the sufferings which my neighbor must endure, I implore You, in Your kindness, to punish them in my person."

How finite works are not sufficient for punishment or recompense without the perpetual affection of love.

Then, the Eternal Truth seized and drew more strongly to Himself her desire, doing as He did in the Old Testament, for when the sacrifice was offered to God, a fire descended and drew to Him the sacrifice that was acceptable to Him; so did the sweet Truth to that soul, in sending down the fire of the clemency of the Holy Spirit, seizing the sacrifice of desire that she made of herself, saying: "Do you not know, dear daughter, that all the sufferings, which the soul endures, or can endure, in this life, are insufficient to punish one smallest fault, because the offense, being done to Me, who am the Infinite Good, calls for an infinite satisfaction? However, I wish that you should know, that not all the pains that are given to men in this life are given as punishments, but as corrections, in order to chastise a son when he offends; though it is true that both the guilt and the penalty can be expiated by the desire of the soul, that is, by true contrition, not through the finite pain endured, but through the infinite desire; because God, who is infinite, wishes for infinite love and infinite grief. Infinite grief I wish from My creature in two ways: in one way, through her sorrow for her own sins, which she has committed against Me her Creator; in the other way, through her sorrow for the sins which she sees her neighbors commit against Me. Of such as these, inasmuch as they have infinite desire, that is, are joined to Me by an affection of love, and therefore grieve when they offend Me, or see Me offended, their every pain, whether spiritual or corporeal, from wherever it may come, receives infinite merit, and satisfies for a guilt which deserved an infinite penalty, although their works are finite and done in finite time; but, inasmuch as they possess the virtue of desire, and sustain their suffering with desire, and contrition, and infinite displeasure against their guilt, their pain is held worthy. Paul explained this when he said: If I had the tongues of angels, and if I knew the things of the future and gave my body to be burned, and have not love, it would be worth nothing to me. The glorious Apostle thus shows that finite works are not valid, either as punishment or recompense, without the condiment of the affection of love."

How desire and contrition of heart satisfies, both for the guilt and the penalty in oneself and in others; and how sometimes it satisfies for the guilt only, and not the penalty.

"I have shown you, dearest daughter, that the guilt is not punished in this finite time by any pain which is sustained purely as such. And I say, that the guilt is punished by the pain which is endured through the desire, love, and contrition of the heart; not by virtue of the pain, but by virtue of the desire of the soul; inasmuch as desire and every virtue is of value, and has life in itself, through Christ crucified, My only begotten Son, in so far as the soul has drawn her love from Him, and virtuously follows His virtues, that is, His Footprints. In this way, and in no other, are virtues of value, and in this way, pains satisfy for the fault, by the sweet and intimate love acquired in the knowledge of My goodness, and in the bitterness and contrition of heart acquired by knowledge of one's self and one's own thoughts. And this knowledge generates a hatred and displeasure against sin, and against the soul's own sensuality, through which, she deems herself worthy of pains and unworthy of reward."

The sweet Truth continued: "See how, by contrition of the heart, together with love, with true patience, and with true humility, deeming themselves worthy of pain and unworthy of reward, such souls endure the patient humility in which consists the above-mentioned satisfaction. You ask me, then, for pains, so that I may receive satisfaction for the offenses, which are done against Me by My Creatures, and you further ask the will to know and love Me, who am the Supreme Truth. Wherefore I reply that this is the way, if you will arrive at a perfect knowledge and enjoyment of Me, the Eternal Truth, that you should never go outside the knowledge of yourself, and, by humbling yourself in the valley of humility, you will know Me and yourself, from which knowledge you will draw all that is necessary. No virtue, my daughter, can have life in itself except through charity, and humility, which is the foster-mother and nurse of charity. In self-knowledge, then, you will humble yourself, seeing that, in yourself, you do not even exist; for your very being, as you will learn, is derived from Me, since I have loved both you and others before you were in existence; and that, through the ineffable love which I had for you, wishing to re-create you to Grace, I have washed you, and re-created you in the Blood of My only-begotten Son, spilt with so great a fire of love. This Blood teaches the truth to him, who, by self-knowledge, dissipates the cloud of self-love, and in no other way can he learn. Then the soul will inflame herself in this knowledge of Me with an ineffable love, through which love she continues in constant pain; not, however, a pain which afflicts or dries up the soul, but one which rather fattens her; for since she has known My truth, and her own faults, and the ingratitude of men, she endures intolerable suffering, grieving because she loves Me; for, if she did not love Me, she would not be obliged to do so; whence it follows immediately, that it is right for you, and My other servants who have learnt My truth in this way, to sustain, even unto death, many tribulations and injuries and insults in word and deed, for the glory and praise of My Name; thus will you endure and suffer pains. Do you, therefore, and My other servants, carry yourselves with true patience, with grief for your sins, and with love of virtue for the glory and praise of My Name. If you act thus, I will satisfy for your sins, and for those of My other servants, inasmuch as the pains which you will endure will be sufficient, through the virtue of love, for satisfaction and reward, both in you and in others. In yourself you will receive the fruit of life, when the stains of your ignorance are effaced, and I shall not remember that you ever offended Me. In others I will satisfy through the love and affection which you have to Me, and I will give to them according to the disposition with which they will receive My gifts. In particular, to those who dispose themselves, humbly and with reverence, to receive the doctrine of My servants, will I remit both guilt and penalty, since they will thus come to true knowledge and contrition for their sins. So that, by means of prayer, and their desire of serving Me, they receive the fruit of grace, receiving it humbly in greater or less degree, according to the extent of their exercise of virtue and grace in general. I say then, that, through your desires, they will receive remission for their sins. See, however, the condition, namely, that their obstinacy should not be so great in their despair as to condemn them through contempt of the Blood, which, with such sweetness, has restored them.

"What fruit do they receive?

"The fruit which I destine for them, constrained by the prayers of My servants, is that I give them light, and that I wake up in them the hound of conscience, and make them smell the odor of virtue, and take delight in the conversation of My servants.

"Sometimes I allow the world to show them what it is, so that, feeling its diverse and various passions, they may know how little stability it has, and may come to lift their desire beyond it, and seek their native country, which is the Eternal Life. And so I draw them by these, and by many other ways, for the eye cannot see, nor the tongue relate, nor the heart think, how many are the roads and ways which I use, through love alone, to lead them back to grace, so that My truth may be fulfilled in them. I am constrained to do so by that inestimable love of Mine, by which I created them, and by the love, desire, and grief of My servants, since I am no despiser of their tears, and sweat, and humble prayers; rather I accept them, inasmuch as I am He who give them this love for the good of souls and grief for their loss. But I do not, in general, grant to these others, for whom they pray, satisfaction for the penalty due to them, but, only for their guilt, since they are not disposed, on their side, to receive, with perfect love, My love, and that of My servants. They do not receive their grief with bitterness, and perfect contrition for the sins they have committed, but with imperfect love and contrition, wherefore they have not, as others, remission of the penalty, but only of the guilt; because such complete satisfaction requires proper dispositions on both sides, both in him that gives and him that receives. Wherefore, since they are imperfect, they receive imperfectly the perfection of the desires of those who offer them to Me, for their sakes, with suffering; and, inasmuch as I told you that they do receive remission, this is indeed the truth, that, by that way which I have told you, that is, by the light of conscience, and by other things, satisfaction is made for their guilt; for, beginning to learn, they vomit forth the corruption of their sins, and so receive the gift of grace.

"These are they who are in a state of ordinary charity, wherefore, if they have trouble, they receive it in the guise of correction, and do not resist over much the clemency of the Holy Spirit, but, coming out of their sin, they receive the life of grace. But if, like fools, they are ungrateful, and ignore Me and the labors of My servants done for them, that which was given them, through mercy, turns to their own ruin and judgment, not through defect of mercy, nor through defect of him who implored the mercy for the ingrate, but solely through the man's own wretchedness and hardness, with which, with the hands of his free will, he has covered his heart, as it were, with a diamond, which, if it be not broken by the Blood, can in no way be broken. And yet, I say to you, that, in spite of his hardness of heart, he can use his free will while he has time, praying for the Blood of My Son, and let him with his own hand apply It to the diamond over his heart and shiver it, and he will receive the imprint of the Blood which has been paid for him. But, if he delays until the time be past, he has no remedy, because he has not used the dowry which I gave him, giving him memory so as to remember My benefits, intellect, so as to see and know the truth, affection, so that he should love Me, the Eternal Truth, whom he would have known through the use of his intellect. This is the dowry which I have given you all, and which ought to render fruit to Me, the Father; but, if a man barters and sells it to the devil, the devil, if he choose, has a right to seize on everything that he has acquired in this life. And, filling his memory with the delights of sin, and with the recollection of shameful pride, avarice, self-love, hatred, and unkindness to his neighbors (being also a persecutor of My servants), with these miseries, he has obscured his intellect by his disordinate will. Let such as these receive the eternal pains, with their horrible stench, inasmuch as they have not satisfied for their sins with contrition and displeasure of their guilt. Now, therefore, you have understood how suffering satisfies for guilt by perfect contrition, not through the finite pain; and such as have this contrition in perfection satisfy not only for the guilt, but also for the penalty which follows the guilt, as I have already said when speaking in general; and if they satisfy for the guilt alone, that is, if, having abandoned mortal sin, they receive grace, and have not sufficient contrition and love to satisfy for the penalty also, they go to the pains of Purgatory, passing through the second and last means of satisfaction.

"So you see that satisfaction is made, through the desire of the soul united to Me, who am the Infinite Good, in greater or less degree, according to the measure of love, obtained by the desire and prayer of the recipient. Wherefore, with that very same measure with which a man measures to Me, do he receive in himself the measure of My goodness. Labor, therefore, to increase the fire of your desire, and let not a moment pass without crying to Me with humble voice, or without continual prayers before Me for your neighbors. I say this to you and to the father of your soul, whom I have given you on earth. Bear yourselves with manful courage, and make yourselves dead to all your own sensuality."

How very pleasing to God is the willing desire to suffer for Him.

"Very pleasing to Me, dearest daughter, is the willing desire to bear every pain and fatigue, even unto death, for the salvation of souls, for the more the soul endures, the more she shows that she loves Me; loving Me she comes to know more of My truth, and the more she knows, the more pain and intolerable grief she feels at the offenses committed against Me. You asked Me to sustain you, and to punish the faults of others in you, and you did not remark that you were really asking for love, light, and knowledge of the truth, since I have already told you that, by the increase of love, grows grief and pain, wherefore he that grows in love grows in grief. Therefore, I say to you all, that you should ask, and it will be given you, for I deny nothing to him who asks of Me in truth. Consider that the love of divine charity is so closely joined in the soul with perfect patience, that neither can leave the soul without the other. For this reason (if the soul elect to love Me) she should elect to endure pains for Me in whatever mode or circumstance I may send them to her. Patience cannot be proved in any other way than by suffering, and patience is united with love as has been said. Therefore bear yourselves with manly courage, for, unless you do so, you will not prove yourselves to be spouses of My Truth, and faithful children, nor of the company of those who relish the taste of My honor, and the salvation of souls."

How every virtue and every defect is obtained by means of our neighbor.

"I wish also that you should know that every virtue is obtained by means of your neighbor, and likewise, every defect; he, therefore, who stands in hatred of Me, does an injury to his neighbor, and to himself, who is his own chief neighbor, and this injury is both general and particular. It is general because you are obliged to love your neighbor as yourself, and loving him, you ought to help him spiritually, with prayer, counseling him with words, and assisting him both spiritually and temporally, according to the need in which he may be, at least with your goodwill if you have nothing else. A man therefore, who does not love, does not help him, and thereby does himself an injury; for he cuts off from himself grace, and injures his neighbor, by depriving him of the benefit of the prayers and of the sweet desires that he is bound to offer for him to Me. Thus, every act of help that he performs should proceed from the charity which he has through love of Me. And every evil also, is done by means of his neighbor, for, if he do not love Me, he cannot be in charity with his neighbor; and thus, all evils derive from the soul's deprivation of love of Me and her neighbor; whence, inasmuch as such a man does no good, it follows that he must do evil. To whom does he evil? First of all to himself, and then to his neighbor, not against Me, for no evil can touch Me, except in so far as I count done to Me that which he does to himself. To himself he does the injury of sin, which deprives him of grace, and worse than this he cannot do to his neighbor. Him he injures in not paying him the debt, which he owes him, of love, with which he ought to help him by means of prayer and holy desire offered to Me for him. This is an assistance which is owed in general to every rational creature; but its usefulness is more particular when it is done to those who are close at hand, under your eyes, as to whom, I say, you are all obliged to help one another by word and doctrine, and the example of good works, and in every other respect in which your neighbor may be seen to be in need; counseling him exactly as you would yourselves, without any passion of self-love; and he (a man not loving God) does not do this, because he has no love towards his neighbor; and, by not doing it, he does him, as you see, a special injury. And he does him evil, not only by not doing him the good that he might do him, but by doing him a positive injury and a constant evil. In this way sin causes a physical and a mental injury. The mental injury is already done when the sinner has conceived pleasure in the idea of sin, and hatred of virtue, that is, pleasure from sensual self-love, which has deprived him of the affection of love which he ought to have towards Me, and his neighbor, as has been said. And, after he has conceived, he brings forth one sin after another against his neighbor, according to the diverse ways which may please his perverse sensual will. Sometimes it is seen that he brings forth cruelty, and that both in general and in particular.

"His general cruelty is to see himself and other creatures in danger of death and damnation through privation of grace, and so cruel is he that he reminds neither himself nor others of the love of virtue and hatred of vice. Being thus cruel he may wish to extend his cruelty still further, that is, not content with not giving an example of virtue, the villain also usurps the office of the demons, tempting, according to his power, his fellow-creatures to abandon virtue for vice; this is cruelty towards his neighbors, for he makes himself an instrument to destroy life and to give death. Cruelty towards the body has its origin in cupidity, which not only prevents a man from helping his neighbor, but causes him to seize the goods of others, robbing the poor creatures; sometimes this is done by the arbitrary use of power, and at other times by cheating and fraud, his neighbor being forced to redeem, to his own loss, his own goods, and often indeed his own person.

"Oh, miserable vice of cruelty, which will deprive the man who practices it of all mercy, unless he turn to kindness and benevolence towards his neighbor!

"Sometimes the sinner brings forth insults on which often follows murder; sometimes also impurity against the person of his neighbor, by which he becomes a brute beast full of stench, and in this case he does not poison one only, but whoever approaches him, with love or in conversation, is poisoned.

"Against whom does pride bring forth evils? Against the neighbor, through love of one's own reputation, whence comes hatred of the neighbor, reputing one's self to be greater than he; and in this way is injury done to him. And if a man be in a position of authority, he produces also injustice and cruelty and becomes a retailer of the flesh of men. Oh, dearest daughter, grieve for the offense against Me, and weep over these corpses, so that, by prayer, the bands of their death may be loosened!

"See now, that, in all places and in all kinds of people, sin is always produced against the neighbor, and through his medium; in no other way could sin ever be committed either secret or open. A secret sin is when you deprive your neighbor of that which you ought to give him; an open sin is where you perform positive acts of sin, as I have related to you. It is, therefore, indeed the truth that every sin done against Me, is done through the medium of the neighbor."

*How virtues are accomplished by means of our neighbor, and how
it is that virtues differ to such an extent in creatures.*

"I have told you how all sins are accomplished by means of your neighbor, through the principles which I exposed to you, that is, because men are deprived of the affection of love, which gives light to every virtue. In the same way self-love, which destroys charity and affection towards the neighbor, is the principle and foundation of every evil. All scandals, hatred, cruelty, and every sort of trouble proceed from this perverse root of self-love, which has poisoned the entire world, and weakened the mystical body of the Holy Church, and the universal body of the believers in the Christian religion; and, therefore, I said to you, that it was in the neighbor, that is to say in the love of him, that all virtues were founded; and, truly indeed did I say to you, that charity gives life to all the virtues, because no virtue can be obtained without charity, which is the pure love of Me.

"Wherefore, when the soul knows herself, as we have said above, she finds humility and hatred of her own sensual passion, for she learns the perverse law, which is bound up in her members, and which ever fights against the spirit. And, therefore, arising with hatred of her own sensuality, crushing it under the heel of reason, with great earnestness, she discovers in herself the bounty of My goodness, through the many benefits which she has received from Me, all of which she considers again in herself. She attributes to Me, through humility, the knowledge which she has obtained of herself, knowing that, by My grace, I have drawn her out of darkness and lifted her up into the light of true knowledge. When she has recognized My goodness, she loves it without any medium, and yet at the same time with a medium, that is to say, without the medium of herself or of any advantage accruing to herself, and with the medium of virtue, which she has conceived through love of Me, because she sees that, in no other way, can she become grateful and acceptable to Me, but by conceiving, hatred of sin and love of virtue; and, when she has thus conceived by the affection of love, she immediately is delivered of fruit for her neighbor, because, in no other way, can she act out the truth she has conceived in herself, but, loving Me in truth, in the same truth she serves her neighbor.

"And it cannot be otherwise, because love of Me and of her neighbor are one and the same thing, and, so far as the soul loves Me, she loves her neighbor, because love towards him issues from Me. This is the means which I have given you, that you may exercise and prove your virtue therewith; because, inasmuch as you can do Me no profit, you should do it to your neighbor. This proves that you possess Me by grace in your soul, producing much fruit for your neighbor and making prayers to Me, seeking with sweet and amorous desire My honor and the salvation of souls. The soul, enamored of My truth, never ceases to serve the whole world in general, and more or less in a particular case according to the disposition of the recipient and the ardent desire of the donor, as I have shown above, when I declared to you that the endurance of suffering alone, without desire, was not sufficient to punish a fault.

"When she has discovered the advantage of this unitive love in Me, by means of which, she truly loves herself, extending her desire for the salvation of the whole world, thus coming to the aid of its neediness, she strives, inasmuch as she has done good to herself by the conception of virtue, from which she has drawn the life of grace, to fix her eye on the needs of her neighbor in particular. Wherefore, when she has discovered, through the affection of love, the state of all rational creatures in general, she helps those who are at hand, according to the various graces which I have entrusted to her to administer; one she helps with doctrine, that is, with words, giving sincere counsel without any respect of persons, another with the example of a good life, and this indeed all give to their neighbor, the edification of a holy and honorable life. These are the virtues, and many others, too many to enumerate, which are brought forth in the love of the neighbor; but, although I have given them in such a different way, that is to say not all to one, but to one, one virtue, and to another, another, it so happens that it is impossible to have one, without having them all, because all the virtues are bound together. Wherefore, learn, that, in many cases I give one virtue, to be as it were the chief of the others, that is to say, to one I will give principally love, to another justice, to another humility, to one a lively faith, to another prudence or temperance, or patience, to another fortitude. These, and many other virtues, I place, indifferently, in the souls of many creatures; it happens, therefore, that the particular one so placed in the soul becomes the principal object of its virtue; the soul disposing herself, for her chief conversation, to this rather than to other virtues, and, by the effect of this virtue, the soul draws to herself all the other virtues, which, as has been said, are all bound together in the affection of love; and so with many gifts and graces of virtue, and not only in the case of spiritual things but also of temporal. I use the word temporal for the things necessary to the physical life of man; all these I have given indifferently, and I have not placed them all in one soul, in order that man should, perforce, have material for love of his fellow. I could easily have created men possessed of all that they should need both for body and soul, but I wish that one should have need of the other, and that they should be My ministers to administer the graces and the gifts that they have received from Me. Whether man will or no, he cannot help making an act of love. It is true, however, that that act, unless made through love of Me, profits him nothing so far as grace is concerned. See then, that I have made men My ministers, and placed them in diverse stations and various ranks, in order that they may make use of the virtue of love.

"Wherefore, I show you that in My house are many mansions, and that I wish for no other thing than love, for in the love of Me is fulfilled and completed the love of the neighbor, and the law observed. For he, only, can be of use in his state of life, who is bound to Me with this love."

How virtues are proved and fortified by their contraries.

"Up to the present, I have taught you how a man may serve his neighbor, and manifest, by that service, the love which he has towards Me.

"Now I wish to tell you further, that a man proves his patience on his neighbor, when he receives injuries from him.

"Similarly, he proves his humility on a proud man, his faith on an infidel, his true hope on one who despairs, his justice on the unjust, his kindness on the cruel, his gentleness and benignity on the irascible. Good men produce and prove all their virtues on their neighbor, just as perverse men all their vices; thus, if you consider well, humility is proved on pride in this way. The humble man extinguishes pride, because a proud man can do no harm to a humble one; neither can the infidelity of a wicked man, who neither loves Me, nor hopes in Me, when brought forth against one who is faithful to Me, do him any harm; his infidelity does not diminish the faith or the hope of him who has conceived his faith and hope through love of Me, it rather fortifies it, and proves it in the love he feels for his neighbor. For, he sees that the infidel is unfaithful, because he is without hope in Me, and in My servant, because he does not love Me, placing his faith and hope rather in his own sensuality, which is all that he loves. My faithful servant does not leave him because he does not faithfully love Me, or because he does not constantly seek, with hope in Me, for his salvation, inasmuch as he sees clearly the causes of his infidelity and lack of hope. The virtue of faith is proved in these and other ways. Wherefore, to those, who need the proof of it, My servant proves his faith in himself and in his neighbor, and so, justice is not diminished by the wicked man's injustice, but is rather proved, that is to say, the justice of a just man. Similarly, the virtues of patience, benignity, and kindness manifest themselves in a time of wrath by the same sweet patience in My servants, and envy, vexation, and hatred demonstrate their love, and hunger and desire for the salvation of souls. I say, also, to you, that, not only is virtue proved in those who render good for evil, but, that many times a good man gives back fiery coals of love, which dispel the hatred and rancor of heart of the angry, and so from hatred often comes benevolence, and that this is by virtue of the love and perfect patience which is in him, who sustains the anger of the wicked, bearing and supporting his defects. If you will observe the virtues of fortitude and perseverance, these virtues are proved by the long endurance of the injuries and detractions of wicked men, who, whether by injuries or by flattery, constantly endeavor to turn a man aside from following the road and the doctrine of truth. Wherefore, in all these things, the virtue of fortitude conceived within the soul, perseveres with strength, and, in addition proves itself externally upon the neighbor, as I have said to you; and, if fortitude were not able to make that good proof of itself, being tested by many contrarieties, it would not be a serious virtue founded in truth."

A TREATISE OF DISCRETION

How the affection should not place reliance chiefly on penance, but rather on virtues; and how discretion receives life from humility, and renders to each man his due.

"These are the holy and sweet works which I seek from My servants; these are the proved intrinsic virtues of the soul, as I have told you. They not only consist of those virtues which are done by means of the body, that is, with an exterior act, or with diverse and varied penances, which are the instruments of virtue; works of penance performed alone without the above-mentioned virtues would please Me little; often, indeed, if the soul perform not her penance with discretion, that is to say, if her affection be placed principally in the penance she has undertaken, her perfection will be impeded; she should rather place reliance on the affection of love, with a holy hatred of herself, accompanied by true humility and perfect patience, together with the other intrinsic virtues of the soul, with hunger and desire for My honor and the salvation of souls. For these virtues demonstrate that the will is dead, and continually slays its own sensuality through the affection of love of virtue. With this discretion, then, should the soul perform her penance, that is, she should place her principal affection in virtue rather than in penance. Penance should be but the means to increase virtue according to the needs of the individual, and according to what the soul sees she can do in the measure of her own possibility. Otherwise, if the soul place her foundation on penance she will contaminate her own perfection, because her penance will not be done in the light of knowledge of herself and of My goodness, with discretion, and she will not seize hold of My truth; neither loving that which I love, nor hating that which I hate. This virtue of discretion is no other than a true knowledge which the soul should have of herself and of Me, and in this knowledge is virtue rooted. Discretion is the only child of self-knowledge, and, wedding with charity, has indeed many other descendants, as a tree which has many branches; but that which gives life to the tree, to its branches, and its root, is the ground of humility, in which it is planted, which humility is the foster-mother and nurse of charity, by whose means this tree remains in the perpetual calm of discretion. Because otherwise the tree would not produce the virtue of discretion, or any fruit of life, if it were not planted in the virtue of humility, because humility proceeds from self-knowledge. And I have already said to you, that the root of discretion is a real knowledge of self and of My goodness, by which the soul immediately, and discreetly, renders to each one his due. Chiefly to Me in rendering praise and glory to My Name, and in referring to Me the graces and the gifts which she sees and knows she has received from Me; and rendering to herself that which she sees herself to have merited, knowing that she does not even exist of herself, and attributing to Me, and not to herself, her being, which she knows she has received by grace from Me, and every other grace which she has received besides.

"And she seems to herself to be ungrateful for so many benefits, and negligent, in that she has not made the most of her time, and the graces she has received, and so seems to herself worthy of suffering; wherefore she becomes odious and displeasing to herself through her guilt. And this founds the virtue of discretion on knowledge of self, that is, on true humility, for, were this humility not in the soul, the soul would be indiscreet, indiscretion being founded on pride, as discretion is on humility.

"An indiscreet soul robs Me of the honor due to Me, and attributes it to herself, through vainglory, and that which is really her own she imputes to Me, grieving and murmuring concerning My mysteries, with which I work in her soul and in those of My other creatures; wherefore everything in Me and in her neighbor is cause of scandal to her. Contrariwise those who possess the virtue of discretion. For, when they have rendered what is due to Me and to themselves, they proceed to render to their neighbor their principal debt of love, and of humble and continuous prayer, which all should pay to each other, and further, the debt of doctrine, and example of a holy and honorable life, counseling and helping others according to their needs for salvation, as I said to you above. Whatever rank a man be in, whether that of a noble, a prelate, or a servant, if he have this virtue, everything that he does to his neighbor is done discreetly and lovingly, because these virtues are bound and mingled together, and both planted in the ground of humility which proceeds from self-knowledge."

A parable showing how love, humility, and discretion are united; and how the soul should conform herself to this parable.

"Do you know how these three virtues stand together? It is, as if a circle were drawn on the surface of the earth, and a tree, with an off-shoot joined to its side, grew in the center of the circle. The tree is nourished in the earth contained in the diameter of the circle, for if the tree were out of the earth it would die, and give no fruit. Now, consider, in the same way, that the soul is a tree existing by love, and that it can live by nothing else than love; and, that if this soul have not in very truth the divine love of perfect charity, she cannot produce fruit of life, but only of death. It is necessary then, that the root of this tree, that is the affection of the soul, should grow in, and issue from the circle of true self-knowledge which is contained in Me, who have neither beginning nor end, like the circumference of the circle, for, turn as you will within a circle, inasmuch as the circumference has neither end nor beginning, you always remain within it.

"This knowledge of yourself and of Me is found in the earth of true humility, which is as wide as the diameter of the circle, that is as the knowledge of self and of Me (for, otherwise, the circle would not be without end and beginning, but would have its beginning in knowledge of self, and its end in confusion, if this knowledge were not contained in Me). Then the tree of love feeds itself on humility, bringing forth from its side the off-shoot of true discretion, in the way that I have already told you, from the heart of the tree, that is the affection of love which is in the soul, and the patience, which proves that I am in the soul and the soul in Me. This tree then, so sweetly planted, produces fragrant blossoms of virtue, with many scents of great variety, inasmuch as the soul renders fruit of grace and of utility to her neighbor, according to the zeal of those who come to receive fruit from My servants; and to Me she renders the sweet odor of glory and praise to My Name, and so fulfills the object of her creation.

"In this way, therefore, she reaches the term of her being, that is Myself, her God, who am Eternal Life. And these fruits cannot be taken from her without her will, inasmuch as they are all flavored with discretion, because they are all united, as has been said above."

How penance and other corporal exercises are to be taken as instruments
for arriving at virtue, and not as the principal affection of the soul; and
of the light of discretion in various other modes and operations.

"These are the fruits and the works which I seek from the soul, the proving, namely, of virtue in the time of need. And yet some time ago, if you remember, when you were desirous of doing great penance for My sake, asking, 'What can I do to endure suffering for You, oh Lord?' I replied to you, speaking in your mind, 'I take delight in few words and many works.' I wished to show you that he who merely calls on me with the sound of words, saying: 'Lord, Lord, I would do something for You,' and he, who desires for My sake to mortify his body with many penances, and not his own will, did not give Me much pleasure; but that I desired the manifold works of manly endurance with patience, together with the other virtues, which I have mentioned to you above, intrinsic to the soul, all of which must be in activity in order to obtain fruits worthy of grace. All other works, founded on any other principle than this, I judge to be a mere calling with words, because they are finite works, and I, who am Infinite, seek infinite works, that is an infinite perfection of love.

"I wish therefore that the works of penance, and of other corporal exercises, should be observed merely as means, and not as the fundamental affection of the soul. For, if the principal affection of the soul were placed in penance, I should receive a finite thing like a word, which, when it has issued from the mouth, is no more, unless it have issued with affection of the soul, which conceives and brings forth virtue in truth; that is, unless the finite operation, which I have called a word, should be joined with the affection or love, in which case it would be grateful and pleasant to Me. And this is because such a work would not be alone, but accompanied by true discretion, using corporal works as means, and not as the principal foundation; for it would not be becoming that that principal foundation should be placed in penance only, or in any exterior corporal act, such works being finite, since they are done in finite time, and also because it is often profitable that the creature omit them, and even that she be made to do so.

"Wherefore, when the soul omits them through necessity, being unable through various circumstances to complete an action which she has begun, or, as may frequently happen, through obedience at the order of her director, it is well; since, if she continued then to do them, she not only would receive no merit, but would offend Me; thus you see that they are merely finite. She ought, therefore, to adopt them as a means, and not as an end. For, if she takes them as an end she will be obliged, some time or other, to leave them, and will then remain empty. This, My trumpeter, the glorious Paul, taught you when he said in his epistle, that you should mortify the body and destroy self-will, knowing, that is to say, how to keep the rein on the body, macerating the flesh whenever it should wish to combat the spirit, but the will should be dead and annihilated in everything, and subject to My will, and this slaying of the will is that due which, as I told you, the virtue of discretion renders to the soul, that is to say, hatred and disgust of her own offenses and sensuality, which are acquired by self-knowledge. This is the knife which slays and cuts off all self-love founded in self-will. These then are they who give Me not only words but manifold works, and in these I take delight. And then I said that I desired few words, and many actions; by the use of the word 'many' I assign no particular number to you, because the affection of the soul, founded in love, which gives life to all the virtues and good works, should increase infinitely, and yet I do not, by this, exclude words, I merely said that I wished few of them, showing you that every actual operation, as such, was finite, and therefore I called them of little account; but they please Me when they are performed as the instruments of virtue, and not as a principal end in themselves.

"However, no one should judge that he has greater perfection, because he performs great penances, and gives himself in excess to the slaying of his body, than he who does less, inasmuch as neither virtue nor merit consists therein; for otherwise he would be in an evil case, who, from some legitimate reason, was unable to do actual penance. Merit consists in the virtue of love alone, flavored with the light of true discretion, without which the soul is worth nothing. And this love should be directed to Me endlessly, boundlessly, since I am the Supreme and Eternal Truth. The soul can therefore place neither laws nor limits to her love for Me; but her love for her neighbor, on the contrary, is ordered in certain conditions. The light of discretion (which proceeds from love, as I have told you) gives to the neighbor a conditioned love, one that, being ordered aright, does not cause the injury of sin to self in order to be useful to others, for, if one single sin were committed to save the whole world from Hell, or to obtain one great virtue, the motive would not be a rightly ordered or discreet love, but rather indiscreet, for it is not lawful to perform even one act of great virtue and profit to others, by means of the guilt of sin. Holy discretion ordains that the soul should direct all her powers to My service with a manly zeal, and, that she should love her neighbor with such devotion that she would lay down a thousand times, if it were possible, the life of her body for the salvation of souls, enduring pains and torments so that her neighbor may have the life of grace, and giving her temporal substance for the profit and relief of his body.

"This is the supreme office of discretion which proceeds from charity. So you see how discreetly every soul, who wishes for grace, should pay her debts, that is, should love Me with an infinite love and without measure, but her neighbor with measure, with a restricted love, as I have said, not doing herself the injury of sin in order to be useful to others. This is St. Paul's counsel to you when he says that charity ought to be concerned first with self, otherwise it will never be of perfect utility to others. Because, when perfection is not in the soul, everything which the soul does for itself and for others is imperfect. It would not, therefore, be just that creatures, who are finite and created by Me, should be saved through offense done to Me, who am the Infinite Good. The more serious the fault is in such a case, the less fruit will the action produce; therefore, in no way should you ever incur the guilt of sin.

"And this true love knows well, because she carries with herself the light of holy discretion, that light which dissipates all darkness, takes away ignorance, and is the condiment of every instrument of virtue. Holy discretion is a prudence which cannot be cheated, a fortitude which cannot be beaten, a perseverance from end to end, stretching from Heaven to earth, that is, from knowledge of Me to knowledge of self, and from love of Me to love of others. And the soul escapes dangers by her true humility, and, by her prudence, flies all the nets of the world and its creatures, and, with unarmed hands, that is through much endurance, discomfits the devil and the flesh with this sweet and glorious light; knowing, by it, her own fragility, she renders to her weakness its due of hatred.

"Wherefore she has trampled on the world, and placed it under the feet of her affection, despising it, and holding it vile, and thus becoming lord of it, holding it as folly. And the men of the world cannot take her virtues from such a soul, but all their persecutions increase her virtues and prove them, which virtues have been at first conceived by the virtue of love, as has been said, and then are proved on her neighbor, and bring forth their fruit on him. Thus have I shown you, that, if virtue were not visible and did not shine in the time of trial, it would not have been truly conceived; for, I have already told you, that perfect virtue cannot exist and give fruit except by means of the neighbor, even as a woman, who has conceived a child, if she do not bring it forth, so that it may appear before the eyes of men, deprives her husband of his fame of paternity. It is the same with Me, who am the Spouse of the soul, if she do not produce the child of virtue, in the love of her neighbor, showing her child to him who is in need, both in general and in particular, as I have said to you before, so I declare now that, in truth, she has not conceived virtue at all; and this is also true of the vices, all of which are committed by means of the neighbor."

*How this soul grew by means of the divine response, and how
her sorrows grew less, and how she prayed to God for the
Holy Church, and for her own people.*

"Then that soul, thirsting and burning with the very great desire that she had conceived on learning the ineffable love of God, shown in His great goodness, and, seeing the breadth of His charity, that, with such sweetness, He had deigned to reply to her request and to satisfy it, giving hope to the sorrow which she had conceived, on account of offenses against God, and the damage of the Holy Church, and through His own mercy, which she saw through self-knowledge, diminished, and yet, at the same time, increased her sorrow.

"For, the Supreme and Eternal Father, in manifesting the way of perfection, showed her anew her own guilt, and the loss of souls, as has been said more fully above. Also because in the knowledge which the soul obtains of herself, she knows more of God, and knowing the goodness of God in herself, the sweet mirror of God, she knows her own dignity and indignity. Her dignity is that of her creation, seeing that she is the image of God, and this has been given her by grace, and not as her due. In that same mirror of the goodness of God, the soul knows her own indignity, which is the consequence of her own fault. Wherefore, as a man more readily sees spots on his face when he looks in a mirror, so, the soul who, with true knowledge of self, rises with desire, and gazes with the eye of the intellect at herself in the sweet mirror of God, knows better the stains of her own face, by the purity which she sees in Him.

"Wherefore, because light and knowledge increased in that soul in the aforesaid way, a sweet sorrow grew in her, and at the same time, her sorrow was diminished by the hope which the Supreme Truth gave her, and, as fire grows when it is fed with wood, so grew the fire in that soul to such an extent that it was no longer possible for the body to endure it without the departure of the soul; so that, had she not been surrounded by the strength of Him who is the Supreme Strength, it would not have been possible for her to have lived any longer. This soul then, being purified by the fire of divine love, which she found in the knowledge of herself and of God, and her hunger for the salvation of the whole world, and for the reformation of the Holy Church, having grown with her hope of obtaining the same, rose with confidence before the Supreme Father, showing Him the leprosy of the Holy Church, and the misery of the world, saying, as if with the words of Moses, 'My Lord, turn the eyes of Your mercy upon Your people, and upon the mystical body of the Holy Church, for You will be the more glorified if You pardon so many creatures, and give to them the light of knowledge, since all will render You praise when they see themselves escape through Your infinite goodness from the clouds of mortal sin, and from eternal damnation; and then You will not only be praised by my wretched self, who have so much offended You, and who am the cause and the instrument of all this evil, for which reason I pray Your divine and eternal love to take Your revenge on me, and to do mercy to Your people, and never will I depart from before Your presence until I see that you grant them mercy. For what is it to me if I have life, and Your people death, and the clouds of darkness cover Your spouse, when it is my own sins, and not those of Your other creatures, that are the principal cause of this? I desire, then, and beg of You, by Your grace, that You have mercy on Your people, and I adjure You that You do this by Your uncreated love which moved You Yourself to create man in Your image and similitude, saying, "Let us make man in our own image," and this You did, oh eternal Trinity, that man might participate in everything belonging to You, the most high and eternal Trinity.'

"Wherefore You gave him memory in order to receive Your benefits, by which he participates in the power of the Eternal Father; and intellect that he might know, seeing Your goodness, and so might participate in the wisdom of Your only-begotten Son; and will, that he might love that which his intellect has seen and known of Your truth, thus participating in the clemency of Your Holy Spirit. What reason had You for creating man in such dignity? The inestimable love with which You saw Your creature in Yourself, and became enamored of him, for You created him through love, and destined him to be such that he might taste and enjoy Your Eternal Good. I see therefore that through his sin he lost this dignity in which You originally placed him, and by his rebellion against You, fell into a state of war with Your kindness, that is to say, we all became Your enemies.

"Therefore, You, moved by that same fire of love with which You created him, willingly gave man a means of reconciliation, so that after the great rebellion into which he had fallen, there should come a great peace; and so You gave him the only-begotten Word, Your Son, to be the Mediator between us and You. He was our Justice, for He took on Himself all our offenses and injustices, and performed Your obedience, Eternal Father, which You imposed on Him, when You clothed Him with our humanity, our human nature and likeness. Oh, abyss of love! What heart can help breaking when it sees such dignity as Yours descend to such lowliness as our humanity? We are Your image, and You have become ours, by this union which You have accomplished with man, veiling the Eternal Deity with the cloud of woe, and the corrupted clay of Adam. For what reason? - Love. Wherefore, You, O God, have become man, and man has become God. By this ineffable love of Yours, therefore, I constrain You, and implore You that You do mercy to Your creatures."

How God grieves over the Christian people, and particularly over His ministers; and touches on the subject of the Sacrament of Christ's Body, and the benefit of the Incarnation.

Then God, turning the eye of His mercy towards her, allowing Himself to be constrained by her tears, and bound by the chain of her holy desire, replied with lamentation - "My sweetest daughter, your tears constrain Me, because they are joined with My love, and fall for love of Me, and your painful desires force Me to answer you; but marvel, and see how My spouse has defiled her face, and become leprous, on account of her filthiness and self-love, and swollen with the pride and avarice of those who feed on their own sin.

"What I say of the universal body and the mystical body of the Holy Church (that is to say the Christian religion) I also say of My ministers, who stand and feed at the breasts of Holy Church; and, not only should they feed themselves, but it is also their duty to feed and hold to those breasts the universal body of Christian people, and also any other people who should wish to leave the darkness of their infidelity, and bind themselves as members to My Church. See then with what ignorance and darkness, and ingratitude, are administered, and with what filthy hands are handled this glorious milk and blood of My spouse, and with what presumption and irreverence they are received. Wherefore, that which really gives life, often gives, through the defects of those who receive it, death; that is to say, the precious Blood of My only-begotten Son, which destroyed death and darkness, and gave life and truth, and confounded falsehood. For I give this Blood and use It for salvation and perfection in the case of that man who disposes himself properly to receive it, for It gives life and adorns the soul with every grace, in proportion to the disposition and affection of him who receives It; similarly It gives death to him who receives It unworthily, living in iniquity and in the darkness of mortal sin; to him, I say, It gives death and not life; not through defect of the Blood, nor through defect of the minister, though there might be great evil in him, because his evil would not spoil nor defile the Blood nor diminish Its grace and virtue, nor does an evil minister do harm to him to whom he gives the Blood, but to himself he does the harm of guilt, which will be followed by punishment, unless he correct himself with contrition and repentance. I say then that the Blood does harm to him who receives it unworthily, not through defect of the Blood, nor of the minister, but through his own evil disposition and defect inasmuch as he has befouled his mind and body with such impurity and misery, and has been so cruel to himself and his neighbor. He has used cruelty to himself, depriving himself of grace, trampling under the feet of his affection the fruit of the Blood which he had received in Holy Baptism, when the stain of original sin was taken from him by virtue of the Blood, which stain he drew from his origin, when he was generated by his father and mother.

"Wherefore I gave My Word, My only-begotten Son, because the whole stuff of human generation was corrupted through the sin of the first man Adam. Wherefore, all of you, vessels made of this stuff, were corrupted and not disposed to the possession of eternal life - so I, with My dignity, joined Myself to the baseness of your human generation, in order to restore it to grace which you had lost by sin; for I was incapable of suffering, and yet, on account of guilt, My divine justice demanded suffering. But man was not sufficient to satisfy it, for, even if he had satisfied to a certain extent, he could only have satisfied for himself, and not for other rational creatures, besides which, neither for himself, nor for others, could man satisfy, his sin having been committed against Me, who am the Infinite Good. Wishing, however, to restore man, who was enfeebled, and could not satisfy for the above reason, I sent My Word, My own Son, clothed in your own very nature, the corrupted clay of Adam, in order that He might endure suffering in that self-same nature in which man had offended, suffering in His body even to the opprobrious death of the Cross, and so He satisfied My justice and My divine mercy. For My mercy willed to make satisfaction for the sin of man and to dispose him to that good for which I had created him. This human nature, joined with the divine nature, was sufficient to satisfy for the whole human race, not only on account of the pain which it sustained in its finite nature, that is in the flesh of Adam, but by virtue of the Eternal Deity, the divine and infinite nature joined to it. The two natures being thus joined together, I received and accepted the sacrifice of My only-begotten Son, kneaded into one dough with the divine nature, by the fire of divine love which was the fetter which held him fastened and nailed to the Cross in this way. Thus human nature was sufficient to satisfy for guilt, but only by virtue of the divine nature. And in this way was destroyed the stain of Adam's sin, only the mark of it remaining behind, that is an inclination to sin, and to every sort of corporeal defect, like the cicatrice which remains when a man is healed of a wound. In this way the original fault of Adam was able still to cause a fatal stain; wherefore the coming of the great Physician, that is to say, of My only-begotten Son, cured this invalid, He drinking this bitter medicine, which man could not drink on account of his great weakness, like a foster-mother who takes medicine instead of her suckling, because she is grown up and strong, and the child is not fit to endure its bitterness. He was man's foster-mother, enduring, with the greatness and strength of the Deity united with your nature, the bitter medicine of the painful death of the Cross, to give life to you little ones debilitated by guilt. I say therefore that the mark alone of original sin remains, which sin you take from your father and your mother when you were generated by them. But this mark is removed from the soul, though not altogether, by Holy Baptism, which has the virtue of communicating the life of grace by means of that glorious and precious Blood. Wherefore, at the moment that the soul receives Holy Baptism, original sin is taken away from her, and grace is infused into her, and that inclination to sin, which remains from the original corruption, as has been said, is indeed a source of weakness, but the soul can keep the bridle on it if she choose. Then the vessel of the soul is disposed to receive and increase in herself grace, more or less, according as it pleases her to dispose herself willingly with affection, and desire of loving and serving Me; and, in the same way, she can dispose herself to evil as to good, in spite of her having received grace in Holy Baptism. Wherefore when the time of discretion is come, the soul can, by her free will, make choice either of good or evil, according as it pleases her will; and so great is this liberty that man has, and so strong has this liberty been made by virtue of this glorious Blood, that no demon or creature can constrain him to one smallest fault without his free consent. He has been redeemed from slavery, and made free in order that he might govern his own sensuality, and obtain the end for which he was created. Oh, miserable man, who delights to remain in the mud like a brute, and does not learn this great benefit which he has received from Me! A benefit so great, that the poor wretched creature full of such ignorance could receive no greater."

How sin is more gravely punished after the Passion of Christ than before; and how God promises to do mercy to the world, and to the Holy Church, by means of the prayers and sufferings of His servants.

"And I wish you to know, My daughter, that, although I have re-created and restored to the life of grace, the human race, through the Blood of My only-begotten Son, as I have said, men are not grateful, but, going from bad to worse, and from guilt to guilt, even persecuting Me with many injuries, taking so little account of the graces which I have given them, and continue to give them, that, not only do they not attribute what they have received to grace, but seem to themselves on occasion to receive injuries from Me, as if I desired anything else than their sanctification.

"I say to you that they will be more hard-hearted, and worthy of more punishment, and will, indeed, be punished more severely, now that they have received redemption in the Blood of My Son, than they would have been before that redemption took place - that is, before the stain of Adam's sin had been taken away. It is right that he who receives more should render more, and should be under great obligations to Him from whom he receives more.

"Man, then, was closely bound to Me through his being which I have given him, creating him in My own image and similitude; for which reason, he was bound to render Me glory, but he deprived Me of it, and wished to give it to himself. Thus he came to transgress My obedience imposed on him, and became My enemy. And I, with My humility, destroyed his pride, humiliating the divine nature, and taking your humanity, and, freeing you from the service of the devil, I made you free. And, not only did I give you liberty, but, if you examine, you will see that man has become God, and God has become man, through the union of the divine with the human nature. This is the debt which they have incurred - that is to say, the treasure of the Blood, by which they have been procreated to grace. See, therefore, how much more they owe after the redemption than before. For they are now obliged to render Me glory and praise by following in the steps of My Incarnate Word, My only-begotten Son, for then they repay Me the debt of love both of Myself and of their neighbor, with true and genuine virtue, as I have said to you above, and if they do not do it, the greater their debt, the greater will

36

be the offense they fall into, and therefore, by divine justice, the greater their suffering in eternal damnation.

"A false Christian is punished more than a pagan, and the deathless fire of divine justice consumes him more, that is, afflicts him more, and, in his affliction, he feels himself being consumed by the worm of conscience, though, in truth, he is not consumed, because the damned do not lose their being through any torment which they receive. Wherefore I say to you, that they ask for death and cannot have it, for they cannot lose their being; the existence of grace they lose, through their fault, but not their natural existence. Therefore guilt is more gravely punished after the Redemption of the Blood than before, because man received more; but sinners neither seem to perceive this, nor to pay any attention to their own sins, and so become My enemies, though I have reconciled them, by means of the Blood of My Son. But there is a remedy with which I appease My wrath - that is to say, by means of My servants, if they are jealous to constrain Me by their desire. You see, therefore, that you have bound Me with this bond which I have given you, because I wished to do mercy to the world.

"Therefore I give My servants hunger and desire for My honor, and the salvation of souls, so that, constrained by their tears, I may mitigate the fury of My divine justice. Take, therefore, your tears and your sweat, drawn from the fountain of My divine love, and, with them, wash the face of My spouse.

"I promise you, that, by this means, her beauty will be restored to her, not by the knife nor by cruelty, but peacefully, by humble and continued prayer, by the sweat and the tears shed by the fiery desire of My servants, and thus will I fulfill your desire if you, on your part, endure much, casting the light of your patience into the darkness of perverse man, not fearing the world's persecutions, for I will protect you, and My Providence shall never fail you in the slightest need."

How the road to Heaven being broken through the disobedience of Adam, God made of His Son a Bridge by which man could pass.

"Wherefore I have told you that I have made a Bridge of My Word, of My only-begotten Son, and this is the truth. I wish that you, My children, should know that the road was broken by the sin and disobedience of Adam, in such a way, that no one could arrive at Eternal Life. Wherefore men did not render Me glory in the way in which they ought to have, as they did not participate in that Good for which I had created them, and My truth was not fulfilled. This truth is that I have created man to My own image and similitude, in order that he might have Eternal Life, and might partake of Me, and taste My supreme and eternal sweetness and goodness. But, after sin had closed Heaven and bolted the doors of mercy, the soul of man produced thorns and prickly brambles, and My creature found in himself rebellion against himself.

37

"And the flesh immediately began to war against the Spirit, and, losing the state of innocence, became a foul animal, and all created things rebelled against man, whereas they would have been obedient to him, had he remained in the state in which I had placed him. He, not remaining therein, transgressed My obedience, and merited eternal death in soul and body. And, as soon as he had sinned, a tempestuous flood arose, which ever buffets him with its waves, bringing him weariness and trouble from himself, the devil, and the world. Every one was drowned in the flood, because no one, with his own justice alone, could arrive at Eternal Life. And so, wishing to remedy your great evils, I have given you the Bridge of My Son, in order that, passing across the flood, you may not be drowned, which flood is the tempestuous sea of this dark life. See, therefore, under what obligations the creature is to Me, and how ignorant he is, not to take the remedy which I have offered, but to be willing to drown."

How God induces the soul to look at the greatness of this Bridge, inasmuch as it reaches from earth to Heaven.

"Open, my daughter, the eye of your intellect, and you will see the accepted and the ignorant, the imperfect, and also the perfect who follow Me in truth, so that you may grieve over the damnation of the ignorant, and rejoice over the perfection of My beloved servants.

"You will see further how those bear themselves who walk in the light, and those who walk in the darkness. I also wish you to look at the Bridge of My only-begotten Son, and see the greatness thereof, for it reaches from Heaven to earth, that is, that the earth of your humanity is joined to the greatness of the Deity thereby. I say then that this Bridge reaches from Heaven to earth, and constitutes the union which I have made with man.

"This was necessary, in order to reform the road which was broken, as I said to you, in order that man should pass through the bitterness of the world, and arrive at life; but the Bridge could not be made of earth sufficiently large to span the flood and give you Eternal Life, because the earth of human nature was not sufficient to satisfy for guilt, to remove the stain of Adam's sin. Which stain corrupted the whole human race and gave out a stench, as I have said to you above. It was, therefore, necessary to join human nature with the height of My nature, the Eternal Deity, so that it might be sufficient to satisfy for the whole human race, so that human nature should sustain the punishment, and that the Divine nature, united with the human, should make acceptable the sacrifice of My only Son, offered to Me to take death from you and to give you life.

"So the height of the Divinity, humbled to the earth, and joined with your humanity, made the Bridge and reformed the road. Why was this done? In order that man might come to his true happiness with the angels. And observe, that it is not enough, in order that you should have life, that My Son should have made you this Bridge, unless you walk thereon."

How this soul prays God to show her those who cross by
the aforesaid Bridge, and those who do not.

Then this soul exclaimed with ardent love, - "Oh, inestimable Charity, sweet above all sweetness! Who would not be inflamed by such great love? What heart can help breaking at such tenderness? It seems, oh, Abyss of Charity, as if you were mad with love of Your creature, as if You could not live without him, and yet You are our God who have no heed of us, Your greatness does not increase through our good, for You are unchangeable, and our evil causes You no harm, for You are the Supreme and Eternal Goodness. What moves You to do us such mercy through pure love, and on account of no debt that You owed us, or need that You had of us? We are rather Your guilty and malignant debtors. Wherefore, if I understand aright, Oh, Supreme and Eternal Truth, I am the thief and You have been punished for me. For I see Your Word, Your Son, fastened and nailed to the Cross, of which You have made me a Bridge, as You have shown me, Your miserable servant, for which reason, my heart is bursting, and yet cannot burst, through the hunger and the desire which it has conceived towards You. I remember, my Lord, that You were willing to show me who are those who go by the Bridge and those who do not; should it please Your goodness to manifest this to me, willingly would I see and hear it."

How this Bridge has three steps, which signify the three states
of the soul; and how, being lifted on high, yet it is not separated
from the earth; and how these words are to be understood:
"If I am lifted up from the earth, I will draw all things unto Me."

Then the Eternal God, to enamor and excite that soul still more for the salvation of souls, replied to her, and said: "First, as I have shown you that for which you wished, and ask Me, I will now explain to you the nature of this Bridge. I have told you, My daughter, that the Bridge reaches from Heaven to earth; this is through the union which I have made with man, whom I formed of the clay of the earth. Now learn that this Bridge, My only-begotten Son, has three steps, of which two were made with the wood of the most Holy Cross, and the third still retains the great bitterness He tasted, when He was given gall and vinegar to drink. In these three steps you will recognize three states of the soul, which I will explain to you below. The feet of the soul, signifying her affection, are the first step, for the feet carry the body as the affection carries the soul. Wherefore these pierced Feet are steps by which you can arrive at His Side,

39

Which manifests to you the secret of His Heart, because the soul, rising on the steps of her affection, commences to taste the love of His Heart, gazing into that open Heart of My Son, with the eye of the intellect, and finds It consumed with ineffable love. I say consumed, because He does not love you for His own profit, because you can be of no profit to Him, He being one and the same thing with Me. Then the soul is filled with love, seeing herself so much loved. Having passed the second step, the soul reaches out to the third - that is - to the Mouth, where she finds peace from the terrible war she has been waging with her sin. On the first step, then, lifting her feet from the affections of the earth, the soul strips herself of vice; on the second she fills herself with love and virtue; and on the third she tastes peace. So the Bridge has three steps, in order that, climbing past the first and the second, you may reach the last, which is lifted on high, so that the water, running beneath, may not touch it; for, in My Son, was no venom of sin. This Bridge is lifted on high, and yet, at the same time, joined to the earth. Do you know when it was lifted on high? When My Son was lifted up on the wood of the most Holy Cross, the Divine nature remaining joined to the lowliness of the earth of your humanity.

"For this reason I said to you that, being lifted on high, He was not lifted out of the earth, for the Divine nature is united and kneaded into one thing with it. And there was no one who could go on the Bridge until It had been lifted on high, wherefore He said, - 'Si exaltatus fuero a terra omnia traham ad me ipsum,' that is, 'If I am lifted on high I will draw all things to Me.' My Goodness, seeing that in no other way could you be drawn to Me, I sent Him in order that He should be lifted on high on the wood of the Cross, making of it an anvil on which My Son, born of human generation, should be re-made, in order to free you from death, and to restore you to the life of grace; wherefore He drew everything to Himself by this means, namely, by showing the ineffable love, with which I love you, the heart of man being always attracted by love. Greater love, then, I could not show you, than to lay down My life for you; perforce, then, My Son was treated in this way by love, in order that ignorant man should be unable to resist being drawn to Me.

"In very truth, then, My Son said, that, being lifted on high, He would draw all things to Him. And this is to be understood in two ways. Firstly, that, when the heart of man is drawn by the affection of love, as I have said, it is drawn together with all the powers of his soul, that is, with the Memory, the Intellect, and the Will; now, when these three powers are harmoniously joined together in My Name, all the other operations which the man performs, whether in deed or thought, are pleasing, and joined together by the effect of love, because love is lifted on high, following the Sorrowful Crucified One; so My Truth said well, 'If I am lifted on high,' &c., meaning, that if the heart and the powers of the soul are drawn to Him, all the actions are also drawn to Him. Secondly, everything has been created for the service of man, to serve the necessities of rational creatures, and the rational creature has not been made for them, but for Me, in order to serve

Me with all his heart, and with all his affection. See, then, that man being drawn, everything else is drawn with him, because everything else has been made for him. It was therefore necessary that the Bridge should be lifted on high, and have steps, in order that it might be climbed with greater facility."

How this Bridge is built of stones which signify virtues; and how on the Bridge is a hostelry where food is given to the travelers; and how he who goes over the Bridge goes to life, while he who goes under It goes to perdition and death.

"This Bridge is built of stones, so that, if the rain come, it may not impede the traveler. Do you know what these stones are? They are the stones of true and sincere virtues. These stones were not built into the walls before the Passion of My Son, and therefore even those who attempted to walk by the road of virtue were prevented from arriving at their journey's end, because Heaven was not yet unlocked with the key of the Blood, and the rain of Justice did not let them pass; but, after the stones were made, and built up on the Body of My sweet Son, My Word, of whom I have spoken to you, He, who was Himself the Bridge, moistened the mortar for its building with His Blood. That is, His Blood was united with the mortar of divinity, and with the fortitude, and the fire of love; and, by My power, these stones of the virtues were built into a wall, upon Him as the foundation, for there is no virtue which has not been proved in Him, and from Him all virtues have their life. Wherefore no one can have the virtue given by a life of grace, but from Him, that is, without following the footsteps of His doctrine. He has built a wall of the virtues, planting them as living stones, and cementing them with His Blood, so that every believer may walk speedily, and without any servile fear of the rain of Divine justice, for he is sheltered by the mercy which descended from Heaven in the Incarnation of this My Son. How was Heaven opened? With the key of His Blood; so you see that the Bridge is walled and roofed with Mercy. His also is the Hostelry in the Garden of the Holy Church, which keeps and ministers the Bread of Life, and gives to drink of the Blood, so that My creatures, journeying on their pilgrimage, may not, through weariness, faint by the way; and for this reason My love has ordained that the Blood and the Body of My only-begotten Son, wholly God and wholly man, may be ministered to you. The pilgrim, having passed the Bridge, arrives at the door which is part of the Bridge, at which all must enter, wherefore He says: 'I am the Way, the Truth, and the Life, he who follows Me does not walk in darkness, but in light.' And in another place My Truth says, 'That no man can come to Me if not by Him,' and so indeed it is. Therefore He says of Himself that He is the Road, and this is the truth, and I have already shown you that He is a Road in the form of the Bridge. And He says that He is the Truth, and so He is, because

He is united with Me who am the Truth, and he who follows Him, walks in the Truth, and in Life, because he who follows this Truth receives the life of grace, and cannot faint from hunger, because the Truth has become your food, nor fall in the darkness, because He is light without any falsehood. And, with that Truth, He confounded and destroyed the lie that the Devil told to Eve, with which he broke up the road to Heaven, and the Truth brought the pieces together again, and cemented them with His Blood. Wherefore, those who follow this road are the sons of the Truth, because they follow the Truth, and pass through the door of Truth and find themselves united to Me, who am the Door and the Road and at the same time Infinite Peace.

"But he, who walks not on this road, goes under the Bridge, in the river where there are no stones, only water, and since there are no supports in the water, no one can travel that way without drowning; thus have come to pass the sins, and the condition of the world. Wherefore, if the affection is not placed on the stones, but is placed, with disordinate love, on creatures, loving them, and being kept by them far from Me, the soul drowns, for creatures are like water that continually runs past, and man also passes continually like the river, although it seems to him that he stands still and the creatures that he loves pass by, and yet he is passing himself continually to the end of his journey - death! And he would gladly retain himself (that is his life, and the things that he loves), but he does not succeed, either, through death, by which he has to leave them, or through my disposition, by which these created things are taken from the sight of My creatures. Such as these follow a lie, walking on the road of falsehood, and are sons of the Devil, who is the Father of Lies; and, because they pass by the door of falsehood, they receive eternal damnation. So then you see, that I have shown you both Truth and Falsehood, that is, My road which is Truth, and the Devil's which is Falsehood."

How traveling on both of these roads, that is the Bridge and the River, is fatiguing; and of the delight which the soul feels in traveling by the Bridge.

"These are the two roads, and both are hard to travel. Wonder, then, at the ignorance and blindness of man, who, having a Road made for him, which causes such delight to those who use It, that every bitterness becomes sweet, and every burden light, yet prefers to walk over the water. For those who cross by the Bridge, being still in the darkness of the body, find light, and, being mortal, find immortal life, tasting, through love, the light of Eternal Truth which promises refreshment to him who wearies himself for Me, who am grateful and just, and render to every man according as he deserves. Wherefore every good deed is rewarded, and every fault is punished. The tongue would not be sufficient to relate the delight felt by him who goes on this road, for, even in this life, he tastes and participates in that good which has been prepared for him in eternal life. He, therefore, is a fool indeed, who despises so great a good, and chooses rather to receive in this life, the earnest money of Hell, walking by the lower road with great toil, and without any refreshment or advantage. Wherefore, through their sins, they are deprived of Me, who am the Supreme and Eternal Good. Truly then have you reason for grief, and I will that you and My other servants remain in continual bitterness of soul at the offense done to Me, and in compassion for the ignorant, and the loss of those who, in their ignorance, thus offend Me. Now you have seen and heard about this Bridge, how it is, and this I have told you in order to explain My words, that My only-begotten Son was a Bridge. And thus, you see that He is the Truth, made in the way that I have shown you, that is - by the union of height and lowliness."

*How this Bridge, having reached to Heaven on the day
of the Ascension, did not for that reason have the earth.*

"When My only-begotten Son returned to Me, forty days after the resurrection, this Bridge, namely Himself, arose from the earth, that is, from among the conversation of men, and ascended into Heaven by virtue of the Divine Nature and sat at the right hand of Me, the Eternal Father, as the angels said, on the day of the Ascension, to the disciples, standing like dead men, their hearts lifted on high, and ascended into Heaven with the wisdom of My Son - 'Do not stand here any longer, for He is seated at the right hand of the Father!' When He, then, had thus ascended on high, and returned to Me the Father, I sent the Master, that is the Holy Spirit, who came to you with My power and the wisdom of My Son, and with His own clemency, which is the essence of the Holy Spirit. He is one thing with Me, the Father, and with My Son. And He built up the road of the doctrine which My Truth had left in the world. Thus, though the bodily presence of My Son left you, His doctrine remained, and the virtue of the stones founded upon this doctrine, which is the way made for you by this Bridge. For first, He practiced this doctrine and made the road by His actions, giving you His doctrine by example rather than by words; for He practiced, first Himself, what He afterwards taught you, then the clemency of the Holy Spirit made you certain of the doctrine, fortifying the minds of the disciples to confess the truth, and to announce this road, that is, the doctrine of Christ crucified, reproving, by this means, the world of its injustice and false judgment, of which injustice and false judgment, I will in time discourse to you at greater length.

"This much I have said to you in order that there might be no cloud of darkness in the mind of your hearers, that is, that they may know that of this Body of Christ I made a Bridge by the union of the divine with the human nature, for this is the truth.

"This Bridge, taking its point of departure in you, rose into Heaven, and was the one road which was taught you by the example and life of the Truth. What has now remained of all this, and where is the road to be found? I will tell you, that is, I will rather tell those who might fall into ignorance on this point. I tell you that this way of His doctrine, of which I have spoken to you, confirmed by the Apostles, declared by the blood of the martyrs, illuminated by the light of doctors, confessed by the confessors, narrated in all its love by the Evangelists, all of whom stand as witnesses to confess the Truth, is found in the mystical body of the Holy Church. These witnesses are like the light placed on a candlestick, to show forth the way of the Truth which leads to life with a perfect light, as I have said to you, and, as they themselves say to you, with proof, since they have proved in their own cases, that every person may, if he will, be illuminated to know the Truth, unless he choose to deprive his reason of light by his inordinate self-love. It is, indeed, the truth that His doctrine is true, and has remained like a lifeboat to draw the soul out of the tempestuous sea and to conduct her to the port of salvation.

"Wherefore, first I gave you the Bridge of My Son living and conversing in very deed amongst men, and when He, the living Bridge, left you, there remained the Bridge and the road of His doctrine, as has been said, His doctrine being joined with My power and with His wisdom, and with the clemency of the Holy Spirit. This power of Mine gives the virtue of fortitude to whoever follows this road, wisdom gives him light, so that, in this road, he may recognize the truth, and the Holy Spirit gives him love, which consumes and takes away all sensitive love out of the soul, leaving there only the love of virtue. Thus, in both ways, both actually and through His doctrine, He is the Way, the Truth, and the Life; that is, the Bridge which leads you to the height of Heaven. This is what He meant when He said, 'I came from the Father, and I return to the Father, and shall return to you'; that is to say, 'My Father sent Me to you, and made Me your Bridge, so that you might be saved from the river and attain to life.' Then He says, 'I will return to you, I will not leave you orphans, but will send you the Paraclete' - as if My Truth should say, 'I will go to the Father and return; that is, that when the Holy Spirit shall come, who is called the Paraclete, He will show you more clearly, and will confirm you in the way of truth, that I have given you.' He said that He would return, and He did return, because the Holy Spirit came not alone, but with the power of the Father, and the wisdom of the Son, and the clemency of His own Essence.

"See then how He returns, not in actual flesh and blood, but, as I have said, building the road of His doctrine, with His power, which road cannot be destroyed or taken away from him who wishes to follow it, because it is firm and stable, and proceeds from Me, who am immovable.

"Manfully, then, should you follow this road, without any cloud of doubt, but with the light of faith which has been given you as a principle in Holy Baptism.

"Now I have fully shown to you the Bridge as it actually is, and the doctrine, which is one and the same thing with it. And I have shown it to the ignorant, in order that they may see where this road of Truth is, and where stand those who teach it; and I have explained that they are the Apostles, Martyrs, Confessors, Evangelists, and Holy Doctors, placed like lanterns in the Holy Church.

"And I have shown how My Son, returning to Me, none the less, returned to you, not in His bodily presence, but by His power, when the Holy Spirit came upon the disciples, as I have said. For in His bodily presence He will not return until the last Day of Judgment, when He will come again with My Majesty and Divine Power to judge the world, to render good to the virtuous, and reward them for their labors, both in body and soul, and to dispense the evil of eternal death to those who have lived wickedly in the world.

"And now I wish to tell you that which I, the Truth, promised you, that is, to show you the perfect, the imperfect, and the supremely perfect; and the wicked, who, through their iniquities, drown in the river, attaining to punishment and torment; wherefore I say to you, My dearest sons, walk over the Bridge, and not underneath it, because underneath is not the way of truth, but the way of falsehood, by which walk the wicked, of whom I will presently speak to you. These are those sinners for whom I beg you to pray to Me, and for whom I ask in addition your tears and sweat, in order that they may receive mercy from Me."

How this soul wondering at the mercy of God, relates
many gifts and graces given to the human race.

Then this soul, as it were, like one intoxicated, could not contain herself, but standing before the face of God, exclaimed, "How great is the Eternal Mercy with which You cover the sins of Your creatures! I do not wonder that You say of those who abandon mortal sin and return to You, 'I do not remember that you have ever offended Me.' Oh, ineffable Mercy! I do not wonder that You say this to those who are converted, when You say of those who persecute You, 'I wish you to pray for such, in order that I may do them mercy.' Oh, Mercy, who proceeds from Your Eternal Father, the Divinity who governs with Your power the whole world, by You were we created, in You were we re-created in the Blood of Your Son. Your Mercy preserves us, Your Mercy caused Your Son to do battle for us, hanging by His arms on the wood of the Cross, life and death battling together; then life confounded the death of our sin, and the death of our sin destroyed the bodily life of the Immaculate Lamb. Which was finally conquered? Death! By what means? Mercy! Your Mercy gives light and life, by which Your clemency is known in all Your creatures, both the just and the unjust. In the height of Heaven Your Mercy shines, that is, in Your saints. If I turn to the earth, it abounds with Your Mercy. In the darkness of Hell Your Mercy shines, for the damned do not receive the pains they deserve; with Your Mercy You temper Justice. By Mercy You have washed us in the Blood, and by Mercy You wish to converse with Your creatures. Oh, Loving Madman! was it not enough for You to become Incarnate, that You must also die? Was not death enough, that You must also descend into Limbo, taking thence the holy fathers to fulfill Your Mercy and Your Truth in them? Because Your goodness promises a reward to them that serve You in truth, You descended to Limbo, to withdraw from their pain Your servants, and give them the fruit of their labors. Your Mercy constrains You to give even more to man, namely, to leave Yourself to him in food, so that we, weak ones, should have comfort, and the ignorant commemorating You, should not lose the memory of Your benefits. Wherefore every day You give Yourself to man, representing Yourself in the Sacrament of the Altar, in the body of Your Holy Church. What has done this? Your Mercy. Oh, Divine Mercy! My heart suffocates in thinking of you, for on every side to which I turn my thought, I find nothing but mercy. Oh, Eternal Father! Forgive my ignorance, that I presume thus to chatter to You, but the love of Your Mercy will be my excuse before the Face of Your loving-kindness."

Of the baseness of those who pass by the river under the Bridge;
and how the soul, that passes underneath, is called by God the
tree of death, whose roots are held in four vices.

After this soul had refreshed a little her heart in the mercy of God, by these words, she humbly waited for the fulfillment of the promise made to her, and God continuing His discourse said: "Dearest daughter, you have spoken before Me of My mercy, because I gave it you to taste and to see in the word which I spoke to you when I said: 'these are those for whom I pray you to intercede with Me,' but know, that My mercy is without any comparison, far more than you can see, because your sight is imperfect, and My mercy perfect and infinite, so that there can be no comparison between the two, except what may be between a finite and an infinite thing. But I have wished that you should taste this mercy, and also the dignity of man, which I have shown you above, so that you might know better the cruelty of those wicked men who travel below the Bridge. Open the eye of your intellect, and wonder at those who voluntarily drown themselves, and at the baseness to which they are fallen by their fault, from which cause, they have first become weak, and this was when they conceived mortal sin in their minds, for they then bring it forth, and lose the life of grace. And, as a corpse which can have no feeling or movement of itself, but only when it is moved and lifted by others, so those, who are drowned in the stream of disordinate love of the world, are dead to grace. Wherefore because they are dead their memory takes no heed of My mercy. The eye of their intellect sees not and knows not My Truth, because their feeling is dead, that is, their intellect has no object before it but themselves, with the dead love of their own sensuality, and so their will is dead to My will because it loves nothing but dead things. These three powers then being dead, all the soul's operations both in deed and thought are dead as far as grace is concerned. For the soul cannot defend herself against her enemies, nor help herself through her own power, but only so far as she is helped by Me. It is true indeed, that every time that this corpse, in whom only free-will has remained (which remains as long as the mortal body lives), asks My help, he can have it, but never can he help himself; he has become insupportable to himself, and, wishing to govern the world, is governed by that which is not, that is by sin, for sin in itself is nothing, and such men have become the servants and slaves of sin. I have made them trees of love with the life of grace which they received in Holy Baptism; and they have become trees of death, because they are dead, as I have already said to you. Do you know how this tree finds such roots? In the height of pride, which is nourished by their own sensitive self-love. Its branch is their own impatience, and its offshoot indiscretion: these are the four principal vices which destroy the soul of him who is a tree of death, because he has not drawn life from grace. Inside the tree is nourished the worm of conscience, which, while man lives in mortal sin, is blinded by self-love, and therefore felt but little; the fruits of this tree are mortal, for they have drawn their nourishment, which should have been humility, from the roots of pride, and the miserable soul is full of ingratitude, whence proceeds every evil. But if she were grateful for the benefits she has received, she would know Me, and knowing Me would know herself, and so would remain in My love: but she, as if blind, goes groping down the river, and she does not see that the water does not support her."

How the fruits of this tree are as diverse as are the sins;
and first, of the sin of sensuality.

"The fruits of this death-giving tree, are as diverse as sins are diverse. See that some of these fruits are the food of beasts who live impurely, using their body and their mind like a swine who wallows in mud, for in the same way they wallow in the mire of sensuality. Oh, ugly soul, where have you left your dignity? You were made sister to the angels, and now you are become a brute beast. To such misery come sinners, notwithstanding that they are sustained by Me, who am Supreme Purity, notwithstanding that the very devils, whose friends and servants they have become, cannot endure the sight of such filthy actions. Neither does any sin, abominable as it may be, take away the light of the intellect from man, so much as does this one. This the philosophers knew, not by the light of grace, because they had it not, but because nature gave them the light to know that this sin obscured the intellect, and for that reason they preserved themselves in continence the better to study. Thus also they flung away their riches in order that the thought of them should not occupy their heart. Not so does the ignorant and false Christian, who has lost grace by sin."

How the fruit of others is avarice; and of the evils that proceed from it.

"A fruit of the earth belongs to some others, who are covetous misers, acting like the mole, who always feeds on earth till death, and when they arrive at death they find no remedy. Such as these, with their meanness, despise My generosity, selling time to their neighbor. They are cruel usurers, and robbers of their neighbor; because in their memory they have not the remembrance of My mercy, for if they had it they would not be cruel to themselves or to their neighbor; on the contrary, they would be compassionate and merciful to themselves, practicing the virtues on their neighbor and succoring him charitably. Oh, how many are the evils that come of this cursed sin of avarice, how many homicides and thefts, and how much pillage with unlawful gain, and cruelty of heart and injustice! It kills the soul and makes her the slave of riches, so that she cares not to observe My commandments.

"A miser loves no one except for his own profit. Avarice proceeds from and feeds pride, the one follows from the other, because the miser always carries with him the thought of his own reputation, and thus avarice, which is immediately combined with pride, full of its own opinions, goes on from bad to worse. It is a fire which always germinates the smoke of vainglory and vanity of heart, and boasting in that which does not belong to it. It is a root which has many branches, and the principal one is that which makes a man care for his own reputation, from whence proceeds his desire to be greater than his neighbor. It also brings forth the deceitful heart that is neither pure nor liberal, but is double, making a man show one thing with his tongue, while he has another in his heart, and making him conceal the truth and tell lies for his own profit. And it produces envy, which is a worm that is always gnawing, and does not let the miser have any happiness out of his own or others' good. How will these wicked ones in so wretched a state give of their substance to the poor, when they rob others? How will they draw their foul soul out of the mire, when they themselves put it there? Sometimes even do they become so brutish, that they do not consider their children and relations, and cause them to fall with them into great misery. And, nevertheless, in My mercy I sustain them, I do not command the earth to swallow them up, that they may repent of their sins. Would they then give their life for the salvation of souls, when they will not give their substance? Would they give their affections when they are gnawed with envy? Oh, miserable vices that destroy the heaven of the soul. Heaven I call her (the soul) because so I made her, living in her at first by grace, and hiding Myself within her, and making of her a mansion through affection of love. Now she has separated herself from Me, like an adulteress, loving herself, and creatures more than Me, and has made a god of herself, persecuting Me with many and diverse sins. And this she does because she does not consider the benefit of the Blood that was shed with so great Fire of Love."

How some others hold positions of authority, and bring forth fruits of injustice.

"There are others who hold their heads high by their position of authority, and who bear the banner of injustice - using injustice against Me, God, and against their neighbor, and against themselves - to themselves by not paying the debt of virtue, and towards Me by not paying the debt of honor in glorifying and praising My Name, which debt they are bound to pay. But they, like thieves, steal what is Mine, and give it to the service of their own sensuality. So that they commit injustice towards Me and towards themselves, like blind and ignorant men who do not recognize Me in themselves on account of self-love, like the Jews and the ministers of the Law who, with envy and self-love, blinded themselves so that they did not recognize the Truth, My only-begotten Son, and rendered not His due to the Eternal Truth, who was amongst them, as said My Truth: 'The Kingdom of God is among you.' But they knew it not, because, in the aforesaid way, they had lost the light of reason, and so they did not pay their debt of honor and glory to Me, and to Him, who was one thing with Me, and like blind ones committed injustice, persecuting Him with much ignominy, even to the death of the Cross.

"Thus are such as these unjust to themselves, to Me, and to their neighbor, unjustly selling the flesh of their dependents, and of any person who falls into their hands."

How through these and through other defects, one falls into
false judgment; and of the indignity to which one comes.

"By these and by other sins men fall into false judgment, as I will explain to you below. They are continually being scandalized by My works, which are all just, and all performed in truth through love and mercy. With this false judgment, and with the poison of envy and pride, the works of My Son were slandered and unjustly judged, and with lies did His enemies say: 'This man works by virtue of Beelzebub.' Thus wicked men, standing in self-love, impurity, pride, and avarice, and founded in envy, and in perverse rashness with impatience, are forever scandalized at Me and at My servants, whom they judge to be feignedly practicing the virtues, because their heart is rotten, and, having spoiled their taste, good things seem evil to them, and bad things, that is to say disorderly living, seem good to them. Oh, how blind is the human generation in that it considers not its own dignity! From being great you have become small, from a ruler you have become a slave, and that in the vilest service that can be had, because you are the servant and slave of sin, and are become like unto that which you do serve.

"Sin is nothing. You, then, have become nothing; it has deprived you of life, and given you death. This life and power were given you by the Word, My only-begotten Son, the glorious Bridge, He drawing you from out of your servitude when you were servants of the devil, Himself becoming as a servant to take you out of servitude, imposing on Himself obedience to do away the disobedience of Adam, and humbling Himself to the shameful death of the Cross to confound pride. By His death He destroyed every vice, so that no one could say that any vice remained that was not punished and beaten out with pains, as I said to you above, when I said that of His Body He had made an anvil. All the remedies are ready to save men from eternal death, and they despise the Blood, and have trampled It under the feet of their disordinate affection; and it is for this injustice and false judgment that the world is reproved, and will be reproved on the Last Day of Judgment.

"This was meant by My Truth when He said: 'I will send the Paraclete, who will reprove the world of injustice and false judgment.' And it was reproved when I sent the Holy Spirit on the Apostles."

Of the words that Christ said: "I will send the Holy Spirit, who will reprove the world of injustice and of false judgment;" and how one of these reproofs is continuous.

"There are three reproofs. One was given when the Holy Spirit came upon the disciples, who, as it is said, being fortified by My power, and illuminated by the wisdom of My beloved Son, received all in the plenitude of the Holy Spirit. Then the Holy Spirit, who is one thing with Me and with My Son, reproved the world by the mouth of the Apostles, with the doctrine of My Truth. They and all others, who are descended from them, following the truth which they understand through the same means, reprove the world.

"This is that continuous reproof that I make to the world by means of the Holy Scriptures, and My servants, putting the Holy Spirit on their tongues to announce My truth, even as the Devil puts himself on the tongues of his servants, that is to say, of those who pass through the river in iniquity. This is that sweet reproof that I have fixed forever, in the aforesaid way, out of My most great affection of love for the salvation of souls. And they cannot say 'I had no one who reproved me,' because the truth is revealed to them showing them vice and virtue. And I have made them see the fruit of virtue, and the hurtfulness of vice, to give them love and holy fear with hatred of vice and love of virtue, and this truth has not been shown them by an angel, so that they cannot say, 'the angel is a blessed spirit who cannot offend, and feels not the vexations of the flesh as we do, neither the heaviness of our body,' because the Incarnate Word of My Truth has been given to them with your mortal flesh.

"Who were the others who followed this Word? Mortal creatures, susceptible of pain like you, having the same opposition of the flesh to the Spirit, as had the glorious Paul, My standard-bearer, and many other saints who, by one thing or another, have been tormented. Which torments I permitted for the increase of grace and virtue in their souls. Thus, they were born in sin like you, and nourished with a like food, and I am God now as then. My power is not weakened, and cannot become weak. So that I can and will succor him who wishes to be succored by Me. Man wants My succor when he comes out of the river, and walks by the Bridge, following the doctrine of My Truth. Thus no one has any excuse, because both reproof and truth are constantly given to them. Wherefore, if they do not amend while they have time, they will be condemned by the second condemnation which will take place at the extremity of death, when My Justice will cry to them, 'Rise, you dead, and come to judgment!' That is to say, 'You, who are dead to grace, and have reached the moment of your corporal death, arise and come before the Supreme Judge with your injustice and false judgment, and with the extinguished light of faith which you received burning in Holy Baptism (and which you have blown out with the wind of pride), and with the vanity of your heart, with which you set your sails to winds which were contrary to your salvation, for with the wind of self-esteem, you filled the sail of self-love.' Thus you hastened down the stream of the delights and dignities of the world at your own will, following your fragile flesh and the temptations of the devil, who, with the sail of your own will set, has led you along the underway which is a running stream, and so has brought you with himself to eternal damnation."

*Of the second reproof of injustice, and of
false judgment, in general and in particular.*

"This second reproof, dearest daughter, is indeed a condemnation, for the soul has arrived at the end, where there can be no remedy, for she is at the extremity of death, where is the worm of conscience, which I told you was blinded self-love. Now at the time of death, since she cannot get out of My hands, she begins to see, and therefore is gnawed with remorse, seeing that her own sin has brought her into so great evil. But if the soul have light to know and grieve for her fault, not on account of the pain of Hell that follows upon it, but on account of pain at her offense against Me, who am Supreme and Eternal Good, still she can find mercy. But if she pass the Bridge of death without light, and alone, with the worm of conscience, without the hope of the Blood, and bewailing herself more on account of her first condemnation than on account of My displeasure, she arrives at eternal damnation. And then she is reproved cruelly by My Justice of injustice and of false judgment, and not so much of general injustice and false judgment which she has practiced generally in all her works, but much more on

51

account of the particular injustice and false judgment which she practices at the end, in judging her misery greater than My mercy. This is that sin which is neither pardoned here nor there, because the soul would not be pardoned, depreciating My mercy. Therefore is this last sin graver to Me than all the other sins that the soul has committed. Wherefore the despair of Judas displeased Me more, and was more grave to My Son than was his betrayal of Him. So that they are reproved of this false judgment, which is to have held their sin to be greater than My mercy, and, on that account, are they punished with the devils, and eternally tortured with them. And they are reproved of injustice because they grieve more over their condemnation than over My displeasure, and do not render to Me that which is Mine, and to themselves that which is theirs. For to Me, they ought to render love, and to themselves bitterness, with contrition of heart, and offer it to Me, for the offense they have done Me. And they do the contrary because they give to themselves love, pitying themselves, and grieving on account of the pain they expect for their sin; so you see that they are guilty of injustice and false judgment, and are punished for the one and the other together. Wherefore, they, having depreciated My mercy, I with justice send them, with their cruel servant, sensuality, and the cruel tyrant the Devil, whose servants they made themselves through their own sensuality, so that, together, they are punished and tormented, as together they have offended Me. Tormented, I say, by My ministering devils whom My judgment has appointed to torment those who have done evil."

Of the four principal torments of the damned, from which
follow all the others; and particularly of the foulness of the Devil.

"My daughter, the tongue is not sufficient to narrate the pain of these poor souls. As there are three principal vices, namely: self-love, whence proceeds the second, that is love of reputation, whence proceeds the third, that is pride, with injustice and cruelty, and with other filthiness and iniquitous sins, that follow upon these. So I say to you, that in Hell, the souls have four principal torments, out of which proceed all the other torments. The first is, that they see themselves deprived of the vision of Me, which is such pain to them, that, were it possible, they would rather choose the fire, and the tortures and torments, and to see Me, than to be without the torments and not to see Me.

"This first pain revives in them, then, the second, the worm of Conscience, which gnaws unceasingly, seeing that the soul is deprived of Me, and of the conversation of the angels, through her sin, made worthy of the conversation and sight of the devils, which vision of the Devil is the third pain and redoubles to them their every toil. As the saints exult in the sight of Me, refreshing themselves with joyousness in the fruit of their toils borne for Me with such abundance of love, and displeasure of themselves, so does the sight of the Devil revive these wretched ones to torments, because in seeing him they know themselves more, that is to say, they know that, by their own sin, they have made themselves worthy of him. And so the worm of Conscience gnaws more and more, and the fire of this Conscience never ceases to burn. And the sight is more painful to them, because they see him in his own form, which is so horrible that the heart of man could not imagine it. And if you remember well, you know that I showed him to you in his own form for a little space of time, hardly a moment, and you chose (after you had returned to yourself) rather to walk on a road of fire, even until the Day of Judgment, than to see him again. With all this that you have seen, even you do not know well how horrible he is, because, by Divine justice, he appears more horrible to the soul that is deprived of Me, and more or less according to the gravity of her sin. The fourth torment that they have is the fire. This fire burns and does not consume, for the being of the soul cannot be consumed, because it is not a material thing that fire can consume. But I, by Divine justice, have permitted the fire to burn them with torments, so that it torments them, without consuming them, with the greatest pains in diverse ways according to the diversity of their sins, to some more, and to some less, according to the gravity of their fault. Out of these four torments issue all others, such as cold and heat and gnashing of the teeth and many others. Now because they did not amend themselves after the first reproof that they had of injustice and false judgment, neither in the second, which was that, in death, they would not hope in Me, nor grieve for the offense done to Me, but only for their own pain, have they thus so miserably received Eternal Punishment."

Of the third reproof which is made on the Day of Judgment.

"Now it remains to tell of the third reproof which is on the Last Day of Judgment. Already I have told you of two, and now, so that you may see how greatly man deceives himself, I will tell you of the third - of the General Judgment, when the pain of the miserable soul is renewed and increased by the union that the soul will make with the body, with an intolerable reproof, which will generate in it confusion and shame. Know that, in the Last Day of Judgment, when will come the Word - My Son, with My Divine Majesty to reprove the world with Divine Power, He will not come like a poor one, as when He was born, coming in the womb of the Virgin, and being born in a stable amongst the animals, and then dying between two thieves. Then I concealed My power in Him, letting Him suffer pain and torment like man, not that My divine nature was therefore separated from human nature, but I let Him suffer like man to satisfy for your guilt. He will not come thus in that last moment, but He will come, with power, to reprove in His Own Person, and will render to everyone his due, and there will be no one in that Day who will not tremble. To the miserable ones who are damned, His aspect will cause such torment and terror that the tongue cannot describe it. To the just it will cause the fear of reverence with great joy; not that His face changes, because He is unchangeable, being one thing with Me according to the divine nature, and, according to the human nature, His face was unchangeable, after it took the glory of the Resurrection. But, to the eye of the damned, it will appear such, on account of their terrible and darkened vision, that, as the sun which is so bright, appears all darkness to the infirm eye, but to the healthy eye light (and it is not the defect of the light that makes it appear other to the blind than to the illuminated one, but the defect of the eye which is infirm), so will the condemned ones see His countenance in darkness, in confusion, and in hatred, not through defect of My Divine Majesty, with which He will come to judge the world, but through their own defect."

How the damned cannot desire any good.

"And their hatred is so great that they cannot will or desire any good, but they continually blaspheme Me. And do you know why they cannot desire good? Because the life of man ended, free-will is bound. Wherefore they cannot merit, having lost, as they have, the time to do so. If they finish their life, dying in hatred with the guilt of mortal sin, their souls, by divine justice, remain forever bound with the bonds of hatred, and forever obstinate in that evil, in which, therefore, being gnawed by themselves, their pains always increase, especially the pains of those who have been the cause of damnation to others, as that rich man, who was damned, demonstrated to you when he begged the favor that Lazarus might go to his brothers, who were in the world, to tell them of his pains. This, certainly, he did not do out of love or compassion for his brothers, for he was deprived of love and could not desire good, either for My honor or their salvation, because, as I have already told you, the damned souls cannot do any good to their neighbor, and they blaspheme Me, because their life ended in hatred of Me and of virtue. But why then did he do it? He did it because he was the eldest, and had nourished them up in the same miseries in which he had lived, so that he was the cause of their damnation, and he saw pain increased to himself, on account of their damnation when they should arrive in torment together with him, to be gnawed forever by hatred, because in hatred they finished their lives."

Of the glory of the Blessed.

"Similarly, the just soul, for whom life finishes in the affection of charity and the bonds of love, cannot increase in virtue, time having come to naught, but she can always love with that affection with which she comes to Me, and that measure that is measured to her. She always desires Me, and loves Me, and her desire is not in vain - being hungry, she is satisfied, and being satisfied, she has hunger, but the tediousness of satiety and the pain of hunger are far from her. In love, the Blessed rejoice in My eternal vision, participating in that good that I have in Myself, everyone according to his measure, that is that, with that measure of love, with which they have come to Me, is it measured to them. Because they have lived in love of Me and of the neighbor, united together with the general love, and the particular, which, moreover, both proceed from the same love. And they rejoice and exult, participating in each other's good with the affection of love, besides the universal good that they enjoy altogether. And they rejoice and exult with the angels with whom they are placed, according to their diverse and various virtues in the world, being all bound in the bonds of love. And they have a special participation with those whom they closely loved with particular affection in the world, with which affection they grew in grace, increasing virtue, and the one was the occasion to the other of manifesting the glory and praise of My name, in themselves and in their neighbor; and, in the life everlasting, they have not lost their love, but have it still, participating closely, with more abundance, the one with the other, their love being added to the universal good, and I would not that you should think that they have this particular good, of which I have told you, for themselves alone, for it is not so, but it is shared by all the proved citizens, My beloved sons, and all the angels - for, when the soul arrives at eternal life, all participate in the good of that soul, and the soul in their good. Not that her vessel or theirs can increase, nor that there be need to fill it, because it is full, but they have an exultation, a mirthfulness, a jubilee, a joyousness in themselves, which is refreshed by the knowledge that they have found in that soul. They see that, by My mercy, she is raised from the earth with the plenitude of grace, and therefore they exult in Me in the good of that soul, which good she has received through My goodness.

"And that soul rejoices in Me, and in the souls, and in the blessed spirits, seeing and tasting in them the beauty and the sweetness of My love. And their desires forever cry out to Me, for the salvation of the whole world. And because their life ended in the love of the neighbor, they have not left it behind, but, with it, they will pass through the Door, My only-begotten Son in the way that I will relate to you. So you see that in those bonds of love in which they finished their life, they go on and remain eternally. They are conformed so entirely to My will, that they cannot desire except what I desire, because their free-will is bound in the bond of love, in such a way that, time failing them, and, dying in a state of grace, they cannot sin any more. And their will is so united with Mine, that a father or a mother seeing their son, or a son seeing his father or his mother in Hell, do not trouble themselves, and even are contented to see them punished as My enemies. Wherefore in nothing do they disagree with Me, and their desires are all satisfied. The desire of the blessed is to see My honor in you wayfarers, who are pilgrims, forever running on towards the term of death. In their desire for My honor, they desire your salvation, and always pray to Me for you, which desire is fulfilled by Me, when you ignorant ones do not resist My mercy. They have a desire too, to regain the gifts of their body, but this desire does not afflict them, as they do not actually feel it, but they rejoice in tasting the desire, from the certainty they feel of having it fulfilled. Their desire does not afflict them, because, though they have it not yet fulfilled, no bliss is thereby lacking to them. Wherefore they feel not the pain of desire. And think not, that the bliss of the body after the resurrection gives more bliss to the soul, for, if this were so, it would follow that, until they had the body, they had imperfect bliss, which cannot be, because no perfection is lacking to them. So it is not the body that gives bliss to the soul, but the soul will give bliss to the body, because the soul will give of her abundance, and will re-clothe herself on the Last Day of Judgment, in the garments of her own flesh which she had quitted. For, as the soul is made immortal, stayed and established in Me, so the body in that union becomes immortal, and, having lost heaviness, is made fine and light. Wherefore, know that the glorified body can pass through a wall, and that neither water nor fire can injure it, not by virtue of itself, but by virtue of the soul, which virtue is of Me, given to her by grace, and by the ineffable love with which I created her in My image and likeness. The eye of your intellect is not sufficient to see, nor your ear to hear, nor your tongue to tell of the good of the Blessed. Oh, how much delight they have in seeing Me, who am every good! Oh, how much delight they will have in being with the glorified body, though, not having that delight from now to the general Judgment, they have not, on that account, pain, because no bliss is lacking to them, the soul being satisfied in herself, and, as I have told you, the body will participate in this bliss.

"I told you of the happiness which the glorified body would take in the glorified humanity of My only-begotten Son, which gives you assurance of your resurrection. There, they exult in His wounds, which have remained fresh, and the Scars in His Body are preserved, and continually cry for mercy for you, to Me, the Supreme and Eternal Father. And they are all conformed with Him, in joyousness and mirth, and you will all be conformed with Him, eye with eye, and hand with hand, and with the whole Body of the sweet Word My Son, and, dwelling in Me, you will dwell in Him, because He is one thing with Me. But their bodily eye, as I told you, will delight itself in the glorified humanity of the Word, My only-begotten Son. Why so? Because their life finished in the affection of My love, and therefore will this delight endure for them eternally. Not that they can work any good, but they rejoice and delight in that good which they have brought with them, that is, they cannot do any meritorious act, by which they could merit anything, because in this life alone can they merit and sin, according as they please, with free-will.

"These then do not await, with fear, the Divine judgment, but with joy, and the Face of My Son will not seem to them terrible, or full of hatred, because they finished their lives in love and affection for Me, and good-will towards their neighbor. So you see then, that the transformation is not in His Face, when He comes to judge with My Divine Majesty, but in the vision of those who will be judged by Him. To the damned He will appear with hatred and with justice. And to the saved with love and mercy."

How, after the General Judgment, the pain of the damned will increase.

"I have told you of the dignity of the Righteous, so that you may the better know the misery of the damned. For this is another of their pains, namely, the vision of the bliss of the righteous, which is to them an increase of pain, as, to the righteous, the damnation of the damned is an increase of exultation in My goodness. As light is seen better near darkness, and darkness near light, so the sight of the Blessed increases their pain. With pain they await the Last Day of Judgment, because they see, following it, an increase of pain to themselves. And so will it be, because when that terrible voice shall say to them, 'Arise, you dead, and come to judgment,' the soul will return with the body, in the just to be glorified, and in the damned to be tortured eternally. And the aspect of My Truth, and of all the blessed ones will reproach them greatly, and make them ashamed, and the worm of conscience will gnaw the pith of the tree, that is the soul, and also the bark outside, which is the body. They will be reproached by the Blood that was shed for them, and by the works of mercy, spiritual and temporal, which I did for them by means of My Son, and which they should have done for their neighbor, as is contained in the Holy Gospel. They will be reproved for their cruelty towards their neighbor, for their pride and self-love, for their filthiness and avarice; and when they see the mercy that they have received from Me, their reproof will seem to be intensified in harshness. At the time of death, the soul only is reproved, but, at the General Judgment, the soul is reproved together with the body, because the body has been the companion and instrument of the soul - to do good and evil according as the free-will pleased. Every work, good or bad, is done by means of the body. And, therefore, justly, My daughter, glory and infinite good are rendered to My elect ones with their glorified body, rewarding them for the toils they bore for Me, together with the soul. And to the perverse ones will be rendered eternal pains by means of their body, because their body was the instrument of evil. Wherefore, being their body, restored, their pains will revive and increase at the aspect of My Son, their miserable sensuality with its filthiness, in the vision of their nature (that is, the humanity of Christ), united with the purity of My Deity, and of this mass of their Adam nature raised above all the choirs of Angels, and themselves, by their own fault, sunk into the depths of Hell. And they will see generosity and mercy shining in the blessed ones, who receive the fruit of the Blood of the Lamb, the pains that they have borne remaining as ornaments on their bodies, like the dye upon the cloth, not by virtue of the body but only out of the fullness of the soul, representing in the body the fruit of its labor, because it was the companion of the soul in the working of virtue. As in the mirror is represented the face of the man, so in the body is represented the fruit of bodily toils, in the way that I have told you.

"The pain and confusion of the darkened ones, on seeing so great a dignity (of which they are deprived), will increase, and their bodies will appear the sign of the wickedness they have committed, with pain and torture. And when they hear that terrible speech, 'Go, cursed ones, to the Eternal Fire,' the soul and the body will go to be with the Devil without any remedy or hope - each one being wrapped up in diverse filth of earth, according to his evil works. The miser with the filth of avarice, wrapping himself up with the worldly substance which he loved disordinately, and the burning in the fire; the cruel one with cruelty; the foul man with foulness and miserable concupiscence; the unjust with his injustice; the envious with envy; and the hater of his neighbor with hatred. And inordinate self-love, whence were born all their ills, will be burnt with intolerable pain, as the head and principle of every evil, in company with pride. So that body and soul together will be punished in diverse ways. Thus miserably do they arrive at their end who go by the lower way, that is, by the river, not turning back to see their sins and My Mercy. And they arrive at the Gate of the Lie, because they follow the doctrine of the Devil, who is the Father of Lies; and this Devil is their Door, through which they go to Eternal Damnation, as has been said, as the elect and My sons, keeping by the way above, that is by the Bridge, follow the Way of Truth, and this Truth is the Door, and therefore said My Truth, 'No one can go to the Father but by Me.' He is the Door and the Way through which they pass to enter the Sea Pacific. It is the contrary for those who have kept the Way of the Lie, which leads them to the water of death. And it is to this that the Devil calls them, and they are as blind and mad, and do not perceive it, because they have lost the light of faith. The Devil says, as it were, to them: 'Whosoever thirsts for the water of death, let him come and I will give it to him.'"

Of the use of temptations, and how every soul in her extremity sees her final place either of pain or of glory, before she is separated from the body.

"The Devil, dearest daughter, is the instrument of My Justice to torment the souls who have miserably offended Me. And I have set him in this life to tempt and molest My creatures, not for My creatures to be conquered, but that they may conquer, proving their virtue, and receive from Me the glory of victory. And no one should fear any battle or temptation of the Devil that may come to him, because I have made My creatures strong, and have given them strength of will, fortified in the Blood of my Son, which will, neither Devil nor creature can move, because it is yours, given by Me. You therefore, with free arbitration, can hold it or leave it, according as you please. It is an arm, which, if you place it in the hands of the Devil, straightway becomes a knife, with which he strikes you and slays you. But if man do not give this knife of his will into the hands of the Devil, that is, if he do not consent to his temptations and molestations, he will never be injured by the guilt of sin in any temptation, but will even be fortified by it, when the eye of his intellect is opened to see My love which allowed him to be tempted, so as to arrive at virtue, by being proved. For one does not arrive at virtue except through knowledge of self, and knowledge of Me, which knowledge is more perfectly acquired in the time of temptation, because then man knows himself to be nothing, being unable to lift off himself the pains and vexations which he would flee; and he knows Me in his will, which is fortified by My goodness, so that it does not yield to these thoughts. And he has seen that My love permits these temptations, for the devil is weak, and by himself can do nothing, unless I allow him. And I let him tempt, through love, and not through hatred, that you may conquer, and not that you may be conquered, and that you may come to a perfect knowledge of yourself, and of Me, and that virtue may be proved, for it is not proved except by its contrary. You see, then, that he is my Minister to torture the damned in Hell, and in this life, to exercise and prove virtue in the soul. Not that it is the intention of the Devil to prove virtue in you (for he has not love), but rather to deprive you of it, and this he cannot do, if you do not wish it. Now you see, then, how great is the foolishness of men in making themselves feeble, when I have made them strong, and in putting themselves into the hands of the Devil. Wherefore, know, that at the moment of death, they, having passed their life under the lordship of the Devil (not that they were forced to do so, for as I told you they cannot be forced, but they voluntarily put themselves into his hands), and, arriving at the extremity of their death under this perverse lordship, they await no other judgment than that of their own conscience, and desperately, despairingly, come to eternal damnation. Wherefore Hell, through their hate, surges up to them in the extremity of death, and before they get there, they take hold of it, by means of their lord the Devil. As the righteous, who have lived in charity and died in love, if they have lived perfectly in virtue, illuminated with the light of faith, with perfect hope in the Blood of the Lamb, when the extremity of death comes, see the good which I have prepared for them, and embrace it with the arms of love, holding fast with pressure of love to Me, the Supreme and Eternal Good. And so they taste eternal life before they have left the mortal body, that is, before the soul be separated from the body. Others who have passed their lives, and have arrived at the last extremity of death with an ordinary charity (not in that great perfection), embrace My mercy with the same light of faith and hope that had those perfect ones, but, in them, it is imperfect, for, because they were imperfect, they constrained My mercy, counting My mercy greater than their sins. The wicked sinners do the contrary, for, seeing, with desperation, their destination, they embrace it with hatred, as I told you. So that neither the one nor the other waits for judgment, but, in departing this life, they receive every one their place, as I have told you, and they taste it and possess it before they depart from the body, at the extremity of death - the damned with hatred and with despair, and the perfect ones with love and the light of faith and with the hope of the Blood. And the imperfect arrive at the place of Purgatory, with mercy and the same faith."

How the Devil gets hold of souls, under pretense of some good: and, how those are deceived who keep by the river, and not by the aforesaid Bridge, for, wishing to fly pains, they fall into them; and of the vision of a tree, that this soul once had.

"I have told you that the Devil invites men to the water of death, that is, to that which he has, and, blinding them with the pleasures and conditions of the world, he catches them with the hook of pleasure, under the pretense of good, because in no other way could he catch them, for they would not allow themselves to be caught if they saw that no good or pleasure to themselves were to be obtained thereby. For the soul, from her nature, always relishes good, though it is true that the soul, blinded by self-love, does not know and discern what is true good, and of profit to the soul and to the body. And, therefore, the Devil, seeing them blinded by self-love, iniquitously places before them diverse and various delights, colored so as to have the appearance of some benefit or good; and he gives to everyone according to his condition and those principal vices to which he sees him to be most disposed - of one kind to the secular, of another to the religious, and others to prelates and noblemen, according to their different conditions. I have told you this, because I now speak to you of those who drown themselves in the river, and who care for nothing but themselves, to love themselves to My injury, and I will relate to you their end.

"Now I want to show you how they deceive themselves, and how, wishing to flee troubles, they fall into them. For, because it seems to them that following Me, that is, walking by the way of the Bridge, the Word, My Son, is great toil, they draw back, fearing the thorn. This is because they are blinded and do not know or see the Truth, as, you know, I showed you in the beginning of your life, when you prayed Me to have mercy on the world, and draw it out of the darkness of mortal sin. You know that I then showed you Myself under the figure of a Tree, of which you saw neither the beginning nor the end, so that you did not see that the roots were united with the earth of your humanity. At the foot of the Tree, if you remember well, there was a certain thorn, from which thorn all those who love their own sensuality kept away, and ran to a mountain of Lolla, in which you figured to yourself all the delights of the world. That Lolla seemed to be of corn and was not, and, therefore, as you saw, many souls thereon died of hunger, and many, recognizing the deceits of the world, returned to the Tree and passed the thorn, which is the deliberation of the will. Which deliberation, before it is made, is a thorn which appears to man to stand in the way of following the Truth. And conscience always fights on one side, and sensuality on the other; but as soon as he, with hatred and displeasure of himself, manfully makes up his mind, saying, 'I wish to follow Christ crucified,' he breaks at once the thorn, and finds inestimable sweetness, as I showed you then, some finding more and some less, according to their disposition and desire. And you know that then I said to you, 'I am your God, unmoving and unchangeable,' and I do not draw away from any creature who wants to come to Me. I have shown them the Truth, making Myself visible to them, and I have shown them what it is to love anything without Me. But they, as if blinded by the fog of disordinate love, know neither Me nor themselves. You see how deceived they are, choosing rather to die of hunger than to pass a little thorn. And they cannot escape enduring pain, for no one can pass through this life without a cross, far less those who travel by the lower way. Not that My servants pass without pain, but their pain is alleviated. And because - by sin, as I said to you above - the world germinates thorns and tribulations, and because this river flows with tempestuous waters, I gave you the Bridge, so that you might not be drowned.

"I have shown you how they are deceived by a disordinate fear, and how I am your God, immovable, who am not an Acceptor of persons but of holy desire. And this I have shown you under the figure of the Tree, as I told you."

How, the world having germinated thorns, who those are whom they do not harm; although no one passes this life without pain.

"Now I want to show you to whom the thorns and tribulations, that the world germinated through sin, do harm, and to whom they do not. And as, so far, I have shown you the damnation of sinners, together with My goodness, and have told you how they are deceived by their own sensuality, now I wish to tell you how it is only they themselves who are injured by the thorns. No one born passes this life without pain, bodily or mental. Bodily pain My servants bear, but their minds are free, that is, they do not feel the weariness of the pain; for their will is accorded with Mine, and it is the will that gives trouble to man. Pain of mind and of body have those, of whom I have narrated to you, who, in this life, taste the earnest money of hell, as My servants taste the earnest money of eternal life. Do you know what is the special good of the blessed ones? It is having their desire filled with what they desire; wherefore desiring Me, they have Me, and taste Me without any revolt, for they have left the burden of the body, which was a law that opposed the spirit, and came between it and the perfect knowledge of the Truth, preventing it from seeing Me face to face. But after the soul has left the weight of the body, her desire is full, for, desiring to see Me, she sees Me, in which vision

61

is her bliss; and seeing she knows, and knowing she loves, and loving she tastes Me, Supreme and Eternal Good, and, in tasting Me, she is satisfied, and her desire is fulfilled, that is, the desire she had to see and know Me; wherefore desiring she has, and having she desires. And as I told you pain is far from the desire, and weariness from the satisfaction of it. So you see that My servants are blessed principally in seeing and in knowing Me, in which vision and knowledge their will is fulfilled, for they have that which they desired to have, and so are they satisfied. Wherefore I told you that the tasting of eternal life consisted especially in having that which the will desires, and thus being satisfied; but know that the will is satisfied in seeing and knowing Me, as I have told you. In this life then, they taste the earnest money of eternal life, tasting the above, with which I have told you they will be satisfied.

"But how have they the earnest money in this present life? I reply to you, they have it in seeing My goodness in themselves, and in the knowledge of My Truth, which knowledge, the intellect (which is the eye of the soul) illuminated in Me, possesses. This eye has the pupil of the most holy faith, which light of faith enables the soul to discern, to know, and to follow the way and the doctrine of My Truth - the Word Incarnate; and without this pupil of faith she would not see, except as a man who has the form of the eye, but who has covered the pupil (which causes the eye to see) with a cloth. So the pupil of the intellect is faith, and if the soul has covered it with the cloth of infidelity, drawn over it by self-love, she does not see, but only has the form of the eye without the light, because she has hidden it. Thus you see, that in seeing they know, and in knowing they love, and in loving they deny and lose their self-will. Their own will lost, they clothe themselves in Mine, and I will nothing but your sanctification. At once they set to, turning their back to the way below, and begin to ascend by the Bridge, and pass over the thorns, which do not hurt them, their feet being shod with the affection of My love. For I told you that My servants suffered corporally but not mentally, because the sensitive will, which gives pain and afflicts the mind of the creature, is dead. Wherefore, the will not being there, neither is there any pain. They bear everything with reverence, deeming themselves favored in having tribulation for My sake, and they desire nothing but what I desire. If I allow the Devil to trouble them, permitting temptations to prove them in virtue, as I told you above, they resist with their will fortified in Me, humiliating themselves, and deeming themselves unworthy of peace and quiet of mind and deserving of pain, and so they proceed with cheerfulness and self-knowledge, without painful affliction. And if tribulations on man's account, or infirmity, or poverty, or change of worldly condition, or loss of children, or of other much loved creatures (all of which are thorns that the earth produced after sin) come upon them, they endure them all with the light of reason and holy faith, looking to Me, who am the Supreme Good, and who cannot desire other than good, for which I permit these tribulations through love, and not through hatred. And they that love Me recognize this, and, examining themselves, they see their sins, and understand by the light of faith, that good must be rewarded and evil punished. And they see that every little sin merits infinite pain, because it is against Me, who am Infinite Good, wherefore they deem themselves favored because I wish to punish them in this life, and in this finite time; they drive away sin with contrition of heart, and with perfect patience do they merit, and their labors are rewarded with infinite good. Hereafter they know that all labor in this life is small, on account of the shortness of time. Time is as the point of a needle and no more; and, when time has passed labor is ended, therefore you see that the labor is small. They endure with patience, and the thorns they pass through do not touch their heart, because their heart is drawn out of them and united to Me by the affection of love. It is a good truth then that these do taste eternal life, receiving the earnest money of it in this life, and that, though they walk on thorns, they are not pricked, because as I told you, they have known My Supreme Goodness, and sought for it where it was to be found, that is in the Word, My only-begotten son."

How this soul was in great bitterness, on account of the
blindness of those who are drowned below in the river.

Then that soul, tormented by desire, considering her own imperfections and those of others, was saddened to hear of and to see the great blindness of creatures, notwithstanding the great goodness of God, in having placed nothing in this life, no matter in what condition, that could be an impediment to the salvation of creatures, but rather arranged for the exercising and proving of virtue in them. And, notwithstanding all this, she saw them, through self-love and disordinate affection, go under by the river and arrive at eternal damnation, and many who were in the river and had begun to come out, turn back again, scandalized at her, because they had heard of the sweet goodness of GOD, who had deigned to manifest Himself to her. And, for this, she was in bitterness, and fixing the eye of her intellect on the Eternal Father, she said: "Oh, Inestimable Love, great is the delusion of Your creatures. I would that, when it is pleasing to Your Goodness, You would more clearly explain to me the three steps figured in the Body of Your only Son, and what method should be used so as to come entirely out of the depths and to keep the way of Your Truth, and who are those who ascend the staircase."

How the three steps figured in the Bridge, that is, in the
Son of GOD, signify the three powers of the soul.

Then the Divine Goodness, regarding with the eye of His mercy, the hunger and desire of that soul, said: "Oh, My most delightful daughter, I am not a

Despiser, but the Fulfiller of holy desire, and therefore I will show and declare to you that which you ask Me. You ask Me to explain to you the figure of three steps, and to tell you what method they who want to come out of the river must use, to be able to ascend the Bridge. And, although above, in relating to you the delusion and blindness of men, tasting in this life the earnest-money of Hell, and, as martyrs of the Devil, receiving damnation, I showed you the methods they should use; nevertheless, now I will declare it to you more fully, satisfying your desire. You know that every evil is founded in self-love, and that self-love is a cloud that takes away the light of reason, which reason holds in itself the light of faith, and one is not lost without the other. The soul I created in My image and similitude, giving her memory, intellect, and will. The intellect is the most noble part of the soul, and is moved by the affection, and nourishes it, and the hand of love - that is, the affection - fills the memory with the remembrance of Me and of the benefits received, which it does with care and gratitude, and so one power spurs on another, and the soul is nourished in the life of grace.

"The soul cannot live without love, but always wants to love something, because she is made of love, and, by love, I created her. And therefore I told you that the affection moved the intellect, saying, as it were, 'I will love, because the food on which I feed is love.' Then the intellect, feeling itself awakened by the affection, says, as it were, 'If you will love, I will give you that which you can love.' And at once it arises, considering carefully the dignity of the soul, and the indignity into which she has fallen through sin. In the dignity of her being it tastes My inestimable goodness, and the increate charity with which I created her, and, in contemplating her misery, it discovers and tastes My mercy, and sees how, through mercy, I have lent her time and drawn her out of darkness. Then the affection nourishes itself in love, opening the mouth of holy desire, with which it eats hatred and displeasure of its own sensuality, united with true humility and perfect patience, which it drew from holy hatred. The virtues conceived, they give birth to themselves perfectly and imperfectly, according as the soul exercises perfection in herself, as I will tell you below. So, on the contrary, if the sensual affection wants to love sensual things, the eye of the intellect set before itself for its sole object transitory things, with self-love, displeasure of virtue, and love of vice, whence she draws pride and impatience, and the memory is filled with nothing but that which the affection presents to it. This love so dazzles the eye of the intellect that it can discern and see nothing but such glittering objects. It is the very brightness of the things that causes the intellect to perceive them and the affection to love them; for had worldly things no such brightness there would be no sin, for man, by his nature, cannot desire anything but good, and vice, appearing to him thus, under color of the soul's good, causes him to sin. But, because the eye, on account of its blindness, does not discern, and knows not the truth, it errs, seeking good and delights there where they are not.

"I have already told you that the delights of the world, without Me, are venomous thorns, and, that the vision of the intellect is deluded by them, and the affection of the will is deluded into loving them, and the memory into retaining remembrance of them. The unity of these powers of the soul is so great that I cannot be offended by one without all the others offending Me at the same time, because the one presents to the other, as I told you, good or evil, according to the pleasure of the free will. This free will is bound to the affection, and it moves as it pleases, either with the light of reason or without it. Your reason is attached to Me when your will does not, by disordinate love, cut it off from Me; you have also in you the law of perversity, that continually fights against the Spirit. You have, then, two parts in you - sensuality and reason. Sensuality is appointed to be the servant, so that, with the instrument of the body, you may prove and exercise the virtues. The soul is free, liberated from sin by the Blood of My Son, and she cannot be dominated unless she consent with her will, which is controlled by her free choice, and when this free choice agrees with the will, it becomes one thing with it. And I tell you truly, that, when the soul undertakes to gather together, with the hand of free choice, her powers in My Name, then are assembled all the actions, both spiritual and temporal, that the creature can do, and free choice gets rid of sensuality and binds itself with reason. I, then, by grace, rest in the midst of them; and this is what My truth, the Word Incarnate, meant, when He said: 'When there are two or three or more gathered together in My name, there am I in the midst of them.' And this is the truth. I have already told you that no one could come to Me except by Him, and therefore I made of Him a Bridge with three steps. And those three steps figure, as I will narrate to you below, the three states of the soul."

How if the three aforesaid powers are not united, there cannot
be perseverance, without which no man arrives at his end.

"I have explained to you the figure of the three steps, in general, as the three powers of the soul, and no one who wishes to pass by the Bridge and doctrine of My Truth can mount one without the other, and the soul cannot persevere except by the union of her three powers. Of which I told you above, when you asked Me, how the voyagers could come out of the river. There are two goals, and, for the attainment of either, perseverance is needful - they are vice and virtue. If you desire to arrive at life, you must persevere in virtue, and if you would have eternal death, you must persevere in vice. Thus it is with perseverance that they who want life arrive at Me who am Life, and with perseverance that they who taste the water of death arrive at the Devil."

An exposition on Christ's words: "Whosoever thirsts,
let him come to Me and drink."

"You were all invited, generally and in particular, by My Truth, when He cried in the Temple, saying: 'Whosoever thirsts, let him come to Me and drink, for I am the Fountain of the Water of Life.' He did not say 'Go to the Father and drink,' but He said 'Come to Me.' He spoke thus, because in Me, the Father, there can be no pain, but in My Son there can be pain. And you, while you are pilgrims and wayfarers in this mortal life, cannot be without pain, because the earth, through sin, brought forth thorns. And why did He say 'Let him come to Me and drink'? Because whoever follows His doctrine, whether in the most perfect way or by dwelling in the life of common charity, finds to drink, tasting the fruit of the Blood, through the union of the Divine nature with the human nature. And you, finding yourselves in Him, find yourselves also in Me, who am the Sea Pacific, because I am one thing with Him, and He with Me. So that you are invited to the Fountain of Living Water of Grace, and it is right for you, with perseverance, to keep by Him who is made for you a Bridge, not being turned back by any contrary wind that may arise, either of prosperity or adversity, and to persevere till you find Me, who am the Giver of the Water of Life, by means of this sweet and amorous Word, My only-begotten Son. And why did He say: 'I am the Fountain of Living Water'? Because He was the Fountain which contained Me, the Giver of the Living Water, by means of the union of the Divine with the human nature. Why did He say 'Come to Me and drink'? Because you cannot pass this mortal life without pain, and in Me, the Father, there can be no pain, but in Him there can be pain, and therefore of Him did I make for you a Bridge. No one can come to Me except by Him, as He told you in the words: 'No one can come to the Father except by Me.'

"Now you have seen to what way you should keep, and how, namely with perseverance, otherwise you shall not drink, for perseverance receives the crown of glory and victory in the life everlasting."

The general method by which every rational creature can come
out of the sea of the world, and go by the aforesaid holy Bridge.

"I will now return to the three steps, which you must climb in order to issue from the river without drowning, and attain to the Living Water, to which you are invited, and to desire My Presence in the midst of you. For in this way, in which you should follow, I am in your midst, reposing, by grace, in your souls. In order to have desire to mount the steps, you must have thirst, because only those who thirst are invited: 'Whosoever thirsts, let him come to Me and drink.' He who

66

has no thirst will not persevere, for either fatigue causes him to stop, or pleasure, and he does not care to carry the vessel with which he may get the water, and neither does he care for the company, and alone he cannot go, and he turns back at the smallest prick of persecution, for he loves it not. He is afraid because he is alone; were he accompanied he would not fear, and had he ascended the three steps he would not have been alone, and would, therefore, have been secure. You must then have thirst and gather yourselves together, as it is said, 'two or three or more.'

"Why is it said 'two or three or more'? Because there are not two without three, nor three without two, neither three nor two without more. The number one is excluded, for, unless a man has a companion, I cannot be in the midst; this is no indifferent trifle, for he who is wrapped up in self-love is solitary.

"Why is he solitary? Because he is separated from My grace and the love of his neighbor, and being, by sin, deprived of Me, he turns to that which is naught, because I am He that is. So that he who is solitary, that is, who is alone in self-love, is not mentioned by My Truth and is not acceptable to Me. He says then: 'If there be two or three or more gathered together in My name, I will be in the midst of them.' I said to you that two were not without three, nor three without two, and so it is. You know that the commandments of the Law are completely contained in two, and if these two are not observed the Law is not observed. The two commandments are to love Me above everything, and your neighbor as yourself, which two are the beginning, the middle and the end of the Law. These two cannot be gathered together in My Name, without three, that is without the congregation of the powers of the soul, the memory, the intellect, and the will; the memory to retain the remembrance of My benefits and My goodness, the intellect to gaze into the ineffable love, which I have shown you by means of My only-begotten Son, whom I have placed as the object of the vision of your intellect, so that, in Him, you behold the fire of My charity, and the will to love and desire Me, who am your End. When these virtues and powers of the soul are congregated together in My Name, I am in the midst of them by grace, and a man, who is full of My love and that of his neighbor, suddenly finds himself the companion of many and royal virtues. Then the appetite of the soul is disposed to thirst. Thirst, I say, for virtue, and the honor of My Name and salvation of souls, and his every other thirst is spent and dead, and he then proceeds securely without any servile fear, having ascended the first step of the affection, for the affection, stripped of self-love, mounts above itself and above transitory things, or, if he will still hold them, he does so according to My will - that is, with a holy and true fear, and love of virtue. He then finds that he has attained to the second step - that is, to the light of the intellect, which is, through Christ crucified, mirrored in cordial love of Me, for through Him have I shown My love to man. He finds peace and quiet, because the memory is filled with My love. You know that an empty thing, when touched, resounds, but not so when it is full. So memory, being filled with the light of the intellect, and the affection with love, on being moved by the tribulations or delights of the world, will not resound with disordinate merriment or with impatience, because they are full of Me, who am every good.

"Having climbed the three steps, he finds that the three powers of the soul have been gathered together by his reason in My Name. And his soul, having gathered together the two commandments, that is love of Me and of the neighbor, finds herself accompanied by Me, who am her strength and security, and walks safely because I am in the midst of her. Wherefore then he follows on with anxious desire, thirsting after the way of Truth, in which way he finds the Fountain of the Water of Life, through his thirst for My honor and his own salvation and that of his neighbor, without which thirst he would not be able to arrive at the Fountain. He walks on, carrying the vessel of the heart, emptied of every affection and disordinate love of the world, but filled immediately it is emptied with other things, for nothing can remain empty, and, being without disordinate love for transitory things, it is filled with love of celestial things, and sweet Divine love, with which he arrives at the Fountain of the Water of Life, and passes through the Door of Christ crucified, and tastes the Water of Life, finding himself in Me, the Sea Pacific."

How this devoted soul looking in the Divine mirror
saw the creatures going in diverse ways.

Then that soul, tormented with intense desire, gazing into the sweet Divine mirror, saw creatures setting out to attain their end in diverse ways and with diverse considerations. She saw that many began to mount, feeling themselves pricked by servile fear, that is, fearing their own personal pain, and she saw others, practicing this first state, arriving at the second state, but few she saw who arrived at the greatest perfection.

How servile fear is not sufficient, without the love of virtue,
to give eternal life; and how the law of fear and that of love are united.

Then the goodness of God, wishing to satisfy the desire of that soul, said, "Do you see those? They have arisen with servile fear from the vomit of mortal sin, but, if they do not arise with love of virtue, servile fear alone is not sufficient to give eternal life. But love with holy fear is sufficient, because the law is founded in love and holy fear. The old law was the law of fear, that was given by Me to Moses, by which law they who committed sin suffered the penalty of it. The new law is the law of love, given by the Word of My only-begotten Son, and is founded in love alone. The new law does not break the old law, but rather fulfills it, as said My Truth, 'I come not to destroy the law, but to fulfill it.' And He united the law of fear with that of love. Through love was taken away the imperfection of the fear of the penalty, and the perfection of holy fear remained, that is, the fear of offending, not on account of one's own damnation, but of offending Me, who am Supreme Good. So that the imperfect law was made perfect with the law of love. Wherefore, after the car of the fire of My only-begotten Son came and brought the fire of My charity into your humanity with abundance of mercy, the penalty of the sins committed by humanity was taken away, that is, he who offended was no longer punished suddenly, as was of old given and ordained in the law of Moses.

"There is, therefore, no need for servile fear; and this does not mean that sin is not punished, but that the punishment is reserved, unless, that is to say, the person punish himself in this life with perfect contrition. For, in the other life, the soul is separated from the body, wherefore while man lives is his time for mercy, but when he is dead comes the time of justice. He ought, then, to arise from servile fear, and arrive at love and holy fear of Me, otherwise there is no remedy against his falling back again into the river, and reaching the waters of tribulation, and seeking the thorns of consolation, for all consolations are thorns that pierce the soul who loves them disordinately."

How, by exercising oneself in servile fear, which is the state of imperfection, by which is meant the first step of the holy Bridge, one arrives at the second step, which is the state of perfection.

"I told you that no one could go by the Bridge or come out of the river without climbing the three steps, which is the truth. There are some who climb imperfectly, and some perfectly, and some climb with the greatest perfection. The first are those who are moved by servile fear, and have climbed so far being imperfectly gathered together; that is to say, the soul, having seen the punishment which follows her sin, climbs; and gathers together her memory to recollect her vice, her intellect to see the punishment which she expects to receive for her fault, and her will to move her to hate that fault. And let us consider this to be the first step and the first gathering together of the powers of the soul, which should be exercised by the light of the intellect with the pupil of the eye of holy faith, which looks, not only at the punishment of sin, but at the fruit of virtue, and the love which I bear to the soul, so that she may climb with love and affection, and stripped of servile fear. And doing so, such souls will become faithful and not unfaithful servants, serving Me through love and not through fear, and if, with hatred of sin, they employ their minds to dig out the root of their self-love with prudence, constancy, and perseverance they will succeed in doing so. But there are many who begin their course climbing so slowly, and render their debt to

Me by such small degrees, and with such negligence and ignorance, that they suddenly faint, and every little breeze catches their sails, and turns their prow backwards. Wherefore, because they imperfectly climb to the first Step of the Bridge of Christ crucified, they do not arrive at the second step of His Heart."

Of the imperfection of those who love GOD
for their own profit, delight, and consolation.

"Some there are who have become faithful servants, serving Me with fidelity without servile fear of punishment, but rather with love. This very love, however, if they serve Me with a view to their own profit, or the delight and pleasure which they find in Me, is imperfect. Do you know what proves the imperfection of this love? The withdrawal of the consolations which they found in Me, and the insufficiency and short duration of their love for their neighbor, which grows weak by degrees, and oftentimes disappears. Towards Me their love grows weak when, on occasion, in order to exercise them in virtue and raise them above their imperfection, I withdraw from their minds My consolation and allow them to fall into battles and perplexities. This I do so that, coming to perfect self-knowledge, they may know that of themselves they are nothing and have no grace, and accordingly in time of battle fly to Me, as their Benefactor, seeking Me alone, with true humility, for which purpose I treat them thus, without drawing from them consolation indeed, but not grace. At such a time these weak ones, of whom I speak, relax their energy, impatiently turning backwards, and sometimes abandon, under color of virtue, many of their exercises, saying to themselves, This labor does not profit me. All this they do, because they feel themselves deprived of mental consolation. Such a soul acts imperfectly, for she has not yet unwound the bandage of spiritual self-love, for, had she unwound it she would see that, in truth, everything proceeds from Me, that no leaf of a tree falls to the ground without My providence, and that what I give and promise to My creatures, I give and promise to them for their sanctification, which is the good and the end for which I created them. My creatures should see and know that I wish nothing but their good, through the Blood of My only-begotten Son, in which they are washed from their iniquities. By this Blood they are enabled to know My Truth, how, in order to give them eternal life, I created them in My image and likeness and re-created them to grace with the Blood of My Son, making them sons of adoption. But, since they are imperfect, they make use of Me only for their own profit, relaxing their love for their neighbor. Thus, those in the first state come to naught through the fear of enduring pain, and those in the second, because they slacken their pace, ceasing to render service to their neighbor, and withdrawing their charity if they see their own profit or consolation withdrawn from them: this happens because their love was originally impure, for they gave to their neighbor the same imperfect love which they gave to Me, that is to say, a love based only on desire of their own advantage. If, through a desire for perfection, they do not recognize this imperfection of theirs, it is impossible that they should not turn back. For those who desire Eternal Life, a pure love, prescinding from themselves, is necessary, for it is not enough for eternal life to fly sin from fear of punishment, or to embrace virtue from the motive of one's own advantage. Sin should be abandoned because it is displeasing to Me, and virtue should be loved for My sake. It is true that, generally speaking, every person is first called in this way, but this is because the soul herself is at first imperfect, from which imperfection she must advance to perfection, either while she lives, by a generous love to Me with a pure and virtuous heart that takes no thought for herself, or, at least, in the moment of death, recognizing her own imperfection, with the purpose, had she but time, of serving Me, irrespectively of herself. It was with this imperfect love that S. Peter loved the sweet and good Jesus, My only-begotten Son, enjoying most pleasantly His sweet conversation, but, when the time of trouble came, he failed, and so disgraceful was his fall, that, not only could he not bear any pain himself, but his terror of the very approach of pain caused him to fall, and deny the Lord, with the words, 'I have never known Him.' The soul who has climbed this step with servile fear and mercenary love alone, falls into many troubles. Such souls should arise and become sons, and serve Me, irrespective of themselves, for I, who am the Rewarder of every labor, render to each man according to his state and his labor; wherefore, if these souls do not abandon the exercise of holy prayer and their other good works, but go on, with perseverance, to increase their virtues, they will arrive at the state of filial love, because I respond to them with the same love, with which they love Me, so that, if they love Me, as a servant does his master, I pay them their wages according to their deserts, but I do not reveal Myself to them, because secrets are revealed to a friend, who has become one thing with his friend, and not to a servant. Yet it is true, that a servant may so advance by the virtuous love, which he bears to his master, as to become a very dear friend, and so do some of these of whom I have spoken, but while they remain in the state of mercenary love, I do not manifest Myself to them. If they, through displeasure at their imperfection, and love of virtue, dig up, with hatred, the root of spiritual self-love, and mount to the throne of conscience, reasoning with themselves, so as to quell the motions of servile fear in their heart, and to correct mercenary love by the light of the holy faith, they will be so pleasing to Me, that they will attain to the love of the friend. And I will manifest Myself to them, as My Truth said in these words: 'He who loves Me shall be one thing with Me and I with him, and I will manifest Myself to him and we will dwell together.' This is the state of two dear friends, for though they are two in body, yet they are one in soul through the affection of love, because love transforms the lover into the object loved, and where two friends have one soul, there can be no secret between them, wherefore My Truth said: 'I will come and we will dwell together,' and this is the truth."

Of the way in which GOD manifests Himself to the soul who loves Him.

"Do you know how I manifest Myself to the soul who loves Me in truth, and follows the doctrine of My sweet and amorous Word? In many is My virtue manifested in the soul in proportion to her desire, but I make three special manifestations. The first manifestation of My virtue, that is to say, of My love and charity in the soul, is made through the Word of My Son, and shown in the Blood, which He spilled with such fire of love. Now this charity is manifested in two ways; first, in general, to ordinary people, that is to those who live in the ordinary grace of God. It is manifested to them by the many and diverse benefits which they receive from Me. The second mode of manifestation, which is developed from the first, is peculiar to those who have become My friends in the way mentioned above, and is known through a sentiment of the soul, by which they taste, know, prove, and feel it. This second manifestation, however, is in men themselves; they manifesting Me, through the affection of their love. For though I am no Acceptor of creatures, I am an Acceptor of holy desires, and Myself in the soul in that precise degree of perfection which she seeks in Me. Sometimes I manifest Myself (and this is also a part of the second manifestation) by endowing men with the spirit of prophecy, showing them the things of the future. This I do in many and diverse ways, according as I see need in the soul herself and in other creatures. At other times the third manifestation takes place. I then form in the mind the presence of the Truth, My only-begotten Son, in many ways, according to the will and the desire of the soul. Sometimes she seeks Me in prayer, wishing to know My power, and I satisfy her by causing her to taste and see My virtue. Sometimes she seeks Me in the wisdom of My Son, and I satisfy her by placing His wisdom before the eye of her intellect, sometimes in the clemency of the Holy Spirit and then My Goodness causes her to taste the fire of Divine charity, and to conceive the true and royal virtues, which are founded on the pure love of her neighbor."

Why Christ did not say "I will manifest
My Father," but "I will manifest myself."

"You see now how truly My Word spoke, when He said: 'He who loves Me shall be one thing with Me.' Because, by following His doctrine with the affection of love, you are united with Him, and, being united with Him, you are united with Me, because We are one thing together. And so it is that I manifest Myself to you, because We are one and the same thing together. Wherefore if My Truth said, 'I will manifest Myself to you,' He said the truth, because, in manifesting Himself, He manifested Me, and, in manifesting Me, He manifested Himself. But why did

He not say, 'I will manifest My Father to you'? For three reasons in particular. First, because He wished to show that He and I are not separate from each other, on which account He also made the following reply to S. Philip, when he said to Him, 'Show us the Father, and it is enough for us.' My Word said, 'Who sees Me sees the Father, and who sees the Father sees Me.' This He said because He was one thing with Me, and that which He had, He had from Me, I having nothing from Him; wherefore, again, He said to Judas, 'My doctrine is not Mine, but My Father's who sent Me,' because My Son proceeds from Me, not I from Him, though I with Him and He with Me are but one thing. For this reason He did not say 'I will manifest the Father,' but 'I will manifest Myself,' being one thing with the Father. The second reason was because, in manifesting Himself to you, He did not present to you anything He had not received from Me, the Father. These words, then, mean, the Father has manifested Himself to Me, because I am one thing with Him, and I will manifest to you, by means of Myself, Me and Him. The third reason was, because I, being invisible, could not be seen by you, until you should be separated from your bodies. Then, indeed, will you see Me, your GOD, and My Son, the Word, face to face. From now until after the general Resurrection, when your humanity will be conformed with the humanity of the Eternal Word, according to what I told you in the treatise of the Resurrection, you can see Me, with the eye of the intellect alone, for, as I am, you cannot see Me now. Wherefore I veiled the Divine nature with your humanity, so that you might see Me through that medium. I, the Invisible, made Myself, as it were, visible by sending you the Word, My Son, veiled in the flesh of your humanity. He manifested Me to you. Therefore it was that He did not say 'I will manifest the Father to you,' but rather, 'I will manifest Myself to you,' as if He should say, 'According as My Father manifests himself to Me, will I manifest myself to you, for in this manifestation of Himself, He manifests Me.' Now therefore you understand why He did not say 'I will manifest the Father to you.' Both, because such a vision is impossible for you, while yet in the mortal body, and because He is one thing with Me."

*How the soul, after having mounted the first step
of the Bridge, should proceed to mount the second.*

"You have now seen how excellent is the state of him who has attained to the love of a friend; climbing with the foot of affection, he has reached the secret of the Heart, which is the second of the three steps figured in the Body of My Son. I have told you what was meant by the three powers of the soul, and now I will show you how they signify the three states, through which the soul passes. Before treating of the third state, I wish to show you how a man becomes a friend and how, from a friend, he grows into a son, attaining to filial love, and how a man may know if he has become a friend. And first of how a man arrives at being a friend. In the beginning, a man serves Me imperfectly through servile fear, but, by exercise and perseverance, he arrives at the love of delight, finding his own delight and profit in Me. This is a necessary stage, by which he must pass, who would attain to perfect love, to the love that is of friend and son. I call filial love perfect, because thereby, a man receives his inheritance from Me, the Eternal Father, and because a son's love includes that of a friend, which is why I told you that a friend grows into a son. What means does he take to arrive thereat? I will tell you. Every perfection and every virtue proceeds from charity, and charity is nourished by humility, which results from the knowledge and holy hatred of self, that is, sensuality. To arrive thereat, a man must persevere, and remain in the cellar of self-knowledge in which he will learn My mercy, in the Blood of My only-begotten Son, drawing to Himself, with this love, My divine charity, exercising himself in the extirpation of his perverse self-will, both spiritual and temporal, hiding himself in his own house, as did Peter, who, after the sin of denying My Son, began to weep. Yet his lamentations were imperfect and remained so, until after the forty days, that is until after the Ascension. But when My Truth returned to Me, in His humanity, Peter and the others concealed themselves in the house, awaiting the coming of the Holy Spirit, which My Truth had promised them. They remained barred in from fear, because the soul always fears until she arrives at true love. But when they had persevered in fasting and in humble and continual prayer, until they had received the abundance of the Holy Spirit, they lost their fear, and followed and preached Christ crucified. So also the soul, who wishes to arrive at this perfection, after she has risen from the guilt of mortal sin, recognizing it for what it is, begins to weep from fear of the penalty, whence she rises to the consideration of My mercy, in which contemplation, she finds her own pleasure and profit. This is an imperfect state, and I, in order to develop perfection in the soul, after the forty days, that is after these two states, withdraw Myself from time to time, not in grace but in feeling. My Truth showed you this when He said to the disciples 'I will go and will return to you.'

"Everything that He said was said primarily, and in particular, to the disciples, but referred in general to the whole present and future, to those, that is to say, who should come after. He said 'I will go and will return to you;' and so it was, for, when the Holy Spirit returned upon the disciples, He also returned, as I told you above, for the Holy Spirit did not return alone, but came with My power, and the wisdom of the Son, who is one thing with Me, and with His own clemency, which proceeds from Me the Father, and from the Son. Now, as I told you, in order to raise the soul from imperfection, I withdraw Myself from her sentiment, depriving her of former consolations. When she was in the guilt of mortal sin, she had separated herself from Me, and I deprived her of grace through her own guilt, because that guilt had barred the door of her desires. Wherefore the sun of grace did not shine, not through its own defect, but through the defect of the creature, who bars the door of desire. When she knows herself and her darkness, she opens the window and vomits her filth, by holy confession. Then I, having returned to the soul by grace, withdraw Myself from her by sentiment, which I do in order to humiliate her, and cause her to seek Me in truth, and to prove her in the light of faith, so that she come to prudence. Then, if she love Me without thought of self, and with lively faith and with hatred of her own sensuality, she rejoices in the time of trouble, deeming herself unworthy of peace and quietness of mind. Now comes the second of the three things of which I told you, that is to say: how the soul arrives at perfection, and what she does when she is perfect. This is what she does. Though she perceives that I have withdrawn Myself, she does not, on that account, look back, but perseveres with humility in her exercises, remaining barred in the house of self-knowledge, and, continuing to dwell therein, awaits, with lively faith, the coming of the Holy Spirit, that is of Me, who am the fire of charity. How does she await me? Not in idleness, but in watching and continued prayer, and not only with physical, but also with intellectual watching, that is, with the eye of her mind alert, and, watching with the light of faith, she extirpates, with hatred, the wandering thoughts of her heart, looking for the affection of My charity, and knowing that I desire nothing but her sanctification, which is certified to her in the Blood of My Son. As long as her eye thus watches, illumined by the knowledge of Me and of herself, she continues to pray with the prayer of holy desire, which is a continued prayer, and also with actual prayer, which she practices at the appointed times, according to the orders of Holy Church. This is what the soul does in order to rise from imperfection and arrive at perfection, and it is to this end, namely that she may arrive at perfection, that I withdraw from her, not by grace but by sentiment. Once more do I leave her, so that she may see and know her defects, so that, feeling herself deprived of consolation and afflicted by pain, she may recognize her own weakness, and learn how incapable she is of stability or perseverance, thus cutting down to the very root of spiritual self-love, for this should be the end and purpose of all her self-knowledge, to rise above herself, mounting the throne of conscience, and not permitting the sentiment of imperfect love to turn again in its death-struggle, but, with correction and reproof, digging up the root of self-love, with the knife of self-hatred and the love of virtue."

How an imperfect lover of GOD loves his neighbor
also imperfectly, and of the signs of this imperfect love.

"And I would have you know that just as every imperfection and perfection is acquired from Me, so is it manifested by means of the neighbor. And simple souls, who often love creatures with spiritual love, know this well, for, if they have received My love sincerely without any self-regarding considerations, they satisfy the thirst of their love for their neighbor equally sincerely. If a man carry away the vessel which he has filled at the fountain and then drink of it, the vessel becomes empty, but if he keep his vessel standing in the fountain, while he drinks, it always remains full. So the love of the neighbor, whether spiritual or temporal, should be drunk in Me, without any self-regarding considerations. I require that you should love Me with the same love with which I love you. This indeed you cannot do, because I loved you without being loved. All the love which you have for Me you owe to Me, so that it is not of grace that you love Me, but because you ought to do so. While I love you of grace, and not because I owe you My love. Therefore to Me, in person, you cannot repay the love which I require of you, and I have placed you in the midst of your fellows, that you may do to them that which you cannot do to Me, that is to say, that you may love your neighbor of free grace, without expecting any return from him, and what you do to him, I count as done to Me, which My Truth showed forth when He said to Paul, My persecutor - 'Saul, Saul, why persecute you Me?' This He said, judging that Paul persecuted Him in His faithful. This love must be sincere, because it is with the same love with which you love Me, that you must love your neighbor. Do you know how the imperfection of spiritual love for the creature is shown? It is shown when the lover feels pain if it appear to him that the object of his love does not satisfy or return his love, or when he sees the beloved one's conversation turned aside from him, or himself deprived of consolation, or another loved more than he. In these and in many other ways can it be seen that his neighborly love is still imperfect, and that, though his love was originally drawn from Me, the Fountain of all love, he took the vessel out of the water, in order to drink from it. It is because his love for Me is still imperfect, that his neighborly love is so weak, and because the root of self-love has not been properly dug out. Wherefore I often permit such a love to exist, so that the soul may in this way come to the knowledge of her own imperfection, and for the same reason do I withdraw myself from the soul by sentiment, that she may be thus led to enclose herself in the house of self-knowledge, where is acquired every perfection. After which I return into her with more light and with more knowledge of My Truth, in proportion to the degree in which she refers to grace the power of slaying her own will. And she never ceases to cultivate the vine of her soul, and to root out the thorns of evil thoughts, replacing them with the stones of virtues, cemented together in the Blood of Christ crucified, which she has found on her journey across the Bridge of Christ, My only-begotten Son. For I told you, if you remember, that upon the Bridge, that is, upon the doctrine of My Truth, were built up the stones, based upon the virtue of His Blood, for it is in virtue of this Blood that the virtues give life."

A TREATISE OF PRAYER

Of the means which the soul takes to arrive at pure
and generous love; and here begins the Treatise of Prayer.

"When the soul has passed through the doctrine of Christ crucified, with true love of virtue and hatred of vice, and has arrived at the house of self-knowledge and entered therein, she remains, with her door barred, in watching and constant prayer, separated entirely from the consolations of the world. Why does she thus shut herself in? She does so from fear, knowing her own imperfections, and also from the desire, which she has, of arriving at pure and generous love. And because she sees and knows well that in no other way can she arrive thereat, she waits, with a lively faith for My arrival, through increase of grace in her. How is a lively faith to be recognized? By perseverance in virtue, and by the fact that the soul never turns back for anything, whatever it be, nor rises from holy prayer, for any reason except (note well) for obedience or charity's sake. For no other reason ought she to leave off prayer, for, during the time ordained for prayer, the Devil is wont to arrive in the soul, causing much more conflict and trouble than when the soul is not occupied in prayer. This he does in order that holy prayer may become tedious to the soul, tempting her often with these words: 'This prayer avails you nothing, for you need attend to nothing except your vocal prayers.' He acts thus in order that, becoming wearied and confused in mind, she may abandon the exercise of prayer, which is a weapon with which the soul can defend herself from every adversary, if grasped with the hand of love, by the arm of free choice in the light of the Holy Faith."

Here, touching something concerning the Sacrament of the Body of Christ,
the complete doctrine is given; and how the soul proceeds from vocal to
mental prayer, and a vision is related which this devout soul once received.

"Know, dearest daughter, how, by humble, continual, and faithful prayer, the soul acquires, with time and perseverance, every virtue. Wherefore should she persevere and never abandon prayer, either through the illusion of the Devil or her own fragility, that is to say, either on account of any thought or movement coming from her own body, or of the words of any creature. The Devil often places himself upon the tongues of creatures, causing them to chatter nonsensically, with the purpose of preventing the prayer of the soul. All of this she should pass by, by means of the virtue of perseverance. Oh, how sweet and pleasant to that soul and to Me is holy prayer, made in the house of knowledge of self and of

Me, opening the eye of the intellect to the light of faith, and the affections to the abundance of My charity, which was made visible to you, through My visible only-begotten Son, who showed it to you with His blood! Which Blood inebriates the soul and clothes her with the fire of divine charity, giving her the food of the Sacrament [which is placed in the tavern of the mystical body of the Holy Church] that is to say, the food of the Body and Blood of My Son, wholly God and wholly man, administered to you by the hand of My vicar, who holds the key of the Blood. This is that tavern, which I mentioned to you, standing on the Bridge, to provide food and comfort for the travelers and the pilgrims, who pass by the way of the doctrine of My Truth, lest they should faint through weakness. This food strengthens little or much, according to the desire of the recipient, whether he receives sacramentally or virtually. He receives sacramentally when he actually communicates with the Blessed Sacrament. He receives virtually when he communicates, both by desire of communion, and by contemplation of the Blood of Christ crucified, communicating, as it were, sacramentally, with the affection of love, which is to be tasted in the Blood which, as the soul sees, was shed through love. On seeing this the soul becomes inebriated, and blazes with holy desire and satisfies herself, becoming full of love for Me and for her neighbor. Where can this be acquired? In the house of self-knowledge with holy prayer, where imperfections are lost, even as Peter and the disciples, while they remained in watching and prayer, lost their imperfection and acquired perfection. By what means is this acquired? By perseverance seasoned with the most holy faith.

"But do not think that the soul receives such ardor and nourishment from prayer, if she pray only vocally, as do many souls whose prayers are rather words than love. Such as these give heed to nothing except to completing Psalms and saying many paternosters. And when they have once completed their appointed tale, they do not appear to think of anything further, but seem to place devout attention and love in merely vocal recitation, which the soul is not required to do, for, in doing only this, she bears but little fruit, which pleases Me but little. But if you ask Me, whether the soul should abandon vocal prayer, since it does not seem to all that they are called to mental prayer, I should reply 'No.' The soul should advance by degrees, and I know well that, just as the soul is at first imperfect and afterwards perfect, so also is it with her prayer. She should nevertheless continue in vocal prayer, while she is yet imperfect, so as not to fall into idleness. But she should not say her vocal prayers without joining them to mental prayer, that is to say, that while she is reciting, she should endeavor to elevate her mind in My love, with the consideration of her own defects and of the Blood of My only-begotten Son, wherein she finds the breadth of My charity and the remission of her sins. And this she should do, so that self-knowledge and the consideration of her own defects should make her recognize My goodness in herself and continue her exercises with true humility. I do not wish defects to be considered in particular, but in general, so that the mind may not be contaminated by the remembrance of particular and hideous sins. But, as I said, I do not wish the soul to consider her sins, either in general or in particular, without also remembering the Blood and the broadness of My mercy, for fear that otherwise she should be brought to confusion. And together with confusion would come the Devil, who has caused it, under color of contrition and displeasure of sin, and so she would arrive at eternal damnation, not only on account of her confusion, but also through the despair which would come to her, because she did not seize the arm of My mercy. This is one of the subtle devices with which the Devil deludes My servants, and, in order to escape from his deceit, and to be pleasing to Me, you must enlarge your hearts and affections in My boundless mercy, with true humility. You know that the pride of the Devil cannot resist the humble mind, nor can any confusion of spirit be greater than the broadness of My good mercy, if the soul will only truly hope therein. Wherefore it was, if you remember rightly, that, once, when the Devil wished to overthrow you, by confusion, wishing to prove to you that your life had been deluded, and that you had not followed My will, you did that which was your duty, which My goodness (which is never withheld from him who will receive it) gave you strength to do, that is you rose, humbly trusting in My mercy, and saying: 'I confess to my Creator that my life has indeed been passed in darkness, but I will hide myself in the wounds of Christ crucified, and bathe myself in His Blood and so shall my iniquities be consumed, and with desire will I rejoice in my Creator.' You remember that then the Devil fled, and, turning round to the opposite side, he endeavored to inflate you with pride, saying: 'You are perfect and pleasing to God, and there is no more need for you to afflict yourself or to lament your sins.' And once more I gave you the light to see your true path, namely, humiliation of yourself, and you answered the Devil with these words: 'Wretch that I am, John the Baptist never sinned and was sanctified in his mother's womb. And I have committed so many sins, and have hardly begun to know them with grief and true contrition, seeing who God is, who is offended by me, and who I am, who offend Him.' Then the Devil, not being able to resist your humble hope in My goodness, said to you: 'Cursed that you are, for I can find no way to take you. If I put you down through confusion, you rise to Heaven on the wings of mercy, and if I raise you on high, you humble yourself down to Hell, and when I go into Hell you persecute me, so that I will return to you no more, because you strike me with the stick of charity.' The soul, therefore, should season the knowledge of herself with the knowledge of My goodness, and then vocal prayer will be of use to the soul who makes it, and pleasing to Me, and she will arrive, from the vocal imperfect prayer, exercised with perseverance, at perfect mental prayer; but if she simply aims at completing her tale, and, for vocal abandons mental prayer, she will never arrive at it. Sometimes the soul will be so ignorant that, having resolved to say so many prayers vocally, and I, visiting her mind sometimes in one way, and sometimes in another, in a flash of self-knowledge or of contrition for sin, sometimes in the broadness of My charity, and sometimes by placing before her mind, in diverse ways, according to My pleasure and the desire of the soul, the presence of My Truth, she (the soul), in order to complete her tale, will abandon My visitation, that she feels, as it were, by conscience, rather than abandon that which she had begun. She should not do so, for, in so doing, she yields to a deception of the Devil. The moment she feels her mind disposed by My visitation, in the many ways I have told you, she should abandon vocal prayer; then, My visitation past, if there be time, she can resume the vocal prayers which she had resolved to say, but if she has not time to complete them, she ought not on that account to be troubled or suffer annoyance and confusion of mind; of course provided that it were not the Divine office which clerics and religious are bound and obliged to say under penalty of offending Me, for, they must, until death, say their office. But if they, at the hour appointed for saying it, should feel their minds drawn and raised by desire, they should so arrange as to say it before or after My visitation, so that the debt of rendering the office be not omitted. But, in any other case, vocal prayer should be immediately abandoned for the said cause. Vocal prayer, made in the way that I have told you, will enable the soul to arrive at perfection, and therefore she should not abandon it, but use it in the way that I have told you.

And so, with exercise in perseverance, she will taste prayer in truth, and the food of the Blood of My only-begotten Son, and therefore I told you that some communicated virtually with the Body and Blood of Christ, although not sacramentally; that is, they communicate in the affection of charity, which they taste by means of holy prayer, little or much, according to the affection with which they pray. They who proceed with little prudence and without method, taste little, and they who proceed with much, taste much. For the more the soul tries to loosen her affection from herself, and fasten it in Me with the light of the intellect, the more she knows; and the more she knows, the more she loves, and, loving much, she tastes much. You see then, that perfect prayer is not attained to through many words, but through affection of desire, the soul raising herself to Me, with knowledge of herself and of My mercy, seasoned the one with the other. Thus she will exercise together mental and vocal prayer, for, even as the active and contemplative life is one, so are they. Although vocal or mental prayer can be understood in many and diverse ways, for I have told you that a holy desire is a continual prayer, in this sense that a good and holy will disposes itself with desire to the occasion actually appointed for prayer in addition to the continual prayer of holy desire, wherefore vocal prayer will be made at the appointed time by the soul who remains firm in a habitual holy will, and will sometimes be continued beyond the appointed time, according as charity commands for the salvation of the neighbor, if the soul see him to be in need, and also her own necessities according to the state in which I have placed her. Each one, according to his condition, ought to exert himself for the salvation of souls, for this exercise lies at the root of a holy will, and whatever he may contribute, by words or deeds, towards the salvation of his neighbor, is virtually a prayer, although it does not replace a prayer which one should make oneself at the appointed season, as My glorious standard-bearer Paul said, in the words, 'He who ceases not to work ceases not to pray.' It was for this reason that I told you that prayer was made in many ways, that is, that actual prayer may be united with mental prayer if made with the affection of charity, which charity is itself continual prayer. I have now told you how mental prayer is reached by exercise and perseverance, and by leaving vocal prayer for mental when I visit the soul. I have also spoken to you of common prayer, that is, of vocal prayer in general, made outside of ordained times, and of the prayers of good-will, and how every exercise, whether performed in oneself or in one's neighbor, with good-will, is prayer. The enclosed soul should therefore spur herself on with prayer, and when she has arrived at friendly and filial love she does so. Unless the soul keep to this path, she will always remain tepid and imperfect, and will only love Me and her neighbor in proportion to the pleasure which she finds in My service."

Of the method by which the soul separates herself from imperfect love, and attains to perfect love, friendly and filial.

"Hitherto I have shown you in many ways how the soul raises herself from imperfection and attains to perfection, which she does after she has attained to friendly and filial love. I tell you that she arrives at perfect love by means of perseverance, barring herself into the House of Self-Knowledge, which knowledge of self requires to be seasoned with knowledge of Me, lest it bring the soul to confusion, for it would cause the soul to hate her own sensitive pleasure and the delight of her own consolations. But from this hatred, founded in humility, she will draw patience, with which she will become strong against the attacks of the Devil, against the persecutions of man, and towards Me, when, for her good, I withdraw delight from her mind. And if her sensuality, through malevolence, should lift its head against reason, the judgment of conscience should rise against it, and, with hatred of it, hold out reason against it, not allowing such evil emotions to get by it. Though sometimes the soul who lives in holy hatred corrects and reproves herself, not only for those things that are against reason, but also for things that in reality come from Me, which is what My sweet servant S. Gregory meant, when he said that a holy and pure conscience made sin where there was no sin, that is, that through purity of conscience, it saw sin where there was no sin.

"Now the soul who wishes to rise above imperfection should await My Providence in the House of Self-Knowledge, with the light of faith, as did the disciples, who remained in the house in perseverance and in watching, and in humble and continual prayer, awaiting the coming of the Holy Spirit. She should remain fasting and watching, the eye of her intellect fastened on the doctrine of My Truth, and she will become humble because she will know herself in humble and continual prayer and holy and true desire."

Of the signs by which the soul knows she has arrived at perfect love.

"It now remains to be told you how it can be seen that souls have arrived at perfect love. This is seen by the same sign that was given to the holy disciples after they had received the Holy Spirit, when they came forth from the house, and fearlessly announced the doctrine of My Word, My only-begotten Son, not fearing pain, but rather glorying therein. They did not mind going before the tyrants of the world, to announce to them the truth, for the glory and praise of My Name. So the soul, who has awaited Me in self-knowledge as I have told you, receives Me, on My return to her, with the fire of charity, in which charity, while still remaining in the house with perseverance, she conceives the virtues by affection of love, participating in My power; with which power and virtues she overrules and conquers her own sensitive passions, and through which charity she participates in the wisdom of My Son, in which she sees and knows, with the eye of her intellect, My Truth and the deceptions of spiritual self-love, that is, the imperfect love of her own consolations, as has been said, and she knows also the malice and deceit of the devil, which he practices on those souls who are bound by that imperfect love. She therefore arises, with hatred of that imperfection and with love of perfection, and, through this charity, which is of the Holy Spirit, she participates in His will, fortifying her own to be willing to suffer pain, and, coming out of the house through My Name, she brings forth the virtues on her neighbor. Not that by coming out to bring forth the virtues, I mean that she issues out of the House of Self-Knowledge, but that, in the time of the neighbor's necessity she loses that fear of being deprived of her own consolations, and so issues forth to give birth to those virtues which she has conceived through affection of love. The souls, who have thus come forth, have reached the fourth state, that is, from the third state, which is a perfect state, in which they taste charity and give birth to it on their neighbors, they have arrived at the fourth state, which is one of perfect union with Me. The two last-mentioned states are united, that is to say, one cannot be without the other, for there cannot be love of Me, without love of the neighbor, nor love of the neighbor without love of Me."

How they who are imperfect desire to follow the Father alone, but they who are perfect desire to follow the Son. And of a vision, which this holy soul had, concerning diverse baptisms, and of many other beautiful and useful things.

"As I have told you, these latter have issued forth from the house, which is a sign that they have arisen from imperfection and arrived at perfection. Open the eye of your intellect and see them running by the Bridge of the doctrine of Christ crucified, which was their rule, way, and doctrine. They place none other before the eye of their intellect than Christ crucified, not the Father, as they do who are in imperfect love and do not wish to suffer pain, but only to have the delight which they find in Me. But they, as if drunken with love and burning with it, have gathered together and ascended the three steps, which I figured to you as the three powers of the soul, and also the three actual steps, figured to you as in the Body of My only Son, Christ crucified, by which steps the soul, as I told you, ascended, first climbing to the Feet, with the feet of the soul's affection, from thence arriving at the Side, where she found the secret of the Heart and knew the baptism of water, which has virtue through the Blood, and where I dispose the soul to receive grace, uniting and kneading her together in the Blood. Where did the soul know of this her dignity, in being kneaded and united with the Blood of the Lamb, receiving the grace in Holy Baptism, in virtue of the Blood? In the Side, where she knew the fire of divine Charity, and so, if you remember well, My Truth manifested to you, when you asked, saying: 'Sweet and Immaculate Lamb, You were dead when Your side was opened. Why then did You want to be struck and have Your heart divided?' And He replied to you, telling you that there was occasion enough for it; but the principal part of what He said I will tell you. He said: Because My desire towards the human generation was ended, and I had finished the actual work of bearing pain and torment, and yet I had not been able to show, by finite things, because My love was infinite, how much more love I had, I wished you to see the secret of the Heart, showing it to you open, so that you might see how much more I loved than I could show you by finite pain. I poured from it Blood and Water, to show you the baptism of water, which is received in virtue of the Blood. I also showed the baptism of love in two ways, first in those who are baptized in their blood, shed for Me, which has virtue through My Blood, even if they have not been able to have Holy Baptism, and also in those who are baptized in fire, not being able to have Holy Baptism, but desiring it with the affection of love. There is no baptism of fire without the Blood, because the Blood is steeped in and kneaded with the fire of Divine charity, because, through love was It shed. There is yet another way by which the soul receives the baptism of Blood, speaking, as it were, under a figure, and this way the Divine charity provided, knowing the infirmity and fragility of man, through which he offends, not that he is obliged, through his fragility and infirmity, to commit sin unless he wish to do so; but, falling, as he will, into the guilt of mortal sin, by which he loses the grace which he drew from Holy Baptism in virtue of the Blood, it was necessary to leave a continual baptism of Blood. This the Divine charity provided in the Sacrament of Holy Confession, the soul receiving the Baptism of Blood, with contrition of heart, confessing, when able, to My ministers, who hold the keys of the Blood, sprinkling It, in absolution, upon the face of the soul. But, if the soul be unable to confess, contrition of heart is sufficient for this baptism, the hand of My clemency giving you the fruit of this precious Blood. But if you are able to confess, I wish you to do so, and if you are able to, and do not, you will be deprived of the fruit of the Blood. It is true that, in the last extremity, a man, desiring to confess and not being able to, will receive the fruit of this baptism, of which I have been speaking. But let no one be so mad as so to arrange his deeds, that, in the hope of receiving it, he puts off confessing until the last extremity of death, when he may not be able to do so. In which case, it is not at all certain that I shall not say to him, in My Divine Justice: 'You did not remember Me in the time of your life, when you could, now will I not remember you in your death.'

"You see then that these Baptisms, which you should all receive until the last moment, are continual, and though My works, that is the pains of the Cross were finite, the fruit of them which you receive in Baptism, through Me, are infinite. This is in virtue of the infinite Divine nature, united with the finite human nature, which human nature endures pain in Me, the Word, clothed with your humanity. But because the one nature is steeped in and united with the other, the Eternal Deity drew to Himself the pain, which I suffered with so much fire and love. And therefore can this operation be called infinite, not that My pain, neither the actuality of the body be infinite, nor the pain of the desire that I had to complete your redemption, because it was terminated and finished on the Cross, when the Soul was separated from the Body; but the fruit, which came out of the pain and desire for your salvation, is infinite, and therefore you receive it infinitely. Had it not been infinite, the whole human generation could not have been restored to grace, neither the past, the present, nor the future. This I manifested in the opening of My Side, where is found the secret of the Heart, showing that I loved more than I could show, with finite pain. I showed to you that My love was infinite. How? By the Baptism of Blood, united with the fire of My charity, and by the general baptism, given to Christians, and to whomsoever will receive it, and by the baptism of water, united with the Blood and the fire, wherein the soul is steeped. And, in order to show this, it was necessary for the Blood to come out of My Side. Now I have shown you (said My Truth to you) what you asked of Me."

How worldly people render glory and praise to GOD, whether they will or no.

"And so perfect is her vision that she sees the glory and praise of My Name, not so much in the angelic nature as in the human, for, whether worldly people will or no, they render glory and praise to My Name, not that they do so in the way they should, loving Me above everything, but that My mercy shines in them, in that, in the abundance of My charity, I give them time, and do not order the earth to open and swallow them up on account of their sins. I even wait for them, and command the earth to give them of her fruits, the sun to give them light and warmth, and the sky to move above them. And in all things created and made for them, I use My charity and mercy, withdrawing neither on account of their sins. I even give equally to the sinner and the righteous man, and often more to the sinner than to the righteous man, because the righteous man is able to endure privation, and I take from him the goods of the world that he may the more abundantly enjoy the goods of heaven. So that in worldly men My mercy and charity shine, and they render praise and glory to My Name, even when they persecute My servants; for they prove in them the virtues of patience and charity, causing them to suffer humbly and offer to Me their persecutions and injuries, thus turning them into My praise and glory.

"So that, whether they will or no, worldly people render to My Name praise and glory, even when they intend to do Me infamy and wrong."

How even the devils render glory and praise to GOD.

"Sinners, such as those of whom I have just spoken, are placed in this life in order to augment virtues in My servants, as the devils are in Hell as My justiciars and augmenters of My Glory; that is, My instruments of justice towards the damned, and the augmenters of My Glory in My creatures, who are wayfarers and pilgrims on their journey to reach Me, their End. They augment in them the virtues in diverse ways, exercising them with many temptations and vexations, causing them to injure one another and take one another's property, and not for the motive of making them receive injury or be deprived of their property, but only to deprive them of charity. But in thinking to deprive My servants, they fortify them, proving in them the virtues of patience, fortitude, and perseverance. Thus they render praise and glory to My Name, and My Truth is fulfilled in them, which Truth created them for the praise and glory of Me, Eternal Father, and that they might participate in My beauty. But, rebelling against Me in their pride, they fell and lost their vision of Me, wherefore they rendered not to Me glory through the affection of love, and I, Eternal Truth, have placed them as instruments to exercise My servants in virtue in this life and as justiciars to those who go, for their sins, to the pains of Purgatory. So you see that My Truth is fulfilled in them, that is, that they render Me glory, not as citizens of life eternal, of which they are deprived by their sins, but as My justiciars, manifesting justice upon the damned, and upon those in Purgatory."

How the soul, after she has passed through this life, sees fully
the praise and glory of My Name in everything, and, though,
in her the pain of desire is ended, the desire is not.

"Thus in all things created, in all rational creatures, and in the devils is seen the glory and praise of My Name. Who can see it? The soul who is denuded of the body and has reached Me, her End, sees it clearly, and, in seeing, knows the truth. Seeing Me, the Eternal Father, she loves, and loving, she is satisfied. Satisfied, she knows the Truth, and her will is stayed in My Will, bound and made stable, so that in nothing can it suffer pain, because it has that which it desired to have, before the soul saw Me, namely, the glory and praise of My Name. She now, in truth, sees it completely in My saints, in the blessed spirits, and in all creatures and things, even in the devils, as I told you. And although she also sees the injury done to Me, which before caused her sorrow, it no longer now can give her pain, but only compassion, because she loves without pain, and prays to Me continually with affection of love, that I will have mercy on the world. Pain in her is ended, but not love, as the tortured desire, which My Word, the Son, had borne from the beginning when I sent Him into the world, terminated on the Cross in His painful death, but His love - no. For had the affection of My charity, which I showed you by means of Him, been terminated and ended then, you would not be, because by love you are made, and had My love been drawn back, that is, had I not loved your being, you could not be, but My love created you, and My love possesses you, because I am one thing with My Truth, and He, the Word Incarnate with Me. You see then, that the saints and every soul in Eternal Life have desire for the salvation of souls without pain, because pain ended in their death, but not so the affection of love.

"Thus, as if drunk with the Blood of the Immaculate Lamb, and clothed in the love of the neighbor, they pass through the Narrow Gate, bathed in the Blood of Christ crucified, and they find themselves in Me, the Sea Pacific, raised from imperfection, far from satiety, and arrived at perfection, satisfied by every good."

How after Saint Paul was drawn to the glory of the blessed,
he desired to be loosened from the body, as they do, who
have reached the aforesaid third and fourth states.

"Paul, then, had seen and tasted this good, when I drew him up into the third heaven, that is into the height of the Trinity, where he tasted and knew My Truth, receiving fully the Holy Spirit, and learning the doctrine of My Truth, the Word Incarnate. The soul of Paul was clothed, through feeling and union, in Me, Eternal Father, like the blessed ones in Eternal Life, except that his soul was not separated from his body, except through this feeling and union. But it being pleasing to My Goodness to make of him a vessel of election in the abyss of Me, Eternal Trinity, I dispossessed him of Myself, because on Me can no pain fall, and I wished him to suffer for My name; therefore I placed before him, as an object for the eyes of his intellect, Christ crucified, clothing him with the garment of His doctrine, binding and fettering him with the clemency of the Holy Spirit and inflaming him with the fire of charity. He became a vessel, disposed and reformed by My Goodness, and, on being struck, made no resistance, but said: 'My Lord, what do You wish me to do? Show me that which it is Your pleasure for me to do, and I will do it.' Which I answered when I placed before him Christ crucified, clothing him with the doctrine of My charity. I illuminated him perfectly with the light of true contrition, by which he extirpated his defects, and founded him in My charity."

How the soul who finds herself in the unitive state desires infinitely to have the barren earthly state and unite herself to GOD.

"And when I depart from the soul in the aforesaid way that the body may return a little to its corporal sentiment, the soul, on account of the union which she had made with Me, is impatient in her life, being deprived of union with Me, and the conversation of the Immortals, who render glory to Me, and finding herself, amid the conversation of mortals, and seeing them so miserably offending Me. This vision of My offense is the torture which such souls always have, and which, with the desire to see Me, renders their life insupportable to them. Nevertheless, as their will is not their own, but becomes one with Mine, they cannot desire other than what I desire, and though they desire to come and be with Me, they are contented to remain, if I desire them to remain, with their pain, for the greater praise and glory of My Name and the salvation of souls. So that in nothing are they in discord with My Will; but they run their course with ecstatic desire, clothed in Christ crucified, and keeping by the Bridge of His doctrine, glorying in His shame and pains. Inasmuch as they appear to be suffering they are rejoicing, because the enduring of many tribulations is to them a relief in the desire which they have for death, for oftentimes the desire and the will to suffer pain mitigates the pain caused them by their desire to quit the body. These not only endure with patience, as I told you they did, who are in the third state, but they glory, through My Name, in bearing much tribulation. In bearing tribulation they find pleasure, and not having it they suffer pain, fearing that I reward not their well-doing or that the sacrifice of their desires is not pleasing to Me; but when I permit to them many tribulations they rejoice, seeing themselves clothed with the suffering and shame of Christ crucified. Wherefore were it possible for them to have virtue without toil they would not want it. They would rather delight in the Cross, with Christ, acquiring it with pain, than in any other way obtain Eternal Life. Why? Because they are inflamed and steeped in the Blood, where they find the blaze of My charity, which charity is a fire proceeding from Me, ravishing their heart and mind and making their sacrifices acceptable. Wherefore, the eye of the intellect is lifted up and gazes into My Deity, when the affection behind the intellect is nourished and united with Me. This is a sight which I grant to the soul, infused with grace, who, in truth, loves and serves Me."

*How they, who are arrived at the aforesaid unitive state, have the eye
of their intellect illuminated by supernatural light infused by grace.
And how it is better to go for counsel for the salvation of the soul,
to a humble and holy conscience than to a proud lettered man.*

"With this light that is given to the eye of the intellect, Thomas Aquinas saw Me, wherefore he acquired the light of much science; also Augustine, Jerome, and the doctors, and my saints. They were illuminated by My Truth to know and understand My Truth in darkness. By My Truth I mean the Holy Scripture, which seemed dark because it was not understood; not through any defect of the Scriptures, but of them who heard them, and did not understand them. Wherefore I sent this light to illuminate the blind and coarse understanding, uplifting the eye of the intellect to know the Truth. And I, Fire, Acceptor of sacrifices, ravishing away from them their darkness, give the light; not a natural light, but a supernatural, so that, though in darkness, they know the Truth. Wherefore that, which at first appeared to be dark, now appears with the most perfect light, to the gross or subtle mind; and everyone receives according as he is capable or disposed to know Me, for I do not despise dispositions. So you see that the eye of the intellect has received supernatural light, infused by grace, by which the doctors and saints knew light in darkness, and of darkness made light. The intellect was, before the Scriptures were formed, wherefore, from the intellect came science, because in seeing they discerned. It was thus that the holy prophets and fathers understood, who prophesied of the coming and death of My Son, and the Apostles, after the coming of the Holy Spirit, which gave them that supernatural light. The evangelists, doctors, professors, virgins, and martyrs were all likewise illuminated by the aforesaid perfect light. And everyone has had the illumination of this light according as he needed it for his salvation or that of others, or for the exposition of the Scriptures. The doctors of the holy science had it, expounding the doctrine of My Truth, the preaching of the Apostles, and the Gospels of the Evangelists. The martyrs had it, declaring in their blood the Most Holy Faith, the fruit and the treasure of the Blood of the Lamb. The virgins had it in the affection of charity and purity. To the obedient ones is declared, by it, the obedience of the Word, showing them the perfection of obedience, which shines in my Truth, who for the obedience that I imposed upon Him, ran to the opprobrious death of the Cross. This light is to be seen in the Old and New Testament; in the Old, by it, were seen by the eye of the intellect, and known the prophecies of the holy prophets. In the New Testament of the evangelical life, how is the Gospel declared to the faithful? By this same light. And because the New Testament proceeded from the same light, the new law did not break the old law; rather are the two laws bound together, the imperfection of the old law, founded in fear alone, being taken from it, by the coming of the Word of My only-begotten Son, with the law of Love, completing the old law by giving it love, and replacing the fear of penalty by holy fear. And, therefore, said My Truth to the disciples, to show that He was not a breaker of laws: 'I came not to dissolve the law, but to fulfill it.' It is almost as if My Truth would say to them - The Law is now imperfect, but with My Blood I will make it perfect, and I will fill it up with what it lacks, taking away the fear of penalty, and founding it in love and holy fear. How was this declared to be the Truth? By this same supernatural light, which was and is given by grace to all, who will receive it? Every light that comes from Holy Scripture comes and came from this supernatural light. Ignorant and proud men of science were blind notwithstanding this light, because their pride and the cloud of self-love had covered up and put out the light. Wherefore they understood the Holy Scripture rather literally than with understanding, and taste only the letter of it, still desiring many other books; and they get not to the marrow of it, because they have deprived themselves of the light, with which is found and expounded the Scripture; and they are annoyed and murmur, because they find much in it that appears to them gross and idiotic. And, nevertheless, they appear to be much illuminated in their knowledge of Scripture, as if they had studied it for long; and this is not remarkable, because they have of course the natural light from whence proceeds science. But because they have lost the supernatural light, infused by grace, they neither see nor know My Goodness, nor the grace of My servants. Wherefore, I say to you, that it is much better to go for counsel for the salvation of the soul, to a holy and upright conscience, than to a proud lettered man, learned in much science, because such a one can only offer what he has himself, and, because of his darkness, it may appear to you, that, from what he says, the Scriptures offer darkness. The contrary will you find with My servants, because they offer the light that is in them, with hunger and desire for the soul's salvation. This I have told you, my sweetest daughter, that you might know the perfection of this unitive state, when the eye of the intellect is ravished by the fire of My charity, in which charity it receives the supernatural light. With this light the souls in the unitive state love Me, because love follows the intellect, and the more it knows the more can it love. Thus the one feeds the other, and, with this light, they both arrive at the Eternal Vision of Me, where they see and taste Me, in Truth, the soul being separated from the body, as I told you when I spoke to you of the blissfulness that the soul received in Me. This state is most excellent, when the soul, being yet in the mortal body, tastes bliss with the immortals, and oftentimes she arrives at so great a union that she scarcely knows whether she be in the body or out of it; and tastes the earnest-money of Eternal Life, both because she is united with Me, and because her will is dead in Christ, by which death her union was made with Me, and in no other way could she perfectly have done so. Therefore do they taste life eternal, deprived of the hell of their own will, which gives to man the earnest-money of damnation, if he yield to it."

Then this soul, yearning with very great desire, and rising as one intoxicated both by the union which she had had with God, and by what she had heard and tasted of the Supreme and Sweet Truth, yearned with grief over the ignorance of creatures, in that they did not know their Benefactor, or the affection of the love of God. And nevertheless she had joy from the hope of the promise that the Truth of God had made to her, teaching her the way she was to direct her will (and the other servants of God as well as herself) in order that He should do mercy to the world. And, lifting up the eye of her intellect upon the sweet Truth, to whom she remained united, wishing to know somewhat of the aforesaid states of the soul of which God had spoken to her, and seeing that the soul passes through these states with tears, she wished to learn from the Truth concerning the different kinds of tears, and how they came to be, and whence they proceeded, and the fruit that resulted from weeping. Wishing then to know this from the Sweet, Supreme and First Truth, as to the manner of being and reason of the aforesaid tears, and inasmuch as the truth cannot be learnt from any other than from the Truth Himself, and nothing can be learnt in the Truth but what is seen by the eye of the intellect, she made her request of the Truth. For it is necessary for him who is lifted with desire to learn the Truth with the light of faith.

Wherefore, knowing that she had not forgotten the teaching which the Truth, that is, God, had given her, that in no other way could she learn about the different states and fruits of tears, she rose out of herself, exceeding every limit of her nature with the greatness of her desire. And, with the light of a lively faith, she opened the eye of her intellect upon the Eternal Truth, in whom she saw and knew the Truth, in the matter of her request, for God Himself manifested it to her, and condescending in His benignity to her burning desire, fulfilled her petition.

How there are five kinds of tears.

Then said the Supreme and Sweet Truth of God, "Oh, beloved and dearest daughter, you beg knowledge of the reasons and fruits of tears, and I have not despised your desire; open well the eye of your intellect and I will show you, among the aforesaid states of the soul, of which I have told you, concerning the imperfect tears caused by fear; but first rather of the tears of wicked men of the world. These are the tears of damnation. The former are those of fear, and belong to men who abandon sin from fear of punishment, and weep for fear. The third are the tears of those who, having abandoned sin, are beginning to serve and taste Me, and weep for very sweetness; but since their love is imperfect, so also is their weeping, as I have told you. The fourth are the tears of those who have arrived at the perfect love of their neighbor, loving Me without any regard whatsoever for themselves. These weep and their weeping is perfect. The fifth are joined to the fourth and are tears of sweetness let fall with great peace, as I will explain to you. I will tell you also of the tears of fire, without bodily tears of the eyes, which satisfy those who often would desire to weep and cannot. And I wish you to know that all these various graces may exist in one soul, who, rising from fear and imperfect love, reaches perfect love in the unitive state. Now I will begin to tell you of these tears in the following way."

Of the difference of these tears, arising from the
explanation of the aforesaid state of the soul.

"I wish you to know that every tear proceeds from the heart, for there is no member of the body that will satisfy the heart so much as the eye. If the heart is in pain the eye manifests it. And if the pain be sensual the eye drops hearty tears which engender death, because proceeding from the heart, they are caused by a disordinate love distinct from the love of Me; for such love, being disordinate and an offense to Me, receives the meed of mortal pain and tears. It is true that their guilt and grief are more or less heavy, according to the measure of their disordinate love. And these form that first class, who have the tears of death, of whom I have spoken to you, and will speak again. Now, begin to consider the tears which give the commencement of life, the tears, that is, of those who, knowing their guilt, set to weeping for fear of the penalty they have incurred.

"These are both hearty and sensual tears, because the soul, not having yet arrived at perfect hatred of its guilt on account of the offense thereby done to Me, abandons it with a hearty grief for the penalty which follows the sin committed, while the eye weeps in order to satisfy the grief of the heart.

"But the soul, exercising herself in virtue, begins to lose her fear, knowing that fear alone is not sufficient to give her eternal life, as I have already told you when speaking of the second stage of the soul. And so she proceeds, with love, to know herself and My goodness in her, and begins to take hope in My mercy in which her heart feels joy. Sorrow for her grief, mingled with the joy of her hope in My mercy, causes her eye to weep, which tears issue from the very fountain of her heart.

"But, inasmuch as she has not yet arrived at great perfection, she often drops sensual tears, and if you ask Me why, I reply: Because the root of self-love is not sensual love, for that has already been removed, as has been said, but it is a spiritual love with which the soul desires spiritual consolations or loves some creature spiritually. (I have spoken to you at length regarding the imperfections of such souls.) Wherefore, when such a soul is deprived of the thing she loves, that is, internal or external consolation, the internal being the consolation received from Me, the external being that which she had from the creature, and when temptations and the persecutions of men come on her, her heart is full of grief. And, as soon as the eye feels the grief and suffering of the heart, she begins to weep with a tender and compassionate sorrow, pitying herself with the spiritual compassion of self-love; for her self-will is not yet crushed and destroyed in everything, and in this way she lets fall sensual tears - tears, that is, of spiritual passion. But, growing, and exercising herself in the light of self-knowledge, she conceives displeasure at herself and finally perfect self-hatred. From this she draws true knowledge of My goodness with a fire of love, and she begins to unite herself to Me, and to conform her will to Mine and so to feel joy and compassion. Joy in herself through the affection of love, and compassion for her neighbor, as I told you in speaking of the third stage. Immediately her eye, wishing to satisfy the heart, cries with hearty love for Me and for her neighbor, grieving solely for My offense and her neighbor's loss, and not for any penalty or loss due to herself; for she does not think of herself, but only of rendering glory and praise to My Name, and, in an ecstasy of desire, she joyfully takes the food prepared for her on the table of the Holy Cross, thus conforming herself to the humble, patient, and immaculate Lamb, My only-begotten Son, of whom I made a Bridge, as I have said. Having thus sweetly traveled by that Bridge, following the doctrine of My sweet Truth, enduring with true and sweet patience every pain and trouble which I have permitted to be inflicted upon her for her salvation, having manfully received them all, not choosing them according to her own tastes, but accepting them according to Mine, and not only, as I said, enduring them with patience, but sustaining them with joy, she counts it glory to be persecuted for My Name's sake in whatever she may have to suffer. Then the soul arrives at such delight and tranquillity of mind that no tongue can tell it. Having crossed the river by means of the Eternal Word, that is, by the doctrine of My only-begotten Son, and, having fixed the eye of her intellect on Me, the Sweet Supreme Truth, having seen the Truth, knows it; and knowing it, loves it. Drawing her affection after her intellect, she tastes My Eternal Deity, and she knows and sees the Divine nature united to your humanity.

"Then she reposes in Me, the Sea Pacific, and her heart is united to Me in love, as I told you when speaking of the fourth and unitive state. When she thus feels Me, the Eternal Deity, her eyes let fall tears of sweetness, tears indeed of milk, nourishing the soul in true patience; an odoriferous ointment are these tears, shedding odors of great sweetness.

"Oh, best beloved daughter, how glorious is that soul who has indeed been able to pass from the stormy ocean to Me, the Sea Pacific, and in that Sea, which is Myself, the Supreme and Eternal Deity, to fill the pitcher of her heart. And her eye, the conduit of her heart, endeavors to satisfy her heart-pangs, and so sheds tears. This is the last stage in which the soul is blessed and sorrowful.

"Blessed she is through the union which she feels herself to have with Me, tasting the divine love; sorrowful through the offenses which she sees done to My goodness and greatness, for she has seen and tasted the bitterness of this in her self-knowledge, by which self-knowledge, together with her knowledge of Me, she arrived at the final stage. Yet this sorrow is no impediment to the unitive state, which produces tears of great sweetness through self-knowledge, gained in love of the neighbor, in which exercise the soul discovers the plaint of My divine mercy, and grief at the offenses caused to her neighbor, weeping with those who weep, and rejoicing with those who rejoice - that is, who live in My love. Over these the soul rejoices, seeing glory and praise rendered Me by My servants, so that the third kind of grief does not prevent the fourth, that is, the final grief belonging to the unitive state; they rather give savor to each other, for, had not this last grief (in which the soul finds such union with Me), developed from the grief belonging to the third state of neighborly love, it would not be perfect. Therefore it is necessary that the one should flavor the other, else the soul would come to a state of presumption, induced by the subtle breeze of love of her own reputation, and would fall at once, vomited from the heights to the depths. Therefore it is necessary to bear with others and practice continually love to one's neighbor, together with true knowledge of oneself.

"In this way will she feel the fire of My love in herself, because love of her neighbor is developed out of love of Me - that is, out of that learning which the soul obtained by knowing herself and My goodness in her. When, therefore, she sees herself to be ineffably loved by Me, she loves every rational creature with the self-same love with which she sees herself to be loved. And, for this reason, the soul that knows Me immediately expands to the love of her neighbor, because she sees that I love that neighbor ineffably, and so, herself, loves the object which she sees Me to have loved still more. She further knows that she can be of no use to Me and can in no way repay Me that pure love with which she feels herself to be loved by Me, and therefore endeavors to repay it through the medium which I have given her, namely, her neighbor, who is the medium through which you can all serve Me. For, as I have said to you, you can perform all virtues by means of your neighbor, I having given you all creatures, in general and in particular, according to the diverse graces each has received from Me, to be ministered unto by you; you should therefore love them with the same pure love with which I have loved you. That pure love cannot be returned directly to Me, because I have loved you without being Myself loved, and without any consideration of Myself whatsoever, for I loved you without being loved by you - before you existed; it was, indeed, love that moved Me to create you to My own image and similitude. This love you cannot repay to Me, but you can pay it to My rational creature, loving your neighbor without being loved by him and without consideration of your own advantage, whether spiritual or temporal, but loving him solely for the praise and glory of My Name, because he has been loved by Me.

"Thus will you fulfill the commandment of the law, to love Me above everything, and your neighbor as yourselves.

"True indeed is it that this height cannot be reached without passing through the second stage, namely the second stage of union which becomes the third (and final) stage. Nor can it be preserved when it has been reached if the soul abandon the affection from which it has been developed, the affection to which the second class of tears belongs. It is therefore impossible to fulfill the law given by Me, the Eternal God, without fulfilling that of your neighbor, for these two laws are the feet of your affection by which the precepts and counsels are observed, which were given you, as I have told you, by My Truth, Christ crucified. These two states united nourish your soul in virtue, making her to grow in the perfection of virtue and in the unitive state. Not that the other state is changed because this further state has been reached, for this further state does but increase the riches of grace in new and various gifts and admirable elevations of the mind, in the knowledge of the truth, as I said to you, which, though it is mortal, appears immortal because the soul's perception of her own sensuality is mortified and her will is dead through the union which she has attained with Me.

"Oh, how sweet is the taste of this union to the soul, for, in tasting it, she sees My secrets! Wherefore she often receives the spirit of prophecy, knowing the things of the future. This is the effect of My Goodness, but the humble soul should despise such things, not indeed in so far as they are given her by My love, but in so far as she desires them by reason of her appetite for consolation, considering herself unworthy of peace and quiet of mind, in order to nourish virtue within her soul. In such a case let her not remain in the second stage, but return to the valley of self-knowledge. I give her this light, My grace permitting, so that she may ever grow in virtue. For the soul is never so perfect in this life that she cannot attain to a higher perfection of love. My only-begotten Son, your Captain, was the only One who could increase in no perfection, because He was one thing with Me, and I with Him, wherefore His soul was blessed through union with the Divine nature. But do you, His pilgrim-members, be ever ready to grow in greater perfection, not indeed to another stage, for as I have said, you have now reached the last, but to that further grade of perfection in the last stage, which may please you by means of My Grace."

How the four stages of the soul, to which belong the five aforesaid states of tears, produce tears of infinite value: and how God wishes to be served as the Infinite, and not as anything finite.

"These five states are like five principal canals which are filled with abundant tears of infinite value, all of which give life if they are disciplined in virtue, as I have said to you. You ask how their value can be infinite. I do not say that in this life your tears can become infinite, but I call them infinite, on account of the infinite desire of your soul from which they proceed. I have already told you how tears

94

come from the heart, and how the heart distributes them to the eye, having gathered them in its own fiery desire. As, when green wood is on the fire, the moisture it contains groans on account of the heat, because the wood is green, so does the heart, made green again by the renovation of grace drawn into itself among its self-love which dries up the soul, so that fiery desire and tears are united. And inasmuch as desire is never ended, it is never satisfied in this life, but the more the soul loves the less she seems to herself to love. Thus is holy desire, which is founded in love, exercised, and with this desire the eye weeps. But when the soul is separated from the body and has reached Me, her End, she does not on that account abandon desire, so as to no longer yearn for Me or love her neighbor, for love has entered into her like a woman bearing the fruits of all other virtues. It is true that suffering is over and ended, as I have said to you, for the soul that desires Me possesses Me in very truth, without any fear of ever losing that which she has so long desired; but, in this way, hunger is kept up, because those who are hungry are satisfied, and as soon as they are satisfied hunger again; in this way their satiety is without disgust, and their hunger without suffering, for, in Me, no perfection is wanting.

"Thus is your desire infinite, otherwise it would be worth nothing, nor would any virtue of yours have any life if you served Me with anything finite. For I, who am the Infinite God, wish to be served by you with infinite service, and the only infinite thing you possess is the affection and desire of your souls. In this sense I said that there were tears of infinite value, and this is true as regards their mode, of which I have spoken, namely, of the infinite desire which is united to the tears. When the soul leaves the body the tears remain behind, but the affection of love has drawn to itself the fruit of the tears, and consumed it, as happens in the case of the water in your furnace. The water has not really been taken out of the furnace, but the heat of the fire has consumed it and drawn it into itself. Thus the soul, having arrived at tasting the fire of My divine charity, and having passed from this life in a state of love towards Me and her neighbor, having further possessed that unitive love which caused her tears to fall, does not cease to offer Me her blessed desires, tearful indeed, though without pain or physical weeping, for physical tears have evaporated in the furnace, becoming tears of fire of the Holy Spirit. You see then how tears are infinite, how, as regards the tears shed in this life only, no tongue can tell what different sorrows may cause them. I have now told you the difference between four of these states of tears."

Of the fruit of worldly men's tears.

"It remains for Me to tell you of the fruit produced by tears shed with desire, and received into the soul. But first will I speak to you of that first class of men whom I mentioned at the beginning of this My discourse; those, that is, who live miserably in the world, making a god of created things and of their own sensuality, from which comes damage to their body and soul. I said to you that every tear proceeded from the heart, and this is the truth, for the heart grieves in proportion to the love it feels. So worldly men weep when their heart feels pain, that is, when they are deprived of something which they loved.

"But many and diverse are their complainings. Do you know how many? There are as many as there exist different loves. And inasmuch as the root of self-love is corrupt, everything that grows from it is corrupt also. Self-love is a tree on which grow nothing but fruits of death, putrid flowers, stained leaves, branches bowed down, and struck by various winds. This is the tree of the soul. For you are all trees of love, and without love you cannot live, for you have been made by Me for love. The soul who lives virtuously, places the root of her tree in the valley of true humility; but those who live thus miserably are planted on the mountain of pride, whence it follows that since the root of the tree is badly planted, the tree can bear no fruits of life but only of death. Their fruits are their actions, which are all poisoned by many and diverse kinds of sin, and if they should produce some good fruit among their actions, even it will be spoiled by the foulness of its root, for no good actions done by a soul in mortal sin are of value for eternal life, for they are not done in grace. Let not, however, such a soul abandon on this account its good works, forevery good deed is rewarded, and every evil deed punished. A good action performed out of a state of grace is not sufficient to merit eternal life, as has been said, but My Justice, My Divine Goodness, grants an incomplete reward, imperfect as the action which obtains it. Often such a man is rewarded in temporal matters; sometimes I give him more time in which to repent, as I have already said to you in another place. This also will I sometimes do, I grant him the life of grace by means of My servants who are pleasing and acceptable to Me. I acted in this way with My glorious apostle Paul, who abandoned his infidelity, and the persecutions he directed against the Christians, at the prayer of St. Stephen. See truly, therefore, that, in whatever state a man may be, he should never stop doing good.

"I said to you that the flowers of this tree were putrid, and so in truth they are. Its flowers are the stinking thoughts of the heart, displeasing to Me, and full of hatred and unkindness towards their neighbor. So if a man be a thief, he robs Me of honor, and takes it himself. This flower stinks less than that of false judgment, which is of two kinds. The first with regard to Me, by which men judge My secret judgments, gauging falsely all My mysteries, that is, judging that which I did in love, to have been done in hatred; that which I did in truth to have been done in falsehood; that which I give them for life, to have been given them for death. They condemn and judge everything according to their weak intellect; for they have blinded the eye of their intellect with sensual self-love, and hidden the pupil of the most holy Faith, which they will not allow to see or know the Truth. The second kind of false judgment is directed against a man's neighbor, from which often come many evils, because the wretched man wishes to set himself up as the judge of the affections and heart of other rational creatures, when he does not yet know himself. And, for an action which he may see, or for a word he may hear, he will judge the affection of the heart. My servants always judge well, because they are founded on Me, the Supreme Good; but such as these always judge badly, for they are founded on evil. Such critics as these cause hatreds, murders, unhappinesses of all kinds to their neighbors, and remove themselves far away from the love of My servants' virtue.

"Truly these fruits follow the leaves, which are the words which issue from their mouth in insult to Me and the Blood of My only-begotten Son, and in hatred to their neighbors. And they think of nothing else but cursing and condemning My works, and blaspheming and saying evil of every rational creature, according as their judgment may suggest to them. The unfortunate creatures do not remember that the tongue is made only to give honor to Me, and to confess sins, and to be used in love of virtue, and for the salvation of the neighbor. These are the stained leaves of that most miserable fault, because the heart from which they proceeded was not clean, but all spotted with duplicity and misery. How much danger, apart from the spiritual privation of grace to the soul, of temporal loss may not occur! For you have all heard and seen how, through words alone, have come revolutions of states, and destructions of cities, and many homicides and other evils, a word having entered the heart of the listener, and having passed through a space not large enough for a knife.

"I say that this tree has seven branches drooping to the earth, on which grow the flowers and leaves in the way I have told you. These branches are the seven mortal sins which are full of many and diverse wickednesses, contained in the roots and trunk of self-love and of pride, which first made both branches and flowers of many thoughts, the leaves of words, and the fruits of wicked deeds. They stand drooping to the earth because the branches of mortal sin can turn no other way than to the earth, the fragile disordinate substance of the world. Do not marvel, they can turn no way but that in which they can be fed by the earth; for their hunger is insatiable, and the earth is unable to satisfy them. They are insatiable and unbearable to themselves, and it is conformable to their state that they should always be unquiet, longing and desiring that thing which they have to satiety. This is the reason why such satiety cannot content them, because they (who are infinite in their being) are always desiring something finite; because their being will never end, though their life to grace ends when they commit mortal sin.

"Man is placed above all creatures, and not beneath them, and he cannot be satisfied or content except in something greater than himself. Greater than himself there is nothing but Myself, the Eternal God. Therefore I alone can satisfy him, and, because he is deprived of this satisfaction by his guilt, he remains in continual torment and pain. Weeping follows pain, and when he begins to weep the wind strikes the tree of self-love, which he has made the principle of all his being."

How this devout soul, thanking God for His explanation of
the above-mentioned states of tears, makes three petitions.

Then this soul, eager with the greatness of her desire, through the sweetness of the explanation and satisfaction which she had received from the Truth, concerning the state of tears, said as one enamored - "Thanks, thanks be to You, Supreme and Eternal Father, Satisfier of holy desires, and Lover of our Salvation, who, through Your Love, gave us Love Himself, in the time of our warfare with You, in the person of Your only-begotten Son. By this abyss of Your fiery Love, I beg of You grace and mercy that I may come to You truly in the light, and not flee far in darkness away from Your doctrine, of which You have clearly demonstrated to me the truth, so that, by the light thereof, I perceive two other points, concerning which I fear that they are, or may become, stumbling-blocks to me. I beg, Eternal Father, that, before I leave the subject of these states of tears, You would explain these points also to me. The first is - when a person desirous of serving You, comes to me, or to some other servant of Yours to ask for counsel, how should I teach him? I know, Sweet and Eternal God, that You replied above to this question - 'I am He who takes delight in few words and many deeds.' Nevertheless, if it please Your Goodness to grant me a few more words on the subject, it will cause me the greatest pleasure. And also, if on some occasion, when I am praying for Your creatures, and in particular for Your servants, and I seem to see the subjects of my prayer, in one I find (in the course of my prayer) a well-disposed mind, a soul rejoicing in You; and in another, as it might seem to me, a mind full of darkness; have I the right, O Eternal Father, to judge the one soul to be in light, and the other in darkness? Or, supposing I should see that the one lives in great penance, and the other does not, should I be right to judge that he who does the greater penance has the higher perfection? I pray You, so that I may not be deceived through my limited vision, that You would declare to me in detail, what You have already said in general on this matter. The second request I have to make is, that You will explain further to me about the sign which You said the soul received on being visited by You - the sign which revealed Your Presence. If I remember well, oh, Eternal Truth, You said that the soul remained in joy and courageous virtue. I would gladly know whether this joy can consist with the delusion of the passion of spiritual self-love; for if it were so, I would humbly confine myself to the sign of virtue. These are the things which I beg You to tell me, so that I may serve You and my neighbor in truth, and not fall into false judgment concerning Your creatures and servants. For it seems to me that the habit of judging keeps the soul far from You, so I do not wish to fall into this snare."

How the light of reason is necessary to every soul that wishes to serve God in truth; and first of the light of reason in general.

Then the Eternal God, delighting in the thirst and hunger of that soul, and in the purity of her heart, and the desire with which she longed to serve Him, turned the eye of His benignity and mercy upon her, saying - "Oh, best-beloved, dearest and sweetest daughter, my spouse! rise out of yourself, and open the eye of your intellect to see Me, the Infinite Goodness, and the ineffable love which I have towards you and My other servants. And open the ear of the desire which you feel towards Me, and remember, that if you do not see, you can not hear, that is to say, that the soul that does not see into My Truth with the eye of her intellect, cannot hear or know My Truth, wherefore in order that you may the better know it, rise above the feelings of your senses.

"And I, who take delight in your request, will satisfy your demand. Not that you can increase My delight, for I am the cause of you and of your increase; not those of Mine. Yet the very pleasure that I take in the work of My own hands causes Me delight."

Then that soul obeyed and rose out of herself, in order to learn the true solution of her difficulty. And the Eternal God said to her, "In order that you may the better understand what I shall say to you, I shall revert to the beginning of your request concerning the three lights which issue from Me, the True Light. The first is a general light dwelling in those who live in ordinary charity. (I shall repeat to you here many things concerning these lights, which I have already told you, in spite of My having done so, in order that your creeping intelligence may better understand that which you wish to know.) The other two lights dwell in those who, having abandoned the world, desire perfection. Besides this I will explain to you your request, telling you in great detail that which I have already pointed out to you in general. You know, as I have told you, that, without the light, no one can walk in the truth, that is, without the light of reason, which light of reason you draw from Me the True Light, by means of the eye of your intellect and the light of faith which I have given you in holy baptism, though you may have lost it by your own defects. For, in baptism, and through the mediation of the Blood of My only-begotten Son, you have received the form of faith; which faith you exercise in virtue by the light of reason, which gives you life and causes you to walk in the path of truth, and, by its means, to arrive at Me, the True Light, for, without it, you would plunge into darkness.

"It is necessary for you to have two lights derived from this primary light, and to these two I will also add a third. The first lightens you all to know the transitory nature of the things of the world, all of which pass like the wind. But this you cannot know thoroughly, unless you first recognize your own fragility, how strong is your inclination, through the law of perversity with which your members are bound, to rebel against Me, your Creator (not that by this law any man can be constrained to commit any, even the smallest sin, against his will, but that this law of perversity fights lustily against the spirit). I did not impose this law upon you, in order that My rational creature should be conquered by it, but in order that he should prove and increase the virtue of his soul, because virtue cannot be proved, except by its contrary. Sensuality is contrary to the spirit, and yet, by means of sensuality, the soul is able to prove the love which she has for Me, her Creator. How does she prove it? When, with anger and displeasure, she rises against herself. This law has also been imposed in order to preserve the soul in true humility. Wherefore you see that, while I created the soul to Mine own image and similitude, placing her in such dignity and beauty, I caused her to be accompanied by the vilest of all things, imposing on her the law of perversity, imprisoning her in a body, formed of the vilest substance of the earth, so that, seeing in what her true beauty consisted, she should not raise her head in pride against Me. Wherefore, to one who possesses this light, the fragility of his body is a cause of humiliation to the soul, and is in no way matter for pride, but rather for true and perfect humility. So that this law does not constrain you to any sin by its strivings, but supplies a reason to make you know yourselves and the instability of the world. This should be seen by the eye of the intellect, with light of the holy faith, of which I said to you that it was the pupil of the eye. This is that light which is necessary in general to every rational creature, whatever may be his condition, who wishes to participate in the life of grace, in the fruit of the Blood of the immaculate Lamb. This is the ordinary light, that is, the light which all persons must possess, as has been said, for, without it, the soul would be in a state of damnation. And, for this reason, because the soul, being without the light, is not in a state of grace, inasmuch as, not having the light, she does not know the evil of her sin or its cause, and therefore cannot avoid or hate it.

"And similarly if the soul know not good, and the reason of good, that is to say virtue, she cannot love or desire either Me, who am the Essential Good, or virtue, which I have given you as an instrument and means for you to receive My grace, and Myself the True Good. See then how necessary is this light, for your sins consist in nothing else than in loving that which I hate, and in hating that which I love. I love virtue and hate vice; he who loves vice and hates virtue offends Me, and is deprived of My grace. Such a one walks as if blind, for he knows not the cause of vice, that is, his sensual self-love, nor does he hate himself on account of it; he is ignorant of vice and of the evil which follows it: he is ignorant of virtue and of Me, who am the cause of his obtaining life-giving virtue; he is ignorant of his own dignity, which he should maintain by advancing to grace, by means of virtue. See, therefore, how his ignorance is the cause of all his evil, and how you also need this light, as has been said."

Of those who have placed their desire rather in the mortification of the body than in the destruction of their own will; and of the second light, more perfect than the former general one.

"When the soul has arrived at the attainment of the general light, of which I have spoken, she should not remain contented, because, as long as you are pilgrims in this life, you are capable of growth, and he who does not go forward, by that very fact, is turning back. She should either grow in the general light, which she has acquired through My Grace, or anxiously strive to attain to the second and perfect light, leaving the imperfect and reaching the perfect. For, if the soul truly have light, she will wish to arrive at perfection. In this second perfect light are to be found two kinds of perfection; for they may be called perfect who have abandoned the general way of living of the world. One perfection is that of those who give themselves up wholly to the castigation of the body, doing great and severe penance. These, in order that their sensuality may not rebel against their reason, have placed their desire rather in the mortification of the body than in the destruction of their self-will, as I have explained to you in another place. These feed their souls at the table of penance, and are good and perfect, if their penance be illuminated by discretion, and founded on Me, if, that is to say, they act with true knowledge of themselves and of Me, with great humility, and wholly conformed to the judgment of My Will, and not to that of the will of man. But, if they were not thus clothed with My Will, in true humility, they would often offend against their own perfection, esteeming themselves the judges of those who do not walk in the same path. Do you know why this would happen to them? Because they have placed all their labor and desire in the mortification of the body, rather than in the destruction of their own will. Such as these wish always to choose their own times, and places, and consolations, after their own fashion, and also the persecutions of the world and of the Devil, as I have narrated to you in speaking of the second state of perfection.

"They say, cheating themselves with the delusion of their own self-will, which I have already called their spiritual self-will, 'I wish to have that consolation, and not these battles, or these temptations of the Devil, not, indeed, for my own pleasure, but in order to please God the more, and in order to retain Him the more in my soul through grace; because it seems to me that I should possess Him more, and serve Him better in that way than in this.' And this is the way the soul often fails into trouble, and becomes tedious and insupportable to herself; thus injuring her own perfection; yet she does not perceive it, nor that, within her, lurks the stench of pride, and there she lies. Now, if the soul were not in this condition, but were truly humble and not presumptuous, she would be illuminated to see that I, the Primary and Sweet Truth, grant condition, and time, and place, and consolations, and tribulations as they may be needed for your salvation, and to complete the perfection to which I have elected the soul. And she would see that I give everything through love, and that therefore, with love and reverence, should she receive everything, which is what the souls in the second state do, and, by doing so, arrive at the third state. Of whom I will now speak to you, explaining to you the nature of these two states which stand in the most perfect light."

Of the third and most perfect state, and of reason, and of the works done by the soul who has arrived at this light. And of a beautiful vision which this devout soul once received, in which the method of arriving at perfect purity is fully treated, and the means to avoid judging our neighbor is spoken of.

"Those who belong to the third state, which immediately follows the last, having arrived at this glorious light, are perfect in every condition in which they may be, and receive every event which I permit to happen to them with due reverence, as I have mentioned to you when speaking of the third and unitive state of the soul. These deem themselves worthy of the troubles and stumbling-blocks caused them by the world, and of the privation of their own consolation, and indeed of whatever circumstance happens to them. And inasmuch as they deem themselves worthy of trouble, so also do they deem themselves unworthy of the fruit which they receive after their trouble. They have known and tasted in the light My Eternal Will, which wishes naught else but your good, and gives and permits these troubles in order that you should be sanctified in Me. Wherefore the soul having known My Will, clothes herself with it, and fixes her attention on nothing else except seeing in what way she can preserve and increase her perfection to the glory and praise of My Name, opening the eye of her intellect and fixing it in the light of faith upon Christ crucified, My only-begotten Son, loving and following His doctrine, which is the rule of the road for perfect and imperfect alike. And see, how My Truth, the Lamb, who became enamored of her when He saw her, gives the soul the doctrine of perfection. She knows what this perfection is, having seen it practiced by the sweet and amorous Word, My only-begotten Son, who was fed at the table of holy desire, seeking the honor of Me, the Eternal Father, and your salvation. And, inflamed with this desire, He ran, with great eagerness, to the shameful death of the Cross, and accomplished the obedience which was imposed on Him by Me, His Father, not shunning labors or insults or withdrawing on account of your ingratitude or ignorance of so great a benefit, or because of the persecutions of the Jews, or on account of the insults, derision, grumbling, and shouting of the people. But all this He passed through like the true Captain and Knight that He was, whom I had placed on the battle-field to deliver you from the hands of the Devil, so that you might be free, and drawn out of the most terrible slavery in which you could ever be, and also to teach you His road, His doctrine, and His rule, so that you might open the Door of Me, Eternal Life, with the key of His precious Blood, shed with such fire of love, with such hatred of your sins. It was as if the sweet and amorous Word, My Son, should have said to you: 'Behold, I have made the road, and opened the door with My Blood.' Do not you then be negligent to follow, laying yourselves down to rest in self-love and ignorance of the road, presuming to choose to serve Me in your own way, instead of in the way which I have made straight for you by means of My Truth, the Incarnate Word, and built up with His Blood. Rise up then, promptly, and follow Him, for no one can reach Me, the Father, if not by Him; He is the Way and the Door by which you must enter into Me, the Sea Pacific.

"When therefore the soul has arrived at seeing, knowing, and tasting, in its full sweetness, this light, she runs, as one enamored and inflamed with love, to the table of holy desire; she does not see herself in herself, seeking her own consolation either spiritual or temporal, but, like one who has placed his all in this light and knowledge, and has destroyed his own will, she shuns no labor from whatever source it comes, but rather enduring the troubles, the insults, the temptations of the Devil, and the murmurings of men, eats at the table of the most holy Cross, the food of the honor of Me, the Eternal God, and of the salvation of souls; seeking no reward, either from Me or from creatures, because she is stripped of mercenary love, that is of love for Me based on interested motives, and is clothed in perfect light, loving Me in perfect purity, with no other regard than for the praise and glory of My Name, serving neither Me for her own delight, nor her neighbor for her own profit, but purely through love alone. Such as these have lost themselves, and have stripped themselves of the Old Man, that is of their own sensuality, and, having clothed themselves with the New Man, the sweet Christ Jesus, My Truth, follow Him manfully. These are they who sit at the table of holy desire, having been more anxious to slay their own will than to slay and mortify their own body. They have indeed mortified their body, though not as an end in itself, but as a means which helps them to stay their own will, as I said to you when explaining that sentence that I wished few words and many deeds, and so ought you to do. Their principal desire should be to slay their own will, so that it may not seek or wish anything else than to follow My sweet Truth, Christ crucified, seeking the honor and glory of My Name and the salvation of souls. Those who are in this sweet light know it, and remain constantly in peace and quiet, and no one scandalizes them, for they have cut away that thing by which stumbling-blocks are caused, namely their own will. And all the persecutions, with which the world and the Devil can attack them, slide under their feet, standing, as they do, in the waters of many tribulations and temptations, and do not hurt them, for they remain attached to Me by the umbilical cord of fiery desire. Such a man rejoices in everything, nor does he make himself judge of My servants, or of any rational creature, but rejoices in every condition and in every manner of holiness which he sees, saying: 'Thanks be to You, Eternal Father, who have in Your House many mansions.' And he rejoices more in the different ways of holiness which he sees, than if he were to see all traveling by one road, because, in this way, he perceives the greatness of My Goodness become more manifest, and thus, rejoicing, draws from all the fragrance of the rose. And not only in the case of good, but even when he sees something evidently sinful, he does not fall into judgment, but rather into true and holy compassion, interceding with Me for sinners and saying, with perfect humility: 'To-day it is your turn, and tomorrow it will be mine unless the Divine Grace preserve me.'

"Enamor yourself, dearest daughter, of this sweet and excellent state, and gaze at those who run in this glorious light and holiness, for they have holy minds, and eat at the table of holy desire, and, with the light, have arrived at feeding on the food of souls, that is, the honor of Me, the Eternal Father, being clothed with burning love in the sweet garment of My Lamb, My only-begotten Son, namely His doctrine. These do not lose their time in passing false judgments, either on My servants or the servants of the world, and they are never scandalized by any murmurings of men, either for their own sake or that of others. That is to say, in their own case they are content to endure anything for My Name's sake; and when an injury is done to some one else, they endure it with compassion of this injured neighbor, and without murmuring against him who caused the injury, or him who received it, because their love is not disordinate, but has been ordered in Me, the Eternal God.

"And, since their love is so ordered, these souls, my dearest daughter, never take offense from those they love, nor from any rational creature, their will being dead and not alive, wherefore they never assume the right to judge the will of men, but only the will of My Clemency. These observe the doctrine which, as you know, was given you by My Truth at the beginning of your life, when you were thinking in what way you could arrive at perfect purity, and were praying to Me with a great desire of doing so. You know what was replied to you, while you were asleep, concerning this holy desire, and that the words resounded not only in your mind, but also in your ear. So much so, that, if you remember truly, you returned to your waking body, when My Truth said, 'Will you arrive at perfect purity, and be freed from stumbling-blocks, so that your mind may not be scandalized by anything?' Unite yourself always to Me by the affection of love, for I am the Supreme and Eternal Purity. I am that Fire which purifies the soul, and the closer the soul is to Me, the purer she becomes, and the further she is from Me, the more does her purity leave her; which is the reason why men of the world fall into such iniquities, for they are separated from Me, while the soul, who, without any medium, unites herself directly to Me, participates in My Purity. Another thing is necessary for you to arrive at this union and purity, namely, that you should never judge the will of man in anything that you may see done or said by any creature whatsoever, either to yourself or to others. My will alone should you consider, both in them and in yourself. And, if you should see evident sins or defects, draw out of those thorns the rose, that is to say, offer them to Me, with holy compassion. In the case of injuries done to yourself, judge that My will permits this in order to prove virtue in yourself, and in My other servants, esteeming that he who acts thus does so as the instrument of My will; perceiving, moreover, that such apparent sinners may frequently have a good intention, for no one can judge the secrets of the heart of man. That which you do not see you should not judge in your mind, even though it may externally be open mortal sin, seeing nothing in others, but My will, not in order to judge, but, as has been said, with holy compassion. In this way you will arrive at perfect purity, because acting thus, your mind will not be scandalized, either in Me or in your neighbor. Otherwise you fall into contempt of your neighbor, if you judge his evil will towards you, instead of My will acting in him. Such contempt and scandal separates the soul from Me, and prevents perfection, and, in some cases, deprives a man of grace, more or less according to the gravity of his contempt, and the hatred which his judgment has conceived against his neighbor.

"A different reward is received by the soul who perceives only My will, which, as has been said, wishes nothing else but your good; so that everything which I give or permit to happen to you, I give so that you may arrive at the end for which I created you. And because the soul remains always in the love of her neighbor, she remains always in Mine, and thus remains united to Me. Wherefore, in order to arrive at purity, you must entreat Me to do three things: to grant you to be united to Me by the affection of love, retaining in your memory the benefits you have received from Me; and with the eye of your intellect to see the affection of My love, with which I love you inestimably; and in the will of others to discern My will only, and not their evil will, for I am their Judge, not you, and, in doing this, you will arrive at all perfection.

"This was the doctrine given to you by My Truth, if you remember well. Now I tell you, dearest daughter, that such as these, who have learnt this doctrine, taste the earnest of eternal life in this life; and, if you have well retained this doctrine, you will not fall into the snares of the Devil, because you will recognize them in the case about which you have asked Me.

"But, nevertheless, in order to satisfy your desire more clearly, I will tell you and show you how men should never discern by judgment, but with holy compassion."

In what way they, who stand in the above-mentioned third
most perfect light, receive the earnest of eternal life in this life.

"Why did I say to you that they received the earnest of eternal life? I say that they receive the earnest-money, but not the full payment, because they wait to receive it in Me, the Eternal Life, where they have life without death, and satiety without disgust, and hunger without pain, for from that divine hunger pain is far away, and though they have what they desire, disgust is far from satiety, for I am the flawless Food of Life. It is true that, in this life, they receive the earnest, and taste it in this way, namely that the soul begins to hunger for the honor of the Eternal God, and for the food of the salvation of other souls, and being hungry, she eats, that is to say, nourishes herself with love of her neighbor, which causes her hunger and desire, for the love of the neighbor is a food which never satiates him who feeds on it, the eater being insatiable and always remains hungry. So this earnest-money is a commencement of a guarantee which is given to man, in virtue of which he expects one day to receive his payment, not through the perfection of the earnest-money in itself, but through faith, through the certitude which he has of reaching the completion of his being and receiving his payment. Wherefore this enamored soul, clothed in My Truth, having already received in this life the earnest of My love, and of her neighbor's, is not yet perfect, but expects perfection in immortal life. I say that this earnest is not perfect, because the soul who tastes it has not, as yet, the perfection which would prevent her feeling pain in herself, or in others. In herself, through the offense done to Me by the law of perversity which is bound in her members and struggles against the spirit, and in others by the offense of her neighbor. She has indeed, in a sense, a perfect grace, but not that perfection of My saints, who have arrived at Me, Eternal Life, for, as has been said, their desires are without suffering, and yours are not. These servants of Mine, as I have said to you in another place, who nourish themselves at this table of holy desire, are blessed and full of grief, even as My only-begotten Son was, on the wood of the holy Cross, because, while His flesh was in grief and torment, His soul was blessed through its union with the divine nature. In like manner these are blessed by the union of their holy desire towards Me, clothed, as has been said, in My sweet Will, and they are full of grief through compassion for their neighbor, and because they afflict their own self-love, depriving it of sensual delights and consolations."

How this soul, rendering thanks to God, humiliates herself; then she prays for the whole world and particularly for the mystical body of the holy Church, and for her spiritual children, and for the two fathers of her soul; and, after these things, she asks to hear something about the defects of the ministers of the holy Church.

"Then that soul, as if, in truth, inebriated, seemed beside herself, as if the feelings of the body were alienated through the union of love which she had made with her Creator, and as if, in elevation of mind, she had gazed into the eternal truth with the eye of her intellect, and, having recognized the truth, had become enamored of it, and said, "Oh! Supreme and Eternal Goodness of God, who am I, miserable one, that You, Supreme and Eternal Father, have manifested to me Your Truth, and the hidden deceits of the Devil, and the deceitfulness of personal feeling, so that I, and others in this life of pilgrimage, may know how to avoid being deceived by the Devil or ourselves! What moved you to do it? Love, because You loved me, without my having loved You. Oh, Fire of Love! Thanks, thanks be to You, Eternal Father! I am imperfect and full of darkness, and You, Perfection and Light, have shown to me perfection, and the resplendent way of the doctrine of Your only-begotten Son. I was dead, and You have brought me to life. I was sick, and You have given me medicine, and not only the medicine of the Blood which You gave for the diseased human race in the person of Your Son, but also a medicine against a secret infirmity that I knew not of, in this precept that, in no way, can I judge any rational creature, and particularly Your servants, upon whom oftentimes I, as one blind and sick with this infirmity, passed judgment under the pretext of Your honor and the salvation of souls. Wherefore, I thank You, Supreme and Eternal Good, that, in the manifesting of Your truth and the deceitfulness of the Devil, and our own passions, You have made me know my infirmity. Wherefore I beseech You, through grace and mercy, that, from today henceforward, I may never again wander from the path of Your doctrine, given by Your goodness to me and to whoever wishes to follow it, because without You is nothing done. To You, then, Eternal Father, do I have recourse and flee, and I do not beseech You for myself alone, Father, but for the whole world, and particularly for the mystical body of the holy Church, that this truth given to me, miserable one, by You, Eternal Truth, may shine in Your ministers; and also I beseech You especially for all those whom You have given me, and whom You have made one thing with me, and whom I love with a particular love, because they will be my refreshment to the glory and praise of Your Name, when I see them running on this sweet and straight road, pure, and dead to their own will and opinion, and without any passing judgment on their neighbor, or causing him any scandal or murmuring. And I pray You, Sweetest Love, that not one of them may be taken from me by the hand of the infernal Devil, so that at last they may arrive at You, their End, Eternal Father.

"Also I make another petition to You for my two fathers, the supports whom You have placed on the earth to guard and instruct me, miserable infirm one, from the beginning of my conversion until now, that You unite them, and of two bodies make one soul, and that they attend to nothing else than to complete in themselves, and in the mysteries that You have placed in their hands, the glory and praise of Your Name, and the salvation of souls, and that I, an unworthy and miserable slave, and no daughter, may behave to them with due reverence and holy fear, for love of You, in a way that will be to Your honor, and their peace and quiet, and to the edification of the neighbor. I now know for certain, Eternal Truth, that You will not despise the desire of the petitions that I have made to You, because I know, from seeing what it has pleased You to manifest, and still more from proof, that You are the Acceptor of holy desires. I, Your unworthy servant, will strive, according as You will give me grace, to observe Your commandments and Your doctrine. Now, O Eternal Father, I remember a word which you said to me in speaking of the ministers of the holy Church, to the effect that You would speak to me more distinctly, in some other place, of the sins which they commit today; wherefore if it should please Your goodness to tell me anything of this matter, I will gladly hear it, so as to have material for increasing my grief, compassion, and anxious desire for their salvation; for I remember that You said, that, on account of the endurance and tears, the grief, and sweat and prayers of Your servants, You would reform the holy Church, and comfort her with good and holy pastors. I ask You this in order that these sentiments may increase in me."

Then the Eternal God, turning the eye of His mercy upon this soul, not despising her desire, but granting her requests, proceeded to satisfy the last petition, which she had made concerning His promise, saying, "Oh! best beloved and dearest daughter, I will fulfill your desire in this request, in order that, on your side, you may not sin through ignorance or negligence; for a fault of yours would be more serious and worthy of graver reproof now than before, because you have learnt more of My truth; wherefore apply yourself attentively to pray for all rational creatures, for the mystical body of the holy Church, and for those friends whom I have given you, whom you love with particular love, and be careful not to be negligent in giving them the benefit of your prayers, and the example of your life, and the teaching of your words, reproving vice and encouraging virtue according to your power.

"Concerning the supports which I have given you, of whom you spoke to Me, know that you are, in truth, a means by which they may each receive, according to their needs and fitness. And as I, your Creator, grant you the opportunity, for without Me you can do nothing, I will fulfill your desires, but do not you fail, or they either, in your hope in Me. My Providence will never fail you, and every man, if he be humble, shall receive that which he is fit to receive; and every minister, that which I have given him to administer, each in his own way, according to what he has received and will receive from My goodness."

"Now I will reply to that which you asked Me concerning the ministers of the holy Church, and, in order that you may the better understand the truth, open the eye of your intellect, and look at their excellence and the dignity in which I have placed them. And, since one thing is better known by means of contrast with its contrary, I will show you the dignity of those who use virtuously the treasure I have placed in their hands; and, in this way, you will the better see the misery of those who today are suckled at the breast of My Spouse." Then this soul obediently contemplated the truth, in which she saw virtue resplendent in those who truly taste it. Then said the Eternal God: "I will first, dearest daughter, speak to you of the dignity of priests, having placed them where they are through My Goodness, over and above the general love which I have had to My creatures, creating you in My image and similitude and re-creating you all to the life of grace in the Blood of My only-begotten Son, whence you have arrived at such excellence, through the union which I made of My Deity with human nature; so that in this you have greater dignity and excellence than the angels, for I took your human nature and not that of the angels. Wherefore, as I have said to you, I, God, have become man, and man has become God by the union of My Divine Nature with your human nature. This greatness is given in general to all rational creatures, but, among these I have especially chosen My ministers for the sake of your salvation, so that, through them, the Blood of the humble and immaculate Lamb, My only-begotten Son, may be administered to you. To them have I given the Sun to administer, giving them the light of science and the heat of Divine Love, united together in the color of the Body and Blood of My Son, whose Body is a Sun, because He is one thing with Me, the True Sun, in such a way that He cannot be separated or divided from Me, as in the case of the natural sun, in which heat and light cannot be separated, so perfect is their union; for, the sun, never leaving its orbit, lights the whole world and warms whoever wishes to be warmed by it, and is not defiled by any impurity on which it shines, for its light and heat and color are united.

"So this Word, My Son, with His most sweet Blood, is one Sun, all God and all man, because He is one thing with Me and I with Him. My power is not separated from His wisdom, nor the fiery heat of the Holy Spirit from Me, the Father, or from Him, the Son; for He is one thing with us, the Holy Spirit proceeding from the Father and the Son, and We together forming one and the same Sun; that is to say, I, the Eternal God, am that Sun whence have proceeded the Son and the Holy Spirit. To the Holy Spirit is attributed fire and to the Son wisdom, by which wisdom My ministers receive the light of grace, so that they may administer this light to others, with gratitude for the benefits received from Me, the Eternal Father, following the doctrine of the Eternal Wisdom, My only-begotten Son. This is that Light, which has the color of your humanity, color and light being closely united. Thus was the light of My Divinity united to the color of your humanity, which color shone brightly when it became perfect through its union with the Divine nature, and, by this means of the Incarnate Word mixed with the Light of My Divine nature and the fiery heat of the Holy Spirit, have you received the Light. Whom have I entrusted with its administration?

"My ministers in the mystical body of the holy Church, so that you may have life, receiving His Body in food and His Blood in drink. I have said to you that this Body is, as it were, a Sun. Wherefore, you cannot receive the Body without the Blood, or the Blood or the Body without the Soul of the Incarnate Word; nor the Soul, nor the Body, without the Divinity of Me, the Eternal God, because none of these can be separated from each other, as I said to you in another place that the Divine nature never left the human nature, either by death or from any other cause. So that you receive the whole Divine Essence in that most Sweet Sacrament concealed under the whiteness of the bread; for as the sun cannot be divided into light, heat, and color, the whole of God and the whole of man cannot be separated under the white mantle of the host; for even if the host should be divided into a million particles (if it were possible) in each particle should I be present, whole God and whole Man. When you break a mirror the reflection to be seen in it is not broken; similarly, when the host is divided God and man are not divided, but remain in each particle. Nor is the Sacrament diminished in itself, except as far as may be in the following example.

"If you have a light, and the whole world should come to you in order to take light from it - the light itself does not diminish - and yet each person has it all. It is true that everyone participates more or less in this light, according to the substance into which each one receives the fire. I will develop this metaphor further that you may the better understand Me. Suppose that there are many who bring their candles, one weighing an ounce, others two or six ounces, or a pound, or even more, and light them in the flame, in each candle, whether large or small, is the whole light, that is to say, the heat, the color, and the flame; nevertheless you would judge that he whose candle weighs an ounce has less of the light than he whose candle weighs a pound. Now the same thing happens to those who receive this Sacrament. Each one carries his own candle, that is the holy desire, with which he receives this Sacrament, which of itself is without light, and lights it by receiving this Sacrament. I say without light, because of yourselves you can do nothing, though I have given you the material, with which you can receive this light and feed it. The material is love, for through love I created you, and without love you cannot live.

"Your being, given to you through love, has received the right disposition in holy baptism, which you receive in virtue of the Blood of the Word, for, in no other way, could you participate in this light; you would be like a candle with no wick inside it, which cannot burn or receive light, if you have not received in your souls the wick which catches this Divine Flame, that is to say, the Holy Faith, which you receive, by grace, in baptism, united with the disposition of your soul created by Me, so fitted for love, that, without love, which is her very food, she cannot live. Where does the soul united in this way obtain light? At the fire of My Divine love, loving and fearing Me, and following the Doctrine of My Truth. It is true that the soul becomes more or less lighted according to the material which it brings to the fire; for although you all have one and the same material, in that you are all created to My image and similitude, and, being Christians, possess the light of holy baptism, each of you may grow in love and virtue by the help of My grace, as may please you. Not that you change the form of what I have given you, but that you increase your strength in love, and your free-will, by using it while you have time, for when time is past you can no longer do so. So that you can increase in love, as has been said, coming with love to receive this Sweet and Glorious Light, which I have given you as Food for your service, through My ministers, and you receive this Light according to the love and fiery desire with which you approach It.

"The Light Itself you receive entire, as I have said (in the example of those, who in spite of the difference in weight of their candles, all receive the entire light), and not divided, because It cannot be divided, as has been said, either on account of any imperfection of yours who receive, or of the minister; but you personally participate in this light, that is in the grace which you receive in this Sacrament, according to the holy desire with which you dispose yourselves to receive it. He who should go to this sweet Sacrament in the guilt of mortal sin, will receive no grace therefrom, though he actually receive the whole of God and the whole of Man. Do you know the condition of the soul who receives unworthily? She is like a candle on which water has fallen, which can do nothing but crackle when brought near the flame, for no sooner has the fire touched it, than it is extinguished, and nothing remains but smoke; so this soul has cast the water of guilt within her mind upon the candle which she received in holy baptism, which has drenched the wick of the grace of baptism, and, not having heated it at the fire of true contrition and confession, goes to the table of the altar to receive this Light with her body, and not with her mind, wherefore the Light, since the soul is not disposed as she should be for so great a mystery, does not remain by grace in that soul, but leaves her, and, in the soul, remains only greater confusion, for her light is extinguished and her sin increased by her darkness. Of the Sacrament she feels nothing but the crackling of a remorseful conscience, not through the defect of the Light Itself, for that can receive no hurt, but on account of the water that was in the soul, which impeded her proper disposition so that she could not receive the Light. See, therefore, that in no way can this Light, united with its heat and its color, be divided, either by the scanty desire of the soul when she receives the Sacrament, or by any defect which may be in the soul, or by any defect of him who administers it, as I told you of the sun which is not defiled by shining on anything foul, so the sweet Light of this Sacrament cannot be defiled, divided, or diminished in any way, nor can it be detached from its orbit.

"If all the world should receive in communion the Light and Heat of this Sun, the Word, My only-begotten Son, would not be separated from Me - the True Sun, His Eternal Father - because in His mystical Body, the holy Church, He is administered to whoever will receive Him. He remains wholly with Me, and yet you have Him, whole God and whole man, as I told you, in the metaphor of the light, that, if all the world came to take light from it, each would have it entire, and yet it would remain whole."

How the bodily sentiments are all deceived in the aforesaid Sacrament, but not those of the soul; therefore it is, with the latter, that one must see, taste, and touch It; and of a beautiful vision this soul had upon this subject.

"Oh, dearest daughter, open well the eye of your intellect and gaze into the abyss of My love, for there is no rational creature whose heart would not melt for love in contemplating and considering, among the other benefits she receives from Me, the special Gift that she receives in the Sacrament.

"And with what eye, dearest daughter, should you and others look at this mystery, and how should you touch it? Not only with the bodily sight and touch, because in this Sacrament all bodily perceptions fail.

"The eye can only see, and the hand can only touch, the white substance of the bread, and the taste can only taste the savor of the bread, so that the grosser bodily sentiments are deceived; but the soul cannot be deceived in her sentiments unless she wish to be - that is, unless she let the light of the most holy faith be taken away from her by infidelity.

"How is this Sacrament to be truly tasted, seen, and touched? With the sentiment of the soul. With what eye is It to be seen? With the eye of the intellect if within it is the pupil of the most holy faith. This eye sees in that whiteness whole God and whole man, the Divine nature united with the human nature, the Body, the Soul, and the Blood of Christ, the Soul united to the Body, the Body and the Soul united with My Divine nature, not detached from Me, as I revealed to you, if you remember well, almost in the beginning of your life; and not so much at first through the eye of your intellect as through your bodily eye, although the light being so great your bodily eyes lost their vision, and only the sight of the eye of your intellect remained. I showed it to you for your enlightenment in the battle that the Devil had been waging against you in this Sacrament; and to make you increase in love in the light of the most holy faith.

"You know that you went one morning to church at sunrise to hear Mass, having beforehand been tormented by the Devil, and you placed yourself upright at the Altar of the Crucifix, while the priest went to the Altar of Mary; you stood there to consider your sin, fearing to have offended Me through the vexation which the Devil had been causing you, and to consider My love, which had made you worthy to hear Mass, seeing that you deemed yourself unworthy to enter into My holy temple. When the minister came to consecrate, you raised your eyes above his head while he was saying the words of consecration, and I manifested Myself to you, and you saw issue from My breast a light, like a ray from the sun, which proceeds from the circle of the sun without being separated from it, out of the midst of which light came a dove and hovered over the host, in virtue of the words which the minister was saying. But sight remained alone in the eye of your intellect, because your bodily sight was not strong enough to stand the light, and in that place you saw and tasted the Abyss of the Trinity, whole God and whole man concealed and veiled in that whiteness that you saw in the bread; and you perceived that the seeing of the Light and the presence of the Word, which you saw intellectually in the whiteness of the bread, did not prevent you seeing at the same time the actual whiteness of the bread, the one vision did not prevent the other vision, that is to say, the sight of the God-Man revealed in the bread did not prevent the sight of the bread, for neither its whiteness, nor its touch, nor its savor were taken away. This was shown you by My goodness, as I have said to you. The eye of the intellect had the true vision, using the pupil of the holy faith, for this eye should be your principal means of vision, inasmuch as it cannot be deceived; wherefore, with it you should look on this Sacrament. How do you touch It? By the hand of love. With this hand alone can you touch that which the eye of the intellect has recognized in this Sacrament. The soul touches Me with the hand of love, as if to certify to herself that which she has seen and known through faith. How do you taste It? With the palate of holy desire. The corporal palate tastes only the savor of the bread; but the palate of the soul, which is holy desire, tastes God and Man. See, therefore, that the perceptions of the body are deluded, but not those of the soul, for she is illuminated and assured in her own perceptions, for she touches with the hand of love that which the eye of her intellect has seen with the pupil of holy faith; and with her palate - that is, with fiery desire - she tastes My Burning Charity, My Ineffable Love, with which I have made her worthy to receive the tremendous mystery of this Sacrament and the Grace which is contained therein. See, therefore, that you should receive and look on this Sacrament, not only with bodily perceptions, but rather with your spiritual perceptions, disposing your soul in the way that has been said, to receive, and taste, and see this Sacrament."

Of the excellent state of the soul who receives the sacrament in grace.

"See, dearest daughter, in what an excellent state is the soul who receives, as she should, this Bread of Life, this Food of the Angels. By receiving this Sacrament she dwells in Me and I in her, as the fish in the sea, and the sea in the fish - thus do I dwell in the soul, and the soul in Me - the Sea Pacific. In that soul grace dwells, for, since she has received this Bread of Life in a state of grace, My grace remains in her, after the accidents of bread have been consumed. I leave you the imprint of grace, as does a seal, which, when lifted from the hot wax upon which it has been impressed, leaves behind its imprint, so the virtue of this Sacrament remains in the soul, that is to say, the heat of My Divine charity, and the clemency of the Holy Spirit. There also remains to you the wisdom of My only-begotten Son, by which the eye of your intellect has been illuminated to see and to know the doctrine of My Truth, and, together with this wisdom, you participate in My strength and power, which strengthen the soul against her sensual self-love, against the Devil, and against the world. You see then that the imprint remains, when the seal has been taken away, that is, when the material accidents of the bread, having been consumed, this True Sun has returned to Its Center, not that it was ever really separated from It, but constantly united to Me. The Abyss of My loving desire for your salvation has given you, through My dispensation and Divine Providence, coming to the help of your needs, the sweet Truth as Food in this life, where you are pilgrims and travelers, so that you may have refreshment, and not forget the benefit of the Blood. See then how straitly you are constrained and obliged to render Me love, because I love you so much, and, being the Supreme and Eternal Goodness, deserve your love."

How the things which have been said about the excellence of this Sacrament, have been said that we might know better the dignity of priests; and how God demands in them greater purity than in other creatures.

"I have told you all this, dearest daughter, that you may the better recognize the dignity to which I have called My ministers, so that your grief at their miseries may be more intense. If they themselves considered their own dignity they would not be in the darkness of mortal sin, or defile the face of their soul. They would not only see their offenses against Me, but also, that, if they gave their bodies to be burned, they would not repay the tremendous grace and favor which they have received, inasmuch as no greater dignity exists in this life. They are My anointed ones, and I call them My Christs, because I have given them the office of administering Me to you, and have placed them like fragrant flowers in the mystical body of the holy Church. The angel himself has no such dignity, for I have given it to those men whom I have chosen for My ministers, and whom I have appointed as earthly angels in this life. In all souls I demand purity and charity, that they should love Me and their neighbor, helping him by the ministration of prayer, as I said to you in another place. But far more do I demand purity in My ministers, and love towards Me, and towards their fellow-creatures, administering to them the Body and Blood of My only-begotten Son, with the fire of charity, and a hunger for the salvation of souls, for the glory and honor of My Name. Even as these ministers require cleanness in the chalice in which this Sacrifice is made, even so do I require the purity and cleanness of their heart and soul and mind. And I wish their body to be preserved, as the instrument of the soul in perfect charity; and I do not wish them to feed upon and wallow in the mire of filth, or to be inflated by pride, seeking great prelacies, or to be cruel to themselves or to their fellow-creatures, because they cannot use cruelty to themselves without being cruel to their fellow-creatures; for, if by sin they are cruel to themselves, they are cruel to the souls of their neighbors, in that they do not give them an example of life, nor care to draw them out of the hands of the Devil, nor to administer to them the Body and Blood of My only-begotten Son, and Me the True Light, as I told you, and the other Sacraments of the holy Church. So that, in being cruel to themselves, they are cruel to others."

Of the excellence, virtues, and holy works of virtuous and holy ministers; and how such are like the sun.

"I will now speak to you, in order to give a little refreshment to your soul, and to mitigate your grief at the darkness of these miserable subjects, of the holy life of some of My ministers, of whom I have spoken to you, who are like the sun, for the odor of their virtues mitigates the stench of the vices of the others, and the light thereof shines in their darkness. And, by means of this light, will you the better be able to understand the darkness and sins of My unworthy ministers. Open then the eye of your intellect and gaze at the Sun of Justice, and you will see those glorious ministers, who, through ministering the Sun, have become like to It, as I told you of Peter, the prince of the Apostles, who received the keys of the kingdom of Heaven. I say the same of these others, who have administered, in the garden of the holy Church, the Light, that is to say, the Body and the Blood of My only-begotten Son, who is Himself the undivided Sun, as has been said, and all the Sacraments of the holy Church, which all give life in virtue of the Blood. Each one, placed in a different rank, has administered, according to his state, the grace of the Holy Spirit. With what have they administered it? With the light of grace, which they have drawn from this True Light. With light alone? No; because the light cannot be separated from the warmth and color of grace, wherefore a man must either have the light, warmth, and color of grace, or none at all. A man in mortal sin is deprived of the life of grace, and he who is in grace has illuminated the eye of his intellect to know Me, who gave him both grace and the virtue which preserves it, and, in that light, he knows the misery and the reason of sin, that is to say, his own self-love, on which account he hates it, and thereby receives the warmth of Divine love into his affection, which follows his intellect, and he receives the color of this glorious Light, following the doctrine of My sweet Truth, by which his memory is filled with the benefit of the Blood. You see, therefore, that no one can receive the light without receiving the warmth and the color, for they are united together and are one thing; wherefore he cannot, as I have said to you, have one power of his soul so ordered as to receive Me, the True Sun, unless all three powers of his soul are brought together and ordered in My Name. For, as soon as the eye of the intellect lifts itself with the pupil of faith above sensual vision in the contemplation of Me, affection follows it, loving that which the intellect sees and knows, and the memory is filled with that which the affection loves; and, as soon as these powers are thus disposed, the soul participates in Me, the Sun who illuminates her with My power, and with the wisdom of My only-begotten Son, and the fiery clemency of the Holy Spirit. See, then, that these have taken on them the condition of the Sun, for, having clothed themselves, and filled the power of their soul with Me, the true Sun, they become like Me. The Sun illuminates them and causes the earth of their souls to germinate with Its heat. Thus do My sweet ministers, elected and anointed and placed in the mystical body of the holy Church, in order to administer Me, the Sun, that is to say, the Body and Blood of My only-begotten Son, together with the other Sacraments, which draw their life from this Blood; this they do in two ways, actually, in administering the Sacraments, and spiritually, by shedding forth in the mystical body of the holy Church, the light of supernatural science, together with the color of an honorable and holy life, following the doctrine of My Truth, which they administer in the ardent love with which they cause barren souls to bear fruit, illuminating them with the light of their science, and driving away the darkness of their mortal sin and infidelity, by the example of their holy and regular life, and reforming the lives of those who live in disorder and darkness of sin, and in coldness, through the privation of charity. So you see that they are the Sun, because they have taken the condition of the Sun from Me, the True Sun, because, through affection of love, they are one thing with Me, and I with them, as I narrated to you in another place, and each one has given light in the holy Church, according to the position to which I have elected him: Peter with preaching and doctrine, and in the end with blood; Gregory with science, and holy scripture, and with the mirror of his life; Sylvester, against the infidels, and with disputation and proving of the most holy faith, which he made in word and in deed, receiving virtue from Me. If you turn to Augustine, and to the glorious Thomas and Jerome, and the others, you will see how much light they have thrown over this spouse, extirpating error, like lamps placed upon the candelabra, with true and perfect humility. And, as if famished for such food, they feed upon My honor, and the salvation of souls, upon the table of the most holy Cross. The martyrs, indeed, with blood, which blood cast up sweet perfume before My countenance; and, with the perfume of blood, and of the virtues, and with the light of science, they brought forth fruit in this spouse and extended the faith, and, by their means, the light of the most holy faith was rekindled in the darkened. And prelates, placed in the position of the prelacy of Christ on earth, offered Me the sacrifice of justice with holy and upright lives. The pearl of justice, with true humility, and most ardent love, shone in them, and in their subjects, with the light of discretion. In them, principally because they justly paid Me My due, in rendering glory and praise to My Name, and, to their own sensuality, hatred and displeasure, despising vice and embracing virtue, with love of Me and of their neighbor. With humility they trampled on pride, and, with purity of heart and of body, came, like angels, to the table of the altar, and, with sincerity of mind, celebrated, burning in the furnace of love. And, because they first had done justice to themselves, they therefore did justice to those under them, wishing to see them live virtuously, and correcting them without any servile fear, because they were not thinking of themselves, but solely of My honor and the salvation of souls, like good shepherds, followers of the Good Shepherd, My Truth, whom I gave you to lead your sheep, having willed that He should give His life for you. These have followed His footsteps, and therefore did they correct them, and did not let their members become putrid for want of correcting, but they charitably corrected them with the unction of benignity, and with the sharpness of fire, cauterizing the wound of sin with reproof and penance, little or much, according to the graveness of the fault. And, in order to correct it and to speak the truth, they did not even fear death. They were true gardeners who, with care and holy tears, took away the thorns of mortal sins, and planted plants odoriferous of virtue. Wherefore, those under them lived in holy, true fear, and grew up like sweet smelling flowers in the mystic body of the holy Church (because they were not deprived of correction, and so were not guilty of sin), for My gardeners corrected them without any servile fear, being free from it, and without any sin, for they balanced exactly the scales of holy justice, reproving humbly and without human respect. And this justice was and is that pearl which shines in them, and which gave peace and light in the minds of the people and caused holy fear to be with them, and unity of hearts. And I would that you know that, more darkness and division have come into the world amongst seculars and religious and the clergy and pastors of the holy Church, through the lack of the light of justice, and the advent of the darkness of injustice, than from any other causes.

"Neither the civil law, nor the divine law, can be kept in any degree without holy justice, because he who is not corrected, and does not correct others, becomes like a limb which putrefies, and corrupts the whole body, because the bad physician, when it had already begun to corrupt, placed ointment immediately upon it, without having first burnt the wound. So, were the prelate, or any other lord having subjects, on seeing one putrefying from the corruption of mortal sin, to apply to him the ointment of soft words of encouragement alone, without reproof, he would never cure him, but the putrefaction would rather spread to the other members, who, with him, form one body under the same pastor. But if he were a physician, good and true to those souls, as were those glorious pastors of old, he would not give salving ointment without the fire of reproof. And, were the member still to remain obstinate in his evil doing, he would cut him off from the congregation in order that he corrupt not the other members with the putrefaction of mortal sin. But they act not so today, but, in cases of evil doing, they even pretend not to see. And do you know why? The root of self-love is alive in them, wherefore they bear perverted and servile fear. Because they fear to lose their position or their temporal goods, or their prelacy, they do not correct, but act like blind ones, in that they see not the real way by which their position is to be kept. If they would only see that it is by holy justice they would be able to maintain it; but they do not, because they are deprived of light. But, thinking to preserve their position with injustice, they do not reprove the faults of those under them; and they are deluded by their own sensitive self-love, or by their desire for lordship and prelacy, and they correct not the faults they should correct in others, because the same or greater ones are their own. They feel themselves comprehended in the guilt, and they therefore lose all ardor and security, and, fettered by servile fear, they make believe not to see. And, moreover, if they do see they do not correct, but allow themselves to be bound over with flattering words and with many presents, and they themselves find the excuse for the guilty ones not to be punished. In such as these are fulfilled the words spoken by My Truth, saying: 'These are blind and leaders of the blind, and if the blind lead the blind, they both fall into the ditch.' My sweet ministers, of whom I spoke to you, who have the properties and condition of the sun, did not, and do not (if there be any now) act so. And they are truly suns, as I have told you, because in them is no darkness of sin, or of ignorance, because they follow the doctrine of My Truth. They are not tepid, because they burn in the furnace of My love, and because they are despisers of the grandeurs, positions, and delights of the world. They fear not to correct, for he who does not desire lordship or prelacy will not fear to lose it, and will reprove manfully, and he whose conscience does not reprove him of guilt, does not fear.

"And therefore this pearl of justice was not dimmed in My anointed ones, My Christs (of whom I have narrated to you), but was resplendent in them, wherefore they embraced voluntary poverty, and sought out vileness with profound humility, and cared not for scorn or villainies, or the detractions of men, or insult, or opprobrium, or pain, or torment.

"They were cursed, and they blessed, and, with true patience, they bore themselves like terrestrial angels, not by nature, but by their ministry, and the supernatural grace given to them, of administering the Body and Blood of My only-begotten Son. And they are truly angels. Because, as the angel, which I give you to be your guardian, ministers to you holy and good inspirations, so were these ministers angels, and were given by My goodness to be guardians, and therefore had they their eye continually over those under them, like real guardian angels, inspiring in their hearts holy and good thoughts, and offering up for them before Me, sweet and amorous desires with continual prayer, and the doctrine of words, and with example of life. So you see that they are angels, placed by My burning love, like lanterns in the mystic body of the holy Church, to be your guardians, so that you blind ones may have guides to direct you into the way of truth, giving you good inspirations, with prayers and example of life, and doctrine as I said. With how much humility did they govern those under them, and converse with them! With how much hope and lively faith, and therefore with liberality, did they distribute to the poor the substance of the holy Church, not fearing, or caring if for them and their subjects temporal substance diminished. And they scarcely observed that which they were really bound to do, that is, to distribute the temporal substance to their own necessity being the poor in the Church. They saved nothing, and after their death there remained no money at all, and there were some even who, for the sake of the poor, left the Church in debt. This was because through the largeness of their charity, and of the hope that they had placed in My Providence, they were without servile fear that anything should diminish to them, either spiritual or temporal.

"The sign that a creature hopes in Me and not in himself, is that he does not fear with a servile fear. They who hope in themselves are the ones who fear, and are afraid of their own shadow, and doubt lest the sky and earth fade away before them. With such fears as these, and a perverted hope in their own small knowledge, they spend so much miserable solicitude in acquiring and preserving temporal things, that they turn their back on the spiritual, caring not for them. But they, miserable, faithless, proud ones consider not that I alone am He who provides all things necessary for the soul and the body, and that with the same measure that My creatures hope in Me, will My providence be measured to them. The miserable presumptuous ones do not regard the fact that I am He who is, and they are they who are not, and that they have received their being, and every other additional grace, from My Goodness. And therefore his labor may be reputed to be in vain, who watches the city if it be not guarded by Me. All his labor will be vain, if he thinks by his labor or solicitude to keep it, because I alone keep it. It is true that I desire you to use your being, and exercise the graces which I have bestowed upon you, in virtue using the free-will which I have given you, with the light of reason, because though I created you without your help I will not save you without it. I loved you before you were, and those My beloved ones saw and knew this, and therefore they loved Me ineffably, and through their love hoped so greatly in Me that they feared nothing. Sylvester feared not when he stood before the Emperor Constantine disputing with those twelve Jews before the whole crowd, but with lively faith he believed that I being for him, no one could be against him; and in the same way the others all lost their every fear, because they were not alone but were accompanied, because being in the enjoyment of love, they were in Me, and from Me they acquired the light of the wisdom of My only-begotten Son, and from Me they received the faculty to be strong and powerful against the princes and tyrants of the world, and from Me they had the fire of the Holy Spirit, sharing the clemency and burning love of that Spirit.

"This love was and is the companion of whosoever desires it, with the light of faith, with hope, with fortitude, true patience and long perseverance even until death. So you see that because they were not alone but were accompanied they feared nothing. He only who feels himself to be alone, and hopes in himself, deprived of the affection of love, fears, and is afraid of every little thing, because he alone is without Me who give supreme security to the soul who possesses Me through the affection of love. And of this did those glorious ones, My beloved, have full experience, for nothing could injure their souls; but they on the contrary could injure men and the devils, who oftentimes remained bound by the virtue and power that I had given My servants over them. This was because I responded to the love, faith, and hope they had placed in Me. Your tongue would not be sufficient to relate their virtues, neither the eye of your intellect to see the fruit which they receive in everlasting life, and that all will receive who follow in their footsteps. They are like precious stones, and as such do they stand in My presence, because I have received their labor and poverty and the light which they shed with the odor of virtues in the mystic body of the holy Church. And in the life eternal I have placed them in the greatest dignity, and they receive blessing and glory in My sight, because they gave the example of an honorable and holy life, and with light administered the Light of the Body and Blood of My only-begotten Son, and all the Sacraments. And these My anointed ones and ministers are peculiarly beloved by Me, on account of the dignity which I placed in them, and because this Treasure which I placed in their hands they did not hide through negligence and ignorance, but rather recognized it to be from Me, and exercised it with care and profound humility with true and real virtues; and because I, for the salvation of souls, having placed them in so much excellency they never rested like good shepherds from putting the sheep into the fold of the holy Church, and even out of love and hunger for souls they gave themselves to die, to get them out of the hands of the devil. They made themselves infirm with those who were infirm, so that they might not be overcome with despair, and to give them more courage in exposing their infirmity, they would oftentimes lend countenance to their infirmity and say, 'I, too, am infirm with you.' They wept with those who wept, and rejoiced with those who rejoiced; and thus sweetly they knew to give everyone his nourishment, preserving the good and rejoicing in their virtues, not being gnawed by envy, but expanded with the broadness of love for their neighbors, and those under them. They drew the imperfect ones out of imperfection, themselves becoming imperfect and infirm with them, as I told you, with true and holy compassion, and correcting them and giving them penance for the sins they committed - they through love endured their penance - together with them. For through love, they who gave the penance, bore more pain than they who received it; and there were even those who actually performed the penance, and especially when they had seen that it had appeared particularly difficult to the penitent. Wherefore by that act the difficulty became changed into sweetness.

"Oh! My beloved ones, they made themselves subjects, being prelates, they made themselves servants, being lords, they made themselves infirm, being whole, and without infirmity and the leprosy of mortal sin, being strong they made themselves weak, with the foolish and simple they showed themselves simple, and with the small insignificant. And so with love they knew how to be all things to all men, and to give to each one his nourishment. What caused them to do thus? The hunger and desire for My honor and the salvation of souls which they had conceived in Me. They ran to feed on it at the table of the holy Cross, not fleeing from or refusing any labor, but with zeal for souls and for the good of the holy Church and the spread of the faith, they put themselves in the midst of the thorns of tribulation, and exposed themselves to every peril with true patience, offering incense odoriferous with anxious desires, and humble and continual prayers. With tears and sweat they anointed the wounds of their neighbor, that is the wounds of the guilt of mortal sin, which latter were perfectly cured, the ointment so made, being received in humility."

A brief repetition of the preceding chapter; and of the reverence which should be paid to priests, whether they are good or bad.

"I have shown you, dearest daughter, a sample of the excellence of good priests (for what I have shown you is only a sample of what that excellence really is), and I have told you of the dignity in which I have placed them, having elected them for My ministers, on account of which dignity and authority I do not wish them to be punished by the hand of seculars on account of any personal defect, for those who punish them offend Me miserably. But I wish seculars to hold them in due reverence, not for their own sakes, as I have said, but for Mine, by reason of the authority which I have given them. Wherefore this reverence should never diminish in the case of priests whose virtue grows weak, any more than in the case of those virtuous ones of whose goodness I have spoken to you; for all alike have been appointed ministers of the Sun - that is of the Body and Blood of My Son, and of the other Sacraments.

"This dignity belongs to good and bad alike - all have the Sun to administer, as has been said, and perfect priests are themselves in a condition of light, that is to say, they illuminate and warm their neighbors through their love. And with this heat they cause virtues to spring up and bear fruit in the souls of their subjects. I have appointed them to be in very truth your guardian angels to protect you; to inspire your hearts with good thoughts by their holy prayers, and to teach you My doctrine reflected in the mirror of their life, and to serve you by administering to you the holy Sacraments, thus serving you, watching over you, and inspiring you with good and holy thoughts as does an angel.

"See, then, that besides the dignity to which I have appointed them, how worthy they are of being loved; when they also possess the adornment of virtue, as did those of whom I spoke to you, which are all bound and obliged to possess, and in what great reverence you should hold them, for they are My beloved children and shine each as a sun in the mystical body of the holy Church by their virtues, forevery virtuous man is worthy of love, and these all the more by reason of the ministry which I have placed in their hands. You should love them therefore by reason of the virtue and dignity of the Sacrament, and by reason of that very virtue and dignity you should hate the defects of those who live miserably in sin, but not on that account appoint yourselves their judges, which I forbid, because they are My Christs, and you ought to love and reverence the authority which I have given them. You know well that if a filthy and badly dressed person brought you a great treasure from which you obtained life, you would not hate the bearer, however ragged and filthy he might be, through love of the treasure and of the lord who sent it to you. His state would indeed displease you, and you would be anxious through love of his master that he should be cleansed from his foulness and properly clothed. This, then, is your duty according to the demands of charity, and thus I wish you to act with regard to such badly ordered priests, who themselves filthy and clothed in garments ragged with vice through their separation from My love, bring you great Treasures - that is to say, the Sacraments of the holy Church - from which you obtain the life of grace, receiving Them worthily (in spite of the great defects there may be in them) through love of Me, the Eternal God, who send them to you, and through love of that life of grace which you receive from the great treasure, by which they administer to you the whole of God and the whole of Man, that is to say, the Body and Blood of My Son united to My Divine nature. Their sins indeed should displease you, and you should hate them, and strive with love and holy prayer to re-clothe them, washing away their foulness with your tears - that is to say, that you should offer them before Me with tears and great desire, that I may re-clothe them in My goodness, with the garment of charity. Know well that I wish to do them grace, if only they will dispose themselves to receive it, and you to pray for it; for it is not according to My will that they should administer to you the Sun being themselves in darkness, not that they should be stripped of the garment of virtue, foully living in dishonor; on the contrary I have given them to you, and appointed them to be earthly angels and suns, as I have said. It not being My will that they should be in this state, you should pray for them, and not judge them, leaving their judgment to Me. And I, moved by your prayers, will do them mercy if they will only receive it, but if they do not correct their life, their dignity will be the cause of their ruin. For if they do not accept the breadth of My mercy, I, the Supreme Judge, shall terribly condemn them at their last extremity, and they will be sent to the eternal fire."

Of the difference between the death of a just man and that of a sinner, and first of the death of the just man.

"Having told you how the world and the devils accuse these wretches, which is indeed the truth, I wish to speak to you in more detail on this point (so that you may have greater compassion on these poor wretches), telling you how different are the struggles of the soul of a just man to those of a sinner, and how different are their deaths, and how the peace of the just man's death is greater or less according to the perfection of his soul. For I wish you to know that all the sufferings which rational creatures endure depend on their will, because if their will were in accordance with mine they would endure no suffering, not that they would have no labors on that account, but because labors cause no suffering to a will which gladly endures them, seeing that they are ordained by My will. Such men as these wage war with the world, the Devil, and their own sensuality through holy hatred of themselves. Wherefore when they come to the point of death, they die peacefully, because they have vanquished their enemies during their life. The world cannot accuse such a man, because he saw through its deceptions and therefore renounced it with all its delights. His sensual fragility and his body do not accuse him, because he bound sensuality like a slave with the rein of reason, macerating his flesh with penance, with watchings, and humble and continual prayer. The will of his senses he slew with hatred and dislike of vice, and with love of virtue. He has entirely lost all tenderness for his body, which tenderness and love between the soul and the body makes death seem difficult, and on account of it man naturally fears death; but since the virtue of a just and perfect man transcends nature, extinguishing his natural fear and overcoming it with holy hatred of himself and desire of arriving at his last end, his natural tenderness cannot make war on him, and his conscience remains in peace; for during his life his conscience kept a good guard, warning him when enemies were coming to attack the city of his soul, like a watch-dog which stands at the door, and when it sees enemies warns the guards by its barking, for in this way the dog of conscience warns the sentry of reason, and the reason together with the free-will know by the light of the intellect whether the stranger be friend or enemy. To a friend, that is to say, to virtue and holy thoughts, he gave his delighted love, receiving and using these with great solicitude; to an enemy, that is to say, to vice and wicked thoughts, he gave hatred and displeasure. And with the knife of hatred of self, and love of Me, and with the light of reason, and the hand of free-will he struck his enemies; so that at the point of death his conscience, having been a faithful guardian, does not gnaw but remains in peace.

"It is true that a just soul, through humility, and because at the moment of death she realizes better the value of time and of the jewels of virtue, reproves herself, seeming to herself to have used her time but little; but this is not an afflictive pain, but rather profitable, for the soul recollected in herself, is caused by it to throw herself before the Blood of the humble and immaculate Lamb My Son. The just man does not turn his head to admire his past virtues, because he neither can nor will hope in his own virtues, but only in the Blood in which he has found mercy; and as he lived in the memory of that Blood, so in death he is inebriated and drowned in the same. How is it that the devils cannot reprove him of sin? Because during his life he conquered their malice with wisdom, yet they come round him to see if they can acquire anything, and appear in horrible shapes in order to frighten him with hideous aspect, and many diverse phantasms, but the poison of sin not being in his soul, their aspect causes him no terror or fear, as it would do to another who had lived wickedly in the world. Wherefore the devils, seeing that the soul has entered into the Blood with ardent love, cannot endure the sight, but stand afar off shooting their arrows. But their war and their shouts cannot hurt that soul, who already is beginning to taste eternal life, as I said to you in another place, for with the eye of the intellect illuminated by the pupil of the holy faith, she sees Me, the Infinite and Eternal Good, whom she hopes to obtain by grace, not as her due, but by virtue of Jesus Christ My Son.

"Wherefore opening the arms of hope and seizing Him with the hands of love, she seems to enter into His possession before she actually does so, in the way which I have narrated to you in another place. Passing suddenly, drowned in the Blood, by the narrow door of the Word she reaches Me, the Sea Pacific. For sea and door are united together. I and the Truth, My only-begotten Son being one and the same thing. What joy such a soul receives who sees herself so sweetly arrived at this pass, for in Truth she tastes the happiness of the angelic nature! This joy is received by all those who pass in this sweet manner, but to a far greater extent by My ministers, of whom I spoke to you, who have lived like angels, for in this life have they lived with greater knowledge, and with greater hunger for the salvation of souls. I do not speak only of the light of virtue which all can have in general, but of the supernatural light which these men possessed over and above the light of virtuous living, the light, that is, of holy science, by which science they knew more of My Truth, and he who knows more loves Me more, and he who loves Me more receives more. Your reward is measured according to the measure of your love, and if you should ask Me, whether one who has no science can attain to this love, I should reply, yes it is possible that he may attain to it, but an individual case does not make a general law and I always discourse to you in general.

"They also receive greater dignity on account of their priesthood, because they have personally received the office of eating souls in My honor. For just as everyone has the office of remaining in charity with his neighbor, to them is given the office of administering the Blood, and of governing souls.

"Wherefore if they do this solicitously and with love of virtue they receive, as has been said, more than others. Oh! how happy are their souls when they come to the extremity of death! For they have been the defenders and preachers of the faith to their neighbor. This faith they have incarnated in their very marrow, and with it they see their place of repose in Me. The hope with which they have lived, confiding in My providence and losing all trust in themselves, in that they did not hope in their own knowledge, and having lost hope in themselves, placed no inordinate love in any fellow-creature or in any created thing; having lived in voluntary poverty, causes them now with great delight to lift their confidence towards Me. Their heart, which was a vessel of love, inscribed by their ardent charity with My name, they showed forth with the example of their good and holy life and by the doctrine of their words to their neighbor. This heart then arises and seizes Me, who am its End, with ineffable love, restoring to Me the pearl of justice which it always carried before it, doing justice to all, and discreetly rendering to each his due. Wherefore this man renders to Me justice with true humility, and renders glory and praise to My Name, because he refers to Me the grace of having been able to run his course with a pure and holy conscience, and with himself he is indignant, deeming himself unworthy of receiving such grace.

"His conscience gives good testimony of him to Me, and I justly give him the crown of justice, adorned with the pearls of the virtues - that is, of the fruit which love has drawn from the virtues. Oh, earthly angel! happy you are in that you have not been ungrateful for the benefits received from Me, and have not been negligent or ignorant, but have solicitously opened your eye by the true light, and kept it on your subjects, and have faithfully and manfully followed the doctrine of the Good Shepherd, sweet Christ Jesus, My only-begotten Son, wherefore you are really now passing through Him, the Door, bathed and drowned in His blood, with your troop of lambs of whom you have brought many by your holy doctrine and example to eternal life, and have left many behind you in a state of grace.

"Oh, dearest daughter! to such as these the vision of the devils can do no harm, because of the vision which they have of Me, which they see by faith and hold by love; the darkness and the terrible aspect of the demons do not give them trouble or any fear, because in them is not the poison of sin. There is no servile fear in them, but holy fear. Wherefore they do not fear the demon's deception, because with supernatural light and with the light of Holy Scripture they know them, so that they do not cause them darkness or disquietude. So thus they gloriously pass, bathed in the blood, with hunger for the salvation of souls, all on fire with love for the neighbor, having passed through the door of the word and entered into Me; and by My goodness each one is arranged in his place, and to each one is measured of the affection of love according as he has measured to Me."

Of the death of sinners, and of their pains in the hour of death.

"Not so excellent, dearest daughter, is the end of these other poor wretches who are in great misery as I have related to you. How terrible and dark is their death! Because in the moment of death, as I told you, the Devil accuses them with great terror and darkness, showing his face, which you know is so horrible that the creature would rather choose any pain that can be suffered in this world than see it; and so greatly does he freshen the sting of conscience that it gnaws him horribly. The disordinate delights and sensuality of which he made lords over his reason, accuse him miserably, because then he knows the truth of that which at first he knew not, and his error brings him to great confusion.

"In his life he lived unfaithfully to Me - self-love having veiled the pupil of the most holy faith - wherefore the Devil torments him with infidelity in order to bring him to despair. Oh! how hard for them is this battle, because it finds them disarmed, without the armor of affection and charity; because, as members of the Devil, they have been deprived of it all. Wherefore they have not the supernatural light, neither the light of science, because they did not understand it, the horns of their pride not letting them understand the sweetness of its marrow. Wherefore now in the great battle they know not what to do. They are not nourished in hope, because they have not hoped in Me, neither in the Blood of which I made them ministers, but in themselves alone, and in the dignities and delights of the world. And the incarnate wretch did not see that all was counted to him with interest, and that as a debtor he would have to render an account to Me; now he finds himself denuded and without any virtue, and on whichever side he turns he hears nothing but reproaches with great confusion. His injustice which he practiced in his life accuses him to his conscience, wherefore he dares not ask other than justice.

"And I tell you that so great is that shame and confusion that unless in their life they have taken the habit of hoping in My mercy, that is, have taken the milk of mercy (although on account of their sins this is great presumption, for you cannot truly say that he who strikes Me with the arm of My mercy has a hope in mercy, but rather has presumption), there is not one who would not despair, and with despair they would arrive with the Devil in eternal damnation.

"But arriving at the extremity of death, and recognizing his sin, his conscience unloaded by holy confession, and presumption taken away, so that he offends no more, there remains mercy, and with this mercy he can, if he will, take hold on hope. This is the effect of Mercy, to cause them to hope therein during their life, although I do not grant them this, so that they should offend Me by means of My mercy, but rather that they should dilate themselves in charity, and in the consideration of My goodness. But they act in a contrary way, because they offend Me in the hope which they have in My mercy. And nevertheless, I keep them in this hope so that at the last moment they may have something which they may lay hold of, and by so doing not faint away with the condemnation which they receive, and thus arrive at despair; for this final sin of despair is much more displeasing to Me and injures them much more than all the other sins which they have committed. And this is the reason why this sin is more dangerous to them and displeasing to Me, because they commit other sins through some delight of their own sensuality, and they sometimes grieve for them, and if they grieve in the right way their grief will procure them mercy. But it is no fragility of your nature which moves you to despair, for there is no pleasure and nothing but intolerable suffering in it. One who despairs despises My mercy, making his sin to be greater than mercy and goodness. Wherefore, if a man fall into this sin, he does not repent, and does not truly grieve for his offense against Me as he should, grieving indeed for his own loss, but not for the offense done to Me, and therefore he receives eternal damnation. See, therefore, that this sin alone leads him to hell, where he is punished for this and all the other sins which he has committed; whereas had he grieved and repented for the offense done to Me, and hoped in My mercy, he would have found mercy, for, as I have said to you, My mercy is greater without any comparison than all the sins which any creature can commit; wherefore it greatly displeases Me that they should consider their sins to be greater.

"Despair is that sin which is pardoned neither here nor hereafter, and it is because despair displeases Me so much that I wish them to hope in My mercy at the point of death, even if their life have been disordered and wicked. This is why during their life I use this sweet trick with them, making them hope greatly in My mercy, for when, having fed themselves with this hope, they arrive at death, they are not so inclined to abandon it, on account of the severe condemnation they receive, as if they had not so nourished themselves.

"All this is given them by the fire and abyss of My inestimable love, but because they have used it in the darkness of self-love, from which has proceeded their every sin, they have not known it in truth, but in so far as they have turned their affections towards the sweetness of My mercy they have thought of it with great presumption. And this is another cause of reproof which their conscience gives them in the likeness of the Devil, reproving them in that they should have used the time and the breadth of My mercy in which they hoped, in charity and love of virtue, and that time which I gave them through love should have been spent in holiness, whereas with all their time and great hope of My mercy they did nothing but offend Me miserably. Oh! blinder than the blind! You have hidden your pearl and your talent which I placed in your hands in order that you might gain more with it, but you in your presumption would not do My will, rather you hid it under the ground of disordinate self-love, which now renders you the fruit of death.

"Your miseries are not hid from you now, for the worm of conscience sleeps no longer, but is gnawing you, the devils shout and render to you the reward which they are accustomed to give their servants, that is to say, confusion and condemnation; they wish to bring you to despair, so that at the moment of death you may not escape from their hands, and therefore they try to confuse you, so that afterwards when you are with them they may render to you of the part which is theirs. Oh, wretch! the dignity in which I placed you, you now see shining as it really is, and you know to your shame that you have held and used in such guilty darkness the substance of the holy Church, that you see yourself to be a thief, a debtor, who ought to pay his debt to the poor and the holy Church. Then your conscience represents to you that you have spent the money on public harlots, and have brought up your children and enriched your relations, and have thrown it away on gluttony and on many silver vessels and other adornments for your house. Whereas you should have lived in voluntary poverty.

"Your conscience represents to you the divine office which you neglected, by which you fell into the guilt of mortal sin, and how even when you recited it with your mouth your heart was far from Me. Conscience also shows you your subjects, that is to say, the love and hunger which you should have felt towards nourishing them in virtue, giving them the example of your life and striking them with the hand of mercy and the rod of justice, and because you did the contrary your conscience and the horrible likeness of the Devil reproves you.

"And if as a prelate you have given prelacies or any charge of souls unjustly to one of your subjects, that is, that you have not considered to whom and how you were giving it, the Devil puts this also before your conscience, because you ought to have given it, not on account of pleasant words, nor in order to please creatures, nor for the sake of gifts, but solely with regard to virtue, My honor and the salvation of souls. And since you have not done so you are reproved, and for your greater pain and confusion you have before your conscience and the light of your intellect that which you have done and ought not to have done, and that which you ought to have done and have not done.

"I wish you to know, dearest daughter, that whiteness is better seen when placed on a black ground, and blackness on a white, than when they are separated. So it happens to these wretches, to these in particular and to all others in general, for at death when the soul begins to see its woes, and the just man his beatitude, his evil life is represented to a wicked man, and there is no reason that any one should remind him of the sins that he has committed, for his conscience places them before him, together with the virtues which he ought to have practiced. Why the virtues? For his greater shame. For vice being placed on a ground of virtue is known better on account of the virtue, and the better he knows his sin, the greater his shame, and by comparison with his sin he knows better the perfection of virtue, wherefore he grieves the more, for he sees that his own life was devoid of any; and I wish you to know that in this knowledge which dying sinners have of virtue and vice they see only too clearly the good which follows the virtue of a just man, and the pain that comes on him who has lain in the darkness of mortal sin. I do not give him this knowledge so that he may despair, but so that he may come to a perfect self-knowledge and shame for his sins, with hope, so that with that pain and knowledge he may pay for his sins, and appease My anger, humbly begging My mercy. The virtuous woman increases thereby in joy and in knowledge of My love, for he attributes the grace of having followed virtue in the doctrine of My truth to Me and not to himself, wherefore he exalts in Me, with this truly illuminated knowledge, and tastes and receives the sweet end of his being in the way which I have related to you in another place. So that the one, that is to say, the just man, who has lived in ardent charity, exults in joy, while the wicked man is darkened and confounded in sorrow.

"To the just man the appearance and vision of the Devil causes no harm or fear, for fear and harm can only be caused to him by sin; but those who have passed their lives lasciviously and in many sins, receive both harm and fear from the appearance of the devils, not indeed the harm of despair if they do not wish it, but the suffering of condemnation, of the refreshing of the worm of conscience, and of fear and terror at their horrible aspect. See now, dearest daughter, how different are the sufferings and the battle of death to a just man and to a sinner, and how different is their end.

"I have shown to the eye of your intellect a very small part of what happens, and so small is what I have shown you with regard to what it really is, to the suffering, that is, of the one, and the happiness of the other, that it is but a trifle. See how great is the blindness of man, and in particular of these ministers, for the more they have received of Me, and the more they are enlightened by the Holy Scripture, the greater are their obligations and more intolerable confusion do they receive for not fulfilling them; the more they knew of Holy Scripture during their life, the better do they know at their death the great sins they have committed, and their torments are greater than those of others, just as good men are placed in a higher degree of excellence. Theirs is the fate of the false Christian, who is placed in Hell in greater torment than a pagan, because he had the light of faith and renounced it, while the pagan never had it.

"So these wretches will be punished more than other Christians for the same sin, on account of the ministry which I entrusted to them, appointing them to administer the sun of the holy Sacrament, and because they had the light of science, in order to discern the truth both for themselves and others had they wished to; wherefore they justly receive the greater pains. But the wretches do not know this, for did they consider their state at all, they would not come to such misery, but would be that which they ought to be and are not. For the whole world has thus become corrupt, they being much more guilty than seculars, according to their state; for with their stench they defile the face of their soul, and corrupt their subjects, and suck the blood from My spouse, that is, the holy Church, wherefore through these sins they make her grow pale, because they divert to themselves the love and charity which they should have to this divine spouse, and think of nothing but stripping her for their own advantage, seizing prelacies, and great properties, when they ought to be seeking souls. Wherefore through their evil life, seculars become irreverent and disobedient to the holy Church, not that they ought on that account to do so, or that their sins are excused through the sins of My ministers."

How this devout soul, praising and thanking GOD,
made a prayer for the Holy Church.

Then this soul, as if inebriated, tormented, and on fire with love, her heart wounded with great bitterness, turned herself to the Supreme and Eternal Goodness, saying: "Oh! Eternal God! oh! Light above every other light, from whom issues all light! Oh! Fire above every fire, because You are the only Fire who burn without consuming, and consume all sin and self-love found in the soul, not afflicting her, but fattening her with insatiable love, and though the soul is filled she is not sated, but ever desires You, and the more of You she has, the more she seeks - and the more she desires, the more she finds and tastes of You - Supreme and Eternal Fire, Abyss of Charity. Oh! Supreme and Eternal Good, who has moved You, Infinite God, to illuminate me, Your finite creature, with the light of Your Truth? You, the same Fire of Love are the cause, because it is always love which constrained and constrains You to create us in Your image and similitude, and to do us mercy, giving immeasurable and infinite graces to Your rational creatures. Oh! Goodness above all goodness! You alone are He who is Supremely Good, and nevertheless You gave the Word, Your only-begotten Son, to converse with us filthy ones and filled with darkness. What was the cause of this? Love. Because You loved us before we were. Oh! Good! oh! Eternal Greatness! You made Yourself low and small to make man great. On whichever side I turn I find nothing but the abyss and fire of Your charity. And can a wretch like me pay back to You the graces and the burning charity that You have shown and show with so much burning love in particular to me beyond common charity, and the love that You show to all Your creatures? No, but You alone, most sweet and amorous Father, are He who will be thankful and grateful for me, that is, that the affection of Your charity itself will render You thanks, because I am she who is not, and if I spoke as being anything of myself, I should be lying by my own head, and should be a lying daughter of the Devil, who is the father of lies, because You alone are He who is. And my being and every further grace that You have bestowed upon me, I have from You, who give them to me through love, and not as my due.

"Oh! sweetest Father, when the human race lay sick through the sin of Adam, You sent it a Physician, the sweet and amorous Word - Your Son; and now, when I was lying infirm with the sickness of negligence and much ignorance, You, most soothing and sweet Physician, Eternal God, have given a soothing, sweet, and bitter medicine, that I may be cured and rise from my infirmity. You have soothed me because with Your love and gentleness You have manifested Yourself to me, Sweet above all sweetness, and have illuminated the eye of my intellect with the light of most holy faith, with which light, according as it has pleased You to manifest it to me, I have known the excellence of grace which You have given to the human race, administering to it the entire God-Man in the mystic body of the holy Church. And I have known the dignity of Your ministers whom You have appointed to administer You to us. I desired that You would fulfill the promise that You made to me, and You gave much more, more even than I knew how to ask for. Wherefore I know in truth that the heart of man knows not how to ask or desire as much as You can give, and thus I see that You are He who is the Supreme and Eternal Good, and that we are they who are not. And because You are infinite, and we are finite, You give that which Your rational creature cannot desire enough; for she cannot desire it in itself, nor in the way in which You can and will satisfy the soul, filling her with things for which she does not ask You. Moreover, I have received light from Your Greatness and Charity, through the love which You have for the whole human race, and in particular for Your anointed ones, who ought to be earthly angels in this life. You have shown me the virtue and beatitude of these Your anointed ones who have lived like burning lamps, shining with the Pearl of Justice in the holy Church. And by comparison with these I have better understood the sins of those who live wretchedly. Wherefore I have conceived a very great sorrow at Your offense and the harm done to the whole world, for they do harm to the world, being mirrors of sin when they ought to be mirrors of virtue. And because You have manifested and grieved over their iniquities to me - a wretch who am the cause and instrument of many sins - I am plunged in intolerable grief.

"You, oh! inestimable love, have manifested this to me, giving me a sweet and bitter medicine that I might wholly arise out of the infirmity of my ignorance and negligence, and have recourse to You with anxious and solicitous desire, knowing myself and Your goodness and the offenses which are committed against You by all sorts of people, so that I might shed a river of tears, drawn from the knowledge of Your infinite goodness, over my wretched self and over those who are dead in that they live miserably. Wherefore I do not wish, oh! Eternal Father, ineffable Fire of Love, that my heart should ever grow weary, or my eyes fail through tears, in desiring Your honor and the salvation of souls, but I beg of You, by Your grace, that they may be as two streams of water issuing from You, the Sea Pacific. Thanks, thanks to You, oh! Father, for having granted me that which I asked You and that which I neither knew nor asked, for by thus giving me matter for grief You have invited me to offer before You sweet, loving, and yearning desires, with humble and continual prayer. Now I beg of You that You will do mercy to the world and to the holy Church. I pray You to fulfill that which You caused me to ask You. Alas! what a wretched and sorrowful soul is mine, the cause of all these evils. Do not put off any longer Your merciful designs towards the world, but descend and fulfill the desire of Your servants.

"Ah me! You cause them to cry in order to hear their voices! Your truth told us to cry out, and we should be answered; to knock, and it would be opened to us; to beg, and it would be given to us. Oh! Eternal Father, Your servants do cry out to Your mercy; do You then reply.

"I know well that mercy is Your own attribute, wherefore You can not destroy it or refuse it to him who asks for it. Your servants knock at the door of Your truth, because in the truth of Your only-begotten Son they know the ineffable love which You have for man, wherefore the fire of Your love ought not and cannot refrain from opening to him who knocks with perseverance. Wherefore open, unlock, and break the hardened hearts of Your creatures, not for their sakes who do not knock, but on account of Your infinite goodness, and through love of Your servants who knock at You for their sakes. Grant the prayer of those, Eternal Father who, as You see, stand at the door of Your truth and pray. For what do they pray? For with the Blood of this door - Your truth - have You washed our iniquities and destroyed the stain of Adam's sin. The Blood is ours, for You have made it our bath, wherefore You can not deny it to any one who truly asks for it. Give, then, the fruit of Your Blood to Your creatures. Place in the balance the price of the blood of Your Son, so that the infernal devils may not carry off Your lambs. You are the Good Shepherd who, to fulfill Your obedience, laid down His life for Your lambs, and made for us a bath of His Blood.

"That Blood is what Your hungry servants beg of You at this door, begging You through it to do mercy to the world, and to cause Your holy Church to bloom with the fragrant flowers of good and holy pastors, who by their sweet odor shall extinguish the stench of the putrid flowers of sin. You have said, Eternal Father, that through the love which You have for Your rational creatures, and the prayers and the many virtues and labors of Your servants, You would do mercy to the world, and reform the Church, and thus give us refreshment; wherefore do not delay, but turn the eye of Your mercy towards us, for You must first reply to us before we can cry out with the voice of Your mercy. Open the door of Your inestimable love which You have given us through the door of Your Word. I know indeed that You open before even we can knock, for it is with the affection of love which You have given to Your servants, that they knock and cry to You, seeking Your honor and the salvation of souls. Give them then the bread of life, that is to say, the fruit of the Blood of Your only-begotten Son, which they ask of You for the praise and glory of My name and the salvation of souls. For more glory and praise will be Yours in saving so many creatures, than in leaving them obstinate in their hardness of heart. To You, Eternal Father, everything is possible, and even though You have created us without our own help, You will not save us without it. I beg of You to force their wills, and dispose them to wish for that for which they do not wish; and this I ask You through Your infinite mercy. You have created us from nothing; now, therefore, that we are in existence, do mercy to us, and remake the vessels which You have created to Your image and likeness. Re-create them to Grace in Your mercy and the Blood of Your Son sweet Christ Jesus."

A TREATISE OF OBEDIENCE

Here begins the treatise of obedience, and first of where obedience may be found, and what it is that destroys it, and what is the sign of a man's possessing it, and what accompanies and nourishes obedience.

The Supreme and Eternal Father, kindly turning the eye of His mercy and clemency towards her, replied: "Your holy desire and righteous request, oh! dearest daughter, have a right to be heard, and inasmuch as I am the Supreme Truth, I will keep My word, fulfilling the promise which I made to you, and satisfying your desire. And if you ask Me where obedience is to be found, and what is the cause of its loss, and the sign of its possession, I reply that you will find it in its completeness in the sweet and amorous Word, My only-begotten Son. So prompt in Him was this virtue, that, in order to fulfill it, He hastened to the shameful death of the Cross. What destroys obedience? Look at the first man and you will see the cause which destroyed the obedience imposed on him by Me, the Eternal Father. It was pride, which was produced by self-love, and desire to please his companion. This was the cause that deprived him of the perfection of obedience, giving him instead disobedience, depriving him of the life of grace, and slaying his innocence, wherefore he fell into impurity and great misery, and not only he, but the whole human race, as I said to you. The sign that you have this virtue is patience, and impatience the sign that you have it not, and you will find that this is indeed so, when I speak to you further concerning this virtue. But observe that obedience may be kept in two ways, of which one is more perfect than the other, not that they are on that account separated, but united as I explained to you of the precepts and counsels. The one way is the most perfect, the other is also good and perfect; for no one at all can reach eternal life if he be not obedient, for the door was unlocked by the key of obedience, which had been fastened by the disobedience of Adam. I, then, being constrained by My infinite goodness, since I saw that man whom I so much loved, did not return to Me, his End, took the keys of obedience and placed them in the hands of My sweet and amorous Word - the Truth - and He becoming the porter of that door, opened it, and no one can enter except by means of that door and that Porter. Wherefore He said in the Holy Gospel that 'no one could come to Me, the Father, if not by Him.' When He returned to Me, rising to Heaven from the conversation of men at the Ascension, He left you this sweet key of obedience; for as you know He left His vicar, the Christ, on earth, whom you are all obliged to obey until death, and whoever is outside His obedience is in a state of damnation, as I have already told you in another place. Now I wish you to see and know this most excellent virtue in that humble and immaculate Lamb, and the source whence it proceeds. What caused the great obedience of the Word? The love which He had for My honor and your salvation. Whence proceeded this love? From the clear vision with which His soul saw the divine essence and the eternal Trinity, thus always looking on Me, the eternal God. His fidelity obtained this vision most perfectly for Him, which vision you imperfectly enjoy by the light of holy faith. He was faithful to Me, His eternal Father, and therefore hastened as one enamored along the road of obedience, lit up with the light of glory. And inasmuch as love cannot be alone, but is accompanied by all the true and royal virtues, because all the virtues draw their life from love, He possessed them all, but in a different way from that in which you do. Among the others he possessed patience, which is the marrow of obedience, and a demonstrative sign, whether a soul be in a state of grace and truly love or not. Wherefore charity, the mother of patience, has given her as a sister to obedience, and so closely united them together that one cannot be lost without the other. Either you have them both or you have neither. This virtue has a nurse who feeds her, that is, true humility; therefore a soul is obedient in proportion to her humility, and humble in proportion to her obedience. This humility is the foster-mother and nurse of charity, and with the same milk she feeds the virtue of obedience. Her raiment given her by this nurse is self-contempt, and insult, desire to displease herself, and to please Me. Where does she find this? In sweet Christ Jesus, My only-begotten Son. For who abased Himself more than He did! He was sated with insults, jibes, and mockings. He caused pain to Himself in His bodily life, in order to please Me. And who was more patient than He? for His cry was never heard in murmuring, but He patiently embraced His injuries like one enamored, fulfilling the obedience imposed on Him by Me, His Eternal Father. Wherefore in Him you will find obedience perfectly accomplished. He left you this rule and this doctrine, which gives you life, for it is the straight way, having first observed them Himself. He is the way, wherefore He said, 'He was the Way, the Truth, and the Life.' For he who travels by that way, travels in the light, and being enlightened cannot stumble, or be caused to fall, without perceiving it. For He has cast from Himself the darkness of self-love, by which he fell into disobedience; for as I spoke to you of a companion virtue proceeding from obedience and humility, so I tell you that disobedience comes from pride, which issues from self-love depriving the soul of humility. The sister given by self-love to disobedience is impatience, and pride, her foster-mother, feeds her with the darkness of infidelity, so she hastens along the way of darkness, which leads her to eternal death. All this you should read in that glorious book, where you find described this and every other virtue."

"Now that I have shown you where obedience is to be found, and whence she comes, and who is her companion, and who her foster-mother, I will continue to speak of the obedient and of the disobedient together, and of obedience in general, which is the obedience of the precepts; and in particular, which is that of the counsels. The whole of your faith is founded upon obedience, for by it you prove your fidelity. You are all in general by My truth to obey the commandments of the law, the chief of which is to love Me above everything, and your neighbor as yourself, and the commandments are so bound up together, that you cannot observe or transgress one without observing or transgressing all. He who observes this principal commandment observes all the others; he is faithful to Me and his neighbor, for he loves Me and My creature, and is therefore obedient, becoming subject to the commandments of the law, and to creatures for My sake, and with humble patience he endures every labor, and even his neighbor's detraction of him. This obedience is of such excellence that you all derive grace from it, just as from disobedience you all derive death. Wherefore it is not enough that it should be only in word, and not practiced by you. I have already told you that this word is the key which opens heaven, which key My Son placed in the hands of His vicar. This vicar placed it in the hands of everyone who receives holy baptism, promising therein to renounce the world and all its pomps and delights, and to obey. So that each man has in his own person that very same key which the Word had, and if a man does not unlock in the light of faith, and with the hand of love the gate of heaven by means of this key, he never will enter there, in spite of its having been opened by the Word; for though I created you without yourselves, I will not save you without yourselves. Wherefore you must take the key in your hand and walk by the doctrine of My Word, and not remain seated, that is to say, placing your love in finite things, as do foolish men who follow the first man, their first father, following his example, and casting the key of obedience into the mud of impurity, breaking it with the hammer of pride, rusting it with self-love. It would have been entirely destroyed had not My only-begotten Son, the Word, come and taken this key of obedience in His hands and purified it in the fire of divine love, having drawn it out of the mud, and cleansed it with His blood, and straightened it with the knife of justice, and hammered your iniquities into shape on the anvil of His own body. So perfectly did He repair it that no matter how much a man may have spoiled his key by his free-will, by the self-same free-will, assisted by My grace, he can repair it with the same instruments that were used by My Word. Oh! blinder than the blind, for, having spoiled the key of obedience, you do not think of mending it! Do you think, forsooth, that the disobedience which closed the door of Heaven will open it? that the pride which fell can rise? Do you think to be admitted to the marriage feast in foul and disordered garments? Do you think that sitting down and binding yourself with the chain of mortal sin, you can walk? or that without a key you can open the door? Do not imagine that you can, for it is a fantastical delusion; you must be firm, you must leave mortal sin by a holy confession, contrition of heart, satisfaction, and purpose of amendment. Then you will throw off that hideous and defiled garment and, clothed in the shining nuptial robe, will hasten, the key of obedience in your hand, to open the door. But bind this key with the cord of self-contempt, and hatred of yourself and of the world, and fasten it to the love of pleasing Me, Your creator, of which you should make a girdle to yourself to bind your loins with it, for fear you lose it. Know, My daughter, there are many who take up this key of obedience, having seen by the light of faith that in no other way can they escape eternal damnation; but they hold it in their hand without wearing this girdle, or fastening the key to it with the cord of self-contempt, that is to say that they are not perfectly clothed with My pleasure, but still seek to please themselves; they do not wear the cord of self-contempt, for they do not desire to be despised, but rather take delight in the praise of men. Such as these are apt to lose their key; for if they suffer a little extra fatigue, or mental or corporal tribulation, and if, as often happens, the hand of holy desire loosens its grasp, they will lose it. They can indeed find it again if they wish to while they live, but if they do not wish they will never find it, and what will prove to them, that they have lost it? Impatience, for patience was united to obedience, and their impatience proves that obedience does not dwell in their soul. Oh! how sweet and glorious is this virtue, which contains all the rest, for she is conceived and born of charity, on her is founded the rock of the holy faith. She is a queen whose consort will feel no trouble, but only peace and quiet; the waves of the stormy sea cannot hurt her, nor can any tempest reach the interior of the soul in whom she dwells. Such a one feels no hatred when injured, because he wishes to obey the precept of forgiveness, he suffers not when his appetites are not satisfied, because obedience has ordered him to desire Me alone, who can and will satisfy all his desires, if he strip himself of worldly riches. And so in all things which would be too long to relate, he who has chosen as spouse Queen Obedience, the appointed key of heaven, finds peace and quiet. Oh! blessed obedience! you voyage without fatigue, and reach without danger the port of salvation, you are conformed to My only-begotten Son, the Word, you board the ship of the holy cross, forcing yourself to endure, so as not to transgress the obedience of the Word, nor abandon His doctrine, of which you make a table when you eat the food of souls, dwelling in the love of your neighbor, being anointed with true humility, which saves you from coveting, contrary to My will, his possessions, you walk erect, without bending, for your heart is sincere and not false, loving generously and truly My creatures, you are a sunrise drawing after you the light of divine grace, you are a sun which makes the earth, that is to say, the organs of the soul, to germinate with the heat of charity, all of which as well as those of the body produce life-giving fruit for yourself and your neighbor. You are even cheerful, for your face is never wrinkled with impatience, but smooth and pleasant with the happiness of patience, and even in its fortitude you are great by your long endurance, so long that it reaches from earth to heaven and unlocks the celestial door. You are a hidden pearl, trampled by the world, abasing yourself, submitting to all creatures. Yet your kingdom is so great that no one can rule you, for you have come out of the mortal servitude of your own sensuality, which destroyed your dignity, and having slain this enemy with hatred and dislike of your own pleasure have re-obtained your liberty."

Here both the misery of the disobedient and the
excellence of the obedient are spoken of.

"All this, dearest daughter, has been done by My goodness and providence as I have told you, for by My providence the Word repaired the key of obedience, but worldly men devoid of every virtue do the contrary; they, like unbridled horses, without the bit of obedience, go from bad to worse, from sin to sin, from misery to misery, from darkness to darkness, from death to death, until they finally reach the edge of the ditch of death, gnawed by the worm of their conscience, and though it is true that they can obey the precepts of the law if they will, and have the time repenting of their disobedience, it is very hard for them to do so, on account of their long habit of sin. Therefore let no man trust to this, putting off his finding of the key of obedience to the moment of his death, for although everyone may and should hope as long as he has life, he should not put such trust in this hope as to delay repentance. What is the reason of all this, and of such blindness that prevents them recognizing this treasure? The cloud of self-love and wretched pride, through which they abandoned obedience, and fell into disobedience. Being disobedient they are impatient, as has been said, and in their impatience endure intolerable pain, for it has seduced them from the way of Truth, leading them along a way of lies, making them slaves and friends of the devils with whom, unless indeed they amend themselves with patience, they will go to the eternal torments. Contrariwise, My beloved sons, obedient and observers of the law, rejoice and exult in My eternal vision with the Immaculate and humble Lamb, the Maker, Fulfiller, and Giver of this law of obedience. Observing this law in this life they taste peace without any disturbance, they receive and clothe themselves in the most perfect peace, for there they possess every good without any evil, safety without any fear, riches without any poverty, satiety without disgust, hunger without pain, light without darkness, one supreme infinite good, shared by all those who taste it truly. What has placed them in so blessed a state? The blood of the Lamb, by virtue of which the key of obedience has lost its rust, so that, by the virtue of the blood, it has been able to unlock the door. Oh! fools and madmen, delay no longer to come out of the mud of impurity, for you seem like pigs to wallow in the mire of your own lust. Abandon the injustice, murders, hatreds, rancors, detractions, murmurings, false judgments, and cruelty, with which you use your neighbors, your thefts and treacheries, and the disordinate pleasures and delights of the world; cut off the horns of pride, by which amputation you will extinguish the hatred which is in your heart against your neighbors. Compare the injuries which you do to Me and to your neighbor with those done to you, and you will see that those done to you are but trifles. You will see that remaining in hatred you injure Me by transgressing My precept, and you also injure the object of your hate, for you deprive him of your love, whereas you have been commanded to love Me above everything, and your neighbor as yourself. No gloss has been put upon these words as if it should have been said, if your neighbor injures you do not love him; but they are to be taken naturally and simply, as they were said to you by My Truth, who Himself literally observed this rule. Literally also should you observe it, and if you do not you will injure your own soul, depriving it of the life of grace. Take, oh! take, then, the key of obedience with the light of faith, walk no longer in such darkness or cold, but observe obedience in the fire of love, so that you may taste eternal life together with the other observers of the law."

Of those who have such love for obedience that they do not remain content with the general obedience of precepts, but take on themselves a particular obedience.

"There are some, My dearest daughter, in whom the sweet and amorous fire of love towards obedience burns so high (which fire of love cannot exist without hatred of self-love, so that when the fire increases so does this self-hatred), that they are not content to observe the precepts of the Law with a general obedience as you are all obliged to do if you will have life and not death, but take upon themselves a particular obedience, following the greatest perfection, so that they become observers of the counsels both in deed and in thought. Such as these wish to bind themselves more tightly through self-hatred, and in order to restrain in everything their own will. They either place themselves under the yoke of obedience in holy religion, or, without entering religion, they bind themselves to some creature, submitting their will to his, so as more expeditiously to unlock the door of Heaven. These are they, as I have told you, who have chosen the most perfect obedience. I have already spoken to you of obedience in general, and as I know it to be your will that I should speak to you of this particular and most perfect obedience, I will now relate to you somewhat of this second kind, which is not divided from the first, but is more perfect, for, as I have already told you, these two kinds of obedience are so closely united together that they cannot be separated. I have told you where general obedience is to be found and whence it proceeds, and the cause of its loss. Now I will speak to you of this particular obedience, not altering, however, the fundamental principle of the virtue."

How a soul advances from general to particular obedience;
and of the excellence of the religious orders.

"The soul who with love has submitted to the yoke of obedience, to the Commandments, following the doctrine of My truth virtuously exercising herself, as has been said, in this general kind of obedience will advance to the second kind by means of the same light which brought her to the first, for by the light of the most holy faith she would have learnt, in the blood of the humble Lamb, My truth - the ineffable love which I have for her, and her own fragility, which cannot respond to Me with due perfection. So she wanders, seeking by that light in what place and in what way she can pay her debt, trampling on her own fragility, and restraining her own will. Enlightened in her search by faith, she finds the place - namely, holy religion - which has been founded by the Holy Spirit, appointed as the ship to receive souls who wish to hasten to perfection, and to bring them to the port of salvation. The Captain of this ship is the Holy Spirit, who never fails in Himself through the defects of any of His religious subjects who may transgress the rule of the order. The ship itself cannot be damaged, but only the offender. It is true that the mistake of the steersman may send her down into the billows, and these are wicked pastors and prelates appointed by the Master of the ship. The ship herself is so delightful that your tongue could not narrate it. I say, then, that the soul, on fire with desire and a holy self-hatred, having found her place by the light of faith, enters there as one dead, if she is truly obedient; that is to say, if she have perfectly observed general obedience. And even if she should be imperfect when she enters, it does not follow that she cannot attain perfection. On the contrary, she attains it by exercising herself in the virtue of obedience; indeed, most of those who enter are imperfect. There are some who enter already in perfection, others in the childhood of virtue, others through fear, others through penance, others through allurements, everything depends on whether after they have entered they exercise themselves in virtue, and persevere till death, for no true judgment can be made on a person's entrance into religion, but only on their perseverance, for many have appeared to be perfect who have afterwards turned back, or remained in the order with much imperfection, so that, as I have said, the act of entrance into this ship ordained by Me, who call men in different ways, does not supply material for a real judgment, but only the love of those who persevere therein with true obedience. This ship is rich, so that there is no need for the subject to think about his necessities either temporal or spiritual, for if he is truly obedient, and observes his order, he will be provided for by his Master, who is the Holy Spirit, as I told you when I spoke to you of My providence, saying that though your servants might be poor, they were never beggars. No more are these, for they find everything they need, and those who observe this order find this to be indeed true. Wherefore, see that in the days when the religious orders lived virtuously, blossoming with true poverty and fraternal charity, their temporal substance never failed them, but they had more than their needs demanded. But because the stench of self-love has entered and caused each to keep his private possessions and to fail in obedience, their temporal substance has failed, and the more they possess to the greater destitution do they come. It is just that even in the smallest matters they should experience the fruit of disobedience, for had they been obedient and observed the vow of poverty, each would not have taken his own, and lived privately. See the riches of these holy rules, so thoughtfully and luminously appointed by those who were temples of the Holy Spirit. See with what judgment Benedict ordered his ship; see with what perfection and order of poverty Francis ordered his ship, decked with the pearls of virtue, steering it in the way of lofty perfection, being the first to give his order for spouse, true and holy poverty, whom he had chosen for himself, embracing self-contempt and self-hatred, not desiring to please any creature but only your will; desiring rather to be thought vile by the world, macerating his body and slaying his will, clothing himself in insults, sufferings, and jibes, for love of the humble Lamb, with whom he was fastened and nailed to the cross by love, so that by a singular grace there appeared in his body the very wounds of your Truth, showing in the vessel of his body that which was in the love of his soul, so he prepared the way.

"But you will say, 'Are not all the other religious orders equally founded on this point?' Yes, but though they are all founded on it, in no other is this the principal foundation; as with the virtues, though all the virtues draw their life from charity, nevertheless, as I explained to you in another place, one virtue belongs especially to one man, and another to another, and yet they all remain in charity, so with the principal foundation of the religious orders. Poverty belonged especially to My poor man Francis, who placed the principal foundation of his order in love for this poverty, and made it very strict for those who were perfect, for the few and the good, not for the majority. I say few because they are not many who choose this perfection, though now through their sins they are multiplied in numbers and deficient in virtue, not through defect of the ship, but through disobedient subjects and wicked rulers. Now look at the ship of your father Dominic, My beloved son: he ordered it most perfectly, wishing that his sons should apply themselves only to My honor and the salvation of souls, with the light of science, which light he laid as his principal foundation, not, however, on that account, being deprived of true and voluntary poverty, but having it also. And as a sign that he had it truly, and that the contrary displeased him, he left as an heirloom to his sons his curse and Mine, if they should hold any possessions, either privately or in community, as a sign that he had chosen for his spouse Queen Poverty. But for his more immediate and personal object he took the light of science in order to extirpate the errors which had arisen in his time, thus taking on him the office of My only-begotten Son, the Word. Rightly he appeared as an apostle in the world, and sowed the seed of My Word with much truth and light, dissipating darkness and giving light. He was a light which I gave the world by means of Mary, placed in the mystical body of the Holy Church as an extirpator of heresies. Why do I say by means of Mary? Because Mary gave him his habit - this office was committed to her by My goodness. At what table does he feed his sons with the light of science? At the table of the cross, which is the table of holy desire, when souls are eaten for My honor. Dominic does not wish his sons to apply themselves to anything, but remaining at this table, there to seek with the light of science, the glory and praise of My name alone, and the salvation of souls. And in order that they might do nothing else, he chose poverty for them, so that they might not have the care of temporal things. It is true that some failed in faith, fearing that they would not be provided for, but he never. Being clothed in faith, and hoping with firm confidence in My providence, He wishes his sons to observe obedience and do their duty, and since impure living obscures the eye of the intellect, and not only the eye of the intellect, but also of the body, he does not wish them to obscure their physical light with which they may more perfectly obtain the light of science; wherefore he imposed on them the third vow of continence, and wishes that all should observe it, with true and perfect obedience, although today it is badly observed. They also prevent the light of science with the darkness of pride, not that this light can be darkened in itself, but only in their souls, for there, where pride is, can be no obedience. I have already told you that a man's humility is in proportion to his obedience, and his obedience to his humility, and similarly, when he transgresses the vow of obedience, it rarely happens that he does not also transgress the vow of continence, either in thought or deed; so that he has rigged his ship with the three ropes of obedience, continence, and true poverty; he made it a royal ship, not obliging his subjects under pain of mortal sin, and illuminated by Me the true light, he provided for those who should be less perfect, for though all who observe the order are perfect in kind, yet one possesses a higher degree of perfection than another, yet all perfect or imperfect live well in this ship. He allied himself with My truth, showing that he did not desire the death of a sinner, but rather that he should be converted and live. Wherefore his religion is a delightful garden, broad and joyous and flagrant, but the wretches who do not observe the order, but transgress its vows, have turned it into a desert and defiled it with their scanty virtue and light of science, though they are nourished at its breast. I do not say that the order itself is in this condition, for it still possesses every delight, but in the beginning its subjects were not as they are now, but blooming flowers, and men of great perfection. Each scented to be another St. Paul, their eyes so illuminated that the darkness of error was dissipated by their glance. Look at My glorious Thomas, who gazed with the gentle eye of his intellect at My Truth, whereby he acquired supernatural light and science infused by grace, for he obtained it rather by means of prayer than by human study. He was a brilliant light, illuminating his order and the mystical body of the Holy Church, dissipating the clouds of heresy. Look at My Peter, virgin and martyr, who by his blood gave light among the darkness of many heresies, and the heretics hated him so that at last they took his life; yet while he lived he applied himself to nothing but prayer, preaching, and disputation with heretics, hearing confessions, announcing the truth, and spreading the faith without any fear, to such an extent that he not only confessed it in his life but even at the moment of his death, for when he was at the last extremity, having neither voice nor ink left, having received his death-blow, he dipped his finger in his blood, and this glorious martyr, having not paper on which to write, leaned over, confessing the faith, and wrote the Credo on the ground. His heart burnt in the furnace of My charity, so that he never slackened his pace nor turned his head back, though he knew that he was to die, for I had revealed to him his death, but like a true knight he fearlessly came forth on to the battlefield; and I could tell you the same of many others, who though they did not actually experience martyrdom, were martyrs in will like Dominic; great laborers were these sent by My Father to labor in His vineyard to extirpate the thorns of vice, planting the virtues in their stead. Of a truth Dominic and Francis were two columns of the holy Church. Francis with the poverty which was specially his own, as has been said, and Dominic with his learning."

Of the excellence of the obedient, and of the misery
of the disobedient members of the religious orders.

"Now that places suitable for obedience have been found, namely, these ships commanded by the Holy Spirit through the medium of their superiors, for, as I told you, the Holy Spirit is the true Master of these ships, which are built in the light of the most holy faith by those who have the light to know that My clemency, the Holy Spirit, will steer them, and having thus shown you the place of obedience and its perfection, I will speak to you of the obedience and of the disobedience of those who travel in such a ship, speaking of all together and not of one ship - that is, one order - in particular, showing you the sin of the disobedient and the virtue of the obedient, so that a man may better know the one by contrast with the other, and how he should walk if he would enter the ship of a religious order. How should he walk who wishes to enter this state of perfect and particular obedience? With the light of holy faith, by which he will know that he must slay his self-will with the knife of hatred of every sensual passion, taking the spouse which charity gives him, together with her sister. The spouse is true and prompt obedience, and the sister, patience; and he must also take the nurse of humility, for without this nurse obedience would perish of hunger, for obedience soon dies in a soul deprived of this little virtue of humility.

"Humility is not alone but has the handmaid of contempt of self and of the world, which causes the soul to hold herself vile, and not to desire honor but shame. Thus dead to himself, should he who is old enough enter the ship of a religious order, but however he may enter it (for I have told you that I call souls in diverse ways), he should acquire and preserve this affection, hurrying generously to seize the key of the obedience of his order, which will open the little door which is in the panel of the door of Heaven. Such as these have undertaken to open the little door, doing without the great key of general obedience, which opens the door of Heaven, as I have said to you. They have taken a little key, passing through a low and narrow opening in the great door. This small door is part of the great door, as you may see in any real door. They should keep this key when they have got it, and not throw it away. And because the truly obedient have seen with the light of faith that they will never be able to pass through this little door with the load of their riches and the weight of their own will without great fatigue and without losing their life, and that they cannot walk with head erect without breaking their neck; whether they wish to or not, they cast from them the load of their riches, and of their own will observing the vow of voluntary poverty, refusing to possess anything, for they see by the light of faith to what ruin they would come if they transgressed obedience, and the and of poverty which they promised to keep. The disobedient walk in pride, holding their heads erect, and if sometimes it suits their convenience to obey they do not incline their heads with humility, but proudly do so, because they must, which force breaks the neck of their will, for they fulfill their obedience with hatred of their order and of their superior. Little by little they are ruined on another point, for they transgress the vow of continence, for he who does not constrain his appetite or strip himself of temporal substance makes many relations and finds plenty of friends who love him for their own profit. From these relations they go on to close intimacies, their body they tend luxuriously, for being without either the nurse of humility or her sister, self-contempt, they live in their own pleasure richly and delicately, not like religious but like nobles, without watching or prayer. This and many other things happen to them because they have money to spend, for if they had it not they could not spend it. They fall into mental and physical impurity, for if sometimes from shame or through lack of means they abstain physically, they indulge themselves mentally, for it is impossible for a man with many worldly relations, of delicate habits and disordinate greediness, who watches not nor prays, to preserve his mind pure. Wherefore the perfectly obedient man sees from afar with the light of holy faith the evil and the loss which would come to him from temporal possessions and from walking weighed down by his own will; he also sees that he is obliged to pass by this narrow door, and that in such a state he would die before he would be able to pass it, having no key of obedience wherewith to open it, for as I said to you, he is obliged to pass through it. Wherefore it is that whether he will or no he should not leave the ship of the order, but should walk the narrow path of obedience to his superior.

"Wherefore the perfectly obedient man rises above himself and his own sensuality, and rising above his own feelings with living faith, places self-hatred as servant in the house of his soul to drive out the enemy of self-love, for he does not wish that his spouse, Obedience, given him with the light of faith by her mother, Charity, should be offended; so he drives out the enemy and puts in his place the nurse and companions of his spouse.

"The love of obedience places in the house of his soul the lovers of his spouse, Obedience, who are the true and royal virtues, the customs and observances of his order, so that this sweet spouse enters his soul with her sister, Patience, and her nurse, Humility, together with Self-contempt and Self-hatred, and when she has entered she possesses peace and quiet, for her enemies have been exiled. She dwells in the garden of true continence, with the sun of intellectual light shining in, the eye of holy faith fixed on the object of My Truth, for her object is My Truth, and the fire of love with which she observes the rules of the order, warms all her servants and companions.

"Who are her enemies who have been expelled? The chief is self-love, producing pride, the enemy of humility and charity. Impatience is the enemy of patience, disobedience of true obedience, infidelity of faith, presumption and self-confidence do not accord with the true hope which the soul should have in Me; injustice cannot be conformed to justice, nor imprudence to prudence, nor intemperance to temperance, nor the transgression of the commandments of the order to perfect observance of them, nor the wicked conversation of those who live in sin to the good conversation of My servants. These are a man's enemies, causing him to leave the good customs and traditions of his order. He has also those other cruel enemies, anger, which wars against his benevolence; cruelty, against his kindness; wrath, against his benignity; hatred of virtue, against the love of virtue; impurity, against chastity; negligence, against solicitude; ignorance, against knowledge; and sloth against watchfulness and continued prayer.

"And since he knew by the light of faith that all these were his enemies who would defile his spouse, holy obedience, he appointed hatred to drive them out, and love to replace them with her friends. Wherefore with the knife of hatred he slew his perverse self-will, who, nourished by self-love, gave life to all these enemies of true obedience, and having cut off the source by which all the others are preserved in life, he remains free and in peace without any war, for there is no one to make war on him, for the soul has cut off from herself that which kept her in bitterness and in sadness. What makes war on obedience? Injuries? No, for the obedient man is patient, patience being the sister of obedience. The weight of the observances of the order? No, for obedience causes him to fulfill them. Does the weight of obedience give him pain? No, for he has trampled on his own will, and does not care to examine or judge the will of his superior, for with the light of faith he sees My will in him, believing truly that My clemency causes him to command according to the needs of his subject's salvation. Is he disgusted and angry at having to perform the humble duties of the order or to endure the mockeries, reproofs, jibes, and insults which are often cast at him, or to be held at little worth? No, for he has conceived love for self-contempt and self-hatred. Wherefore he rejoices with patience, exulting with delight and joy in the company of his spouse, true obedience, for the only thing which saddens him is to see Me, his Creator, offended. His conversation is with those who truly fear Me, and if he should converse with those who are separated from My Will, it is not in order to conform himself to their sins, but to draw them out of their misery, for through the brotherly love which he has in his heart towards them he would like to give them the good which he possesses, seeing that more glory and praise would be given to My name by many observing aright their order than by him doing so alone. Wherefore he endeavors to convert religious and seculars by his words and by prayer, and by every means by which he can draw them out of the darkness of mortal sin. Thus the conversations of a truly obedient man are good and perfect, whether they be with just men or with sinners, through his rightly ordered love and the breadth of his charity. Of his cell he makes a heaven, delighting there to converse with Me, his supreme and eternal Father, with the affection of love, flying idleness with humble and continual prayer, and when, through the illusion of the Devil, thoughts come crowding into his cell, he does not sit down on the bed of negligence embracing idleness, nor care to examine by reason the thoughts or opinions of his heart, but he flies sloth, rising above himself and his senses with hatred and true humility, patiently enduring the weariness which he feels in his mind, and resisting by watching and humble prayer, fixing the eye of his intellect on Me, and seeing with the light of faith that I am his helper, and both can and will help him, and open to him the eyes of My kindness, and that it is I who permit this suffering in order that he may be more eager to fly himself and come to Me. And if it should seem to him that on account of his great weariness and the darkness of his mind, mental prayer is impossible, he recites vocal prayers, or busies himself with some corporal exercises, so that by these means he may avoid idleness. He looks at Me with the light which I give him through love, which draws forth true humility, for he deems himself unworthy of the peace and quiet of mind of My other servants, but rather worthy of pain, for he despises himself in his own mind with hatred and self-reproach, thinking that he can never endure enough pain, for neither his hope nor My providence fail him, but with faith and the key of obedience he passes over this stormy sea in the ship of his order, dwelling thus in his cell as has been said, and avoiding idleness.

"The obedient man wishes to be the first to enter choir and the last to leave it, and when he sees a brother more obedient than himself he regards him in his eagerness with a holy envy, stealing from him the virtue in which he excels, not wishing, however, that his brother should have less thereof, for if he wished this he would be separated from brotherly love. The obedient man does not leave the refectory, but visits it continually and delights at being at table with the poor. And as a sign that he delights therein, and so as to have no reason to remain without, he has abandoned his temporal substance, observing so perfectly the vow of poverty that he blames himself for considering even the necessities of his body. His cell is full of the odor of poverty, and not of clothes; he has no fear that thieves will come to rob him, or that rust or moths will corrupt his garments; and if anything is given to him, he does not think of laying it by for his own use, but freely shares it with his brethren, not thinking of the morrow, but rather depriving himself today of what he needs, thinking only of the kingdom of heaven and how he may best observe true obedience.

"And in order that he may better keep to the path of humility, he submits to small and great, to poor and rich, and becomes the servant of all, never refusing labor, but serving all with charity. The obedient man does not wish to fulfill his obedience in his own way, or to choose his time or place, but prefers the way of his order and of his superior. All this the truly and perfectly obedient man does without pain and weariness of mind. He passes with this key in his hand through the narrow door of the order, easily and without violence, because he observes the vows of poverty, true obedience, and continence, having abandoned the heights of pride, and bowed his head to obedience through humility. He does not break his neck through impatience, but is patient with fortitude and enduring perseverance, the friends of obedience. Thus he passes by the assaults of the devils, mortifying and macerating his flesh, stripping it bare of all pleasures and delights and clothing it with the labors of the order in a faith which despises nothing, for as a child who does not remember the blows and injuries inflicted on him by his father, so this child of the spirit does not remember the injuries, pains, or blows inflicted on him by his superior in the order, but calling him humbly, turns to him without anger, hatred, or rancor, but with meekness and benevolence.

"These are those little ones of whom My Truth spoke to the disciples, who were contending among themselves which of them should be the greater, for calling a child, He said: 'Allow the little ones to come to Me, for of such is the kingdom of heaven to be; whoever will not humble himself like this child (that is, who will not keep this childlike condition), shall not enter the kingdom of heaven. For he who humbles himself, dearest daughter, will be exalted, and he who exalts himself will be humbled,' which also was said to you by My Truth. Justly, therefore, are these humble little ones, humiliated and subjected through love, with true and holy obedience, who do not kick against the pricks of their order or superior, exalted by Me, the supreme and eternal Father, with the true citizens of the blessed life, when they are rewarded for all their labors, and in this life also do they taste eternal life."

How the truly obedient receive a hundredfold for one, and also
eternal life; and what is meant by this one, and this hundredfold.

"In them is fulfilled the saying of the sweet and amorous Word, My only-begotten Son, in the gospel when He replied to Peter's demand, 'Master, we have left everything for your love's sake, and have followed You, what will you give us?' My Truth replied, 'I will give you a hundredfold for one, and you shall possess eternal life.' As if My Truth had wished to say, 'You have done well, Peter, for in no other way could you follow Me. And I, in this life, will give you a hundredfold for one.' And what is this hundredfold, beloved daughter, besides which the apostle obtained eternal life? To what did My Truth refer? To temporal substance?

"Properly speaking, no. Do I not, however, often cause one who gives alms to multiply in temporal goods? In return for what do I this? In return for the gift of his own will. This is the one for which I repay him a hundredfold. What is the meaning of the number a hundred? A hundred is a perfect number, and cannot be added to except by recommencing from the first. So charity is the most perfect of all the virtues, so perfect that no higher virtue can be attained except by recommencing at the beginning of self-knowledge, and thus increasing many hundredfold in merit; but you always necessarily arrive at the number one hundred. This is that hundredfold which is given to those who have given Me the unit of their own will, both in general obedience, and in the particular obedience of the religious life. And in addition to this hundred you also possess eternal life, for charity alone enters into eternal life, like a mistress bringing with her the fruit of all the other virtues, while they remain outside, bringing their fruit, I say, into Me, the eternal life, in whom the obedient taste eternal life. It is not by faith that they taste eternal life, for they experience in its essence that which they have believed through faith; nor by hope, for they possess that for which they had hoped, and so with all the other virtues, Queen Charity alone enters and possesses Me, her possessor. See, therefore, that these little ones receive a hundredfold for one, and also eternal life, for here they receive the fire of divine charity figured by the number of a hundred (as has been said). And because they have received this hundredfold from Me, they possess a wonderful and hearty joy, for there is no sadness in charity, but the joy of it makes the heart large and generous, not narrow or double. A soul wounded by this sweet arrow does not appear one thing in face and tongue while her heart is different. She does not serve, or act towards her neighbor with dissembling and ambition, because charity is an open book to be read by all. Wherefore the soul who possesses charity never falls into trouble, or the affliction of sadness, or jars with obedience, remains obedient until death."

Of the perversities, miseries, and labors of the disobedient man;
and of the miserable fruits which proceed from disobedience.

"Contrariwise, a wicked disobedient man dwells in the ship of a religious order with so much pain to himself and others, that in this life he tastes the earnest of hell, he remains always in sadness and confusion of mind, tormented by the sting of conscience, with hatred of his order and superior, insupportable to himself. What a terrible thing it is, My daughter, to see one who has once taken the key of obedience of a religious order, living in disobedience, to which he has made himself a slave, for of disobedience he has made his mistress with her companion impatience, nourished by pride, and his own pleasure, which pride (as has been said) issues from self-love. For him everything is the contrary to what it would be for the obedient man. For how can this wretch be in any other state than suffering, for he is deprived of charity, he is obliged by force to incline the neck of his own will, and pride keeps it erect, all his desires are in discord with the will of the order. The order commands obedience, and he loves disobedience; the order commands voluntary poverty, and he avoids it, possessing and acquiring riches; the order commands continence and purity, and he desires lewdness. By transgressing these three vows, My daughter, a religious comes to ruin, and falls into so many miseries, that his aspect is no longer that of a religious but of an incarnate devil, as in another place I related to you at greater length. I will, however, tell you something now of their delusion, and of the fruit which they obtained by disobedience to the commendation and exhortation of obedience. This wretched man is deluded by his self-love, because the eye of his intellect is fixed, with a dead faith, on pleasing his self-will, and on things of the world. He left the world in body, but remained there in his affections, and because obedience seems wearisome to him he wishes to disobey in order to avoid weariness; whereby he arrives at the greatest weariness of all, for he is obliged to obey either by force or by love, and it would have been better and less wearisome to have obeyed by love than without it. Oh! how deluded he is, and no one else deceives him but himself. Wishing to please himself he only gives himself displeasure, for the actions which he will have to do, through the obedience imposed on him, do not please him. He wishes to enjoy delights and make this life his eternity, but the order wishes him to be a pilgrim, and continually proves it to him; for when he is in a nice pleasant resting place, where he would like to remain for the pleasures and delights he finds there, he is transferred elsewhere, and the change gives him pain, for his will was active against his obedience, and yet he is obliged to endure the discipline and labors of the order, and thus remains in continual torment. See, therefore, how he deludes himself; for, wishing to fly pain, he on the contrary falls into it, for his blindness does not let him know the road of true obedience, which is a road of truth founded by the obedient Lamb, My only-begotten Son, who removed pain from it, so that he walks by the road of lies, believing that he will find delight there, but finding on the contrary pain and bitterness. Who is his guide? Self-love, that is his own passion for disobedience. Such a man thinks like a fool to navigate this tempestuous sea, with the strength of his own arms, trusting in his own miserable knowledge, and will not navigate it in the arms of his order, and of his superior. Such a one is indeed in the ship of the order in body, and not in mind; he has quitted it in desire, not observing the regulations or customs of the order, nor the three vows which he promised to observe at the time of his profession; he swims in the tempestuous sea, tossed to and fro by contrary winds, fastened only to the ship by his clothes, wearing the religious habit on his body but not on his heart. Such a one is no friar, but a masquerader, a man only in appearance. His life is lower than an animal's, and he does not see that he labors more swimming with his arms, than the good religious in the ship, or that he is in danger of eternal death; for if his clothes should be suddenly torn from the ship, which will happen at the moment of death, he will have no remedy. No, he does not see, for he has darkened his light with the cloud of self-love, whence has come his disobedience, which prevents him seeing his misery, wherefore he miserably deceives himself. What fruit is produced by this wretched tree?

"The fruit of death, because the root of his affection is planted in pride, which he has drawn from self-love. Wherefore everything that issues from this root - flowers, leaves, and fruit - is corrupt, and the three boughs of this tree, which are obedience, poverty, and continence, which spring from the foot of the tree; that is, his affections are corrupted. The leaves produced by this tree, which are his words, are so corrupt that they would be out of place in the mouth of a ribald secular; and if he have to preach My doctrine, he does so in polished terms, not simply, as one who should feed souls with the seed of My Word, but with eloquent language. Look at the stinking flowers of this tree, which are his diverse and various thoughts, which he voluntarily welcomes with delight and pleasure, not flying the occasions of them, but rather seeking them in order to be able to accomplish a sinful act, the which is the fruit which kills him, depriving him of the light of grace, and giving him eternal death. And what stench comes from this fruit, sprung from the flowers of the tree? The stench of disobedience, for, in the secret of his heart, he wishes to examine and judge unfaithfully his superior's will; a stench of impurity, for he takes delight in many foul conversations, wretchedly tempting his penitents.

"Wretch that you are, do you not see that under the color of devotion you conceal a troop of children? This comes from your disobedience. You have not chosen the virtues for your children as does the truly obedient religious; you strive to deceive your superior when you see that he denies you something which your perverse will desires, using the leaves of smooth or rough words, speaking irreverently and reproving him. You can not endure your brother, nor even the smallest word and reproof which he may make to you, but in such a case you immediately bring forth the poisoned fruit of anger and hatred against him, judging that to be done to your hurt which was done for your good, and thus taking scandal, your soul and body living in pain. Why has your brother displeased you? Because you live for your own sensual pleasure, you fly your cell as if it were a prison, for you have abandoned the cell of self-knowledge, and thus fallen into disobedience, wherefore you can not remain in your material cell. You will not appear in the refectory against your will whilst you have anything to spend; when you have nothing left necessity takes you there.

"Therefore the obedient have done well, who have chosen to observe their vow of poverty, so that they have nothing to spend, and therefore are not led away from the sweet table of the refectory, where obedience nourishes both body and soul in peace and quiet. The obedient religious does not think of laying a table, or of providing food for himself like this wretched man, to whose taste it is painful to eat in the refectory, wherefore he avoids it; he is always the last to enter the choir, and the first to leave it; with his lips he approaches Me, with his heart he is far from Me. He gladly escapes from the chapter-house when he can through fear of penance. When he is obliged to be there, he is covered with shame and confusion for the faults which he felt it no shame to commit. What is the cause of this? Disobedience. He does not watch in prayer, and not only does he omit mental prayer, but even the Divine office to which he is obliged. He has no fraternal charity, because he loves no one but himself, and that not with a reasonable but with a bestial love. So great are the evils which fall on the disobedient; so many are the fruits of sorrow which he produces, that your tongue could not relate them. Oh! disobedience, which deprives the soul of the light of obedience, destroying peace, and giving war! Disobedience destroys life and gives death, drawing the religious out of the ship of the observance of his order, to drown him in the sea, making him swim in the strength of his own arms, and not repose on those of the order. Disobedience clothes him with every misery, causes him to die of hunger, taking away from him the food of the merit of obedience, it gives him continual bitterness, depriving him of every sweetness and good, causing him to dwell with every evil in life it gives him the earnest of cruel torments to endure, and if he do not amend before his clothes are loosened from the ship at death, disobedience will lead the soul to eternal damnation, together with the devils who fell from heaven, because they rebelled against Me. In the same way have you, oh! disobedient man, having rebelled against obedience and cast from you the key which would have opened the door of heaven, opened instead the door of hell with the key of disobedience."

How God does not reward merit according to the labor of the obedient, nor according to the length of time which it takes, but according to the love and promptitude of the truly obedient; and of the miracles which God has performed by means of this virtue; and of discretion in obedience, and of the works and reward of the truly obedient man.

"I have appointed you all to labor in the vineyard of obedience in different ways, and every man will receive a price, according to the measure of his love, and not according to the work he does, or the length of time for which he works, that is to say, that he who comes early will not have more than he who comes late, as My Truth told you in the holy gospel by the example of those who were standing idle and were sent by the lord of the vineyard to labor; for he gave as much to those who went at dawn, as to those who went at prime or at tierce, and those who went at sext, at none, and even at vespers, received as much as the first: My Truth showing you in this way that you are rewarded not according to time or work, but according to the measure of your love. Many are placed in their childhood to work in the vineyard; some enter later in life, and others in old age; sometimes these latter labor with such fire of love, seeing the shortness of the time, that they rejoin those who entered in their childhood, because they have advanced but slowly. By love of obedience, then, does the soul receive her merit, filling the vessel of her heart in Me, the Sea Pacific. There are many whose obedience is so prompt, and has become, as it were, so incarnate in them, that not only do they wish to see reason in what is ordered them by their superior, but they hardly wait until the word is out of his mouth, for with the light of faith they understand his intention. Wherefore the truly obedient man obeys rather the intention than the word, judging that the will of his superior is fixed in My will, and that therefore his command comes from My dispensation, and from My will, wherefore I say to you that he rather obeys the intention than the word. He also obeys the word, having first spiritually obeyed in affection his superior's will, seeing and judging it by the light of faith to be Mine. This is well shown in the lives of the fathers, where you read of a religious, who at once obeyed in his affection the command of his superior, commencing to write the letter o, though he had not space to finish it; wherefore to show how pleasing his prompt obedience was to Me, My clemency gave him a proof by writing the other half of the letter in gold. This glorious virtue is so pleasing to Me, that to no other have I given so many miraculous signs and testimonies, for it proceeds from the height of faith.

"In order to show how pleasing it is to Me, the earth obeys this virtue, the animals obey it - water grows solid under the feet of the obedient man. And as for the obedience of the earth, you remember having read of that disciple who, being given a dry stick by his abbot, and being ordered by obedience to plant it in the earth and water it every day, did not proceed to ask how could it possibly do any good, but, without inquiring about possibilities, he fulfilled his obedience in such virtue of faith that the dry wood brought forth leaves and fruits, as a sign that that soul had risen from the dryness of disobedience, and, covered by the green leaves of virtue, had brought forth the fruit of obedience, wherefore the fruit of this tree was called by the holy fathers the fruit of obedience. You will also find that animals obey the obedient man; for a certain disciple, commanded by obedience, through his purity and virtue caught a dragon and brought it to his abbot, but the abbot, like a true physician of the soul, in order that he might not be tossed about by the wind of vainglory, and to prove his patience, sent him away with harsh words, saying: 'Beast that you are, you have brought along another beast with yourself.' And as to fire, you have read in the holy scripture that many were placed in the fire, rather than transgress My obedience, and, at My command were not hurt by it. This was the case of the three children, who remained happily in the furnace - and of many others of whom I could tell you.

The water bore up Maurus who had been sent by obedience to save a drowning disciple; he did not think of himself, but thought only with the light of faith of how to fulfill the command of his superior, and so walked upon the water as if he had been on dry land, and so saved the disciple. In everything, if you open the eye of the intellect, you will find shown forth the excellence of this virtue. Everything else should be abandoned for the sake of obedience. If you were lifted up in such contemplation and union of mind with Me, that your body was raised from the earth, and an obedience were imposed on you (speaking generally, and not in a particular case, which cannot give a law), you ought, if possible, to force yourself to arise, to fulfill the obedience imposed on you, though you should never leave prayer, except for necessity, charity, or obedience. I say this in order that you may see how prompt I wish the obedience of My servants to be, and how pleasing it is to Me. Everything that the obedient man does is a source of merit to him. If he eats, obedience is his food; if he sleeps, his dreams are obedience; if he walks, if he remains still, if he fasts, if he watches - everything that he does is obedience; if he serve his neighbor, it is obedience that he serves. How is he guided in the choir, in the refectory, or his cell? By obedience, with the light of the most holy faith, with which light he has slain and cast from him his humbled self-will, and abandoned himself with self-hatred to the arms of his order and superior. Reposing with obedience in the ship, allowing himself to be guided by his superior, he has navigated the tempestuous sea of this life, with calm and serene mind and tranquillity of heart, because obedience and faith have taken all darkness from him; he remains strong and firm, having lost all weakness and fear, having destroyed his own will, from which comes all feebleness and disordinate fear. And what is the food of this spouse obedience? She eats knowledge of self, and of Me, knowing her own non-existence and sinfulness, and knowing that I am He who is, thus eating and knowing My Truth in the Incarnate Word. What does she drink? The Blood, in which the Word has shown her, My Truth, and the ineffable love which I have for her, and the obedience imposed on Him by Me, His Eternal Father, so she becomes inebriated with the love and obedience of the Word, losing herself and her own opinions and knowledge, and possessing Me by grace, tasting Me by love, with the light of faith in holy obedience.

"The obedient man speaks words of peace all his life, and at his death receives that which was promised him at his death by his superior, that is to say, eternal life, the vision of peace, and of supreme and eternal tranquillity and rest, the inestimable good which no one can value or understand, for, being the infinite good, it cannot be understood by anything smaller than itself, like a vessel, which, dipped into the sea, does not comprehend the whole sea, but only that quantity which it contains. The sea alone contains itself. So I, the Sea Pacific, am He who alone can comprehend and value Myself truly. And in My own estimate and comprehension of Myself I rejoice, and this joy, the good which I have in Myself, I share with you, and with all, according to the measure of each. I do not leave you empty, but fill you, giving you perfect beatitude; each man comprehends and knows My goodness in the measure in which it is given to him. Thus, then, the obedient man, with the light of faith in the truth burning in the furnace of charity, anointed with humility, inebriated with the Blood, in company with his sister patience, and with self-contempt, fortitude, and enduring perseverance, and all the other virtues (that is, with the fruit of the virtues), receives his end from Me, his Creator."

This is a brief repetition of the entire book.

"I have now, oh dearest and best beloved daughter, satisfied from the beginning to the end your desire concerning obedience.

"If you remember well, you made four petitions of Me with anxious desire, or rather I caused you to make them in order to increase the fire of My love in your soul: one for yourself, which I have satisfied, illuminating you with My Truth, and showing you how you may know this truth which you desired to know; explaining to you how you might come to the knowledge of it through the knowledge of yourself and Me, through the light of faith. The second request you made of Me was that I should do mercy to the world. In the third you prayed for the mystical body of the holy Church, that I would remove darkness and persecutions from it, punishing its iniquities at own desire in your person. As to this I explained that no penalty inflicted in finite time can satisfy for a sin committed against Me, the Infinite Good, unless it is united with the desire of the soul and contrition of the heart. How this is to be done I have explained to you. I have also told you that I wish to do mercy to the world, proving to you that mercy is My special attribute, for through the mercy and the inestimable love which I had for man, I sent to the earth the Word, My only-begotten Son, whom, that you might understand things quite clearly, I represented to you under the figure of a Bridge, reaching from earth to heaven, through the union of My divinity with your human nature.

"I also showed you, to give you further light concerning My truth, how this Bridge is built on three steps; that is, on the three powers of the soul. These three steps I also represented to you, as you know, under figures of your body - the feet, the side, and the mouth - by which I also figured three states of soul - the imperfect state, the perfect state, and the most perfect state, in which the soul arrives at the excellence of unitive love. I have shown you clearly in each state the means of cutting away imperfection and reaching perfection, and how the soul may know by which road she is walking and of the hidden delusions of the devil and of spiritual self-love. Speaking of these three states I have also spoken of the three judgments which My clemency delivers - one in this life, the second at death on those who die in mortal sin without hope, of whom I told you that they went under the Bridge by the Devil's road, when I spoke to you of their wretchedness. And the third is that of the last and universal judgment. And I who told you somewhat of the suffering of the damned and the glory of the blessed, when all shall have reassumed their bodies given by Me, also promised you, and now again I repeat my promise, that through the long endurance of My servants I will reform My spouse. Wherefore I invite you to endure, Myself lamenting with you over her iniquities. And I have shown you the excellence of the ministers I have given her, and the reverence in which I wish seculars to hold them, showing you the reason why their reverence towards My ministers should not diminish on account of the sins of the latter, and how displeasing to me is such diminution of reverence; and of the virtue of those who live like angels. And while speaking to you on this subject, I also touched on the excellence of the sacraments. And further wishing you to know of the states of tears and whence they proceed, I spoke to you on the subject and told you that all tears issue from the fountain of the heart, and pointed out their causes to you in order.

"I told you not only of the four states of tears, but also of the fifth, which germinates death. I have also answered your fourth request, that I would provide for the particular case of an individual; I have provided as you know. Further than this, I have explained My providence to you, in general and in particular, showing you how everything is made by divine providence, from the first beginning of the world until the end, giving you and permitting everything to happen to you, both tribulations and consolations temporal and spiritual, and every circumstance of your life for your good, in order that you may be sanctified in Me, and My Truth be fulfilled in you, which truth is that I created you in order to possess eternal life, and manifested this with the blood of My only-begotten Son, the Word.

"I have also in My last words fulfilled your desire and My promise to speak of the perfection of obedience and the imperfection of disobedience; and how obedience can be obtained and how destroyed. I have shown it to you as a universal key, and so it is. I have also spoken to you of particular obedience, and of the perfect and imperfect, and of those in religion, and of those in the world, explaining the condition of each distinctly to you, and of the peace given by obedience, and the war of disobedience, and how the disobedient man is deceived, showing you how death came into the world by the disobedience of Adam, and how I, the Eternal Father, supreme and eternal Truth, give you this conclusion of the whole matter, that in the obedience of the only-begotten Word, My Son, you have life, and as from that first old man you contracted the infection of death, so all of you who will take the key of obedience have contracted the infection of the life of the new Man, sweet Jesus, of whom I made a Bridge, the road to Heaven being broken. And now I urge you and My other servants to grief, for by your grief and humble and continual prayer I will do mercy to the world. Die to the world and hasten along this way of truth, so as not to be taken prisoner if you go slowly. I demand this of you now more than at first, for now I have manifested to you My Truth. Beware that you never leave the cell of self-knowledge, but in this cell preserve and spend the treasure which I have given you, which is a doctrine of truth founded upon the living stone, sweet Christ Jesus, clothed in light which scatters darkness, with which doctrine clothe yourself, My best beloved and sweetest daughter, in the truth."

How this most devout soul, thanking and praising God, makes prayer for the whole world and for the Holy Church, and commending the virtue of faith brings this work to an end.

Then that soul, having seen with the eye of the intellect, and having known by the light of holy faith the truth and excellence of obedience, hearing and tasting it with love and ecstatic desire, gazed upon the divine majesty and gave thanks to Him, saying, "Thanks, thanks to You, oh eternal Father, for You have not despised me, the work of Your hands, nor turned Your face from me, nor despised my desires; You, the Light, have not regarded my darkness; You, true Life, have not regarded my living death; You, the Physician, have not been repelled by my grave infirmities; You, the eternal Purity, have not considered the many miseries of which I am full; You, who are the Infinite, have overlooked that I am finite; You, who are Wisdom, have overlooked my folly; Your wisdom, Your goodness, Your clemency, Your infinite good, have overlooked these infinite evils and sins, and the many others which are in me. Having known the truth through Your clemency, I have found Your charity, and the love of my neighbor. What has constrained me? Not my virtues, but only Your charity. May that same charity constrain You to illuminate the eye of my intellect with the light of faith, so that I may know and understand the truth which You have manifested to me. Grant that my memory may be capable of retaining Your benefits, that my will may burn in the fire of Your charity, and may that fire so work in me that I give my body to blood, and that by that blood given for love of the Blood, together with the key of obedience, I may unlock the door of Heaven. I ask this of You with all my heart, for every rational creature, both in general and in particular, in the mystical body of the holy Church. I confess and do not deny that You loved me before I existed, and that Your love for me is ineffable, as if You were mad with love for Your creature. Oh, eternal Trinity! Oh Godhead! which Godhead gave value to the Blood of Your Son, You, oh eternal Trinity, are a deep Sea, into which the deeper I enter the more I find, and the more I find the more I seek; the soul cannot be satiated in Your abyss, for she continually hungers after You, the eternal Trinity, desiring to see You with light in Your light. As the hart desires the spring of living water, so my soul desires to leave the prison of this dark body and see You in truth. How long, oh! Eternal Trinity, fire and abyss of love, will Your face be hidden from my eyes? Melt at once the cloud of my body. The knowledge which You have given me of Yourself in Your truth, constrains me to long to abandon the heaviness of my body, and to give my life for the glory and praise of Your Name, for I have tasted and seen with the light of the intellect in

Your light, the abyss of You - the eternal Trinity, and the beauty of Your creature, for, looking at myself in You, I saw myself to be Your image, my life being given me by Your power, oh! eternal Father, and Your wisdom, which belongs to Your only-begotten Son, shining in my intellect and my will, being one with Your Holy Spirit, who proceeds from You and Your Son, by whom I am able to love You. You, Eternal Trinity, are my Creator, and I am the work of Your hands, and I know through the new creation which You have given me in the blood of Your Son, that You are enamored of the beauty of Your workmanship. Oh! Abyss, oh! Eternal Godhead, oh! Sea Profound! what more could You give me than Yourself; You are the fire which ever burns without being consumed; You consume in Your heat all the soul's self-love; You are the fire which takes away all cold; with Your light You do illuminate me so that I may know all Your truth; You are that light above all light, which illuminates supernaturally the eye of my intellect, clarifying the light of faith so abundantly and so perfectly, that I see that my soul is alive, and in this light receives You - the true light. By the Light of faith I have acquired wisdom in the wisdom of the Word - Your only-begotten Son. In the light of faith I am strong, constant, and persevering. In the light of faith I hope, suffer me not to faint by the way. This light, without which I should still walk in darkness, teaches me the road, and for this I said, Oh! Eternal Father, that You have illuminated me with the light of holy faith. Of a truth this light is a sea, for the soul revels in You, Eternal Trinity, the Sea Pacific. The water of the sea is not turbid, and causes no fear to the soul, for she knows the truth; it is a deep which manifests sweet secrets, so that where the light of Your faith abounds, the soul is certain of what she believes. This water is a magic mirror into which You, the Eternal Trinity, bid me gaze, holding it with the hand of love, that I may see myself, who am Your creature, there represented in You, and Yourself in me through the union which You made of Your godhead with our humanity. For this light I know to represent to myself You - the Supreme and Infinite Good, Good Blessed and Incomprehensible, Good Inestimable. Beauty above all beauty; Wisdom above all wisdom - for You are wisdom itself. You, the food of the angels, have given Yourself in a fire of love to men; You, the garment which covers all our nakedness, feed the hungry with Your sweetness. Oh! Sweet, without any bitter, oh! Eternal Trinity, I have known in Your light, which You have given me with the light of holy faith, the many and wonderful things You have declared to me, explaining to me the path of supreme perfection, so that I may no longer serve You in darkness, but with light, and that I may be the mirror of a good and holy life, and arise from my miserable sins, for through them I have hitherto served You in darkness. I have not known Your truth and have not loved it. Why did I not know You? Because I did not see You with the glorious light of the holy faith; because the cloud of self-love darkened the eye of my intellect, and You, the Eternal Trinity, have dissipated the darkness with Your light. Who can attain to Your Greatness, and give You thanks for such immeasurable gifts and benefits as You have given me in this doctrine of truth, which has been a special grace over and above the ordinary graces which You give also to Your other creatures? You have been willing to condescend to my need and to that of Your creatures - the need of introspection. Having first given the grace to ask the question, You reply to it, and satisfy Your servant, penetrating me with a ray of grace, so that in that light I may give You thanks. Clothe me, clothe me with You, oh! Eternal Truth, that I may run my mortal course with true obedience and the light of holy faith, with which light I feel that my soul is about to become inebriated afresh."

Here ends the Dialogue of St Catherine of Sienna

Letter of Ser Barduccio di Piero Canigiani, containing the Transit of the Seraphic Virgin, Saint Catherine of Siena, to Sister Catherine Petriboni in the Monastery of San Piero a Monticelli near Florence.

In the Name of Jesus Christ.

Dearest Mother in Christ Jesus, and Sister in the holy memory of our blessed mother Catherine, I, Barduccio, a wretched and guilty sinner, recommend myself to your holy prayers as a feeble infant, orphaned by the death of so great a mother. I received your letter and read it with much pleasure, and communicated it to my afflicted mothers here, who, supremely grateful for your great charity and tender love towards them, recommend themselves greatly, for their part, to your prayers, and beg you to recommend them to the Prioress and all the sisters that they may be ready to do all that may be pleasing to God concerning themselves and you. But since you, as a beloved and faithful daughter, desire to know the end of our common mother, I am constrained to satisfy your desire; and although I know myself to be but little fitted to give such a narration, I will write in any case what my feeble eyes have seen, and what the dull senses of my soul have been able to comprehend.

This blessed virgin and mother of thousands of souls, about the feast of the Circumcision, began to feel so great a change both in soul and body, that she was obliged to alter her mode of life, the action of taking food for her sustenance becoming so loathsome to her, that it was only with the greatest difficulty that she could force herself to take any, and, when she did so, she swallowed nothing of the substance of the food, but had the habit of rejecting it. Moreover, not one drop of water could she swallow for refreshment, whence came to her a most violent and tedious thirst, and so great an inflammation of her throat that her breath seemed to be fire, with all which, however, she remained in very good health, robust and fresh as usual. In these conditions we reached Sexagesima Sunday, when, about the hour of vespers, at the time of her prayer, she had so violent a stroke that from that day onwards she was no longer in health. Towards the night of the following Monday, just after I had written a letter, she had another stroke so terrific, that we all mourned her as dead, remaining under it for a long time without giving any sign of life. Then, rising, she stood for an equal space of time, and did not seem the same person as she who had fallen.

From that hour began new travail and bitter pains in her body, and, Lent having arrived, she began, in spite of her infirmity, to give herself with such application of mind to prayer that the frequency of the humble sighs and sorrowful plaints which she exhaled from the depth of her heart appeared to us a miracle. I think, too, that you know that her prayers were so fervent that one hour spent in prayer by her reduced that dear tender frame to greater weakness than would be suffered by one who should persist for two whole days in prayer. Meanwhile, every morning, after communion, she arose from the earth in such a state that any one who had seen her would have thought her dead, and was thus carried back to bed. Thence, after an hour or two, she would arise afresh, and we would go to St. Peter's, although a good mile distant, where she would place herself in prayer, so remaining until vespers, finally returning to the house so worn out that she seemed a corpse.

These were her exercises up till the third Sunday in Lent, when she finally succumbed, conquered by the innumerable sufferings, which daily increased, and consumed her body, and the infinite afflictions of the soul which she derived from the consideration of the sins which she saw being committed against God, and from the dangers ever more grave to which she knew the Holy Church to be exposed, on account of which she remained greatly overcome, and both internally and externally tormented. She lay in this state for eight weeks, unable to lift her head, and full of intolerable pains, from the soles of her feet to the crown of her head, to such an extent that she would often say: "These pains are truly physical, but not natural; for it seems that God has given permission to the devils to torment this body at their pleasure." And, in truth, it evidently was so; for, if I were to attempt to explain the patience which she practiced, under this terrible and unheard-of agony, I should fear to injure, by my explanations, facts which cannot be explained. This only will I say, that, every time that a new torment came upon her, she would joyously raise her eyes and her heart to God and say: "Thanks to You, oh eternal Spouse, for granting such graces afresh every day to me, Your miserable and most unworthy handmaid!"

In this way her body continued to consume itself until the Sunday before the Ascension; but by that time it was reduced to such a state that it seemed like a corpse in a picture, though I speak not of the face, which remained ever angelical and breathed forth devotion, but of the bosom and limbs, in which nothing could be seen but the bones, covered by the thinnest skin, and so feeble was she from the waist downwards that she could not move herself, even a little, from one side to another. In the night preceding the aforesaid Sunday, about two hours or more before dawn, a great change was produced in her, and we thought that she was approaching the end. The whole family was then called around her, and she, with singular humility and devotion, made signs to those who were standing near that she desired to receive Holy Absolution for her faults and the pains due to them, and so it was done. After which she became gradually reduced to such a state that we could observe no other movement than her breathing, continuous, sad, and feeble. On account of this it seemed right to give her extreme unction, which our abbot of Sant' Antimo did, while she lay as it were deprived of feeling.

After this unction she began altogether to change, and to make various signs with her head and her arms as if to show that she was suffering from grave assaults of demons, and remained in this calamitous state for an hour and a half, half of which time having been passed in silence, she began to say: "I have sinned! Oh Lord, have mercy on me!" And this, as I believe, she repeated more than sixty times, raising each time her right arm, and then letting it fall and strike the bed. Then, changing her words, she said as many times again, but without moving her arms, "Holy God, have mercy on me!" Finally she employed the remainder of the above-mentioned time with many other formulas of prayer both humble and devout, expressing various acts of virtue, after which her face suddenly changed from gloom to angelic light, and her tearful and clouded eyes became serene and joyous, in such a manner that I could not doubt that, like one saved from a deep sea, she was restored to herself, which circumstance greatly mitigated the grief of her sons and daughters who were standing around in the affliction you can imagine.

Catherine had been lying on the bosom of Mother Alessia and now succeeded in rising, and with a little help began to sit up, leaning against the same mother. In the meantime we had put before her eyes a pious picture, containing many relics and various pictures of the saints. She, however, fixed her eyes on the image of the cross set in it, and began to adore it, explaining, in words, certain of her most profound feelings of the goodness of God, and while she prayed, she accused herself in general of all her sins in the sight of God, and, in particular, said: "It is my fault, oh eternal Trinity, that I have offended You so miserably with my negligence, ignorance, ingratitude, and disobedience, and many other defects. Wretch that I am! for I have not observed Your commandments, either those which are given in general to all, or those which Your goodness laid upon me in particular! Oh mean creature that I am!" Saying which, she struck her breast, repeating her confession, and continued: "I have not observed Your precept, with which You commanded me to seek always to give You honor, and to spend myself in labors for my neighbor, while I, on the contrary, have fled from labors, especially where they were necessary. Did You not command me, oh, my God! to abandon all thought of myself and to consider solely the praise and glory of Your Name in the salvation of souls, and with this food alone, taken from the table of the most holy Cross, to comfort myself? But I have sought my own consolation. You did ever invite me to bind myself to You alone by sweet, loving, and fervent desires, by tears and humble and continuous prayers for the salvation of the whole world and for the reformation of the holy Church, promising me that, on account of them, You would use mercy with the world, and give new beauty to Your Spouse; but I, wretched one, have not corresponded with Your desire, but have remained asleep in the bed of negligence.

"Oh, unhappy that I am! You have placed me in charge of souls, assigning to me so many beloved sons, that I should love them with singular love and direct them to You by the way of Life, but I have been to them nothing but a mirror of human weakness; I have had no care of them; I have not helped them with continuous and humble prayer in Your presence, nor have I given them sufficient examples of the good life or the warnings of salutary doctrine. Oh, mean creature that I am! with how little reverence have I received Your innumerable gifts, the graces of such sweet torments and labors which it pleased You to accumulate on this fragile body, nor have I endured them with that burning desire and ardent love with which You sent them to me. Alas! oh, my Love, through Your excessive goodness You chose me for Your spouse, from the beginning of my childhood, but I was not faithful enough; in fact, I was unfaithful to You, because I did not keep my memory faithful to You alone and to Your most high benefits; nor have I fixed my intelligence on the thought of them only or disposed my will to love You immediately with all its strength."

Of these and many other similar things did that pure dove accuse herself, rather, as I think, for our example than for her own need, and then, turning to the priest, said: "For the love of Christ crucified, absolve me of all these sins which I have confessed in the presence of God, and of all the others which I cannot remember." That done, she asked again for the plenary indulgence, saying that it had been granted her by Pope Gregory and Pope Urban, saying this as one an hungered for the Blood of Christ. So I did what she asked, and she, keeping her eyes ever fixed on the crucifix, began afresh to adore it with the greatest devotion, and to say certain very profound things which I, for my sins, was not worthy to understand, and also on account of the grief with which I was laboring and the anguish with which her throat was oppressed, which was so great that she could hardly utter her words, while we, placing our ears to her mouth, were able to catch one or two now or again, passing them on from one to the other. After this she turned to certain of her sons, who had not been present at a memorable discourse, which, many days previously, she had made to the whole family, showing us the way of salvation and perfection, and laying upon each of us the particular task which he was to perform after her death. She now did the same to these others, begging most humbly pardon of all for the slight care which she seemed to have had of our salvation. Then she said certain things to Lucio and to another, and finally to me, and then turned herself straightway to prayer.

Oh! had you seen with what humility and reverence she begged and received many times the blessing of her most sorrowful mother, all that I can say is that it was a bitter sweet to her. How full of tender affection was the spectacle of the mother, recommending herself to her blessed child, and begging her to obtain a particular grace from God - namely, that in these melancholy circumstances she might not offend Him. But all these things did not distract the holy virgin from the fervor of her prayer; and, approaching her end, she began to pray especially for the Catholic Church, for which she declared she was giving her life. She prayed again for Pope Urban VI., whom she resolutely confessed to be the true Pontiff, and strengthened her sons never to hesitate to give their life for that truth. Then, with the greatest fervor, she besought all her beloved children whom the Lord had given her, to love Him alone, repeating many of the words which our

Savior used, when He recommended the disciples to the Father, praying with such affection, that, at hearing her, not only our hearts, but the very stones might have been broken. Finally, making the sign of the cross, she blessed us all, and thus continued in prayer to the end of her life for which she had so longed, saying: "You, oh Lord, call me, and I come to You, not through my merits, but through Your mercy alone, which I ask of You, in virtue of Your Blood!" and many times she called out: "Blood, Blood!" Finally, after the example of the Savior, she said: "Father, into Your Hands I commend my soul and my spirit," and thus sweetly, with a face all shining and angelical, she bent her head, and gave up the ghost.

Her transit occurred on the Sunday at the hour of Sext, but we kept her unburied until the hour of Compline on Tuesday, without any odor being perceptible, her body remaining so pure, intact, and fragrant, that her arms, her neck and her legs remained as flexible as if she were still alive. During those three days the body was visited by crowds of people, and lucky he thought himself who was able to touch it. Almighty God also worked many miracles in that time, which in my hurry I omit. Her tomb is visited devoutly by the faithful, like those of the other holy bodies which are in Rome, and Almighty God is granting many graces in the name of His blessed spouse, and I doubt not that there will be many more, and we are made great by hearing of them. I say no more.

Recommend me to the Prioress and all the sisters, for I have, at present, the greatest need of the help of prayer. May Almighty God preserve you and help you to grow in His grace.

Parchment Books is committed to publishing high quality
Esoteric/Occult classic texts at a reasonable price.

With the premium on space in modern dwellings, we also strive - within the limits of good book design - to make our products as slender as possible, allowing more books to be fitted into a given bookshelf area.

Parchment Books is an imprint of Aziloth Books, which has established itself as a publisher boasting a diverse list of powerful, quality titles, including novels of flair and originality, and factual publications on controversial issues that have not found a home in the rather staid and politically-correct atmosphere of many publishing houses.

Titles Include:

The Interior Castle	St Teresa of Avila
The Everlasting Man	G K Chesterton
Heaven and Hell	Emanuel Swedenborg
The Signature of All Things	Jacob Boehme
Psychic Self-Defence	Dion Fortune
The Ancient Wisdom	Annie Besant
The Masters and the Path	C W Leadbeater
Man, His True Nature & Ministry	Louis-Claude de St.-Martin
Secret Doctrines of the Rosicrucians	Magus Incognito
Corpus Hermeticum	(trans. GRS Mead)
The Virgin of the World	Hermes Trismegistus
Raja Yoga	Yogi Ramacharaka
Theosophy	Rudolf Steiner
The Gospel of Thomas	Anonymous
Pistis Sophia	(trans. GRS Mead)
The Secret Destiny of America	Manly P Hall
Practical Mysticism	Evelyn Underhill
The Rosicrucian Mysteries	Max Heindel
The Conference of Birds	Farid ud-Din Attar
Meetings With Remarkable Men	G I Gurdjieff
War Is A Racket	Maj.-General Smedley D. Butler

Obtainable at all good online and local bookstores.

View Parchment Books' full list at: www.azilothbooks.com

We are a small, approachable company and would love to hear any of your comments and suggestions on our plans, products, or indeed on absolutely anything. Aziloth is also interested in hearing from aspiring authors whom we might publish. We look forward to meeting you. Contact us at:

info@azilothbooks.com

CATHEDRAL CLASSICS

Parchment Book's sister imprint, Cathedral Classics, hosts an array of classic literature, from ancient tomes to twentieth-century masterpieces, all of which deserve a place in your home. A small selection is detailed below:

Mary Shelley	*Frankenstein*
H G Wells	*The Time Machine; The Invisible Man*
Niccolo Machiavelli	*The Prince*
Omar Khayyam	*The Rubaiyat of Omar Khayyam*
Joseph Conrad	*Heart of Darkness; The Secret Agent*
Jane Austen	*Persuasion; Northanger Abbey*
Oscar Wilde	*The Picture of Dorian Gray*
Voltaire	*Candide*
Bulwer Lytton	*The Coming Race*
Arthur Conan Doyle	*The Adventures of Sherlock Holmes*
John Buchan	*The Thirty-Nine Steps*
Friedrich Nietzsche	*Beyond Good and Evil*
George Eliot	*Silas Marner*
Henry James	*Washington Square*
Stephen Crane	*The Red Badge of Courage*
Ralph Waldo Emmerson	*Self-Reliance, and Other Essays, (series 1&2)*
Sun Tzu	*The Art of War*
Charles Dickens	*A Christmas Carol*
Fyodor Dostoyevsky	*The Gambler; The Double*
Virginia Wolf	*To the Lighthouse; Mrs Dalloway.*
Johann W Goethe	*The Sorrows of Young Werther*
Walt Whitman	*Leaves of Grass - 1855 edition*
Confucius	*Analects*
Anonymous	*Beowulf*
Anne Bronte	*Agnes Grey*
More	*Utopia*
Farid ud-Din Attar	*The Conference of Birds*
Jack London	*Call of the Wild*
Edwin A. Abbott	*Flatland*

full list at: www.azilothbooks.com

Obtainable at all good online and local bookstores.

Lightning Source UK Ltd.
Milton Keynes UK
UKOW04f2315010514

230986UK00014B/493/P